Company Law Handbook

Related titles by Law Society Publishing:

Companies Act 2006
Gary Scanlan, Andrew Harvey, Terence Prime and Tunde Ogowewo

Consumer Credit Act 2006
Julia Smith and Sandra McCalla

Data Protection Handbook
General Editor: Peter Carey

Drafting Confidentiality Agreements (2nd edn)
Mark Anderson and Simon Keevey-Kothari

Execution of Documents (2nd edn) (due Spring 2008)
Mark Anderson and Victor Warner

Freedom of Information Handbook (2nd edn) (due Spring 2008)
General Editors: Peter Carey and Marcus Turle

Insolvency Law Handbook (2nd edn) (due Autumn 2007)
Vernon Dennis

Intellectual Property Law Handbook (due Autumn 2007)
Bird & Bird, General Editor: Lorna Brazell

Titles from Law Society Publishing can be ordered from all good legal bookshops or direct from our distributors, Prolog (tel. 0870 850 1422 or email **lawsociety@prolog.uk.com**). For further information or a catalogue, email our editorial and marketing office at **publishing@lawsociety.org.uk**.

COMPANY LAW HANDBOOK

Stephen Griffin

with contributions by David Southern

The Law Society

Crown copyright material is reproduced with the permission of the Controller of Her Majesty's Stationery Office

ISBN: 978 1 85328 952 1

Published in 2008 by the Law Society
113 Chancery Lane, London WC2A 1PL

Typeset by IDSUK (DataConnection) Ltd
Printed by Antony Rowe Ltd, Chippenham, Wilts

Contents

Preface   *ix*
Table of cases   *xi*
Table of statutes   *xxi*
Table of statutory instruments   *xxx*
List of abbreviations   *xxxi*

1   The registered company   **1**

1.1   Introduction – the legislative framework   1
1.2   The corporate entity   2
1.3   The promotion and formation of a company   5
1.4   The registration procedure   7
1.5   The certificate of incorporation   11
1.6   The choice of a company name   14

2   The legal consequences of incorporation   **19**

2.1   Introduction   19
2.2   The corporate veil   19
2.3   The personal liability of a director – statutory provisions 23
2.4   Misfeasance proceedings   24
2.5   Fraudulent trading   26
2.6   Wrongful trading   30
2.7   The phoenix syndrome   35

3   The types and classification of companies   **39**

3.1   Introduction   39
3.2   Types of companies   39
3.3   Changing the status of a company   42
3.4   Groups of companies   48
3.5   Accounting purposes   50

3.6	The community interest company	51
3.7	Other forms of business structures	52
3.8	European structures	55

4	**Accounts and reporting structures**	**57**
4.1	Introduction	57
4.2	Accounting reference date	58
4.3	The accounts obligation	58
4.4	The 'true and fair' requirement	64
4.5	Accounting regulators	65
4.6	Small and medium-sized companies	66
4.7	Group accounts	68
4.8	The audit requirement	70

5	**Taxation of companies**	**74**
5.1	Introduction	74
5.2	Legislation	75
5.3	Profits	76
5.4	Company residence	78
5.5	Close companies	79
5.6	Charge to corporation tax	80
5.7	Administration and payment of corporation tax	82
5.8	Interest and distributions	83
5.9	Groups of companies	88
5.10	All income treatment	91
5.11	Transfer pricing	93
5.12	Taxation of foreign profits	94
5.13	Capital allowances	95

6	**A company's constitution**	**97**
6.1	Introduction	97
6.2	The articles of association	98
6.3	Independent contractual rights	103
6.4	Altering a company's articles	105
6.5	Statement of a company's objects	107
6.6	The weighted voting clause	107
6.7	Membership agreements	108

7   The legal nature and characteristics of holding shares in a limited company   **110**

  7.1   Introduction   110
  7.2   Identifying a member of a company   111
  7.3   Issuing and acquiring shares   113
  7.4   Types of shares   117
  7.5   Class rights   120
  7.6   Types of share issues   123

8   Share capital and capital maintenance   **126**

  8.1   Introduction   126
  8.2   Reducing share capital   127
  8.3   The purchase of a company's own shares   131
  8.4   Payment out of capital (private companies only)   133
  8.5   Financial assistance for the purchase of a company's shares   136

9   Loan capital and the registration of charges   **139**

  9.1   Introduction   139
  9.2   The debenture   139
  9.3   Security interests   141
  9.4   The registration of charges   147
  9.5   Priority rights   151

10   Directors and the management of a company   **155**

  10.1   Introduction   155
  10.2   Identifying company directors   155
  10.3   The *de jure* director   156
  10.4   The *de facto* and shadow director   159
  10.5   The board of directors   161
  10.6   Service contracts and directors' remuneration   163
  10.7   The removal of directors   165
  10.8   The company secretary   167
  10.9   The auditor   169

11   Directors' duties   **171**

  11.1   Introduction   171
  11.2   The duties   171
  11.3   Other statutory duties and obligations   186

12 Directors' authority and the validity of corporate transactions   **191**

    12.1   Introduction   191
    12.2   Corporate capacity – the *ultra vires* rule   191
    12.3   The authority of directors and others to bind the company   195

13 The disqualification of company directors   **201**

    13.1   Introduction   201
    13.2   The disqualification regime   201
    13.3   Discretionary disqualification orders   202
    13.4   Mandatory disqualification – CDDA 1986, s.6   204

14 The company in general meeting   **215**

    14.1   Introduction   215
    14.2   Types of general meeting   217
    14.3   Formal requirements for meetings   219
    14.4   Types of resolution   223
    14.5   Voting procedure   227

15 The protection of minority shareholders   **230**

    15.1   Introduction   230
    15.2   The derivative action   230
    15.3   The unfair prejudice remedy   236
    15.4   The just and equitable winding-up provision   242

16 The criminal liability of a company   **245**

    16.1   Introduction   245
    16.2   Corporate manslaughter   248

Appendices   **253**

    1   The provisions of the Companies Act 2006   253
    2   Draft model articles for private companies limited by shares   309

    Index   327

Preface

This book has been designed to present the essential constituents of company law in a detailed but clear and accessible manner. The work aims to benefit the understanding of general practitioners and is specifically targeted at those who require an insight into the legal regulation of private limited companies. However, in part, the work also covers the regulation of public companies. While this book has been written with the general practitioner in mind, the work may, as a means of guidance and reference, also be of interest to the more specialist practitioner.

The regulation of company law is currently the subject of significant change in the form of the Companies Act 2006. This new legislation is the primary legislative source for this work and is subject to extensive analysis. The book, in the context of each subject chapter, explains all the relevant provisions of the new Act and details if, and how, established corporate law principles have been affected by the new legislation. The book is written as if all the provisions of the new Act are in place. However, it should be noted that not all the provisions of the new Act will become law until October 2008 (see Appendix 1 of this book for a timetable of the proposed legislation). At the time of writing, a new format for the model set of articles (to replace Table A of the 1985 Act) is still to be decided upon. However, a DTI (BERR) draft of the model articles is in place and it is most probable that this draft version will duplicate or at least closely resemble the final format for the model articles. The draft set of model articles for a private company limited by shares is reproduced in Appendix 2.

Although company law is primarily a creature of statute, the subject area is significantly influenced by the common law and equity. The interpretation of the companies legislation, together with the construction of common law and equitable principles generates an abundance of case law. While this work does not seek to analyse deeply, specific case facts, the principles derived from the decided cases are fully explained and case references are alluded to. Working examples are also included within the text as a means to best explain complex principles.

I sincerely hope that this book will be instructive and a useful guide to those who require its assistance. Finally, I would like to thank David Southern for contributing his expertise to the writing of Chapter 4 (Accounts and reporting structures) and Chapter 5 (Taxation of companies). Also, my sincere thanks to my publishers and all of their staff. I would especially wish to commend the encouragement and assistance of Simon Blackett (commissioning editor) and Jennifer Cowan (production editor).

I have endeavoured to state the law as of 1 May 2007. However, at proof stage, I was able to include some additional material, to include commentary on the Corporate Manslaughter and Corporate Homicide Act 2007. The Act received Royal Assent on 26 July 2007.

Stephen Griffin
September 2007

Table of cases

A & BC Chewing Gum Ltd, Re (1975) 1 WLR 579 243
Abbey Leisure, Re [1990] BCC 60 244
Adams v. Cape Industries [1990] 2 WLR 657 . . . . .21, 22
Adams v. R [1995] BCC 376 (Privy Council) 182
Agnew v. Commissioner of Inland Revenue (Re Brumark) [2001] 2 AC 710 147
Aktieselskabet Dansk v. Brothers [2001] 2 BCLC 324 29
Allen v. Gold Reef [1900] 1 Ch 656 106
Aluminium Industrie Vaasen BV v. Romalpa Aluminium Ltd [1976] 2 All
   ER 552; [1976] 1 WLR 676 . . . . .148, 149
Alvona Developments Ltd v. The Manhattan Loft Corporation (AC) Ltd
   [2006] BCC 119 223
Anderson v. Hogg [2002] BCC 923 242
Anglo Austrian Printing & Publishing Union, Re [1892] 2 Ch 158 104
Archer Structures Ltd v. Griffiths [2004] BCC 156 37
Armagh Shoes Ltd, Re [1982] NI 59 146
Armour & Anor v. Thyssen Edelstahlweke AG [1990] BCC 929 149
Ashbury Railway Carriage and Iron Co v. Riche (1875) LR 7 HL 653 191
Association of Certified Public Accountants of Britain v. Secretary of State
   for Trade and Industry [1997] 2 BCLC 307 15–16
Atlas Wright (Europe) Ltd v. Wright [1999] BCC 163 165
Attorney-General's Reference (No.2 of 1999) [2000] 3 WLR 195 . . . . .249, 250
Atwool v. Merryweather (1868) LR 5 Eq 231
Augustus Barnett & Son Ltd, Re [1986] BCLC 170 29
Automatic Bottle Markers Ltd, Re [1926] Ch 412 152

Baltic Real Estate Ltd, Re [1992] BCC 629 236
Bank of Credit and Commerce International SA (in liq) (No.14), Re [2004]
   2 BCLC 236 30
Barclays Bank Ltd v. TOSG [1984] BCLC 1 192
Barclays Bank plc v. British & Commonwealth Holdings plc [1996] 1 BCLC 1 . . .136
Barleycorn Enterprises Ltd, Re [1970] Ch 465 153
Barry Artist Ltd, Re [1985] BCLC 283 . . . . .226, 227
Bath Glass Ltd, Re [1988] BCLC 329 210
Baumler Ltd, Re [2005] BCC 181 242
Baumler (UK), Re [2005] 1 BCLC 92 237
Beckett Investment Group Ltd v. Itall (2007) *The Times*, 11 July 21

Bede Steam Shipping Co Ltd, Re [1917] 1 Ch 123 116
Bell Houses Ltd v. City Wall Properties [1966] 2 QB 656 .192
Belmont Finance Corporation v. Williams Furniture Ltd (No.2) [1980] 1 All
    ER 393 136
Benjamin Cope & Sons Ltd, Re [1914] Ch 800 152
Bentley-Stevens v. Jones [1974] 1 WLR 638 163
Bhullar v. Bhullar [2003] 2 BCLC 241 178
Birch v. Cropper (1889) 14 App Cas 525 119
Bishopsgate Investment Management Ltd v. Maxwell [1993] BCC 140 174
Blackspur Group plc (No.3), Re; Secretary of State for Trade and Industry v.
    Eastaway [2003] BCC 520 211
Bond Worth, Re [1979] 3 All ER 919; [1980] Ch 228 149
Bonus Breaks Ltd, Re [1991] BCC 546 36
Borax, Re [1901] Ch 326 142
Boschoek Proprietary Co Ltd v. Fuke [1906] 1 Ch 148 .217
Brady v. Brady [1989] AC 755 137
Bratton Seymour Service Co Ltd v. Oxborough [1992] BCC 471 99
Braymist Ltd v. Wise Finance Co Ltd [2002] BCC 514 7
Breckland Group Holdings Ltd v. London & Suffolk Properties [1989]
    BCLC 100 . . . . .108, 231
Brenfield Squash Racquets Club, Re [1996] 2 BCLC 184 240
Brian D Pierson (Contractors) Ltd, Re [1999] BCC 26 203
Brightlife Ltd, Re [1986] BCLC 418; [1987] Ch 200 . . . . .142, 145, 146
Brightview Ltd, Re [2004] BCC 542 242
Bristol & West Building Society v. Mothew [1998] Ch 1 .172
British Murac Syndicate v. Alperton Rubber Ltd [1915] 2 Ch 168 105
British Sugar Refining Co, Re (1857) 3 K & J 408 101
Brooks v. Secretary of State for Trade and Industry [1999] BCC 232 4
Browne v. La Trinidad (1887) 37 Ch D 1 . . . . .6, 163
Buchler v. Talbot [2004] 2 WLR 582 153
Burdett v. Standard Exploration (1899) 16 TLR 112 100
Bushell v. Faith [1970] 1 All ER 53 108
Byng v. London Life Association Ltd [1990] Ch 170 229

Campbell's case (1876) 4 Ch D 470 139
Cane v. Jones [1980] 1 WLR 1451 226
Carecraft Construction Co Ltd, Re [1994] 1 WLR 172 205
Carman v. The Cronos Group SA [2006] BCC 451 28
Cayne v. Global Natural Resources plc [1984] 1 All ER 225 173
Centrebind Ltd, Re [1967] 1 WLR 377 37
Charterhouse Investment Trust Ltd v. Tempest Diesels Ltd [1985] 1
    BCC 99, 544 136
Chaston v. SWP Group plc [2003] BCLC 675 137
Cheah Theam Swee v. Equiticorp Finance Group Ltd [1992] BCC 98 143
Ciro Citterio Menswear plc v. Thakrar [2002] 1 BCLC 672 189
Civica Investments Ltd, Re [1983] BCLC 456 209
Clark v. Cutland [2003] 2 BCLC 393 241
Clemens v. Clemens Bros Ltd [1976] 2 All ER 268 216

Clough Mill v. Martin [1984] 3 All ER 982 149
CMS Dolphin Ltd v. Simonet [2002] BCC 600 179
Coleman Taymar Ltd v. Oakes [2001] 2 BCLC 749 ....182, 184
a Company (No.005287 of 1985), Re (1985) 1 BCC 99, 586 242
a Company (No.008699 of 1985), Re [1986] BCLC 382 237
a Company (No.005136 of 1986), Re [1987] BCLC 82 241
a Company (No.00370 of 1987), Re [1988] 1 WLR 1068 243
a Company (No.005009 of 1987), Re (1988) 4 BCC 424 161
a Company (No.001418 of 1988), Re [1991] BCLC 197 30
a Company, ex p. Burr [1992] BCLC 724 242
Compaq Computers Ltd v. Abercorn Group Ltd & Ors [1991] BCC 484 149
Cook v. Deeks [1916] 1 AC 554 231
County Farm Inns Ltd, Re; Secretary of State v. Ivens [1997] BCC 801 209
Creasey v. Breachwood Motors Ltd [1992] BCC 639 ....21, 22
Credit Lyonnais Bank Nederland N.V. v. Export Credits Guarantee
    Department [1999] 2 WLR 540 245
Crown Bank Ltd, Re (1890) 44 Ch D 634 243
Cumbrian Newspapers Group Ltd v. Cumberland & Westmorland Herald
    Newspaper & Printing Co Ltd [1987] Ch 1 120
Customs & Excise Commissioners v. Royal Bank of Scotland Plc [2006]
    EWHC 2813 (Ch) 153

Dafen Tin Plate v. Llanelly Steel Ltd [1920] 2 Ch 124 106
Daimler v. Continental Tyre & Rubber Co [1916] 2 AC 307 20
Daniels v. Daniels [1978] Ch 406 231
Davies v. United Kingdom [2005] BCC 401 211
Day v. Cook [2002] 1 BCLC 1 235
DC, HS and AD v. United Kingdom [2000] BCC 710 211
De Beers Consolidated Gold Mines v. Howe (1906) 5 TC 198 78
Demite Ltd v. Proctec Health Ltd [1998] BCC 638 226
DHN Food Distributors Ltd v. Tower Hamlets LBC [1976] 1 WLR 852 20–1
Dimbleby & Sons Ltd v. NUJ [1984] 1 All ER 751 24
D'Jan of London Ltd, Re [1993] BCC 646 ....25, 177, 184
Dorchester Finance Co Ltd v. Stebbing [1989] BCLC 498 177
DPP v. Gomez [1993] AC 442 3
DPP v. Kent & Sussex Contractors Ltd [1944] KB 146 246
DR Chemicals Ltd, Re [1989] 5 BCC 39 240
Dubai Aluminium Co Ltd v. Salaam [2003] 2 AC 366 54
Duckwari plc (No.2), Re [1998] 2 BCLC 315 186
Duckwari plc (No.3), Re [1999] 1 BCLC 168 186
Duomatic, Re [1969] 2 Ch 365 ....177, 225
Dyment v. Boyden [2005] BCC 79 137

Ebrahimi v. Westbourne Galleries [1973] AC 360 ....243, 244
EDC v. United Kingdom [1998] BCC 370 211
EIC Services Ltd & Anor v. Phipps & Ors [2003] BCC 931 226
EIC Services v. Phipps [2004] 2 BCLC 589 ....124, 200
Eley v. Positive Government Security Life Insurance (1876) 1 Ex D 88 101

Elgindata Ltd, Re [1991] BCLC 959 237
Ellis v. Property Leeds (UK) Ltd [2002] 2 BCLC 175 235
English & Scottish Mercantile Investment Trust v. Brunton [1892] 12
    Ch D 707 151
Estmanco v. Greater London Council [1982] 1 All ER 437 231
Euro Brokers Holdings Ltd v. Monecor (London) Ltd [2003] BCC 573 108
Eurofinance Group Ltd, Re [2001] BCC 551 238
Ewing v. Buttercup Margarine Co Ltd [1917] 2 Ch 1 16
Exeter City AFC Ltd v. The Football Conference Ltd & Anor [2004]
    BCC 498 . . . . .100, 109
Expanded Plugs Ltd, Re [1966] 1 WLR 514 242
Export Finance Ltd v. Umunna [1986] BCLC 460 179
Extrasure Travel Insurances Ltd v. Scattergood [2003] 1 BCLC 598 173–4

Fiorentino Comm. Giuseppe Srl v. Farnesi [2005] BCC 771 18
Firestone Tyre & Rubber Co v. Lewellin [1957] 1 WLR 464 24
First Energy Ltd v. Hungarian International Bank Ltd [1993] BCC 533 195
Floyd & Ors v. Fairhurst & Co [2004] EWCA Civ 604 .235
Folkes Group plc v. Alexander [2002] 2 BCLC 254 99
Foss v. Harbottle (1843) 2 Hare 461 230
Framlington Group plc v. Anderson [1995] BCC 611 179
Freeman & Lockyer v. Buckhurst Park Properties Ltd [1964] 2 QB 480 195
Fulham Football Club Ltd v. Cabra Estates plc [1992] BCC 863 176
Fusion Interactive Communication Solutions Ltd v. Venture Investment
    Placement Ltd [2006] BCC 187 173

G E Tunbridge Ltd, Re [1994] BCC 563 145
Gardner v. Parker [2005] BCC 46 235
Garnac Grain Co Inc v. HMF Faure and Fairclough Ltd [1968] AC 1130 21
Gerald Cooper Chemicals Ltd, Re [1978] Ch 262 27
Gibson Davies Ltd, Re [1995] BCC 11 214
Giles v. Rhind [2001] 2 BCLC 582 235
Gilford Motor Co v. Horne [1933] Ch 935 20
Globalink Hackney Pavilion Ltd, Re [1924] 1 Ch 276 162
Gluckstein v. Barnes [1900] AC 200 6
Grace v. Biagioli [2006] BCC 85 238
Grant v. United Kingdom Switchback Railways Co (1888) 40 Ch D 135 217
Greenhalgh v. Arderne Cinemas Ltd [1946] 1 All ER 512 121
Griffith v. Paget (1877) 6 Ch D 511 100
Griffiths v. Yorkshire Bank plc [1994] 1 WLR 1427 . . . . .142, 152
Guidezone Ltd, Re [2001] BCC 692 243
Guinness v. Saunders [1990] 2 AC 663 163

Hackney Pavilion Ltd, Re [1924] 1 Ch 276 162
Halt Garage, Re [1982] 3 All ER 1016 216
Hamilton Windsor Ironworks Co Ltd, Re (1879) 12 Ch D 707 151
Harman v. BML Group Ltd [1994] 2 BCLC 674 120
Harmer Ltd, Re [1959] 1 WLR 62 240

Hease v. Secretary of State for Trade and Industry [2006] BPIR 425 214
Hedley Byrne v. Heller & Partners Ltd [1964] AC 465 23
Heinl v. Jyske Bank (Gibraltar) Ltd [1999] LloydÆs Rep 511 196
Hely Hutchinson v. Brayhead Ltd [1968] 1 QB 549 .182, 195
Hendon v. Adelman (1973) 117 SJ 631 18
Heron International v. Lord Grade [1983] BCLC 244 174
Hickman v. Kent and Romney Sheepbreeders Association [1915] 1 Ch 881 99
Hills Waterfall Estate & Gold Mining Co, Re [1896] 1 Ch 947 24
Hogg v. Cramphorn [1967] Ch 254 172
Home & Colonial Insurance Co Ltd, Re [1930] 1 Ch 102 .26
Home Treat Ltd, Re [1991] BCC 165 226
Hong Kong & China Gas Co v. Glen [1914] 1 Ch 527 117
House of Fraser plc v. ACGE Investments Ltd [1987] AC 387 119
Howard Smith Ltd v. Ampol Petroleum Ltd [1974] AC 821 172
Howard v. Patent Ivory Manufacturing Co (1833) 38 Ch D 156 196
Hurst v. Bryk [2002] 1 AC 185 54

igroup Ltd v. Owen [2004] BCLC 61 150
Illingworth v. Houldsworth see Yorkshire Woolcombers, Re, sub nom
    Illingworth v. Houldsworth (HL) [1903] 2 Ch 284
Imperial Chemical Industries plc v. Colmer (Case C-264/96) [1998] STC 874 89
Industrial Development Consultants Ltd v. Cooley [1972] 1 WLR 443 179
Inland Revenue Commissioners v. Nash [2004] BCC 150 .36
International Championship Management Ltd, Re [2007] BCC 95 24
International Sales and Agencies Ltd v. Marcus [1982] 3 All ER 551 192
Irvine v. Union Bank of Australia (1877) 2 App Cas 366 .196
ISIS Factors plc, Re [2004] BCC 359 111

J E Cade & Son Ltd, Re [1991] BCC 360 . . . . .238, 242
Jayflex Construction Ltd, Re [2004] 2 BCLC 145 243
Jenice v. Dan [1993] BCLC 1349 18
Jesner v. Jarrad Properties Ltd [1992] BCC 807 243
John Reid & Sons (Strucsteel) Ltd, Re [2003] 2 BCLC 319 238
Johnson v. Gore Wood & Co [2002]2 AC 1 . . . . .234, 235, 242
Jones v. Sherwood Computer Services plc [1992] 1 WLR 277 116
Jubilee Cotton Mills Ltd v. Lewis [1924] AC 958 12

Kaytech International plc, Re; Portier v. Secretary of State for Trade and
    Industry [1999] BCC 390 160
Keenan Bros Ltd, Re [1986] 2 BCC 98, 970 146
Kenyon Swansea Ltd, Re [1987] 3 BCC 259; [1987] BLCL 514 . . . . .237, 241
Kirby's Coaches Ltd, Ltd [1991] BCC 130 184
Kodak v. Clarke [1902] 2 KB 450 21

L Todd (Swanscombe) Ltd, Re [1990] BCLC 454 28
Langunas Nitrate Co v. Langunas Syndicate [1899] 2 Ch 392 6
Lee Panavision Ltd v. Lee Lighting Ltd [1992] BCLC 22 . . . . .172, 181
Lee v. Lee's Air Farming [1961] AC 12 4

Legal Costs Negotiators Ltd, Re [1999] BCC 547 236
Lennard's Carrying Co Ltd *v.* Asiatic Petroleum Co Ltd [1915] AC 705 245
Lightning Electrical Contractors, Re [1996] BCC 950 36
Lindholst & Co *v.* Fowler [1988] BCLC 166 18
Lister *v.* Romford Ice & Cold Storage Ltd [1957] AC 555 177
Little Olympian Each Ways Ltd, Re [1994] 2 BCLC 420 242
Loch *v.* John Blackwood Ltd [1924] AC 783 243
London & Mashonaland Exploration Co Ltd *v.* New Mashonaland
    Exploration Co Ltd [1891] WN 165 182
London Sack & Bag Co Ltd *v.* Dixon & Lugton Ltd [1943] 2 All ER 767 102
London School of Electronics Ltd, Re [1986] Ch 211 240
Loquitur Ltd, Re [2003] 2 BCLC 442 . . . . .26, 184
Lyme Bay Canoe case (noted in (1994) *The Times*, 9 December) 248

Macaura *v.* Northern Assurance Co [1925] AC 619 3
MacDougall *v.* Gardiner (1875) 1 Ch D 13 . . . . .101, 102
MacPherson & Anor *v.* European Strategic Bureau Ltd [2002] BCC 39 136
Macro (Ipswich) Ltd, Re [1994] 2 BCLC 354 . . . . .237, 242
Maidstone Buildings Ltd, Re [1971] 1 WLR 1085 28
Manifest Shipping Co Ltd *v.* Uni-Polaris Shipping Co Ltd [2003] 1 AC 469 30
Marks & Spencer plc *v.* Halsey (Case C-446/03) [2006] STC 237 89
Marquis of Bute's case [1892] 2 Ch 100 157
Maxform *v.* Mariani & Goodville Ltd [1981] 2 Lloyd's Rep 54 18
MDA Investment Management Ltd, Re; Whalley (liquidator of MDA
    Investment Management Ltd) *v.* Doney [2005] BCC 783 184
Melcast (Wolverhampton) Ltd, Re [1991] BCLC 288 213
Mercia Safetywear Ltd *v.* Dodd [1988] BCLC 250 175
Millennium Advanced Technology, Re [2004] 2 BCLC 77 244
Modelboard Ltd *v.* Outer Box Ltd [1992] BCC 945 149
Moore *v.* I Bresler Ltd [1944] 2 All ER 515 246
Morecambe Bowling Ltd, Re [1969] 1 All ER 753 24
Morphitis *v.* Bernasconi [2003] Ch 552 . . . . .27, 30
Morris *v.* Kansen [1946] AC 459 196
Movitex Ltd *v.* Bulfield [1988] BCLC 104 182
MT Realisations Ltd (in liq.) *v.* Digital Equipment Co Ltd [2003] 2 BCLC 117 . . .137

Natal Land & Colonisation Co *v.* Pauline Colliery Syndicate [1904] AC 120 6
National Westminster *v.* Spectrum Plus Ltd [2005] 2 AC 680 . . . . .146, 147
Neptune (Vehicle Washing Equipment) Ltd *v.* Fitzgerald [1995] BCC 474 181
New British Iron Co, *ex p.* Beckwith, Re (1898) 1 Ch 324 104
New Bullas Trading Ltd, Re [1994] 1 BCLC 485 147
Newtherapeutics Ltd *v.* Katz [1991] Ch 226 104
Nisbet *v.* Shepherd [1994] BCC 91 116
Noble (R A) & Sons (Clothing) Ltd, Re [1983] BCLC 273 243
Norgard *v.* DFCT (1987) ACLR 527 146
Norman *v.* Theodore Goddard [1991] BCLC 1028 177
Northern Engineering Industries plc, Re [1994] 2 BCLC 704 121
Northumberland Avenue Hotel Co, Re (1886) 33 Ch D 16 .6

Nuneaton Borough AFC Ltd (No.2), Re [1991] BCC 44 240
Nye, Re [1971] Ch 1052 150

Oasis Mechanising Services Ltd, Re [1997] 1 WLR 764 34–5
Odeon Associated Theatres Ltd *v.* Jones (1972) 48 TC 257 76
Old Silkstone Collieries Ltd, Re [1954] Ch 169 120
Oliver *v.* Dalgleish [1963] 3 All ER 330 228
O'Neill *v.* Phillips [1999] 1 WLR 1092 . . . . .238, 239
Ooregum Gold Mining Co of India *v.* Roper [1892] AC 125 110
Opera Photographic, Re [1989] 5 BCC 601 223
Ord *v.* Belhaven Pubs Ltd [1998] 2 BCLC 447 22
Oshkosh B'Gosh Inc *v.* Dan Marbel Ltd [1989] BCLC 507 7
Oval 1742 Ltd (in liq.), Re; Customs & Excise Commissioners *v.* Royal Bank
    of Scotland Plc [2006] EWHC 2813 (Ch) 153

Pamstock Ltd, Re [1994] 1 BCLC 716 . . . . .211, 213
Panama case (1870) 5 Ch App 318 141
Panorama Developments Ltd *v.* Fidelis Furnishing Fabrics Ltd [1971] 2
    QB 711 168
Park Properties Ltd, Re [1997] 2 BCLC 530 213
Parker & Cooper Ltd *v.* Reading [1926] Ch 975 225
Patrick Lyon Ltd, Re [1933] Ch 786 29
Pender *v.* Lushington (1870) 6 Ch D 70 101
Penrose *v.* Official Receiver [1996] 1 BCLC 389 36
Percival *v.* Wright [1902] 2 Ch 421 174
Peskin *v.* Anderson [2001] BCC 874 174
Pfieffer Weinkellerei Weineinkauf GmbH & Co *v.* Arbuthnot Factors Ltd
    [1988] 1 WLR 150 149
Phillips *v.* Symes [2002] 1 WLR 853 53
Phonogram *v.* Lane [1982] QB 938 7
Plus Group Ltd & Ors *v.* Pyke [2003] BCC 332 182
Poole *v.* National Bank of China [1907] AC 229 131
Portbase (Clothing) Ltd, Re [1993] BCC 96 143
POW Services Ltd *v.* Clare [1995] 2 BCLC 205 111
Practice Direction No.1 of 1990 [1990] 1 WLR 1089 243
Produce Marketing Consortium Ltd, Re [1989] 5 BCC 569 33
Profinance Trust SA *v.* Gladstone [2002] 1 WLR 1024 .240
Prudential Assurance Co Ltd *v.* Newman Industries (No.2) [1982] Ch 204 231
Prudential Assurance Co *v.* Newman Industries [1982] Ch 204 234
Punt *v.* Symons & Co Ltd [1903] 2 Ch 506 . . . . .104, 105

Quarter Master UK *v.* Pyke [2005] 1 BCLC 245 179
Quinlan *v.* Essex Hinge Co Ltd [1996] 2 BCLC 417 238
Quinn & Axtens *v.* Salmon [1909] AC 442 101

R & H Electrical Ltd *v.* Haden Bill Electrical Ltd [1995] BCC 958 238
R *v.* Adomako [1995] 1 AC 171 249
R *v.* British Steel plc [1995] 1 WLR 1356 248

R v. Cole, Lees & Birch [1998] BCC 87 36
R v. Grantham [1984] QB 675 29
R v. ICR Haulage Ltd [1944] KB 551 246
R v. IRC Holdings [1944] 1 All ER 691 247
R v. K [2006] BCC 362 20
R v. Lockwood (1985) 2 BCC 99, 333 29
R v. McDonnell [1966] 1 All ER 193 247
R v. Miles [1992] Cr LR 657 28
R v. Philippou (1989) 89 Cr App R 290 28
R v. Registrar of Companies, ex p. Attorney General [1991] BCLC 476 12
R v. Registrar of Companies, ex p. Bowen [1914] 3 KB 1161 14
R v. Registrar of Companies, ex p. Central Bank of India [1986] 2 QB 1114 150
R v. Registrar of Companies, ex p. More [1931] 2 KB 197 14
R v. Secretary of State for Trade and Industry, ex p. McCormick [1998]
    BCC 379 211
Rainham Chemical Works Ltd v. Belvedere Fish Guano Ltd [1921] 2 AC 465 23
Ratners Group plc, Re [1988] 4 BCC 293 131
Ravenhart Service (Holdings) Ltd, Re [2004] 2 BCLC 376 236
Rayfield v. Hands [1960] Ch 1 102
Read v. Astoria Garage (Streatham) Ltd [1952] Ch 637 104
The Real Meat Co Ltd, Re [1996] BCC 254 143
Regal (Hastings) Ltd v. Gulliver [1942] 1 All ER 378; [1967] 2 AC 134 . . . . . .25, 178
Richardson v. Blackmore [2006] BCC 276 239
Richmond-on-Thames BC v. Pinn [1989] RTR 354 246
Ricketts v. Ad Valorem Factors Ltd [2004] BCC 164 37
Rights and Issues Investment Trust v. Stylo Shoes [1956] Ch 250 231
Ringtower Holdings plc, Re [1989] 5 BCC 82 240
Rock Nominees Ltd v. RCO (Holdings Ltd) plc [2004] 1 BCLC 439 236
Rosemary Simmons Memorial Housing Association Ltd v. UDT Ltd [1986]
    1 WLR 1440 193
Rover International Ltd v. Cannon Film Sales Ltd [1988] BCLC 710 6
Royal British Bank v. Turquand (1856) 6 E & B 327 196
Royal Mutual Benefit Building Society v. Sharman [1963] 1 WLR 581 220
Royal Trust Bank v. National Westminster Bank plc [1996] 2 BCLC 682 145
Ruben v. Great Fingall Consolidated [1906] AC 439 196
Rubin v. Gunner [2004] 2 BCLC 110 33
Runciman v.Walter Runciman plc [1992] BCLC 1084 181
Russell v. Northern Bank Development Corporation Ltd [1992] 1
    WLR 588, HL 108, 109
Russell v. Northern Bank Development Corporation Ltd [1992] BCLC 431,
    CA 109
R.W. Peak (King's Lynn) Ltd, Re [1998] BCC 596 226

Salomon v. A Salomon Ltd [1897] AC 22 . . . . .3, 19
Saltdean Estate Co Ltd, Re [1968] 1 WLR 1844 121
Sarfax Ltd, Re [1979] 1 Ch 592 28
Saul D Harrison & Sons plc, Re [1994] BCC 475 .237
Scandinavian Bank Corp plc, Re [1987] BCLC 220 .60

Scottish Insurance Corporation Ltd v. Wilsons & Clyde [1949] AC 462 118
Secretary of State for Trade and Industry v. Eastaway [2003] BCC 520 211
Secretary of State for Trade and Industry v. Gill [2006] BCC 725 32
Secretary of State for Trade and Industry v. Gray [1995] 1 BCLC 276 209
Secretary of State for Trade and Industry v. Hollier [2007] BCC 11 160
Secretary of State for Trade and Industry v. Rosenfield [1999] BCC 413 213
Secretary of State v. Bottrill [1999] BCC 177 4
Secretary of State v. Deverell [2000] 2 All ER 365; [2001] Ch 340 . . . . .160, 210
Secretary of State v. Gash [1997] 1 BCLC 341 210
Secretary of State v. Gray [1995] 1 BCLC 276 211
Secretary of State v. Ivens [1997] BCC 801 209
Sevenoaks Stationers (Retail) Ltd, Re [1991] Ch 164 . . . . .205, 209, 212
Shaker v. Al-Bedrawi [2003] BCC 465 235
Sherbourne Associates Ltd, Re [1995] BCC 40 33
Siebe Gorman & Co Ltd v. Barclays Bank [1979] 2 Lloyd's Rep 142 146
Simmonds v. Heffer [1983] BCLC 298 193
Smith & Fawcett Ltd, Re [1942] Ch 304 173
Smith Stone & Knight Ltd v. Birmingham Corp [1939] 4 All ER 116 21
Smith v. Croft (No.2) [1987] BCLC 206 231
Smith v. Croft (No.3) [1987] BCLC 355 231
Smith v. Henniker-Major & Co [2003] Ch 182 . . . . .199, 200
Southern Foundries Ltd v. Shirlaw [1940] AC 701 .105, 166
Standard Charter Bank v. Pakistan National Shipping Corporation [2002]
    1 WLR 1547 23
Standard Chartered Bank v. Walker [1992] BCLC 603 101
Supply of Ready Mixed Concrete (No.2), Re [1995] 1 AC 456 247
Swaeby v. Port Darwin Mining Co (1899) 1 Meg 385 106

Tasbian Ltd (No.3), Re [1992] BCC 358 161
Telomatic Ltd, Re [1993] BCC 404 150
Tesco Supermarkets Ltd v. Nattrass [1972] AC 153 246
Tett v. Phoenix Property Ltd [1986] BCLC 149 99
Thorne v. Silverleaf [1994] BCC 109 38
Thundercrest Ltd, Re [1994] BCC 857 111
Trevor v. Whitworth (1887) 12 App Cas 409 . . . . .113, 128
Trustor AB v. Smallbone [2001] 1 WLR 1177 20

Underwood v. Bank of Liverpool & Martins Ltd [1924] 1 KB 755 196
Union Music Ltd & Anor v. Watson & Anor [2004] BCC 37 . . . . .109, 223
Unisoft Group Ltd (No.3), Re [1994] 2 BCLC 609 236
Uno Plc, Re; Secretary of State for Trade and Industry v. Gill [2006]
    BCC 725 . . . . .32, 210

Vectone Entertainment Holding Ltd v. South Entertainment Ltd [2004]
    BCLC 224 223
VGM Holdings Ltd, Re [1942] Ch 235 26

Wallersteiner v. Moir (No.2) [1975] QB 373 . . . . .232, 241

Webb *v.* Earle (1875) LR 20 Eq 556 118
West Mercia Safetywear Ltd *v.* Dodd [1988] BCLC 250 ....25, 34
Westminster Property Management Ltd, Re [2001] BCC 121 211
WGS and MSLS *v.* United Kingdom [2000] BCC 719 211
Whaley Bridge Calico Printing Co *v.* Green (1879) 5 QBD 109 5
Whalley (Liquidator of MDA Investment Management Ltd) *v.* Doney
    [2004] BPIR 75; [2005] BCC 783 ....175, 184
William C Leitch Bros Ltd, Re [1932] 2 Ch 71 28
Williams *v.* Natural Life Health Ltd [1998] 1 BCLC 689 23
Willow International Investments Ltd *v.* Smiths of Smithfield Ltd [2003]
    BCC 769 ....119, 122
Wilson *v.* Kellard [1910] 2 Ch 306 151
Wilton Davies *v.* Kirk [1997] BCC 770 241
Windward Islands (Enterprises Ltd), Re (1988) 4 BCC 158 219
Wood *v.* Holden [2006] STC 443 78
Wood *v.* Odessa Waterworks Co (1889) 42 Ch D 639 100
Woodroffes (Musical Instruments) Ltd, Re [1985] BCLC 227 143
Wragg, Re [1871] 1 Ch 796 117

Yorkshire Woolcombers, Re, *sub nom* Illingworth *v.* Houldsworth (HL)
    [1903] 2 Ch 284 ....141, 142
Yukong Lines Ltd of Korea *v.* Rendsburg Investments [1998] BCC 870 23

Zinotty Properties Ltd, Re [1984] 1 WLR 1249 243

Table of statutes

Arbitration Act 1996
   s.9 100

Business Names Act 1985 17

Capital Allowances Act 2001 . . . .75, 95
   ss.83–9 .96
   ss.91–104 96
Companies Act 1862 3
Companies Act 1948
   Table A 98
Companies Act 1985 . . . . . . .1, 8, 39, 46,
               53, 57, 61, 98, 100,
               122, 156, 187, 217
   s.2 97
   s.3A 192, 193
   s.14 . . . . .99, 100, 101, 103
   s.23 49
   s.23(1) 49
   s.26(1) 16
   s.30 41
   s.35 . . . . .192, 194
   s.35(1) .192
   s.35(2) .194
   s.35(3) .193
   s.35A 197, 198, 199, 200
   s.35A(1) 197
   s.36(4) 6
   s.36C(1) .6
   ss.43–8 .42
   s.49 46
   s.49(3) 46
   s.50 46
   s.51 47
   s.53 .16, 45
   s.54 .17, 45

s.55 45
s.57 17
s.80 114
s.80A 115
s.121 127
s.125 122
s.143 129
ss.151–8 136
s.162 131
ss.221–2 207
s.226 207
s.228 207
s.233 207
s.258 50
s.259 76
s.283(1) .168
s.289 157
s.293(1) .159
s.303 . . . . .104, 166
s.303(1) .166
s.304 167
s.306 222
s.310 . . . . .181, 182
s.320 186
s.322A 199
s.324 228
s.330 . . . . .187, 189, 190
s.342 190
s.348 17
s.349 17
s.349(1) 17, 18
s.349(4) 17, 18
ss.352–3 207
s.363 207
s.371 . . . . .109, 222, 223
s.378(1) .224

s.381A 225
s.387 220
s.396(1) .147
s.399 207
s.415 207
s.459 . . . . .100, 109, 236, 238,
      241, 242, 244
s.652 22
s.727 . . . . .184, 185
s.736 49
s.741(1) 155
s.741(2) 156, 161
Sched.4 . . . . .61, 68
   paras.9–14 61
   para.36A 76
Sched.4A .61
Sched.5 61
Sched.7A 164
Sched.8 . . . . .61, 68
Sched.8A .61
Sched.9 61
Sched.9A .61
Companies Act 1989 . . . . .192, 193, 194
   s.110 .192
Companies Act 2006 . . . . .ix, 1, 2, 8,
      39, 40, 48, 53, 98, 122, 153,
      159, 171, 181, 194, 201, 215,
      217, 220, 224, 253–308
   Part 3 . . . . .97, 115
   Part 20 .11
   Part 26 . . . . .45, 122
   Part 30 . . . . .113, 122
   s.1(1) 39
   s.2 39
   s.3 .2, 40
   s.4 40
   s.5 39
   ss.8–16 8
   s.10 110
   s.11 40
   s.12(2) 168
   s.14 14
   s.15 . . . . .11, 12
   s.16 2
   s.18 98
   s.18(2) 98
   s.19 . . . . .98, 99
   s.20 98

s.21 . . . . .98, 105
s.22 . . . . .106, 107
s.22(3) .107
s.23 106
s.24 107
ss.25–6 .105
s.28 98
s.29 . . . . .97, 102
s.30 . . . . .97, 227
s.31 . . . . .107, 194
s.31(1)–(2) 194
s.32 . . . . .102, 103
s.33 . . . . .99, 100, 101, 102,
      103, 104
s.34 105
s.34(2) .102
s.35 105
s.35(2)(a) 102
s.39 194
s.40 . . . . .195, 197, 198, 199
s.40(1) 197, 198
s.40(4) .198
s.41 199
s.41(2)–(5) 199
s.51 . . . . .6, 7
s.56 16
s.58 40
s.59 . . . . .16, 41
s.60 16
s.62 41
s.64 15
s.64(3)–(4) 15
s.66 14
ss.67–75 15
s.76 16
s.77 14
s.90 42
s.90(3) 43
s.91 42
s.91(1) 43
s.91(1)(b)–(d) 43
s.92 . . . . .42, 43
s.92(2) 44
s.92(3) 43
s.93 . . . . .42, 44
s.93(2)(a) 44
s.93(2)(b) 44
s.93(2)(b)(i)–(ii) 44

ss.94–5 . . . . .42, 45
ss.96–7 45
s.98 . . . . .45, 46, 113, 122
s.99 45
s.100 45
s.100(2) .45
s.101 46
s.102 . . . . .46, 47
ss.103–4 46
s.105 . . . . .42, 47
s.105(2) .48
ss.106–8 . . . . .42, 47
s.109 46
s.109(2) .47
ss.110–11 46
s.112 111
s.113 111
s.113(5) 112
s.114 . . . . .13, 112, 207
s.115 . . . . .13, 112
s.116 . . . . .13, 113, 207
ss.117–18 . . . . .13, 113
s.122 111
s.123 . . . . .11, 40, 112
ss.125–26 111
s.127 . . . . .111, 207
s.128 111
s.136 49
s.137(1) .49
s.137(4) .50
s.139 49
s.141 50
s.154 . . . . .40, 156
s.155 . . . . .40, 156, 169
s.156(4) 156
s.157 . . . . .157, 158
s.158 158
s.161 156
s.162 . . . . .157, 160, 207
ss.163–4 160
s.165 . . . . .157, 160
s.167 157
s.168 . . . . .104, 225
s.169 166
s.169(2) 166
s.169(5) 166
s.170 166
s.170(4) 171

s.170(5) 166
s.171 . . . . .172, 174
s.171(1) 174
s.172 . . . . .173, 233
s.172(1)–(2) 173
s.172(3) 173, 175
s.173 175
s.173(1)–(2) 175
s.174 176
s.174(1)–(2) 176
s.175 . . . . .177, 178, 183
s.175(1)–(4) 177
s.175(5)–(7) 178
s.176 180
s.176(1)–(5) 180
s.177 . . . . .180, 183
s.177(1)–(2) 180
s.177(3)–(6) 181
s.180(5) 182
s.182 183
ss.184–5 180
s.189 . . . . .164, 165
s.190 . . . . .186, 187
ss.191–4 187
s.195 186
s.197 . . . . .187, 188, 189, 190
s.197(3) 188
s.198 . . . . .188, 189, 190
s.199 188
ss.200–1 . . . . .188, 189, 190
s.202 . . . . .188, 190
s.203 . . . . .188, 189, 190
s.203(4) 189
ss.204–9 189
s.212 190
s.213 189
s.213(4)(a)–(d) 190
s.217 167
s.220 190
s.222 167
ss.227–9 164
s.232 . . . . .181, 182, 183, 185
ss.232–8 185
s.239 . . . . .184, 186, 233
s.250 155
s.251 . . . . .156, 161
ss.252–5 187
s.260 . . . . .25, 230, 232, 233

s.260(1) 241
s.260(2)–(4) 232
ss.261–2 . . . . .232, 233
s.263 . . . . .232, 233
s.263(2)–(4) 233
s.264 . . . . .232, 233
s.264(3)–(4) 232
s.264(5) 232, 234
s.270 11
s.271 40
s.273(2) 11
s.275 .207
s.277 .168
s.280 .168
s.281 .223
s.282 .224
s.283 .224
s.288 . . . . .224, 225
s.288(2) 225
s.300 .225
s.303 . . . . .218, 219
s.305 .219
s.306 . . . . .109, 219, 222, 223
s.307 .220
s.307(2) 217
s.308 .219
s.309 .220
ss.311–13 220
ss.314–15 221
s.317 . . . . .183, 221
s.318 .219
s.319 .165
s.321 .228
s.321(2) 228
s.322 .228
s.324 .228
s.336(1) 63, 217
s.337 .217
s.338 .218
ss.362–79 193
ss.380–9 57
s.380 68
s.381 66
s.382 . . . . .66, 67
s.383 . . . . .50, 66, 67
s.384 66
s.384(2)(a) 68
s.386 . . . . .73, 207

s.386(2) 73
s.387 73
s.388 . . . . .73, 207
s.389 73
ss.390–2 58
s.393 5
s.393(1) 64
s.393(3) 61
s.394 . . . . .59, 207
s.395 70
s.395(1)–(5) 59
s.396 . . . . .59, 65, 70, 133
s.396(3)–(4) 61
s.396(5) 61, 65
s.397 60
s.398 68
ss.399–414 50
s.399 . . . . .68, 69
ss.400–1 . . . . .50, 69
s.402 50
s.403(3) 69
s.404 . . . . .65, 69
s.404(3) 61
s.405 . . . . .69, 70
s.406 70
s.407(1)(a) 70
s.409(1) 61
s.411 . . . . .62, 67, 68
ss.412–13 62
s.414 . . . . .61, 67, 207
s.415 5
s.416 67
s.416(3) 62
s.417 67
s.417(5)–(6) 62
ss.418–19 62
s.421 . . . . .62, 170
ss.423–24 . . . . .63, 71
s.426 . . . . .63, 164
ss.427–8 63
s.430 63
s.433 61
s.434(1) 63
s.434(3) 58
s.435 63
s.437(3) 71
s.439 62
s.441 . . . . .58, 63

s.443 63
s.444 .63, 67
s.444(4) 60
s.445 .63, 67
s.445(3)–(4) 60
ss.446–7 63
s.448 . . . . .42, 63, 64
s.449 . . . . .60, 64
ss.450–7 64
s.464 . . . . .65, 76
s.467 68
s.469 60
s.471 .58, 59
s.472 59
s.474 60
s.475 70
s.476 71
s.477 . . . . .60, 70, 71, 169
s.479 71
s.480 . . . . .70, 71
ss.481–4 71
s.485 . . . . .71, 169
s.487 . . . . .71, 169
s.487(2) 71
s.489 . . . . .71, 169
s.490 71
s.491 72
s.492 . . . . .72, 169
s.495(1) 72
s.495(2) .169
s.495(3) 65, 72
s.495(3)(a) 169
s.495(4)(a) 72
s.496 72
ss.498–502 72
s.504 72
s.510 . . . . .72, 225
s.516 72
s.519(1)–(3) 72
ss.533–4 72
s.535 72
s.535(2) 72
ss.536–7 72
s.542 110
s.549 115
s.549(2) .115
s.550 . . . . .114, 115
s.551 . . . . . . .114, 115, 124, 139, 170

s.551(2) .114
s.551(7) .114
s.554 115
s.556 119
s.558 114
s.561 . . . . .123, 139
s.569 124
ss.570–1 .124
s.580 . . . . .2, 116
s.582 117
ss.585–7 .117
s.593 117
s.593(1) 44
s.610 . . . . .110, 127
s.618 121
s.630 . . . . .122, 123
s.630(5) .120
s.630(6) .121
s.633 123
s.641 128
s.641(1)–(2) 128
s.642 128
s.643 129
s.644(2) 129, 130
s.645 . . . . .128, 129
s.646 129
s.648 130
s.649 130
s.649(2) .130
s.652 131
s.653 130
s.654 128
s.656 126
s.658 113
s.659(2) .113
s.660 115
ss.677–8 .136
ss.681–2 .137
s.684 124
s.684(3)–(4) 125
s.687 125
ss.690–2 .131
s.693(2) .132
s.693(4) .132
s.694 132
s.694(2)–(3) 132
s.694(5) .132
s.695 132

s.696(2) .132
s.701 . . . . .132, 133
s.702(2) 132
s.705 . . . . .132, 134
s.706 .132
s.706(b) .86
s.707 .132
s.707(4) 133
s.709 .133
s.712 .133
s.714 . . . . .134, 135
ss.716–17 135
s.718(2) 135
s.719 .135
s.721 .135
s.721(6) 113
s.733 .127
s.738 .139
s.739 .140
s.741 .139
ss.743–4 140
s.755 .40
s.759 .113
s.761 . . . . .13, 40
s.763 .110
s.767 .153
s.768 .114
s.771 .116
s.854 . . . . .5, 207
s.855 .207
s.857 .207
s.860 .147
s.860(7) 147
s.869 . . . . .147, 149
s.870 .147
ss.873–6 150
ss.899–900 102
s.993 . . . . .26, 27, 203
s.994 . . . . .100, 106, 109, 223,
        230, 232, 235, 236, 238,
        239, 241, 242, 243, 244
s.996 . . . . .103, 239, 241
s.996(2) 239
s.996(2)(a) 240
s.996(2)(b)–(c) 241
s.1043 .14
s.1046 .14
s.1099 .14

s.1100 .14
s.1157 . . . . .184, 185
s.1158 .59
s.1159 .48
s.1159(2) 49
s.1161 .50
s.1162 . . . . .50, 69
s.1166 .119
ss.1192–228 17
Sched.4 .13
Sched.5 .13
Sched.6
  para.2 49
  para.3(1)–(2) 49
  para.7 49
Sched.7 . . . . .50, 51, 69
Sched.15
  Part 2 51
Sched.16 .1
Draft Model Articles 309–26
Companies (Audit, Investigations
  and Community Enterprise)
  Act 2004 . . . . .1, 185
  Part II 39, 51
  s.35(2) 51
Companies Consolidation
  (Consequential Provisions) Act
  1985 39
Company Directors Disqualification
  Act 1986 . . . . .201, 211
  s.1 214
  s.1(1) .201
  s.1A .206
  s.1A(a)–(b) 206
  s.2 202
  s.2(2) .202
  s.2A .206
  ss.3–5 203
  s.6 . . . . .155, 201, 204, 205,
          209, 210, 211, 213
  s.6(1) 204, 211
  s.6(1)(b) 209
  s.6(2) .204
  s.6(4) 204, 211
  s.7(1) .204
  s.7(2)–(3) 205
  s.8 . . . . .201, 203, 205
  s.8A .206

s.9 . . . . .201, 204, 206, 214
s.10 . . . . .203, 204
s.13 202
s.15 202
s.17 . . . . .206, 212, 213, 214
s.18(2)–(3) 202
s.22(4) .201
Sched.1 205
    Part 1 206
    Part 2 . . . . .206, 207
Corporate Manslaughter and
    Corporate Homicide
    Act 2007 . . . . .x, 248, 249, 250,
                              251, 252

Electronic Communications
    Act 2000 .13
Enterprise Act 2002 . . . . . . .1, 142, 143,
                                152, 153
European Communities Act 1972 . . .196
    s.9 196
    s.9(2) 7
Finance Act 1988
    s.66(1) 78
Finance Act 1996 76
    s.81 91
    s.87 92
    s.87A 92
    Sched.9
        para.5(5) 92
        para.6(3) 92
Finance Act 1998
    s.42 76
    Sched.18 75
Finance Act 2002 76
    Sched.26 . . . . .75, 92
    Sched.29 . . . . .75, 93
Finance Act 2003
    s.148 79
Finance Act 2004
    s.50A 57
Finance Acts 75
Financial Services and Markets Act
    2000 68

Government Resources and
    Accountability Act 2000
    s.25(6) 71

Health and Safety at Work Act
    1974 248
Human Rights Act 1998 210

Income and Corporation Taxes
    Act 1988 .75
    s.1B 87
    s.6(4)(a) .76
    s.9(1) 74
    s.11 79
    s.12 82
    s.13A 81
    s.14(3) 84
    s.75 77
    s.75A 77
    s.130 77
    s.208 .81, 87
    s.209(2)(d) 84
    s.209(2)(e)(iii) 84
    s.212(1) .84
    ss.219–29 86
    s.231 87
    s.249 85
    s.338 77
    s.338A 77
    s.349 83
    s.349(4) .83
    s.393 77
    s.393(1) .78
    s.393A 77
    s.402 77
    s.402(1)–(2) 88
    s.413(3) .88
    s.414 79
    ss.416–17 79
    s.419 80
    ss.806A–M 95
    s.832(1) 74, 88
    s.836A 57
    Sched.18
        paras.2–3 88
    Sched.28AA
        para.1(1) 94
        para.4 93
    Sched.D
        Case I 75, 76, 77, 92
        Case II 76
        Case III 92

Case III(a) 77, 92
Case V 77
Case VI 77, 93
Income Tax (Trading and Other
Income) Act 2005
s.383 87
s.410 85
Industrial and Provident Societies
Act 1965 .14
Insolvency Act 1986 . . . . .1, 17
Part XVI 207
s.22 208
s.29(2) .143
s.40 153
s.47 208
s.66 208
s.74(2) .41
s.76 134
s.77 48
s.84(1) .224
ss.98–9 . . . . .37, 208
s.110 45
s.114 37
s.115 35
s.122(1)(g) 230, 238, 242,
243, 244
s.123 .175
s.124 .242
s.125(2) 244
s.131 .208
s.166 .37
s.175 .153
s.176 .153
s.176A 154
s.176ZA 153
s.190 .37
s.212 . . . . .24, 25, 26
s.212(1) 26
s.212(3) 25, 26
s.213 . . . . .26, 27, 28, 29, 30,
35, 155, 203, 204
s.213(1)–(2) 27
s.214 . . . . .30, 31, 32, 33, 34,
35, 155, 177, 204
s.214(1) 30, 31
s.214(2) 30–1
s.214(2)(b) 31

s.214(3) 30, 31, 34
s.214(4) 30, 32
s.214(4)(b) 33
s.214(5)–(8) 30
s.214A 53
s.216 . . . . .35, 36, 37, 38
s.216(1) 35
s.216(2)–(4) 36
s.217 . . . . .35, 38
ss.234–5 208
ss.238–40 207
ss.242–3 207
s.245 .145
s.388 .37
Sched.1 143
Sched.6 . . . . .152, 153
paras.1–5C 153
paras.6–7 153
Sched.B1
para.14 144
para.15(1) 144
para.15(2) 143, 144
para.22 144
Insolvency Act 2000 205–6
Interpretation Act 1978
s.5 246
Sched.1 246
Limited Liability Partnerships
Act 2000 52
s.1(2) .52
s.1(3) .53
s.5(1) .53
s.6(1) .52
Limited Partnership Act 1907 . . . .53, 54

Partnership Act 1890 53
s.1 53
s.5 54
s.10 54
Political Parties, Elections and
Referendum Act 2000 193
Proceeds of Crime Act 2002
s.80(3) 20
Restrictive Trade Practices Act
1976 247

Stock Transfer Act 1963 116

Taxation of Chargeable Gains
  Act 1992 75
    s.8(3) 74
    s.17(1) 90
    s.18 90
    s.53 76
    s.170 89
    s.171(1) .90
    s.171A 90
    s.179(1)–(3) 91
    s.179(5)–(8) 91
    s.179A 91
    s.179B 91
    s.286 90
    Sched.A1 87
Taxes Management Act 1970 75
    s.59D 83
    s.118(1) .74
Trade Union and Labour Relations
  (Consolidated) Act 1992

s.10(3) 2

European legislation
European Convention on Human Rights
    art.6 210
    art.6(1) 210–11

Secondary legislation
Company Law First Directive 13, 14
    art.9 192
Directive 76/222/EC
    art.2(3) .65
Directive 2001/86 55
Directive 2002/1606/EC 70
Regulation 2137/85 56
Regulation 2157/2001 55

International legislation
OECA Model Convention
    art.6(3) .79

Table of statutory instruments

Accounting Standards (Prescribed Body) Regulations 2005 (SI 2005/697) 65

Companies (Acquisition of Own Shares) (Treasury Shares) (No.2) Regulations
  2003 (SI 2003/3031) 119
Companies (Acquisition of Own Shares) (Treasury Shares) Regulations 2003
  (SI 2003/1116) 119
Companies Act 1985 (International Accounting Standards and Other
  Accounting Amendments) Regulations 2004 (SI 2004/2947) 70
Companies (Table A to F) Regulations 1985 (SI 1985/805)
    reg.102 85
    reg.103 85
    Table A . . . . .ix, 98
      art.85 181
Corporation Tax (Instalment Payments) Regulations 1998 (SI 1998/3175) 75
    reg.5 82

Directors' Remuneration Report Regulations 2002 (SI 2002/1986) 164

European Public Limited Liability Company Regulations 2004 (SI 2004/2326) 55

Insolvency Rules 1986
    rr.4.227–4.230 36
Insolvency Rules 1996
    rr.4.218(1)(a) 35

Limited Liability Partnerships Regulations 2001 (SI 2001/1090) 52, 53

Membership of Holding Company (Dealers in Securities) Regulations 1997
  (SI 1997/2306) 50

Regulatory Reform Order 2002 (SI 2002/3203) 54

Transitional Provisions (Insolvency) Order 2003 (SI 2003/2332) 153

Uncertificated Securities Regulations 2001 (SI 2001/3755) 113

List of abbreviations

AGM	annual general meeting
AIM	Alternative Investment Market
APB	Auditing Practice Board
ARC	Accounting Regulatory Committee
ASB	Accounting Standards Board
ASC	Accounting Standards Committee
BERR	Department for Business, Enterprise and Regulatory Reform
CA	Companies Act
CAA 2001	Capital Allowances Act 2001
CDDA 1986	Company Directors Disqualification Act 1986
CIC	community interest company
CMCHA 2007	Corporate Manslaughter and Corporate Homicide Act 2007
CTSA	corporation tax self-assessment
DTI	Department of Trade and Industry
EA 2002	Enterprise Act 2002
ECHR	European Convention on Human Rights
EEIG	European Economic Interest Group
EFRAG	European Financial Reporting Advisory Group
EGM	extraordinary general meeting
FA	Finance Act
FII	franked investment income
FRC	Financial Reporting Council
FRRP	Financial Reporting Review Panel
FRC	Financial Reporting Council
FRS	Financial Reporting Standard
FRSSE	Financial Reporting Standards for Small Entities
FSA	Financial Services Authority
GAAP	General Accepted Accounting Practice
HMRC	HM Revenue and Customs
HRMA	higher relevant maximum amount
IA 1986	Insolvency Act 1986

IAS	International Accounting Standards
IASB	International Accounting Standards Board
IFRS	International Financial Reporting Standard
IFRSIC	International Financial Reporting Standard Interpreting Committee
ITTOIA 2005	Income Tax (Trading and Other Income) Act 2005
LLP	limited liability partnership
LLPA 2000	Limited Liability Partnerships Act 2000
LRMA	lower relevant maximum amount
PA 1890	Partnership Act 1890
SE	Sócietas Europaea
SME	small or medium-sized enterprise
SORP	Statement of Recommended Practice
SSAP	Statement of Standard Accounting Practice
STRGL	Statement of Total Reported Gains and Losses
TA 1988	Income and Corporation Taxes Act 1988
TCGA 1992	Taxation of Chargeable Gains Act 1992
TMA 1970	Taxes Management Act 1970
UCITS	Undertakings for collective investments in transferable securities
UITF	Urgent Issues Task Force

CHAPTER 1

The registered company

1.1 INTRODUCTION – THE LEGISLATIVE FRAMEWORK

In the last decade, the regulation of the registered company has been subject to an extensive consultation exercise with proposals for reform being advanced by both the Law Commission and the Department for Business, Enterprise and Regulatory Reform (BERR)'s (formerly the Department of Trade and Industry's (DTI)) Company Law Review. The upshot of this exercise was the issue of the Company Law Reform Bill in November 2005. The Company Law Reform Bill was not prepared as a consolidating Act of Parliament; however, given the wealth of changes during committee stage and the extent of the Bill, the government decided to consolidate much of the existing companies legislation into the Bill, which was re-named the Companies Bill 2006. On 8 November 2006, the Companies Act (CA) 2006 received Royal Assent, although with a proviso that the majority of its provisions would not come into force until 2007/2008. (The BERR expects all the provisions of the CA 2006 to be in force by 1 October 2008. See **Appendix 1** of this book for the proposed timetable of the legislation.) It should also be noted that the CA 2006 will be supplemented by substantial secondary legislation to invoke powers of the Secretary of State (see the DTI document issued in February 2007: *Implementation of the Companies Act 2006: A Consultative Document,* available at **www.berr.gov.uk**).

Although the CA 2006 consolidates a great part of the companies legislation, a limited number of provisions from the Companies Act (CA) 1985 remain in force. Other Acts of Parliament which specifically regulate the registered company include the Insolvency Act 1986, the Enterprise Act 2002 and the Companies (Audit, Investigations and Community Enterprise) Act 2004. In the case of the said Acts, a limited number of provisions have also been amended or repealed by the CA 2006. For the repeals, see CA 2006, Sched.16.

It is expected that the majority of the provisions of the CA 2006 will be implemented, to have immediate effect in relation to both existing companies and new companies formed under the CA 2006. However, a minority of the provisions of the CA 2006 will require transitional provisions.

1.2 THE CORPORATE ENTITY

A company, when registered in accordance with CA 2006 is, as from the date of its incorporation, deemed to be a body corporate (CA 2006, s.16). A registered company is a distinct and separate legal entity, divorced from its membership. The corporate entity possesses rights and is subject to duties in a manner akin to a natural person. Although a company may be registered with unlimited status (where its members have unlimited liability for its obligations), in the vast majority of cases, a registered company will be incorporated with a limited liability status. A company may be limited by shares or by guarantee. The former method of incorporation is by far the most common (unless otherwise stated this book will be concerned with a company limited by shares). A company is a limited company if the liability of its members is limited by its constitution (CA 2006, s.3). Companies limited by guarantee are commonly used as vehicles for charities or other 'not-for-profit' entities where the raising of capital has little relevance. Unlimited companies are generally only used in specialist corporate structures, which are beyond the scope of this work. It should be noted that a trade union cannot be registered as a company under the Trade Union and Labour Relations (Consolidation) Act 1992, s.10(3)).

A company limited by shares will issue shares in its capital to its members (its 'shareholders'), usually denominated in a UK currency value (the 'nominal value'). The purchase price for the new shares is paid to the company ('subscribed') and the new shares are issued to the subscriber ('allotted'). The subscription price of a share can be its nominal value or a higher amount than this (the excess being the share 'premium'). Shares cannot be allotted at a 'discount' (that is, at less than their nominal value, see, CA 2006, s.580).

Shares can be issued 'nil paid' (where none of the subscription price is paid upon allotment), 'partly paid' (where only part of the subscription price is paid) or 'fully paid' (where the whole of the subscription price is paid). Where shares are not 'fully paid' the company can generally demand ('call') payment of the unpaid subscription monies at such times and in such manner as will be set out in its constitutional documents.

Limited liability

A member of a company incorporated with limited liability status by shares, will only be liable to contribute to the debts of the company to the extent that his or her shares are not fully paid. Once the shares held by that member are fully paid, the member ceases to be liable to contribute towards the company's debts. Where a company is limited by guarantee, its members are only liable for the company's debts to the extent of their guarantee liability, which may be any amount, and is usually £1 to £10.

A registered company with a limited-liability status will therefore be liable for its own debts. The judicial acceptance of this principle was established by the House of Lords in *Salomon* v. *A Salomon Ltd* [1897] AC 22. Here, the proprietor of a small but successful leather business, a Mr Salomon, incorporated the business as a limited company in accordance with the registration provisions (then contained within the Companies Act 1862). Despite efforts on the part of Mr Salomon to keep the company afloat, less than a year after its incorporation, the company became insolvent. The company was subsequently put into liquidation. The liquidation (sale) of the company's assets realised sufficient funds to meet the terms of a secured debt but not debts which were owed to the company's unsecured creditors. The liquidator contended that the company (and therefore in effect the company's unsecured creditors) was entitled to be personally reimbursed by Mr Salomon. The House of Lords ruled that the company, having been formed for a lawful purpose and with no intent to fraudulently abuse the incorporation process had, in complying with the correct registration provisions of the 1862 Act, been properly and legally incorporated. A Salomon Ltd was an independent entity and as such responsible for its own debts. The legal entity was totally separate and distinct from its founder, to the extent that Mr Salomon had no responsibility for the repayment of the company's debts.

The immediate result of a company's incorporation is the creation of two independent bodies: the company and its membership. The membership of the company will take shares in the company; this represents the member's interest in the company. The nature and extent of this interest will determine a member's right to participate in dividend payments and in addition will determine the extent of the member's right to participate in the decision-making process of the company at meetings of the shareholders. Subject to any prohibition contained in a company's constitution, a shareholder may freely sell or dispose of his or her shareholding interest. In respect of the company's existence, it is irrelevant that the identity of its shareholders may change. A company's legal existence is not dependent upon the survival of individual shareholders.

Although, prior to incorporation, an individual or partnership may have exclusively owned the property and assets of the business, following the incorporation of that business the individual or partnership transfers the business and assets to the new company. The property vested in the newly formed company will be in the ownership of the company (see, e.g. *Macaura* v. *Northern Assurance Co* [1925] AC 619). Accordingly, while a company holds its property and assets for the ultimate benefit of the associated rights of its membership, a member of a company may still be convicted of theft from the company, notwithstanding that the member in question holds all or a majority of the company's shares (see, e.g. *DPP* v. *Gomez* [1993] AC 442).

While an individual may control the affairs of a company and may occupy several positions in the corporate structure, for example, as the majority shareholder/managing director, such a person cannot, in law, be identified as 'the company' or the owner of the company. In law, the company is a separate legal entity; it is not a slave, to be owned by any individual (*Lee* v. *Lee's Air Farming* [1961] AC 12). Indeed an individual who, as a majority shareholder and director of a company, controls the affairs and destiny of the company, may still be regarded as an employee of the company, for example, if he or she holds a valid service contract (see, e.g. *Secretary of State* v. *Bottrill* [1999] BCC 177; by contrast, see *Brooks* v. *Secretary of State for Trade and Industry* [1999] BCC 232).

Advantages and disadvantages of the limited liability company

The creation of a limited liability company is a means by which businessmen may limit the risk of investing funds into a business enterprise. In addition to possible tax advantages (discussed in **Chapter 4**), the principal advantage of incorporating a business is undoubtedly the limited liability status of the enterprise, coupled with the favourable and respectable standing that the public (often mistakenly) afford to a limited liability status. However, in small private companies, the advantage of trading an enterprise with a limited liability status may be somewhat illusory. Here, major creditors of the enterprise (usually its bankers and landlords) will often demand personal guarantees from the member(s) of the company to secure the company's indebtedness. In such a case, should the company's fortunes decline, the member(s) of the company may gain little from the limited liability status of the company as they will remain personally liable to repay the secured debts under their guarantees.

In relation to public companies, limited liability offers greater advantages and protection to the company's shareholders and directors. Unlike private companies, the expectation of personal guarantees is less obvious in the wake of security represented in the form of substantive corporate assets and significant levels of paid up capital. Further, unlike the private company, a public company is permitted to offer its shares to the general public (usually by having its shares 'listed' on a public stock exchange, which provides a marketplace in which the shares can be bought and sold), which is an advantageous method of raising substantial amounts of investment capital.

The principal disadvantage of incorporation is a loss of privacy for the business. Disclosure is a regulatory requirement that is imposed on companies for the general benefit and safeguard of the public interest. Information relating to the functioning and financial state of a company offers a degree of transparency, providing investors and creditors with an opportunity to obtain an insight into a company's business affairs. Public disclosure requirements are imposed by law and are made to the registrar of companies at Companies House (where registration documents and certain public information are filed). The disclosure requirements include the basic registration procedures, filing details of the directors' register, details of changes to the constitutional

4

structure of the company, copies of all the special resolutions passed by the general meeting of a company, details of most types of security created by companies over their assets and their annual accounts.

Every company must complete an annual return (report of company's affairs and details of its shareholders); this must be filed with the registrar of companies, at Companies House (CA 2006, s.854). In addition to the annual return, all companies must submit a directors' report for each financial year to include matters such as the development and business activities of the company and the amount (if any) which the directors recommend be paid as a dividend (CA 2006, s.415). Simplified 'shuttle' returns can be used where there have been no significant changes since the last annual return was filed.

A company must also provide an annual report of its accounts that must give a 'true and fair' view of the company's financial affairs (CA 2006, s.393). In the case of small and medium companies, the return of the accounts may be in an abbreviated form, and need not be audited. The annual accounts must be accompanied (where applicable) by an auditor's report. (Accounting and reporting matters are dealt with in **Chapter 5**.)

1.3   THE PROMOTION AND FORMATION OF A COMPANY

For a company to obtain the benefits of a limited liability status, it must first comply with the registration provisions contained in the companies legislation. However, prior to obtaining a certificate of registration, the formation of a company must be undertaken by a promoter. Although the companies legislation has never sought to define a promoter, the promoter is nevertheless essential to the creation of a new corporate entity. To establish a person as a promoter, case law illustrates that it is necessary to show the contribution of some essential element towards the incorporation of the company (see, e.g. *Whaley Bridge Calico Printing Co* v. *Green* (1879) 5 QBD 109). The level of contribution may be substantial, for example, the negotiation of the purchase of business premises or, on the other hand, it may be less extensive, for example, a person may be deemed to be a promoter by organising the appointment of a company director.

A promoter cannot be considered an agent or trustee of the company which he or she undertakes to promote, because prior to its incorporation the company will have no legal existence. Nevertheless, a promoter occupies a position which is liable to abuse, to the extent that the position is made subject to fiduciary duties similar to those owed by company directors. A promoter is also subject to the common law duty to exercise reasonable care and skill in the performance of his or her duties. As a consequence of the promoter's assumed fiduciary position, a promoter must make full disclosure of any personal interest in the promotion process. Accordingly, the promoter must disclose whether he or she has obtained a profit as a result of the promotion of the company concerned. Failure to do so may render the promoter liable to account to the company for the amount of the undisclosed profit (see, e.g. *Gluckstein* v. *Barnes* [1900] AC 200). Disclosure of a promoter's personal interest in the promotion of a company must be made to those persons who have invested in or are about to invest in the company, i.e. the company's shareholders or potential shareholders (see, e.g. *Langunas Nitrate Co* v. *Langunas Syndicate* [1899] 2 Ch 392). Where a promoter fails to disclose any benefit obtained by him as a result of entering into a contract connected to the company's promotion, the contract will be voidable.

Pre-incorporation contracts

Prior to incorporation, the promoter(s) of a company will be required to enter into contractual agreements relating to the pre-incorporated company. However, until a company is incorporated it has no existence as a separate legal entity and therefore cannot be bound by contracts made in its name or on its behalf (see, e.g. *Natal Land & Colonisation Co* v. *Pauline Colliery Syndicate* [1904] AC 120). Even after its incorporation, a company cannot expressly, or by conduct, retrospectively ratify or adopt a contract made in its name or on its behalf (see, e.g. *Re Northumberland Avenue Hotel Co* (1886) 33 Ch D 16). Neither may a company claim to have adopted a pre-incorporation contract by including the terms of the contract within its constitution (see, e.g. *Browne* v. *La Trinidad* (1887) 37 Ch D 1). However, following the Court of Appeal's decision in *Rover International Ltd* v. *Cannon Film Sales Ltd* [1988] BCLC 710, monies paid by a newly incorporated company to a third party in the mistaken belief that a pre-incorporation contract was valid, may be recovered as against the third party. In addition, the court may grant a *quantum meruit* award to the company for services which it provided, i.e. for the period in which the company was under the mistaken belief that the pre-incorporation contract was valid. The aforementioned remedies may also be awarded against a company in circumstances where a third party mistakenly believed that the business entity with which it had contracted was, at the time of the contract, an incorporated company.

The liability of a promoter

Section 51 of the CA 2006 provides:

> A contract which purports to be made by or on behalf of a company at a time when the company has not been formed has effect, subject to any agreement to the contrary, as one made with the person purporting to act for the company or as agent for it, and he is personally liable on the contract accordingly.

The wording of CA 2006, s.51 follows its predecessors CA 1985, ss.36C(1) and 36(4), the statutory language of all the provisions being derived from the

European Communities Act 1972, s.9(2). The effect of CA 2006, s.51 is to render a promoter personally liable in respect of a pre-incorporation contract, irrespective of whether the promoter signed the contract in the company's name or on behalf of the company (see, e.g. *Phonogram* v. *Lane* [1982] QB 938). For a promoter to avoid the threat of being made personally liable on a pre-incorporation contract, an express statement excluding the promoter's liability must be included within the contract. Despite the theoretical possibility of the appearance of such a clause, its practical effect would be to prevent the party with whom the promoter dealt from seeking specific performance or damages for non-performance or non-compliance with the terms of the pre-incorporation contract, i.e. neither the company (when incorporated) or its promoter, would be deemed liable.

Section 51 of the CA 2006 provides that a person who purports to contract for a company which was not then formed, as of the date of the contract, may, in relevant circumstances, be made personally liable on the contract. Somewhat surprisingly, the section makes no specific reference to the promoter's right to enforce the terms of a pre-incorporation contract. However, in the light of basic contract law principles, both parties will be able to enforce the contract (see, e.g. *Braymist Ltd* v. *Wise Finance Co Ltd* [2002] BCC 514).

Given a wide, but nonetheless plausible, interpretation of s.51, the possible application of the section would not appear to be exclusively confined to the standard type of mischief against which it is aimed, i.e. a promoter's ability to escape personal liability in respect of pre-incorporation contracts. Indeed, it is possible to interpret the section as applicable to any situation whereby a person contracts on behalf of a company which was not, as of the date on which the contract was made, legally incorporated in accordance with registration procedures. For example, in theory, s.51 could be applicable to a situation where a company sought to change its name and subsequently entered into a contract under its new name but in error of the fact that the new name had not been properly registered. However, notwithstanding the potential merit of such theory, the judicial interpretation of s.51 has specifically restricted the provision's applicability and relevance to the case of pre-incorporation contracts (see, e.g. *Oshkosh B'Gosh Inc* v. *Dan Marbel Ltd* [1989] BCLC 507).

1.4 THE REGISTRATION PROCEDURE

A company is required to be incorporated in accordance with the registration procedures specified by the companies legislation. Prior to the passing of the CA 2006, the registration of a company involved the delivery of two principal constitutional documents to the registrar of companies (i) the company's memorandum of association; and (ii) the company's articles of association (signed by the subscriber(s) named in the memorandum). In addition, a statement of compliance was required. For companies registered after the implementation of the CA 2006, the registration procedure is dealt with by CA 2006, ss.9–16. The following documents must now be delivered to the registrar to complete the registration procedure:

- The memorandum of association.
- An application for registration. If no articles of association are included with the application the company will be registered without a formal set of articles, in which case the statutory model of articles prescribed for the specific type of company in question will be deemed to take effect as the company's articles (considered further in **Chapter 6**). If 'bespoke' articles are required, these must be filed with the registration application.
- A statement of compliance (a statutory declaration by a solicitor engaged in the formation of the company or a person named as a director or secretary of the company) to the effect that the statutory requirements of registration have been complied with. If the company is a public company the declaration must provide that the nominal value of the allotted share capital is not less than £50,000 and that the amount paid up on the allotted share capital is equal to not less than one-quarter of its aggregate nominal value.

The memorandum and application for registration

In accordance with CA 2006, s.8, a memorandum of association must state that the subscribers:

(a) wish to form a company under this Act; and
(b) agree to become members of the company and, in the case of a company that is to have a share capital, to take at least one share each.

The memorandum must be in the prescribed form and must be authenticated by each subscriber. The effect of the 2006 Act weakens greatly the previous significance of the memorandum. The memorandum is no longer of any legal relevance to the constitutional structure of a company. For example, a company is no longer obliged to maintain an objects clause within its memorandum, the purpose of which was to spell out and bind the company in respect of its intended business purposes (discussed further in **Chapter 12**). In effect, for companies incorporated in accordance with the CA 2006, a company's constitutional framework will now be determined by the company's articles of association (discussed further in **Chapter 6**).

Further, specific obligatory information relevant to a company's registration that, by the terms of CA 1985, had been an obligatory requirement of the memorandum, is, following the CA 2006, now deemed to be an obligatory requirement of the 'application for registration'. The following information must be included in the 'application for registration' (see CA 2006, s.9):

(a) the company's proposed name;

8

(b) whether the company's registered office is to be situated in England and Wales (or in Wales), in Scotland or in Northern Ireland;

(c) whether the liability of the members of the company is to be limited, and if so whether it is to be limited by shares or by guarantee; and

(d) whether the company is to be a private or a public company.

The application must also contain:

(a) in the case of a company that is to have a share capital:

    (i) a statement of initial shareholdings; and

    (ii) a statement of capital;

(b) in the case of a company that is to be limited by guarantee, a statement of guarantee;

(c) a statement of the company's proposed officers;

(d) a statement of the intended address of the company's registered office; and

(e) a copy of any proposed articles of association (to the extent that these are not supplied by the default application of the model articles).

The application must be delivered:

(a) to the registrar of companies for England and Wales, if the registered office of the company is to be situated in England and Wales (or in Wales);

(b) to the registrar of companies for Scotland, if the registered office of the company is to be situated in Scotland;

(c) to the registrar of companies for Northern Ireland, if the registered office of the company is to be situated in Northern Ireland.

If the application is delivered by a person as agent for the subscribers to the memorandum of association, it must state the agent's name and address.

Statement of initial shareholdings

The statement of initial shareholdings must contain the names and addresses of the subscribers to the memorandum of association and it must state, with respect to each subscriber to the memorandum:

(a) the number and nominal value of the shares to be taken by the sub-scriber on formation; and

(b) the amount (if any) payable in respect of each share on formation, whether on account of the nominal value or by way of a premium.

Statement of share capital

The statement of share capital must contain the names and addresses of the subscribers to the memorandum of association and it must state, with respect to the company's share capital to be taken by them on formation:

(a) the total number of shares of the company;
(b) the aggregate nominal value of those shares;
(c) for each class of shares:

   (i)   prescribed particulars of the rights attached to the shares;
   (ii) the total number of shares of that class; and
   (iii) the aggregate nominal value of shares of that class; and

(d) the amount paid up and the amount (if any) unpaid on each share (whether on account of the nominal value of the share or by way of premium).

Statement of guarantee

In the case of a company limited by guarantee the statement of guarantee must contain the names and addresses of the subscribers to the memorandum, and must state that each member undertakes, if the company is wound up while he or she is a member, or within one year after ceasing to be a member, that he or she will contribute to the assets of the company such amount as may be required for:

(a) payment of the debts and liabilities of the company contracted before ceasing to be a member;
(b) payment of the costs, charges and expenses of winding up; and
(c) adjustment of the rights of the contributories among themselves, not exceeding a specified limit.

Statement of proposed officers

The statement of the company's proposed officers must contain the required particulars of:

(a) the person who is, or persons who are, to be the first director or directors of the company;
(b) in the case of a company that is to be a public company, the person who is (or the persons who are) to be the first secretary (or joint secretaries) of the company.

The required particulars are the particulars that will be required to be stated in the company's register of directors or register of secretaries. The statement must also contain the consent of each of the persons named as a director, as secretary or as one of the joint secretaries, to act in the relevant capacity. If all the partners in a firm are to be joint secretaries, consent may be given by one partner on behalf of all of them.

1.5   THE CERTIFICATE OF INCORPORATION

On the registration of a company, the registrar of companies will issue a certificate to the effect that the company is incorporated (CA 2006, s.15). The certificate must be signed by the registrar or authenticated by the registrar's official seal. The certificate of incorporation must state:

- the name and registered number of the company;
- the date of its incorporation;
- whether it is a limited or unlimited company, and if it is limited whether it is limited by shares or limited by guarantee;
- whether it is a private or a public company; and
- whether the company's registered office is situated in England and Wales (or in Wales), in Scotland or in Northern Ireland.

The certificate is conclusive evidence that the statutory requirements for registration have been complied with and that the company:

(a)   is duly registered under this Act; and
(b)   where relevant, is duly registered as a limited company or public company.

Prior to the CA 2006, a public company had to be incorporated with at least two members. However, following the implementation of the 2006 Act, it is now possible to incorporate a single member public company insofar as the CA 2006 does not distinguish between private and public companies in respect of a 'membership' qualification (CA 2006, s.123). (For the major differences between a public and private company see CA 2006, Part 20.) A public company must also be incorporated with a named secretary although this requirement is no longer applicable to a private company (CA 2006, s.270). In the case of a single member public company, the single member cannot be appointed as the company's secretary. It is the duty of the directors of a public company to take all reasonable steps to ensure that the secretary (or each joint secretary) of the company is a person who appears to them to have the requisite knowledge and experience to discharge the functions of secretary of the company. Section 273(2) of the CA 2006 provides that a secretary must have one or more of the following qualifications, namely:

(2)   The qualifications are –
    (a)   that he has held the office of secretary of a public company for at least three of the five years immediately preceding his appointment as secretary;
    (b)   that he is a member of any of the bodies specified in subsection (3);
    (c)   that he is a barrister, advocate or solicitor called or admitted in any part of the United Kingdom;
    (d)   that he is a person who, by virtue of his holding or having held any other position or his being a member of any other body, appears to the

directors to be capable of discharging the functions of secretary of the company.

(3) The bodies referred to in subsection (2)(b) are –

   (a) the Institute of Chartered Accountants in England and Wales;
   (b) the Institute of Chartered Accountants of Scotland;
   (c) the Association of Chartered Certified Accountants;
   (d) the Institute of Chartered Accountants in Ireland;
   (e) the Institute of Chartered Secretaries and Administrators;
   (f) the Chartered Institute of Management Accountants;
   (g) the Chartered Institute of Public Finance and Accountancy.

Incorporation

A company is legally incorporated upon the issue of a certificate of incorporation (CA 2006, s.15). The certificate of incorporation identifies the company registered by its name and allotted serial number and is conclusive of the fact that all the requirements of the statutory registration procedures have been complied with. The certificate is also conclusive of the status of the company registered, i.e. if the certificate provides that a company is registered as a public limited company, then the certificate is conclusive of that fact.

A company, having obtained a certificate of incorporation, is permitted, from the date of the certificate, to enter into business activities as a registered company (see, e.g. *Jubilee Cotton Mills Ltd* v. *Lewis* [1924] AC 958). Once the certificate of incorporation is issued, the legal existence of a company cannot be challenged; save in a case where the Crown challenges the legality of a company's business. The Crown may challenge and rescind the incorporation of a company for the purpose of protecting the public interest. For example, the Crown would seek to implement its power where the business of the company was associated with an illegal objective, for example, the manufacture of prohibited drugs or explosives, or as in the case of *R* v. *Registrar of Companies, ex p. Attorney General* [1991] BCLC 476, to prevent a company from running a prostitution business.

Where, in such circumstances, the Crown successfully brings proceedings to strike a company off the companies register, the company's existence is retrospectively denied. In law, the company will be regarded as an enterprise which never achieved incorporation in accordance with the provisions of companies legislation. As such, any outstanding contractual obligations that were incurred by the business whilst it was on the companies register, will be rendered void.

Commencement of business

A private company may commence business from the date of its incorporation, whereas a public limited company must, prior to the commencement of its business, wait until it has received a trading certificate (CA 2006, s.761). Where a public company commences business prior to receipt of a trading certificate, any party with whom the company dealt will nevertheless be protected and the contract will not be set aside. However, the company and any officer in default of the provision will be liable to a fine.

'Off-the-shelf' companies

A registered company may be purchased from an agency specialising in the sale of 'off-the-shelf' companies. An off-the-shelf company is one incorporated in accordance with the registration provisions of the Companies Act, normally having a minimal share capital (usually two £1 shares). The ultimate purpose for its incorporation is its subsequent sale. The advantage to a prospective purchaser of an off-the-shelf company is the speed, relatively low cost and ease by which a business can attain a corporate form. On the payment of a fee (to the agency supplying the off-the-shelf company) the relevant transfers of shares and company's registers will be conveyed to the purchasers of the company. Notification in the change of address of the company's registered office, company directors and secretary, will then be made. The new shareholders of the company may also, if they so wish, change, in accordance with the relevant statutory procedures, the company's name and make any other amendment to the company's constitution as they see fit, for example, alter the company's articles.

Electronic communications

Following the enactment of the Electronic Communications Act 2000, companies have been permitted to submit registration documents electronically (companies have also been able to communicate annual general meeting (AGM) notices and the contents of their annual report and accounts to shareholders by electronic means). Electronic incorporation is basically a process of registration via e-mail with appropriate attachments (the memorandum and articles and other registration forms, etc.) being sent to and processed electronically by Companies House.

Sections 114–8 of the CA 2006 (supplemented by CA 2006, Scheds.4 and 5) deal generally with electronic communications. The purpose behind the company communications provisions is that unless otherwise provided for, companies should be able to use hard copy or electronic communications (or both) in the communication of dealings between the company and others. The said provisions were brought into force in January 2007. As such, the First Company Law Directive is amended to reflect the use of information technology and electronic communications. The First Company Law Directive requires that basic company documents be disclosed via filing with a company registry, and by publication in the national gazette either of the full or partial text of the document or by reference to the document deposited in the company registry. It also requires that those documents be made available for inspection. In addition, the First Company Law Directive specifies minimum information that companies must include on their letters and order forms.

The refusal to register a company

Prior to the issue of a registration certificate, the registrar of companies must be satisfied that the requirements of the statutory registration procedure have been complied with (CA 2006, s.14). The registrar may refuse to register a company if its proposed activities are illegal or contrary to public policy (see, e.g. *R* v. *Registrar of Companies, ex p. More* [1931] 2 KB 197). However, the decision of the registrar to refuse to register a company is subject to judicial review and the registrar's decision may be reversed (see, e.g. *R* v. *Registrar of Companies, ex p. Bowen* [1914] 3 KB 1161).

1.6   THE CHOICE OF A COMPANY NAME

A company's name must be stated in its application for registration. The name may be subsequently changed by special resolution or by other means provided for by the company's articles (CA 2006, s.77). The name with which a company is registered must not be one already included in the index of registered company names (CA 2006, s.66). In accordance with CA 2006, s.1099 the registrar must keep an index of the names of companies (and other specific bodies to which the section applies). The index applies to:

- UK-registered companies; any body to which any provision of the Companies Acts applies by virtue of regulations under CA 2006, s.1043 (unregistered companies);
- overseas companies that have registered particulars with the registrar under CA 2006, s.1046 other than companies that appear to the registrar not to be required to do so;
- limited partnerships registered in the UK;
- limited liability partnerships incorporated in the UK;
- European Economic Interest Groupings registered in the UK;
- open-ended investment companies authorised in the UK;
- societies registered under the Industrial and Provident Societies Act 1965.

Any person may inspect the registrar's index of company names (CA 2006, s.1100). However, the registrar of companies is not responsible for checking the companies name index prior to the registration of a company; the responsibility for that task falls on the person in control of the company's promotion process. In respect of the registration of a company's name and in accordance with CA 2006, s.64 the Secretary of State may make such regulations:

- under s.64(3):

    (a) as to matters that are to be disregarded, and
    (b) as to words, expressions, signs or symbols that are, or are not, to be regarded as the same, for the purposes of this section.

- under s.64(4):

    (a) that registration by a name that would otherwise be prohibited is permitted:

        (i)   in specified circumstances, or
        (ii) with specified consent, and

    (b) that if those circumstances obtain or that consent is given at the time a company is registered by a name, a subsequent change of circumstances or withdrawal of consent does not affect the registration.

Sections 67–8 of the CA 2006 provide that within 12 months of a company's registration the Secretary of State may direct a company to change its name in circumstances where the choice of name was the same as or too similar to the name of a company already listed on the register. Any such direction must specify the period within which the company is to change its name. The Secretary of State may, by a further direction, extend that period. If a company fails to comply with the direction, an offence is committed by (a) the company, and (b) every officer of the company who is in default. For this purpose a shadow director is treated as an officer of the company. A person guilty of an offence under this section is liable on summary conviction to a fine.

The CA 2006 also introduces new provisions (CA 2006, ss.69–74) whereby a person (the applicant) may object to a company's registered name on the ground that it is the same as or sufficiently similar to a name associated with the applicant in which he or she has goodwill, whereby the use of the name would be likely to mislead by suggesting a connection between the company and the applicant. The objection must be made by application to a company names adjudicator. The adjudicator may make an order requiring the respondent company to change its name to one that is not an offending name.

Change of name due to misleading information or indication of activities

Section 75 of the CA 2006 provides that if misleading information has been given for the purposes of a company's registration by a particular name, or that an undertaking or assurance has been given for that purpose and has not been fulfilled, the Secretary of State may direct the company to change its name. Any such direction must be given in writing within five years of the company's registration by that name, and must specify the period within which the company is to change its name (see, e.g. *Association of Certified*

Public Accountants of Britain v. *Secretary of State for Trade and Industry* [1997] 2 BCLC 307).

In accordance with CA 2006, s.76 if the name by which a company is registered gives so misleading an indication of the nature of its activities as to be likely to cause harm to the public, the Secretary of State may direct the company, in writing, to change its name. The direction must be complied with within a period of six weeks from the date of the direction or such longer period as the Secretary of State may determine. The company may, within three weeks of the Secretary of State's direction, apply to the court to set the direction aside. In order to establish liability, it is not sufficient to show that a name is misleading; a likelihood of harm must also be shown.

The passing off action

Where the Secretary of State refuses to exercise his or her powers under the companies legislation a company already in existence may, by means of a passing off action, challenge a name adopted by a newly incorporated company on the premise that the reputation of the existing enterprise was exploited by the new enterprise's choice of name and business activity. The passing off action is a common law remedy and may be invoked by an incorporated or unincorporated business in circumstances where a newly formed business adopts the name of an existing enterprise or a name which is similar to the existing enterprise. It should be stressed that in addition to a similarity in the name of the new enterprise, it must also be established that the new enterprise is engaged in a similar type of business activity to the claimant (see, e.g. *Ewing* v. *Buttercup Margarine Co Ltd* [1917] 2 Ch 1).

General restrictions on the use of a company name

- 'The name of a limited company that is a public company must end with public limited company' or 'plc' (or Welsh equivalents) (CA 2006, s.58). Subject to limited exceptions under CA 2006, s.60, the name of a limited company that is a private company must end with 'limited' or 'ltd.' (or Welsh equivalents) (CA 2006, s.59). Previously, under CA 1985, s.26(1) it was provided that otherwise than at the end of a company's name it was prohibited to insert the words limited, unlimited or public limited company (or their Welsh equivalents) into a company's name. However there is no equivalent to this provision within the CA 2006 (but note below).
- Where the Secretary of State is of the opinion that the use of a company name may constitute a criminal offence or is otherwise offensive, the use of the name may be prohibited (CA 2006, s.53).
- The Secretary of State may, by regulations, specify what letters, symbols, etc. may be used in a company's registered name; the regulations may also

specify a permitted format for a name (for example, to prevent the use of superscript or subscript; see CA 2006, s.57).

- If the Secretary of State considers that the use of a company name implies a connection with HM Government or any local government authority or agency, the Secretary of State may refuse to allow the company name to be registered (CA 2006, s.54).
- Prior to the CA 2006, any business was restricted from adopting a name governed by the terms of the Business Names Act 1985. In the context of companies, CA 2006, ss.1192–9 replace the Business Names Act 1985, with CA 2006, ss.1200–28 replacing the Act in relation to individuals and partnerships. The restrictions contained in ss.1192–9 apply to all companies and not, as under the Business Names Act 1985, just to any company capable of being wound up under the Insolvency Act 1986 which trades under a name other than that under which it is registered. The restrictions apply to any partnership whose members include a company. The Secretary of State may also by regulations make it an offence to carry on business under names using indicators of a particular legal status (e.g. 'ltd.' and 'plc') in companies' registered names (other than legitimately at the end of the business name). Finally, it is an offence to use a business name that gives so misleading an indication of the nature of the activities carried on by the business that it would be likely to cause harm to the public.
- By CA 1985, s.349(1) (this provision is retained in the CA 1985), a company may be fined where it fails to legibly make mention of its name (including its limited liability status) in all its business letters, notices, websites, invoices, receipts, letters of credit, bills of exchange, cheques and other instruments which confer a monetary obligation on the part of the company. Further, the company's business letters, order forms and websites must include fuller particulars, namely, the company's place of registration and the number with which it is registered, and the address of its registered office.
- A company's registered name must be clearly and conspicuously affixed or painted on the outside of every office or other premises from where it conducts its business. A company (and every officer of it who is in default) which fails to do so will be liable to a fine (CA 1985, s.348). The abbreviation 'Ltd' for a private limited company and 'plc' for a public limited company will suffice for the purposes of ss.348 and 349 as will the abbreviation 'Co' to represent company. The word 'and' may also be represented by the abbreviation '&'.

CA 1985, s.349(4)

Although CA 1985, s.349(4) is rarely invoked, the potential consequences of a breach of the provision are severe.

Section 349(4) of the Companies Act 1985 provides that:

> If an officer of a company or a person on its behalf signs or authorises to be signed on behalf of the company any bill of exchange, promissory note, endorsement, cheque or order for money or goods in which the company's name is not mentioned as required by section 349(1), he is liable to a fine; and he is further personally liable to the holder of the bill of exchange, promissory note, cheque or order for money or goods for the amount of it (unless it is duly paid by the company).

The protection afforded by s.349(4) is therefore one of an assurance to the person receiving the relevant instrument which contains a misdescribed corporate name that if the liability evidenced by the instrument is not met by the debtor company, then the person(s) responsible for signing the instrument will be deemed personally liable to discharge that liability. A breach of the provision is also punishable as a fine under the criminal law. In practice, s.349(4) is more likely to be invoked where a company is, itself, unable to meet the terms of the relevant instrument, i.e. where the company is insolvent. In addition, personal liability may be attached to any officer of a company who knowingly authorised the endorsement of an instrument containing a misdescribed form of the company's name unless, in applying a reasonable man test, that officer was unaware (and could not reasonably have been expected to have been aware) that the instrument in question contained a misdescription of the company's name.

In adopting a strict adherence to the literal rule of construction, the provision is construed by the courts as restrictive of any mistake in the linguistical characteristics of the representation of a company's name. As a consequence of its rigid interpretation, even a minor spelling mistake or error in the order in which a company's name is properly represented may invoke the implementation of the provision. For example, in *Hendon* v. *Adelman* (1973) 117 SJ 631 a cheque endorsed in the name 'L.R. Agencies Ltd' was, insofar as the correct name of the company should have been represented as 'L & R Agencies Ltd', held to be contrary to the terms of the provision. The rigid construction of s.349(4) is such that a person authorised to endorse an instrument on behalf of a company may not rely, in an attempt to avoid personal liability, on the fact that the misdescription of a corporate name had no adverse effect on the decision of the recipient of the instrument to enter into the transaction to which the instrument related. A defendant's potential liability is not determined by a subjective or even objective consideration of motive or intent in relation to the nature of the misdescription (see, e.g. *Maxform* v. *Mariani & Goodville Ltd* [1981] 2 Lloyd's Rep 54). Despite an occasional authority to the contrary (see, e.g. *Jenice* v. *Dan* [1993] BCLC 1349), motive or intent are factors which should be quite irrelevant to the determination of the issue (see, e.g. *Lindholst & Co* v. *Fowler* [1988] BCLC 166, *Fiorentino Comm. Giuseppe Srl* v. *Farnesi* [2005] BCC 771).

CHAPTER 2

The legal consequences of incorporation

2.1 INTRODUCTION

In law, a company is regarded as a distinct legal entity with a separate existence from its membership and management team. The independent legal status of the corporate entity is said to cast a veil between the company and its human constituents, 'the corporate veil'. A company's separate legal existence represents a fundamental and essential characteristic of company law; it is rarely impugned. However, in exceptional circumstances, the corporate veil may be dislodged to impose some degree of liability against the human constituents of the company. Nevertheless, in the majority of situations the veil will merely be pierced and not completely removed to the extent that the company's legal status will still be recognised. The corporate veil may be displaced at common law and by statute. In respect of the latter, the majority of statutory provisions that have a capacity to displace the corporate veil seek to penalise the irresponsible conduct of company directors involved in the management of insolvent companies.

2.2 THE CORPORATE VEIL

Displacing the corporate veil

Although the courts are generally reluctant to depart from the principles enunciated in *Salomon* v. *A Salomon Ltd,* specific examples of when the courts will displace the corporate veil may be categorised as follows.

Displacing the corporate veil in times of national emergency

When the nation is engaged in a serious political or economic conflict, it may be expedient for the court to displace the corporate veil to protect the nation's interests. Here, the justification for interfering with the corporate veil is to penalise individuals who have a significant connection with an enemy state. For example, when the nation is in conflict with another state, the corporate veil of a company registered in the UK may be pierced to discover whether the shareholders of that company are connected with the enemy state. If the membership of the company is so connected, the company may not be treated as distinct from its shareholders. Accordingly, a UK-registered company which is, for example, in debt to an 'enemy' company, may be discharged from that liability as it would be contrary to the public interest to have UK monies indirectly transferred to persons connected with an enemy state (see, e.g. *Daimler* v. *Continental Tyre & Rubber Co* [1916] 2 AC 307).

Displacing the corporate veil in cases of fraud

The ability to displace the corporate veil may be justified in cases where the formation of a company is considered a fraud, a sham or a facade, i.e. where a company was incorporated for an improper and/or illegitimate purpose. Case law is indicative of the fact that the fraud exception will ordinarily be invoked where the motive for incorporation was to enable the company's human constituent(s) to impugn a pre-existing obligation (see, e.g. *Gilford Motor Co* v. *Horne* [1933] Ch 935).

Another example of the displacement of the corporate veil based upon the fraud exception, is the decision in *Trustor AB* v. *Smallbone* [2001] 1WLR 1177. Here, the defendant (D), misappropriated moneys from a company (T) of which he was the managing director and transferred the funds to another company (X). D controlled X, and the incoming funds from T were used to make payments to D's wife and another company controlled by D. T sought the return of the monies misappropriated by D. D was held personally liable for the return of the funds on the basis that X was a sham, a facade, a vehicle used by D for the purpose of collecting the misappropriated funds.

The corporate veil of a company may also be dislodged in circumstances where assets of the company have been enriched by persons engaged in a criminal activity, notwithstanding that the company in question was substantially engaged in a legitimate business activity. As such, the assets of a company may be treated as 'property held by a defendant' within the Proceeds of Crime Act 2002, s.80(3) in circumstances where a defendant has used a corporate structure as a device or facade to conceal his or her criminal activities (see, e.g. *R* v. *K* [2006] BCC 362).

Displacing the veil to establish a controlling interest

Exceptionally, in a holding company-subsidiary relationship or where a group of companies is under the control of a dominant individual(s), the group relationship may be viewed as a single economic entity, to the extent that the corporate veil of the subservient subsidiary company(ies) may be removed to merge that entity with the dominant entity (holding company or individual(s)). Although there are cases that illustrate the courts' acceptance of an economic entity (see, e.g. *DHN Food Distributors Ltd* v. *Tower Hamlets LBC*

[1976] 1 WLR 852), following the decision of the Court of Appeal in *Adams* v. *Cape Industries* [1990] 2WLR 657, the qualifying characteristics deemed necessary to establish a dominant company's (or individual's) control over the subservient entity will be difficult to establish. However, note *Beckett Investment Group Ltd* v. *Itall* (2007) *The Times,* 11 July.

Prior to *Adams* v. *Cape Industries,* it was possible to establish a group of companies as one economic entity where the holding company (or individual) exerted a substantial degree of control over the affairs of the subservient company, to the extent that the holding company (or individual) controlled and dictated the corporate policy of its subsidiary. Following *Adams* v. *Cape Industries,* a company's (or an individual's) ability to control the overall policy structure of another company is, of itself, unlikely to be sufficient to justify displacing the corporate veil. The case of *Adams* v. *Cape Industries* provides that, in addition to establishing a holding company's control over the policy structure of its subsidiary, there must be a facade in relation to the incorporation of the subsidiary company. In *Adams,* the Court of Appeal gave two independent examples of what would constitute a facade. First, in relation to a group of companies, an entity could be described as a facade where it was created on the pretext of a lack of any corporate independence of its own, i.e. it was an agent, a mere alias for its master. Secondly, a subservient company could be described as a facade where it was a device created for the purpose of exploiting the corporate form in a manner that satisfied an improper or illegitimate purpose (basically akin to the fraud exception, see above).

Agency in a group relationship

Following the decision of the Court of Appeal in *Adams* v. *Cape Industries,* an agency relationship between a holding company and a subsidiary will facilitate a finding that the holding company (the principal) was totally responsible for the actions of its subsidiary (the agent) (see, e.g. *Smith Stone & Knight Ltd* v. *Birmingham Corp* [1939] 4 All ER 116). In the context of an agency relationship between corporate entities, agency may be tentatively defined as a relationship which is based upon the express or implied consent of both the subsidiary company and its holding company, whereby the subsidiary company is made subject to the holding company's control and will, to the extent that the subsidiary conducts its business affairs for the ultimate benefit of the holding company (see, e.g. *Garnac Grain Co Inc* v. *HMF Faure and Fairclough Ltd* [1968] AC 1130 at 1137). In *Adams* v. *Cape Industries,* Cape's relationship with its subsidiary was not deemed to be an agency relationship because of a lack of absolute control on the part of Cape over the subsidiary's affairs. The subsidiary employed its own staff, rented its own warehouses, occasionally purchased materials on its own behalf, earned its own profits and paid tax in a foreign jurisdiction (USA). Similarly, in *Kodak* v. *Clarke* [1902] 2 KB 450, the court denied the existence of an agency relationship between an English holding company and its overseas subsidiary because the English company, which held 98 per cent of the subsidiary's shares, never attempted to interfere with the management of the subsidiary.

Summary

A court's ability to lift the corporate veil is indicative of the existence of a state of national emergency, a fraud/facade or an agency relationship. It may be argued that the accepted headings mask the fundamental justification for denying the preservation of the corporate veil, namely, to prevent injustice, a perversion of the corporate form. However, if justice was the fundamental criteria in displacing the corporate veil, the said accepted headings would not be closed and it would be possible for the courts to extend their boundaries. This is most unlikely following *Adams* v. *Cape Industries*. Here, the Court of Appeal strongly denied that justice issues were to be given any distinct relevance in determining whether to displace the corporate veil.

Notwithstanding that in *Adams* v. *Cape Industries*, the Court of Appeal unequivocally denied that issues of justice could form the basis of a decision to displace the corporate veil, the first instance judgment of Richard Southwell QC, sitting as a deputy High Court judge in *Creasey* v. *Breachwood Motors Ltd* [1992] BCC 639, attempted to reassert the necessity of considering equitable issues in determining whether to displace the corporate veil. Here, it was held that even where a case fell outside the accepted headings (provided in *Adams* v. *Cape*), it was still possible to exercise a judicial discretion to displace the corporate veil. In *Creasey* an employee (C) of W Ltd (W) claimed unfair dismissal. W carried on business at premises owned by B Ltd (B); the same two individuals controlled both companies. C commenced an action against W for wrongful dismissal. However, before proceedings were commenced against W, the company ceased trading. B took over all of W's assets and paid off W's trade creditors, with the exception of C's claim for compensation. W Ltd was subsequently struck off the Companies Register pursuant to Companies Act (CA) 1985, s.652, i.e. for not carrying on any business. As the effect of the order was to end the legal existence of W, C's solicitors successfully applied to have W substituted by B as the defendant to the order made in favour of C. B appealed to the High Court but failed. In removing the corporate veil of W, the court considered that W was but a part of B. Therefore, B was deemed responsible for the payment of any compensation order in favour of C. In *Creasey*, the corporate veil was lifted for justice's sake.

Nevertheless, subsequent decisions of the English courts have, in reaffirming the lengthy and powerful comments of the Court of Appeal in *Adams* v. *Cape Industries*, sought to deny that individual issues of justice may facilitate the removal of the corporate veil. In *Ord* v. *Belhaven Pubs Ltd* [1998] 2 BCLC 447, the Court of Appeal condemned the reasoning applied in *Creasey*, stating that the case should no longer be treated as authoritative. (See also *Yukong Lines Ltd of Korea* v. *Rendsburg Investments* [1998] BCC 870.)

Liability in tort

Where a director of a limited liability company causes the company to be involved in a tortious act, liability will, in accordance with agency principles, ordinarily be imposed against the principal (the company) and not the agent (the individual officer) (see, e.g. *Rainham Chemical Works Ltd* v. *Belvedere Fish Guano Ltd* [1921] 2 AC 465). However, a director, as an agent of the company, may be deemed personally liable if it can be established that he or she exhibited a personal as opposed to a corporate competence for directing or procuring the wrongful act. Accordingly, if the tort in question is of a fraudulent character, the director will not be permitted to escape the consequences of his or her own fraudulent conduct, a position affirmed by the House of Lords in *Standard Charter Bank* v. *Pakistan National Shipping Corporation* [2002] 1 WLR 1547.

In cases involving a tort of a negligent character, the ability to establish a director's personal liability will be dependent upon complying with the principles of law invoked by the House of Lords in *Hedley Byrne* v. *Heller & Partners Ltd* [1964] AC 465, i.e. it will be necessary to establish a special relationship between the plaintiff and tortfeasor (director) and to ascertain whether the director assumed a personal responsibility for the negligent act. Further, the plaintiff must have relied upon the director's assumption of responsibility.

The evidence to substantiate a claim that a company director should be made personally responsible for the company's commission of the negligent act must be little short of overwhelming, a fact illustrated by the decision of the House of Lords in *Williams* v. *Natural Life Health Ltd* [1998] 1 BCLC 689. Here, the director in question was not personally liable in negligence because, although the company relied almost exclusively on the director's personal expertise, such expertise was never marketed or advanced otherwise than under the company's corporate umbrella. In dealings with the company, the respondents never identified the managing director other than as a part of the company. Therefore, although a director may be portrayed by the company as the instrumental figure behind its trading venture, the director may not be taken to have assumed any personal responsibility for that venture other than where the director, himself or herself, expressly or impliedly affirms an assumption of personal responsibility.

2.3   THE PERSONAL LIABILITY OF A DIRECTOR – STATUTORY PROVISIONS

In exceptional circumstances a director may, by the operation of a statutory provision, be held personally liable for wrongs committed in the company's name. For liability to accrue, the statutory provision must be clear and unambiguous in its intention to displace the corporate veil (see the comments of Lord Diplock in *Dimbleby & Sons Ltd* v. *NUJ* [1984] 1 All ER 751 at 758). For example, legislation specifically concerned with the taxation of companies is usually interpreted in a manner to prevent the use of the corporate form as an instrument for tax avoidance (see, e.g. *Firestone Tyre & Rubber Co* v. *Lewellin* [1957] 1 WLR 464).

In the context of imposing personal liability against a director, statutory provisions targeting the delinquent activities of directors of insolvent companies are particularly relevant.

2.4 MISFEASANCE PROCEEDINGS

The Insolvency Act (IA) 1986, s.212, commonly referred to as the misfeasance provision, is applicable at a time when a company is in liquidation. The provision provides, by way of a summary remedy, that persons who, prior to the company's liquidation, were involved in the management of the company may be held accountable for any breach of duty or other act of misfeasance. Proceedings under s.212 may only be pursued where, prior to its liquidation, the misconduct which formed the subject matter of the misfeasance claim could have been made the subject of an action by the company. Accordingly, the wrong that forms the basis of the proceedings must have been perpetrated against the company and not in violation of the interests of an individual shareholder or individual corporate creditor (see, e.g. *Re Hills Waterfall Estate & Gold Mining Co* [1896] 1 Ch 947).

Under s.212, where a company is in the course of being wound up, the court may examine the conduct of any person who is, or who acted as, a promoter, officer, liquidator, administrator or administrative receiver of the company, where it is suspected that the said person misapplied or retained, or became accountable for, any money or other property of the company or was guilty of any misfeasance or breach of any fiduciary or other duty in relation to the company (see, e.g. *Re International Championship Management Ltd* [2007] BCC 95). An application under s.212 may be made by the official receiver, liquidator or any creditor or contributory of the company. In circumstances where a person's liability is established, the court may compel that person to:

- repay, restore or account for the money or property or any part of it, with interest at such rate as the court thinks just; or
- to contribute such a sum to the company's assets by way of compensation in respect of the misfeasance or breach of fiduciary or other duty as the court thinks just (e.g. *Re Morecambe Bowling Ltd* [1969] 1 All ER 753).

As a prerequisite to successfully pursuing a misfeasance claim, the applicant must establish that the breach of duty or other act of misfeasance resulted in a pecuniary loss to the company. Pecuniary loss is, however, defined in terms whereby misfeasance proceedings may still be sustained notwithstanding that a company's financial loss is not of a quantifiable nature. For example, misfeasance proceedings may still be invoked against a director where the director exploits his fiduciary position to obtain a secret profit, irrespective of the fact that the company did not suffer any accountable financial loss. In such a case the secret profit will be recoverable on the premise that in equity, it belongs to the company (see, e.g. *Regal Hastings Ltd* v. *Gulliver* [1942] 1 All ER 378, [1967] 2 AC 134). Under s.212, misfeasance proceedings may be commenced where a director is in breach of any of his corporate duties. Following the decision in *Re D'Jan of London Ltd* [1993] BCC 646, the term 'any duty' is indicative of the provision's applicability to both a breach of fiduciary duty and a breach of a director's duty of care.

A potential difficulty in implementing s.212 may arise in circumstances where, prior to the company's liquidation, a breach of duty or other act of misfeasance was ratified by the company's general meeting. Other than where the director's wrongful act results in the ability to purse a statutory derivative action (see Companies Act (CA) 2006, s.260 – discussed in **Chapter 15**), ratification will ordinarily absolve the delinquent director from the incursion of any personal liability incurred as a consequence of the wrongful act. As s.212 is a procedural device only, and does not create any new form of liability, the implementation of s.212 would, *prima facie*, appear to be inappropriate in circumstances where the alleged misfeasance had been previously ratified by the general meeting. However, where the ratification of the breach of duty or other act of misfeasance occurred at a time when the company was insolvent, the effectiveness of ratification may be questionable. Where a company is insolvent, the interests of the company's creditors will effectively override the interests of its shareholders insofar as the latter's financial interest in the company will be superseded by the former's expectation of participating in the liquidation of the company's assets. The effectiveness of the ratification of a wrongful act by the members of a company will be particularly dubious in a situation where the company's liquidation was an inescapable certainty (see, e.g. *West Mercia Safetywear Ltd* v. *Dodd* [1988] BCLC 250).

The extent and nature of a director's liability

Although in the course of misfeasance proceedings, an applicant may be successful in establishing a director's breach of duty or other act of misfeasance, the court, in accordance with IA 1986, s.212(3), is not compelled to make an order against the director to account for, to return or to compensate the company in respect of property or monies that were misapplied as a result of the misfeasance. Section 212(3) provides that:

The court may, on the application of the official receiver or the liquidator, or of any creditor or contributory, examine into the conduct of the person falling within subsection (1) and compel him –

(a)   to repay, restore or account for the money or property or any part of it, with interest at such rate as the court thinks just, or

(b)   to contribute such sum to the company's assets by way of compensation in respect of the misfeasance or breach of fiduciary or other duty as the court thinks just.

While the court may exercise its discretion not to compel a director to make some form of restitution for a breach of duty or other act of misfeasance, in the majority of cases it is unlikely that the court's discretion will be applied in this manner. However, a possible example of where the discretion could be employed, so absolving a director's responsibility, would be in a situation where a restitutionary order would have the effect of affording the company an unjust or undeserved benefit. In accordance with IA 1986, s.212(3), where a director is ordered to restore or account for money or property or to contribute to the company's assets, the extent of the director's liability may not necessarily correspond with the extent of the actual loss sustained by the company. Following the company's liquidation, the calculation of the director's liability may, in part, depend upon the company's liability to its corporate creditors. For example, where a director's potential liability for the misfeasance is of a greater monetary value than the company's debt to its creditors, then the s.212(3) order may reflect this fact, to the extent that the amount of the order, while at a sufficient level to compensate creditor interests, may be of a sum which falls short of the actual loss sustained by the company (see, e.g. *Re VGM Holdings Ltd* [1942] Ch 235, *Re Home & Colonial Insurance Co Ltd* [1930] 1 Ch 102 and *Re Loquitur Ltd* [2003] 2 BCLC 442).

As the purpose for pursuing proceedings under s.212 is to enforce a pre-existing right of the company, it follows that the ability to pursue misfeasance proceedings is a property right of the company and that any proceeds obtained as a consequence of the proceedings will form part of the company's general assets. Accordingly, the ability of the company's unsecured creditors to participate in the fruits of the s.212 proceedings will be subject to the prior claims of the holder of any floating charge where the charge is capable, on crystallisation, of attaching itself to the company's general assets.

2.5   FRAUDULENT TRADING

Although fraudulent trading constitutes a breach of the civil law, it is also punishable as a distinct criminal offence. The constituent elements of liability for fraudulent trading, under both civil law and criminal law, are virtually identical. Civil liability for fraudulent trading is dealt with by IA 1986, s.213, whereas criminal liability is dealt with by CA 2006, s.993. IA 1986, s.213 provides:

(1) If in the course of the winding up of a company it appears that any business of the company has been carried on with intent to defraud creditors of the company or creditors of any other person, or for any fraudulent purpose, the following has effect.

(2) The court, on the application of the liquidator may declare that any persons who were knowingly parties to the carrying on of the business in the manner above-mentioned are to be liable to make such contributions (if any) to the company's assets as the court thinks proper.

CA 2006, s.993 provides:

If any business of a company is carried on with intent to defraud creditors of the company or creditors of any other person, or for any fraudulent purpose, every person who is knowingly a party to the carrying on of the business in that manner commits an offence.

The procedural differences between IA 1986, s.213 and CA 2006, s.993 are as follows:

- The burden of proof in civil proceedings should, as with any other civil provision, be established on a balance of probabilities.
- A criminal prosecution, unlike a civil action, may be commenced irrespective of whether a company has been put into liquidation.
- In a civil action, the only party who may make an application to commence proceedings is the company's liquidator. In criminal proceedings, the applicant will be the Crown.

Protection afforded by the fraudulent trading provisions

Both IA 1986, s.213 and CA 2006, s.993 are applicable in circumstances where a person knowingly participated in the carrying on of a company's business with intent to defraud creditors of the company or creditors of any other person, or for any fraudulent purpose. The carrying on of a business may include a single transaction designed to defraud a single creditor (e.g. *Re Gerald Cooper Chemicals Ltd* [1978] Ch 262).

Carrying on the company's business

Section 213 is only applicable where the business of the company has been carried on with an intent to defraud (e.g. *Morphitis* v. *Bernasconi* [2003] Ch 552). In *Morphitis*, the Court of Appeal declined to invoke s.213, on the premise that the provision only applied where any business activity of the company (one may assume, an activity related to the commercial objectives which define the business), was carried on with an intent to defraud creditors. Therefore, not every fraudulent act or misrepresentation perpetrated by a company (for example, in *Morphitis*, delaying tactics incorporating a false representation in relation to the payment of rent for business premises), may be classified as carrying on trade in satisfaction of the company's business. Accordingly, the Court of Appeal's interpretation is perhaps bizarre in that a company is permitted to act as a vehicle or catalyst in respect of a fraudulent act, providing the sum of that fraud cannot be said to involve carrying on trade in relation to the business of the company.

However, a company which ceases to trade but continues to exist for the purpose of collecting and distributing its assets may be deemed to be carrying on its business, and in the pursuit of that business may be liable for fraudulent trading (see, e.g. *Re Sarfax Ltd* [1979] 1 Ch 592 and *Carman* v. *The Cronos Group SA* [2006] BCC 451). Similarly, where, for example, a company fraudulently obtains a licence to operate its business, the fraudulent act, although unrelated to the company's physical trading activities, may, insofar as it fundamentally affects the company's capacity to 'carry on its business', give rise to a potential liability for fraudulent trading (see, e.g. *R* v. *Philippou* (1989) 89 Cr App R 290).

Establishing fraud

In civil cases, the most obvious example of establishing that a company was allowed to trade fraudulently will be where the company continues to trade and incur liabilities, portraying itself (by its continued trading) to be solvent, when in reality it is insolvent, having little or no prospect of repaying its creditors and avoiding liquidation (see, e.g. *Re William C Leitch Bros Ltd* [1932] 2 Ch 71). To determine whether a company has been privy to an act of fraudulent trading the court will assess the nature and degree of the alleged fraudulent conduct in respect of the company's present and potential capacity to repay its debts. In addition to the non-payment of trade creditors, a company's evasion of Crown debts, for example, the non-payment of corporation tax, value added tax (VAT) and national insurance contributions, may also be tantamount to a presumption of fraudulent trading (see, e.g. *Re L Todd (Swanscombe) Ltd* [1990] BCLC 454).

Establishing liability

For an individual to incur liability for fraudulent trading under IA 1986, s.213, first it must be established that the defendant was knowingly a party to the carrying on of the company's business. The courts have construed this requirement as indicative of a person's active involvement in the commission of an act of fraudulent trading (see, e.g. *Re Maidstone Buildings Ltd* [1971] 1 WLR 1085). Although fraudulent trading may be committed by any person who was actively involved in the commission of the fraud, in practice, liability will ordinary fall on a person who is construed to have been a part of a company's 'directing mind' (see, e.g. *R* v. *Miles* [1992] Cr LR 657). A person who acts as a part of a company's directing mind will normally be actively involved in the management of the company's affairs, as such, executive directors (and/or shadow directors) will be the most probable candidates to incur liability for acts of fraudulent trading.

To establish an individual's liability for fraudulent trading one must show that the individual intended to defraud creditors of the company, or creditors of any other person. In seeking to prove that a person intended to commit the fraudulent act, it is unnecessary to establish that, as a consequence of the fraud, the victim of the fraudulent trading suffered any actual economic loss (see, e.g. *R* v. *Grantham* [1984] QB 675). The essential requirement of the provision is, quite simply, to establish that there was an intention to perpetrate the fraudulent act; it must be established that the defendant acted dishonestly. In accordance with IA 1986, s.213, a person's dishonesty will be measured in accordance with the notions of ordinary decent business people (see, e.g. *Re Patrick Lyon Ltd* [1933] Ch 786). In relation to criminal liability, dishonesty may, insofar as it is a question to be determined by a jury, be more aptly measured against the moral standards of ordinary and honest people (see, e.g. *R* v. *Lockwood* (1985) 2 BCC 99, 333).

Basically, dishonesty will be ascertained on the basis of whether, at the time of the incursion of a corporate debt, the defendant was aware that the debt would not be met on the date it was due, or shortly after that date (see, e.g. *R* v. *Grantham* [1984] QB 675). In ascertaining whether a person's participation in the fraudulent trading activities of a company was of an intentional nature, the courts will employ a subjective test to determine the state of mind of the respondent at the time of the alleged fraudulent trading (see, e.g. *Aktieselskabet Dansk* v. *Brothers* [2001] 2 BCLC 324). However, although the court's perception of whether a person intended to defraud will be measured by a subjective test, it would be misleading to suggest that objective considerations are completely ignored in the court's assessment. Realistically, a person's subjective perception of having being unaware that he or she actively participated in a company's fraudulent trading must be viewed in the light of the circumstances surrounding the alleged acts of fraudulent trading. For example, although a person who is accused of fraudulent trading may genuinely believe that the company in which he or she was involved would soon escape from its insolvent state, that belief may be without any reasonable foundation. Accordingly, where a company is privy to fraudulent trading, it would be most difficult to discount a person's active involvement in the perpetration of the fraudulent conduct unless he or she honestly and reasonably believed that he or she was not participating in the fraudulent conduct (see, e.g. *Re Augustus Barnett & Son Ltd* [1986] BCLC 170).

In determining whether a director(s) had knowledge of the fact that there was no reasonable prospect of the company's creditor(s) ever being paid, knowledge may be assumed in circumstances where a director(s) deliberately ignored the obvious, that is, by deliberately shutting his or her eyes to the obvious (it is suggested that a matter, as obvious, will be determined in the sense of whether a reasonable diligent person would consider the matter to be obvious given all the circumstances of the case (see, e.g. *Re Bank of Credit and Commerce International SA (in liq) (No.14)* [2004] 2 BCLC 236)). In *Manifest Shipping Co Ltd* v. *Uni-Polaris Shipping Co Ltd* [2003] 1 AC 469, the House of Lords identified the essential constituents of the 'blind-eye' knowledge test, namely, blind-eye knowledge required a strong suspicion that the relevant facts did exist and that there was a deliberate decision to avoid confirming their existence.

The nature and extent of the liability

Where a person is found liable under IA 1986, s.213, that person may be subject to make such contributions (if any) to the company's assets as the court thinks proper. The court's declaration will primarily be of a compensatory nature and will take account of the company's trading loss during the period of fraudulent trading. It has been suggested that the declaration may also include a punitive element and accordingly the contribution may exceed the totality of debts owed to creditors affected during the period of the company's fraudulent trading (see, e.g. *Re a Company (No 001418 of 1988)* [1991] BCLC 197). However, in *Morphitis* v. *Bernasconi*, the Court of Appeal opined that there was no power by which the court could include a punitive element in the amount of any contribution under s.213. Notwithstanding that the fraudulent trading activities of a company may have predominantly caused damage to an individual creditor, any contribution which the court orders to be paid will be allocated to discharge the collective debts of the company's unsecured creditors.

2.6 WRONGFUL TRADING

IA 1986, s.214 seeks to curb and deter the irresponsible conduct of directors who have prejudiced the interests of corporate creditors in a manner that abuses the privilege of limited liability. The essential requirements for determining a person's liability for wrongful trading are contained in IA 1986, s.214(1)–(3). The remaining subsections of the wrongful trading provision, namely, s.214(4)–(8), are relevant to the interpretation of s.214(1)–(3). Section 214(1) provides that:

> Subject to subsection (3) below, if in the course of the winding up of a company it appears that subsection (2) of this section applies in relation to a person who is or has been a director of the company, the court, on the application of the liquidator, may declare that person is to be liable to make such contribution (if any) to the company's assets as the court thinks proper.

Section 214(2) provides that:

> This subsection applies in relation to a person if –

(a) the company has gone into insolvent liquidation,

(b) at some time before the commencement of the winding up of the company, that person knew or ought to have concluded that there was no reasonable prospect that the company would avoid going into insolvent liquidation, and

(c) that person was a director of the company at that time;

but the court shall not make a declaration under this section in any case where the time mentioned in paragraph (b) above was before 28th April 1986.

Section 214(3) limits the ability of the court to make a declaration in the following circumstances:

The court shall not make a declaration under this section with respect to any person if it is satisfied that after the condition specified in subsection (2)(b) was first satisfied in relation to him that person took every step with a view to minimising the potential loss to the company's creditors as (assuming him to have known that there was no reasonable prospect that the company would avoid going into insolvent liquidation) he ought to have taken.

Therefore, by s.214(1) and (2), liability under the wrongful trading provision will arise in circumstances where a company is in insolvent liquidation and where a person who was acting, or who had previously acted as a director of the company, knew, or ought to have concluded at some time before the commencement of the winding up of the company, that there was no reasonable prospect that the company would avoid going into insolvent liquidation. On hearing an application under s.214, the court may declare (other than where the s.214(3) defence applies) that a director is to be made liable to make such a contribution (if any) to the company's assets, as the court thinks proper.

Conduct giving rise to an action under IA 1986, s.214

In the absence of any specific statutory guidance as to the type of conduct that will give rise to the implementation of the provision, the scope of s.214 would appear very wide and applicable to any situation whereby a director is responsible for misconduct in carrying on the affairs of a company at a time when he or she knew or ought to have concluded that there was no reasonable prospect that the company would avoid going into insolvent liquidation. However, the scope of the provision is impliedly limited by reference to the nature of a director's potential liability. As the nature of that liability is a personal contribution to the company's assets, it is logical to assume that the type of misconduct which the provision was intended to govern is conduct that a director knew or ought to have known would, at a time prior to the commencement of the winding up of the company, deplete the available assets against which creditors could lay claim. The width of the provision is such that it will be applicable to any type of conduct that had the effect of depleting a company's distributable assets. Examples of such conduct would, during a period in which a company was insolvent, include over generous dividend payments, the sale of corporate assets at an undervalue and excessive payments of directors' remuneration.

Establishing liability – the reasonable diligent person test

In determining liability, s.214(4) provides that:

> . . . the facts which a director of a company ought to know or ascertain, the conclusions which he ought to reach and the steps which he ought to take are those which would be known or ascertained, or reached or taken, by a reasonably diligent person having both –
>
> (a) the general knowledge, skill and experience that may reasonably be expected of a person carrying out the same functions as those which were carried out by that director in relation to the company, and
> (b) the general knowledge, skill and experience of the director.

In ascertaining whether to proceed with an action under s.214, the liquidator will need to undertake a retrospective consideration of the financial state of the company. The liquidator must establish that the director's expectation of the company's ability to halt its decline into liquidation was unreasonable. Accordingly, a director's expectation of the company's future survival, based solely upon business instinct and which is speculative in nature will be viewed with much caution, whereas an expectation based upon factual evidence and professional advice, indicative of a possible reversal in the company's fortunes, will be more apt in convincing the court that the company had a reasonable prospect of avoiding liquidation (see, e.g. *Re Uno Plc, Secretary of State for Trade and Industry* v. *Gill* [2006] BCC 725). The determination of the state of a company's financial health will be gauged by, for example, examining the company's profit and loss accounts, its purchase and sales figures, its order books and its banking accounts. In respect of ascertaining whether, at a specified date, a director ought to have concluded that there was no reasonable prospect of the company avoiding liquidation, the court will also be mindful of evidence that may be supportive of a finding that the company was unable to escape from its insolvent state. Examples of this type of evidence may include:

- corporate creditors pressing for judgment orders in respect of outstanding debts;
- the withdrawal, suspension or reduction of financial support from the company's bankers;
- the withdrawal of support from the company's holding company;
- the resignation of directors, in an attempt to divorce themselves from any potential liability following the collapse of the company;
- the loss of contracts, or the inability to attain new contracts;
- the non-payment of Crown debts;
- an unrealistic forecast of expected profits; and
- an inadequate or non-existent business plan.

Section 214(4)(b) creates a flexible standard against which a director's awareness of a company's pending liquidation should be measured. The particular level of skill, knowledge and experience attributable to any given director must be viewed through the eyes of and in accordance with the expectations of the reasonably diligent person (see, e.g. *Rubin* v. *Gunner* [2004] 2 BCLC 110).

As the competence of a director is measured in the context of the standard of a reasonably diligent person, a level of skill, experience or general knowledge which falls below that objective standard will be ignored in relation to the subjective part of the assessment. However, in some circumstances, the subjective part of s.214(4)(b) allows different levels of competency against which the standards of company directors will be measured. For example, the subjective element will be particularly relevant where the director in question possesses skills which are beyond those ordinarily expected of a reasonably diligent director. Accordingly, if the director in question is, for example, a qualified solicitor or accountant, such skills will be relevant in determining whether the actions of the director were reasonable. Similarly, a director involved in the management of a small private company may be considered to have less competence than a director of a large plc (see, e.g. *Re Produce Marketing Consortium Ltd* [1989] 5 BCC 569).

While, prior to its liquidation, a company may, to the knowledge of its directors, have been trading in an insolvent state, it does not necessarily follow that such knowledge will automatically imply that the directors should have presumed that there was no reasonable prospect of the company avoiding liquidation. In determining liability under s.214, the courts will be mindful that their assessment of the alleged wrongful trading will be made with the benefit of hindsight. Accordingly, a director's judgment, in allowing a company to continue to trade while in an insolvent state must be assessed in relation to the circumstances prevailing at the time that decision was made (see, e.g. *Re Sherbourne Associates Ltd* [1995] BCC 40). Although a company is insolvent, a director may conclude that there is a reasonable prospect of the company avoiding liquidation. In such circumstances the court will be mindful of evidence which portrays a creditable and realistic attempt to reverse the fortunes of the company. Examples of evidence which may be supportive of a regeneration of the company may include the following:

- an injection of share capital which significantly reduces the level of the company's indebtedness;
- a review of the levels of directors' and employees' remuneration and in appropriate circumstances a reduction in them;
- the employment of cost-cutting measures to reduce corporate expenditure;
- support from the company's creditors in respect of the company's continued trading;
- holding regular board meetings and the constant review and monitoring of corporate policy;

- the production of up-to-date accounts and a detailed and realistic business plan;
- a reorganisation or restructuring of the day-to-day management of the company;
- a reasonable expectation of securing a new and lucrative contract, the effect of which would seek to reverse the company's dire financial position; and
- professional advice that was supportive of the company's continued trading.

The 'every step' defence (IA 1986, s.214(3))

The s.214(3) defence will be established where the court is convinced that a director, after first becoming aware that there was no reasonable prospect of the company avoiding liquidation, took every step possible with a view to minimising the potential loss to company creditors. In deciding whether there is compliance with s.214(3), the director will be assessed by applying the reasonable diligent person test. To satisfy the s.214(3) defence, the court must be persuaded that a reasonable diligent person, imputed with the director's own skill, experience and knowledge, in seeking to minimise loss to corporate creditors, would have been unable to take any further steps than those that had actually been taken by the director in question, i.e. following the director's realisation that there was no reasonable prospect of the company avoiding liquidation. The defence, in requiring that 'every step' must be taken with a view to minimising the potential loss to the company's creditors, sets a daunting standard which, if construed literally, may, save in the most exceptional cases, render its application to be most improbable.

In the absence of any detailed judicial pronouncements on the scope and the requirements for establishing the s.214(3) defence, its potential application remains uncertain. However, in seeking to establish the defence, a director would be advised to attend all board meetings, ensuring that his or her opinions were recorded in the board minutes. In addition, a director should seek to ensure that the company's accounts are kept up to date and where necessary he or she should be an active player in instigating meetings with the company's creditors. It is also important that the company's creditors are kept aware of and support the company's proposed methods for minimising losses, because following the company's slide into insolvency, the creditors will, in effect, become the beneficial owners of the company's assets and as such the company's directors will have a duty to safeguard their interests (see, e.g. *West Mercia Safetywear Ltd* v. *Dodd* [1988] BCLC 250.)

The beneficiaries of a contribution order

In circumstances where a court finds a director liable under the terms of s.214, the contribution order (if any) must be paid into the general assets of the company. Following the Court of Appeal's decision in *Re Oasis Mechanising*

Services Ltd [1997] 1 WLR 764, the potential beneficiaries of the contribution order are the company's unsecured creditors. Here the Court of Appeal held that the fruits of a s.214 action (the sum of a contribution order) were not to be regarded as a property right of a company and therefore the sum of any contribution order was incapable of being made the subject of a secured charge. The extent of a director's liability will be determined at the discretion of the court. The court may declare that the director make such contributions (if any) to the company's assets as it thinks proper.

Financing an application under IA 1986, s.214

IA 1986, s.115 provides that all the expenses incurred in the winding up of a company are payable out of the company's assets in priority to all other claims. The expenses in question relate to the realising or getting in of any of the assets of the company. However, in respect of proceedings under s.214 (and IA 1986, s.213), such an action is not regarded as an attempt to realise or get in an asset of the company. Although a s.214 action may result in a contribution being made to the company's assets, the said contribution (assets) had no existence at the time when the action was commenced (Insolvency Rules 1996, rule 4.218(1)(a)). However, as from 1 January 2003, rule 4.218(1)(a) was amended so that litigation costs, in respect of legal proceedings of which the liquidator has the power to bring or defend (i.e. ss.213 and 214 proceedings) are now included as winding-up expenses.

2.7   THE PHOENIX SYNDROME

IA 1986, ss.216 and 217, seek to constrain and penalise directors who, having liquidated a debt-ridden company, subsequently seek to form a new company with the intention of carrying on business activities previously associated with the liquidated company. This scenario is commonly referred to as the 'phoenix syndrome'. The potentially prejudicial effect of the phoenix syndrome is most evident where, prior to the liquidation of the failed company, the company's assets are purchased by its controllers at a significant under-value, and then the same assets are employed for the benefit of the phoenix company. The prejudicial effect is compounded where the phoenix company adopts a name which is the same as or closely associated with the name of the liquidated company, i.e. in an attempt to benefit from any goodwill associated with the name of the liquidated company.

IA 1986, s.216 provides that:

(1)   This section applies to a person where a company ('the liquidating company') has gone into insolvent liquidation on or after the appointed day and he was a director or shadow director of the company at any time in the period of 12 months ending with the day before it went into liquidation.

(2)   For the purposes of this section, a name is a prohibited name in relation to such a person if –

    (a)   it is a name by which the liquidating company was known at any time in that period of 12 months, or

    (b)   it is a name which is so similar to a name falling within paragraph (a) as to suggest an association with that company.

(3)   Except with leave of the court or in such circumstances as may be prescribed, a person to whom this section applies shall not at any time in the period of 5 years beginning with the day on which the liquidating company went into liquidation –

    (a)   be a director of any other company that is known by a prohibited name, or

    (b)   in any way, whether directly or indirectly, be concerned or take part in the promotion, formation or management of any such company, or

    (c)   in any way, whether directly or indirectly, be concerned or take part in the carrying on of the business carried on (otherwise than by a company) under a prohibited name.

(4)   If a person acts in contravention of this section, he is liable to imprisonment or a fine, or both.

Therefore, s.216 prohibits a director or shadow director of a company which is in liquidation (the section applies to a director who had held office up to 12 months before the company's liquidation) from being involved, for the next five years from the date of the company's liquidation, in the management of another company where the other company adopts the name of the insolvent company, or a name closely associated with the insolvent company. It is to be observed that it is not essential, in establishing liability, for the director of the liquidated company to be appointed as a director of the successor company, albeit that his or her involvement in the successor company must at least be at a managerial level (see, e.g. *Inland Revenue Commissioners* v. *Nash* [2004] BCC 150).

Although s.216 may be viewed as a strict liability offence (see, e.g. *R* v. *Cole, Lees & Birch* [1998] BCC 87), there are important exceptions to preclude the operation of the provision (see Insolvency Rules 1986, rules 4.227–4.230). Potentially, the most far-reaching exception is the courts' discretionary power to grant leave to a person to be associated with the management of a company that adopts a prohibited name (see, e.g. *Re Bonus Breaks Ltd* [1991] BCC 546, *Penrose* v. *Official Receiver* [1996] 1 BCLC 389 and *Re Lightning Electrical Contractors* [1996] BCC 950). Basically, leave may be granted providing the applicant's conduct in the affairs of the liquidated company is not deemed to be unfit in the sense that the conduct would justify the imposition of a disqualification order (see **Chapter 13**). Unfortunately, this judicial approach fails to recognise that there may be circumstances in which the public interest is prejudiced by the successor company's adoption of a prohibited name, even if an applicant's conduct falls below the standard justifying a disqualification order.

Section 216 fails to completely eradicate the phoenix syndrome as it is only applicable where the successor company adopts a name which is the same as or very similar to the liquidated company. The provision fails to regulate the practice whereby the controllers of an insolvent company purchase that company's assets at a significant undervalue for the ultimate benefit of a successor company. However, in an attempt to curb the prejudice suffered by corporate creditors as a consequence of the phoenix syndrome, specific provisions of the IA 1986 (ss.98, 99, 114, 166 and 388) restrict the ease by which the directors of a company in liquidation are allowed to purchase the company's assets at an undervalue; a practice known as 'centrebinding', so called after the case of *Re Centrebind Ltd* [1967] 1 WLR 377. In addition, CA 2006, s.190 (discussed in **Chapter 11**) prohibits, other than where approved by the general meeting, a company from entering into an arrangement, whereby a director or connected person acquires, or is to acquire, one or more non-cash assets of the requisite value from the company. However, here s.190 may be of little worth, given that a party with an interest in the transaction will be permitted to vote to sanction the arrangement at the general meeting.

Prohibition as to name

In relation to the prohibition of the name of a successor company, this is not confined to the first company's registered name but will also apply where the first company's business was pursued via a trade name. The court, in determining whether the name of the successor company is sufficiently similar to that of the liquidated company, employs an objective test to ascertain whether the name of the successor company is so similar to the name of the first company as to indicate an association with the first company. To establish liability there must be an obvious and definite linguistic link between the name of the successor company and the original (liquidated) company.

In *Archer Structures Ltd* v. *Griffiths* [2004] BCC 156, Kirkham J found that it was patently obvious that the name of the successor company 'MPJ Contractors Ltd' was so similar to that of the liquidated company 'MPJ Construction Ltd', as to suggest an association between the two enterprises. Further, following the decision of the Court of Appeal in *Ricketts* v. *Ad Valorem Factors Ltd* [2004] BCC 164, where there is any doubt in the similarity between the corporate names of the liquidated company and its successor company, the court may (although s.216 does not so provide!) take into consideration any similarity in the products dealt in, the locations of the business, the types of customers dealing with the respective companies and those involved in the management of the two companies. In *Ricketts* v. *Ad Valorem Factors Ltd*, after an examination of the aforementioned factors, the Court of Appeal held that the name of the liquidated company 'Air Component Co Ltd' was sufficiently similar to the successor company 'Air Equipment Co Ltd'.

IA 1986, s.217

Section 217 provides that a person who commits an offence under s.216 is also deemed personally liable for the debts of the company. However, it should be noted that liability under s.217 is not dependent upon an actual conviction under s.216, albeit that the constituent elements of s.216 must be met before liability can be invoked under s.217. Following a contravention of s.216, any creditor of the successor company may seek to recover a debt or other outstanding liability from any person who, in accordance with s.217, is deemed to be personally responsible for the relevant debts of the successor company. The said person will be jointly and severally liable with the company and any other person who may also be deemed liable (i.e. liability will be in respect of the debts of the successor company which adopted the name of the insolvent company). A person will be personally liable to discharge the debts of a corporate creditor under s.217, irrespective of the fact that the creditor was aware and possibly aided and abetted the commission of the criminal offence under s.216 (see, e.g. *Thorne* v. *Silverleaf* [1994] BCC 109).

CHAPTER 3

The types and classification of companies

3.1 INTRODUCTION

A company registered in accordance with the provisions of the Companies Acts will take one of the following forms:

- a public company limited by shares;
- a private company limited by shares;
- a private company limited by guarantee; or
- a private company that is unlimited.

Prior to 22 December 1980, it was possible to register a fifth type of company, namely, a private or public company limited by guarantee and with a share capital. It is no longer possible to register this type of company (Companies Act (CA) 2006, s.5).

In the context of the 'Companies Acts', 'company' means a company formed and registered under the CA 2006, or a company that immediately before the commencement of the CA 2006, was formed and registered pursuant to the Companies Act (CA) 1985 or was otherwise an existing company for the purposes of that Act (CA 2006, s.1(1)). CA 2006, s.2 provides that the 'Companies Acts' means:

- the company law provisions of the CA 2006;
- Part 2 of the Companies (Audit, Investigations and Community Enterprise) Act 2004 (community interest companies); and
- the provisions of the CA 1985 and the Companies Consolidation (Consequential Provisions) Act 1985 that remain in force.

3.2 TYPES OF COMPANIES

Public companies limited by shares

A company which proposes to operate as a public company must, as from 22 December 1980, have been specifically registered as a public limited company. Prior to the passing of the CA 2006, a public company was required to be registered with at least two shareholders and two directors, whereas the minimum requirement for the registration of a private company was one shareholder and one director. Following the implementation of the CA 2006, a public company may now also be registered with one shareholder (CA 2006, s.123) but must still have two directors (CA 2006, s.154). In relation to both private and public companies, at least one of the registered directors of the company must be a natural person (CA 2006, s.155). Unlike a private company, a public company must also be registered with a company secretary (CA 2006, s.271). Before a public company can trade it must be registered with a minimum share capital, currently £50,000 (CA 2006, s.761). A public company must be identified (at the end of its name) as a public limited company, although the abbreviation 'plc' will suffice (CA 2006, s.58).

In accordance with CA 2006, s.4, any company which is not registered as a public company is construed to be a private company. Unlike a private company, a public company may offer its securities to the general public (CA 2006, s.755). While a public company is entitled to offer its securities to the general public, it is not bound to do so, but where its shares are so offered, it has the option of applying to have them listed for dealing on the stock exchange.

Private companies limited by shares

Private companies limited by shares represent the vast majority (approximately 98 per cent) of all limited companies registered in the UK. Many private limited companies are small concerns and the shareholders of such companies are often the major participants in the management of the enterprise. Unlike a public company, a private company cannot offer its securities to the general public. The relationship between the shareholders of a small private company may ordinarily be viewed as one built upon mutual trust and confidence, a fact which is often reflected in a more flexible application of company law to these small concerns by the courts. This flexibility is born from equitable considerations that are closely related to partnership law principles.

Private companies limited by guarantee

While the vast majority of private limited companies are limited by shares, a private company may be limited by guarantee (CA 2006, s.3). Prior to the passing of the CA 2006, the memorandum of a company limited by guarantee would provide that should the company be wound up, the members of the company would be liable to contribute a fixed sum of money, the amount guaranteed (usually a nominal sum, for example, £1) towards the debts of the company. Following the passing of the CA 2006, the said guarantee contribution must be contained in a statement of guarantee which is required to be delivered to the registrar as part of the procedure for the company's registration (see CA 2006, s.11). A member's fixed sum liability cannot be altered and continues during the term of the membership of the company or, where the company's liquidation occurs, within a year of the member having left the company (see Insolvency Act (IA) 1986, s.74(2)).

The most appropriate type of company to be registered as a private company limited by guarantee is one with a charitable or non-profit seeking objective, such as a local club or association. As the company will not have shareholders, any profits made by the company will not be distributed as dividend payments. The members' capital (amount of guarantee) will be kept in reserve and may be called upon in the case of the company's liquidation. Unlike the uncalled share capital of a company limited by shares, the sum of money guaranteed is not deemed to be an asset of the company and therefore cannot be used as a means to repay or secure any of the company's debts.

Although a private company must have a name which ends in 'limited' (CA 2006, s.59), a company limited by guarantee was not compelled to include the word 'limited' after its name, if it satisfied CA 1985, s.30. Section 62 of the CA 2006 continues the exemption for companies limited by guarantee in circumstances where the company was exempted by virtue of CA 1985, s.30, but the provision only applies to existing companies and will not apply to companies formed pursuant to the CA 2006. The s.62 exception applies providing the company does not change its name and the following conditions are met:

(2) The first condition is that the objects of the company are the promotion of commerce, art, science, education, religion, charity or any profession, and anything incidental or conducive to any of those objects.

(3) The second condition is that the company's articles –

    (a) require its income to be applied in promoting its objects,

    (b) prohibit the payment of dividends to its members, and

    (c) require all the assets that would otherwise be available to its members generally to be transferred on its winding up either –

        (i) to another body with objects similar to its own, or

        (ii) to another body the objects of which are the promotion of charity and anything incidental or conducive thereto,

(whether or not the body is a member of the company).

The unlimited company

The unlimited company is a separate legal entity; formed as a private company and possessing the characteristics of a corporate entity. While an unlimited company may have a share capital, the members of an unlimited company are without the advantage of a limited liability status. Nevertheless, an unlimited liability company is regulated by the companies legislation, albeit that the regulation is naturally more relaxed than for a limited company. For example, unlimited companies must, as with limited companies, prepare accounts for the benefit of their members; however, an unlimited

41

company is not required to file accounts at Companies House, save in a situation where the company is a subsidiary of a limited liability company (CA 2006, s.448). Further, because the members of an unlimited company are, following the winding up of the company, ultimately responsible for the company's debts, an unlimited company is not subject to the rules and disclosure requirements in respect of the maintenance of share capital.

A private unlimited company is similar to a business partnership concern. However, unlike a partnership, the creditors of an unlimited company will not be able to sue the company's individual members for the repayment of business debts (save for where the debts have been personally guaranteed) unless the creditors seek an order for the company to be wound up. On the winding up of an unlimited company, the members' contribution towards the repayment of the company's debts will be in accordance with the terms of the company's constitution. Where the constitution fails to specify a procedure for such contributions, calls are made equally upon all the contributories; if a member cannot meet the terms of his or her contribution, the other members of the company will be obliged to make good this loss.

3.3 CHANGING THE STATUS OF A COMPANY

A registered company may change the status with which it was originally registered. For example, in a desire to secure further capital to finance future growth, a private company may wish to offer securities to the general public. In order legitimately to offer securities to the general public, the company must re-register itself as a public company. Conversely, where a public company's issued share capital falls below the minimum requirement of share capital permitted for a public company, the public company must re-register itself as a private company. The following statutory rules provide the framework by which a company may change its registered status.

Private company limited by shares (or unlimited) company to a public limited company

A private company limited by shares may change its status to become a public company by complying with the procedures and conditions for application laid down in CA 2006, ss.90–5 (previously governed by CA 1985, ss.43–8). An unlimited company may also change its status to that of a public company, providing it complies with the said procedures and additionally makes such changes to its constitution in relation to the company becoming a company limited by shares (CA 2006, ss.105–8).

The specific procedures for re-registration from a private company to a public company are contained in CA 2006, ss.90–5. First, the general meeting of the company concerned must pass a special resolution to effect the company's re-registration as a public company. In addition, specific conditions must be met. The conditions are summarised below:

1. Constitutional changes: CA 2006, s.90(3):

> (3) The company must make such changes –
>
>> (a) in its name, and
>> (b) in its articles,
>
> that are necessary in connection with its becoming a public company.

2. Requirements as to share capital (CA 2006, s.91(1)):

> (1) The following requirements must be met at the time the special resolution is passed that the company should re-register as a public company –
>
>> (a) the nominal value of the company's allotted share capital must be not less than the authorised minimum;
>> (b) each of the company's allotted shares must be paid up at least as to one-quarter of the nominal value of that share and the whole of any premium on it;
>> (c) if any shares in the company or any premium on them have been fully or partly paid up by an undertaking given by any person that he or another should do work or perform services (whether for the company or any other person), the undertaking must have been performed or otherwise discharged;
>> (d) if shares have been allotted as fully or partly paid up as to their nominal value or any premium on them otherwise than in cash, and the consideration for the allotment consists of or includes an undertaking to the company (other than one to which paragraph (c) applies), then either –
>>
>>> (i) the undertaking must have been performed or otherwise discharged, or
>>> (ii) there must be a contract between the company and some person pursuant to which the undertaking is to be performed within five years from the time the special resolution is passed.

CA 2006, s.90(2) provides an exception in the context of CA 2006, s.90(1)(b)–(d), namely, shares may be disregarded in respect of an allotment in pursuance of an employees' share scheme or in relation to shares allotted before 22 June 1982. Shares that qualify under this exemption must not amount to more than one-tenth of the nominal value of the company's allotted share capital.

3. Requirements as to net assets (CA 2006, s.92):

> (1) A company applying to re-register as a public company must obtain –
>
>> (a) a balance sheet prepared as at a date not more than seven months before the date on which the application is delivered to the registrar,
>> (b) an unqualified report [see CA 2006, s.92(3)] by the company's auditor on that balance sheet, and
>> (c) a written statement from the company's auditor that in his opinion at the balance sheet date the amount of the company's net assets was not

less than the aggregate of its called-up share capital and undistributable reserves.

The financial position of the company, so determined by the auditor, must not change between the balance sheet date and the date on which the application for re-registration is delivered to the registrar, to the extent that the amount of its net assets must not become less than the aggregate of its called-up share capital and undistributable reserves (CA 2006, s.92(2)).

4. Recent allotment of shares for non-cash consideration (CA 2006, s.93): Where shares are allotted by the company in the period between the date as at which the balance sheet is prepared and the passing of the special resolution to enable the company to re-register as a public company and the shares are allotted as fully or partly paid up as to their nominal value or any premium on them otherwise than in cash, then the registrar shall not entertain the application by the company's re-registration as a public company unless:

(a) s.93(2)(a): the consideration for the allotment has been valued in accordance with CA 2006, s.593(1) and a report with respect to the value of the consideration has been made to the company during the six months immediately preceding the allotment; or

(b) s.92(2)(b): the allotment is in connection with:

(i) a share exchange, namely the shares are allotted in connection with an arrangement under which the whole or part of the consideration for the shares allotted is provided by the transfer to the company allotting the shares, of shares (or shares of a particular class) in another company, or the cancellation of shares (or shares of a particular class) in another company and the allotment is open to all the holders of the shares of the other company in question (or, where the arrangement applies only to shares of a particular class, to all the holders of the company's shares of that class) to take part in the arrangement in connection with which the shares are allotted; or

(ii) there is a proposed merger with another company if one of the companies concerned proposes to acquire all the assets and liabilities of the other in exchange for the issue of its shares or other securities to shareholders of the other (whether or not accompanied by a cash payment). Here 'another company' includes any body corporate.

In determining whether a person is a holder of shares for the purposes of a share exchange (i.e. CA 2006, s.93(2)(b)(i)), the following will be disregarded: shares held by a nominee of the company allotting the shares, shares held by a nominee of the holding company of the company allotting the shares, a subsidiary of the company allotting the shares, or a subsidiary of the holding company of the company allotting the shares. The consideration for an allotment is defined to exclude any amount standing to the credit of any of the company's reserve accounts, or of its profit and loss account, that has been applied in paying up (to any extent) any of the shares allotted or any premium on those shares. An 'arrangement' means any agreement, scheme or arrangement, including an arrangement sanctioned in accordance with CA 2006, Part 26 or IA 1986, s.110.

The actual application to the registrar for re-registration as a public company (CA 2006, ss.94–6) must contain a statement of the company's proposed name on re-registration and in the case of a company that does not have a secretary, a statement of the company's proposed secretary.

An application must be accompanied by:

(a) a copy of a special resolution to the effect that the company should re-register as a public company;
(b) a copy of the company's articles as proposed to be amended (i.e. to comply with a plc status);
(c) a copy of the balance sheet; and
(d) if there has been a recent allotment of shares for non-cash considera-tion, a copy of the valuation report (if any).

A statement of compliance must be delivered with the application. A state-ment of compliance is a statement that provides that the requirements of re-registration as a public company have been complied with. The registrar may accept the statement of compliance as sufficient evidence that the company is entitled to be re-registered as a public company. If the registrar of companies is satisfied that a private limited company has complied with all the necessary statutory requirements applicable to its re-registration, the company will be issued with a new certificate of incorporation confirming its status as a public limited company. The certificate must state that it is issued on re-registration and the date on which it is issued. The certificate is conclusive evidence that the requirements of the Act as to re-registration have been complied with.

Public limited company to a private limited company

In accordance with CA 2006, ss.97–9 (previously CA 1985, ss.53–5), a public company may alter its status to that of a private company limited by shares or guarantee. A public company may be re-registered as a private company where the general meeting pass a special resolution to that effect. The com-pany must make necessary changes to its name and articles in connection with becoming a private company limited by shares or guarantee (CA 2006, s.100). An application for re-registration must be delivered to the registrar together with a statement of compliance (a copy of the special resolution must also be forwarded to the registrar: CA 2006, s.100(2)). When the registrar is satisfied that the requirements of the re-registration process have been complied with, the company will be issued with a certificate of incorporation confirming the company's new status as a private company (CA 2006, s.101). The certificate must state that it is issued on re-registration and the date on which it is issued. The certificate is conclusive evidence that the requirements of the Act as to re-registration have been complied with. However, the application may be challenged as follows.

Application to court to cancel a resolution (CA 2006, s.98)

Where a special resolution by a public company to be re-registered as a private limited company has been passed, an application to the court for the cancellation of the resolution may be made within 28 days after the passing of the resolution. The application may be made by:

(a) the holders of not less in the aggregate than 5 per cent in nominal value of the company's issued share capital or any class of the company's issued share capital (disregarding any shares held by the company as treasury shares);

(b) not less than 5 per cent of its members if the company is not limited by shares; or

(c) not less than 50 of the company's members; but not by a person who has consented to or voted in favour of the resolution.

The ability to challenge the application provides a possible safeguard for shareholders who hold shares for investment or speculative reasons, because the loss of public limited status may severely weaken the shareholders' ability to realise their investment in the company, i.e. the possible market in which shares can be sold will be greatly restricted from when the company is re-registered as a private company. On hearing the application the court may make an order either cancelling or confirming the resolution but may make the order on such terms and conditions as it thinks fit. For example, it may compel the company to purchase the shares of the dissentient members.

A limited company to an unlimited company

A private or public limited company may seek re-registration as an unlimited company. CA 2006, ss.102–4 provide the procedures to enable a private limited company to re-register as an unlimited company (formerly CA 1985, ss.49–50) whereas CA 2006, ss.109–11 deal with the situation where a public limited company resolves to become an unlimited company. The procedures are very similar. It is to be noted that under the CA 1985, a public company could not as of a direct right, re-register as an unlimited company (CA 1985, s.49(3)). Under the CA 1985, if a public company wished to re-register as an unlimited company, it would first need to re-register as a private limited company and then subsequently re-register as an unlimited company.

Under CA 2006, s.102, for a private company limited by shares or guarantee to re-register as an unlimited company, the company must not have been previously re-registered as a limited company (i.e. the private company had never previously been in existence as an unlimited company or a public company) and likewise in the case of a public company proposing to re-register as an unlimited company, the public company must not have been previously re-registered as a limited or unlimited company (i.e. the company was never previously a private company or an unlimited company) (CA 2006, s.109(2)).

To comply with the re-registration formalities, the entire membership of the limited company must assent to the change in status because if, as an unlimited company, the company became insolvent, the membership would be exposed to the risk of having to contribute to the company's debts. The prescribed form of assent to the company being registered as an unlimited company subscribed by or on behalf of all the members of the company, together with the application for re-registration and a statement of compliance must be delivered to the registrar. The statement must contain a statement by the directors of the company that the persons by whom or on whose behalf the form of assent is subscribed constitute the whole membership of the company. The registrar may accept the statement of compliance as sufficient evidence that the company is entitled to be re-registered as an unlimited company. The application is subject to additional conditions, summarised below.

The company must make such necessary changes in its name and to its articles in connection with its transformation into an unlimited company (a copy of the company's articles as amended must be delivered to the registrar). The company must deliver a statement of compliance containing a statement by the directors of the company:

(a) that the persons by whom or on whose behalf the form of assent is authenticated constitute the whole membership of the company; and
(b) if any of the members have not authenticated that form themselves, that the directors have taken all reasonable steps to satisfy themselves that each person who authenticated it on behalf of a member was lawfully empowered to do so.

Following compliance with the requirements of the CA 2006, the registrar will issue the company with a certificate of incorporation confirming the company's new status as unlimited. The certificate must state that it is issued on re-registration and the date on which it is issued. The certificate is conclusive evidence that the requirements of the Act have been complied with.

Unlimited company to a private limited company

Provided an unlimited company complies with the statutory requirements contained in CA 2006, ss.105–8 (formerly CA 1985, s.51), it is entitled to re-register as a private limited company. In compliance with the said procedures, the general meeting of the unlimited company must pass a special resolution that must stipulate whether the company wishes to be limited by shares or by guarantee. An unlimited company that previously had an existence as a limited company cannot subsequently be re-registered as a limited company (CA 2006, s.105(2)). In circumstances where an unlimited company re-registers as a private limited company but is then subsequently wound up within three years of its re-registration as a limited company, both the present and past members of the company may be personally liable to contribute towards its debts (see IA 1986, s.77).

An application for the re-registration of an unlimited company as a private limited company must be delivered to the registrar together with a statement of compliance. The registrar may accept the statement of compliance as sufficient evidence that the company is entitled to re-register as a private limited company. The application is subject to the following conditions:

- The special resolution (a copy of which must be forwarded to the registrar) must state whether the company is to be limited by shares or by guarantee.
- The company must make such changes in its name and in its articles to equate itself with the status of a company limited by shares or guarantee.
- If the company is to be limited by shares and has not previously had a share capital it must provide (i) a statement of initial shareholdings, and (ii) a statement of capital.
- If the company is to be limited by guarantee, it must provide a statement of guarantee and a copy of the company's articles as proposed to be amended.

Following compliance with the requirements of the CA 2006, the registrar will issue the company with a certificate of incorporation confirming the company's new status as unlimited. The certificate must state that it is issued on re-registration and the date on which it is issued. The certificate is conclusive evidence that the requirements of the Act as to re-registration have been complied with.

3.4 GROUPS OF COMPANIES

Although a registered company, as a separate legal entity, is responsible in law for its own actions and liable for its own debts, companies may be tied to a group structure, a structure controlled by a holding company. A company which is directly or indirectly under the control of the holding company, is termed a 'subsidiary' company. A holding company/subsidiary relationship is legally defined by CA 2006, s.1159. This provision provides that a company is a subsidiary of another company, if the other company:

- holds a majority of the voting rights in the company; or

- is a member of the company and has the right to appoint or remove a majority of the company's board of directors; or
- is a member of the company and controls alone or in agreement with other shareholders or members of the company, a majority of the voting rights in the company.

A company (A) will also be classed as a subsidiary of a holding company (B) where that company (A) is a subsidiary of another company (C) and C is a subsidiary of the holding company (B).

A company is classed as a wholly owned subsidiary of another company if its shares are exclusively owned by the holding company and/or other subsidiaries of the holding company, or persons acting on behalf of the holding company and/or its subsidiaries (CA 2006, s.1159(2), previously CA 1985, s.736). CA 2006, Sched.6, para.2 provides that in calculating voting control, the 'voting rights' are those rights held by the shareholders (or members where a company does not have a share capital) in relation to their ability to vote at general meetings on all or substantially all matters. In accordance with CA 2006, Sched.6, para.3(1), the right to appoint or remove a majority of the directors is defined as the right to appoint or remove directors holding the majority of voting rights at board meetings on all or substantially all matters. A company is treated as having the right to appoint a person to a directorship (of the subsidiary) if the appointment necessarily follows from that person's appointment as a director of the company, or where the company itself holds the directorship (CA 2006, Sched.6, para.3(2)). It is to be noted that rights are deemed to be held by a holding company if they are held by any of its subsidiary companies (CA 2006, Sched.6, para.7).

The membership of a holding company

A subsidiary or a subsidiary's nominee is not permitted to be a member of its holding company and any allotment of shares to the subsidiary from its holding company will be void (see CA 2006, s.136). However, the general prohibition so provided by s.136 is subject to exceptions (previously contained in CA 1985, s.23), namely a subsidiary may continue to be a member of its holding company if:

- it was a member of its holding company before 1 July 1948 (CA 2006, s.137(1));
- the prohibition in CA 1985, s.23(1) (or any corresponding earlier enactment), as it then had effect, did not apply, or where the prohibition in s.136 does not apply;
- the subsidiary or its nominee holds shares in the holding company in the capacity of a personal representative or trustee. However, this exception will not apply where the holding company or subsidiary has a beneficial interest under the trust (see CA 2006, s.139). An interest in the

holding company's shares, held only by way of security for the purposes of a transaction entered into by the holding company or subsidiary in the ordinary course of business, which includes the lending of money, will be disregarded for the purposes of determining whether the holding company or subsidiary is beneficially interested;

- the subsidiary is concerned as an 'intermediary' (CA 2006, s.141). An intermediary is a person who holds himself out and is permitted by a recognised investment exchange, other than an overseas investment exchange, as willing to buy and sell securities in accordance with the rules of the exchange (Membership of Holding Company (Dealers in Securities) Regulations 1997 (SI 1997/2306)).

Where a subsidiary company can bring itself within one of the above exceptions it is nevertheless denied a right to vote in respect of the shares it holds in the holding company (CA 2006, s.137(4)).

3.5   ACCOUNTING PURPOSES

For auditing and accounting matters, the definition of a group of companies is provided by CA 2006, s.1162 and Sched.7 (formerly dealt with by CA 1985, s.258). For accounting purposes a holding company is referred to as a parent company and save for when a parent company qualifies under the small companies regime (CA 2006, s.383) or is exempt by CA 2006, ss.400–2, the parent company must prepare group financial statements in addition to the preparation of individual accounts. The group accounts must be prepared in a consolidated form (CA 2006, ss.399–414). A group relationship is expressed in terms of a parent undertaking/subsidiary undertaking relationship. An undertaking is defined by CA 2006, s.1161 as a body corporate or partnership or an unincorporated association carrying on a trade or business, with or without a view to profit. CA 2006, s.1162 states that an undertaking is a parent undertaking in relation to another undertaking (the subsidiary undertaking), if:

- it (parent) holds a majority of the voting rights in the undertaking; or
- it (parent) is a member of the undertaking in its own right (or it has a subsidiary that is a member of the undertaking, or shares held in the undertaking are held by a person acting on behalf of it (parent) or any of its subsidiary undertakings) and has the right to appoint or remove a majority of the board of directors of the undertaking;
- it has the right to exercise a dominant influence over the undertaking by virtue of provisions contained in its articles or by virtue of a control contract; or
- it is a member of the undertaking (or it has a subsidiary that is a member of the undertaking) and controls alone, pursuant to an agreement with

other shareholders or members, a majority of the voting rights in the undertaking; or

- it has the power to exercise, or actually exercises, dominant influence or control over the undertaking; or
- it and the undertaking are managed on a unified basis.

The existence of a parent/subsidiary undertaking relationship in the situation where an undertaking (parent) is found to have exercised a dominant influence over another undertaking, is defined in CA 2006, Sched.7 as one whereby a dominant undertaking (parent) has the right to give directions with which its directors are required to comply with respect to the operating and financial policies of the other undertaking, whether or not they are for the benefit of that other undertaking.

The accounts must be comprised of a consolidated balance sheet dealing with the state of affairs and the profit and loss accounts of the parent and its subsidiary undertakings. It is to be noted that the statutory requirement for a parent company to prepare consolidated accounts ignores the individual characteristic of the subsidiary company as a distinct and separate legal entity. Therefore, for accounting purposes, a group of companies is treated as a single economic entity (explained at **4.5**).

3.6   THE COMMUNITY INTEREST COMPANY

A new type of company, the 'community interest company' (CIC), was created by the Companies (Audit, Investigations and Community Enterprise) Act 2004, Part II (as amended by CA 2006, Sched.15, Part 2). In introducing the CIC the government's aim is to increase (although not necessarily replace) existing forms of social enterprises such as charitable companies and Industrial and Provident Societies, with an ultimate objective of expanding and improving the transparency of the social enterprise sector. The government fears that without the CIC and the flexibility of a corporate form, the sector may be unable to achieve sustainable financing for the good of the community.

All in all, CICs are regulated by the companies legislation although they will be tailored to the needs of non-profit social enterprises. CICs are under the supervisory control of an independent regulator. Social enterprises suited to becoming CICs include those geared to promoting public services, for example, providers of community care services. However, s.35(2) of the 2004 Act provides a rather general definition, namely:

> A company satisfies the community interest test if a reasonable person might consider that its activities are being carried on for the benefit of the community.

As CICs are formed as limited companies (by shares or guarantee) they take the benefits of a limited liability status but as with any other type of limited company will be subject to the disclosure and reporting requirements imposed by the companies legislation. In addition to complying with the usual registration requirements for a limited liability company, a CIC must comply, and continue to comply during its lifetime, with specific 'community interest rules'. For example:

- A CIC must ensure that its profits or financial assets are not ordinarily distributed to its members or investors during its lifetime. However, a CIC may issue shares upon which a capped dividend may be paid, the capped amount to be decided by the CIC Regulator.
- Together with the annual accounts, a CIC must submit an annual 'community interest report' to the CIC Regulator. The community interest report must give a detailed account of the activities the company has undertaken in pursuit of its community interest objectives.

However, unlike existing registered charities, CICs will not be afforded any special tax concessions, a fact that may ultimately deter many organisations from choosing this type of business structure.

3.7 OTHER FORMS OF BUSINESS STRUCTURES

The limited liability partnership

Legislation to establish the limited liability partnership (LLP) was enacted by the Limited Liability Partnerships Act (LLPA) 2000 (supplemented by the Limited Liability Partnerships Regulations 2001, SI 2001/1090). This form of business structure is applicable to a business that seeks to retain the benefits of trading as a partnership but one that also wishes to take advantage of a limited liability status. An LLP is potentially applicable to all business partnerships comprising two or more members. The LLP is a distinct legal entity, a body corporate (LLPA 2000, s.1(2)) and therefore the membership of an LLP will have no personal liability for the acts or obligations of the LLP except as provided by statute or under the general law. Accordingly, where an LLP becomes insolvent, the LLP's assets and not those of its members will be used to discharge its debts. A member will have no liability to contribute to the repayment of the debts of the LLP, save if the member had previously agreed to contribute a guaranteed amount. The members, as agents of the LLP (LLPA 2000, s.6(1)), owe duties to the LLP that are similar to those owed by the directors of registered companies. Minority members of an LLP will be able to avail themselves of the protective provisions of the companies legislation.

However, an LLP is taxed as a partnership and not as a company and its internal structure remains more identifiable with a traditional partnership, for example, it has no share capital and a member's income will not be in the form of dividend payments. An LLP is obliged to register an incorporation document which is similar in content to a company's constitutional documents and has an unlimited capacity to enter into a contract or other transaction (LLPA 2000, s.1(3)). Although without formal articles in the manner prescribed for a registered company, the members of an LLP are obliged to enter into an LLP agreement, the purpose of which is to regulate the relationship between the members and the LLP and the rights of the members *inter se* (LLP 2000, s.5(1)).

In taking the benefit of a limited liability status an LLP must comply with the requirements and safeguards of the companies legislation in a manner akin to that of a registered company. (At the time of writing, the regulation of LLPs in respect of the companies legislation, is, unless specifically provided for by the CA 2006, governed by the CA 1985, insofar as the CA 2006 has, as yet, no general application in respect of LLPs. However, it is most probable that legislation will be enacted to correct this lacuna.) Accordingly, an LLP must file financial and other information on a regular basis, for example, a LLP will be obliged to file accounts and an annual return with the registrar of companies and will need to keep a register of charges. Further, the delinquent activities of members of the partnership are subject to similar sanctions to those imposed against company directors in respect of, for example, wrongful and fraudulent trading and disqualification. In respect of wrongful trading it is to be noted that IA 1986, s.214A (introduced by the 2001 Regulations) is specific to an LLP. This provision provides a liquidator with the right to 'claw back' any withdrawals of assets from the LLP which were made by a member(s) within the two years prior to the commencement of liquidation in a situation where the member(s) knew or had a reasonable ground to believe that at the time of withdrawal, or as a consequence of the withdrawal, the LLP was unable to pay its debts and as such the member(s) knew or ought to have concluded that there was no reasonable prospect of the LLP avoiding liquidation.

Business partnerships

A business partnership is a contractual relationship, but is subject to equitable principles and the provisions of the Partnership Act (PA) 1890. The PA 1890 defines a business partnership as a relationship (an association) between persons carrying on a business in common with a view to profit (PA 1890, s.1). The association may be constituted formally or informally (*Phillips* v. *Symes* [2002] 1 WLR 853). The property of the business belongs to its members and not the actual partnership business. Unlike a registered company, a partnership is not a separate legal entity, although it may sue or be sued using the partnership name. Although the Limited Partnership Act 1907 allows a member of a partnership to attain a limited liability status, a partner with such a status is precluded from taking an active role in the management of the partnership firm and therefore other than for a 'sleeping' partner, the 1907 Act will have little application.

A partnership is, in accordance with PA 1890, s.5, contractually bound by an agreement entered into on its behalf in the ordinary course of the firm's business by any of its members other than where a member enters into a contract without the authority of the other members and the 'lack of authority' point is known to the other contracting party. Further, PA 1890, s.10 provides that:

> Where, by any wrongful act or omission of any partner acting in the ordinary course of business of the firm, or with the authority of his co-partners, loss or injury is caused to any person not being a partner in the firm, or any penalty is incurred, the firm is liable therefor to the same extent as the partner so acting or omitting to act.

The vicarious liability principle established by s.10 extends to any wrongful act providing the act in question was undertaken in the ordinary course of the partnership's business. Here, a wrongful act includes an act involving dishonesty (see, e.g. the decision of the House of Lords in *Dubai Aluminium Co Ltd v. Salaam* [2003] 2 AC 366).

In contrast to a company, a partnership does not have perpetual succession. A partner's interest in the partnership business is a property right and while this right may be transferred, the transferee will not be admitted as a member of the partnership firm without first obtaining the consent of the partnership's existing members. In theory, the acceptance of a new member into the partnership will have the effect of dissolving the old partnership, that is, by creating a new one. Where a member leaves a partnership, the retiring member (or his or her estate) must be paid his or her share of the partnership business. Here, again in theory, the partnership will be dissolved, although in practice the partnership will, with the consent of the remaining partners, continue its existence. (On the dissolution of a partnership, see generally, the House of Lords decision in *Hurst* v. *Bryk* [2002] 1 AC 185.)

In an attempt to raise finance, a partnership may borrow funds and collectively the partners may give security for loans in the form of the partnership's assets. It must be noted that a partnership's ability to grant security over its assets is subject to statutory restrictions that prevent individuals and partnerships from creating floating charges over fluctuating assets (the nature of a floating charge is discussed in **Chapter 9**). Previously business partnerships were required to have a limit of 20 members (but with exemptions); however, this rule was removed by the Regulatory Reform Order 2002, SI 2002/3203. A principal advantage of forming a partnership business is that a partnership business does not have to comply with the many formalities required of a registered company. However, it should be noted that the current trend in legislative policy, aimed towards the deregulation of private companies, may eventually weaken the partnership's advantage in respect of the formality rules.

3.8 EUROPEAN STRUCTURES

The Sócietas Europaea

As a result of EC Regulation 2157/2001 (and its supplementing Directive (2001/86)) legislation to create a new European Company structure (the Sócietas Europaea (SE)) was introduced into the UK by the European Public Limited Liability Company Regulations 2004, SI 2004/2326. The SE is an available corporate vehicle for at least two commercial bodies with operations in more than one Member State. A SE may be created as a European public limited liability company registered in one of the Member States, provided it has a minimum share capital of €120,000. The SE will be governed by the terms of the regulation and more especially the applicable corporate laws of the Member State in which it is registered. If registered in the UK, the SE will therefore be governed by the terms of the Regulation but will primarily be regulated by the UK companies legislation as applicable to plcs. There are five ways in which a SE may be created, namely:

1. *Merger:* Two or more public limited companies or existing SEs may merge to form an SE provided at least two of them are governed by the laws of different Member States.
2. *A holding SE:* Two or more private or public limited companies (including existing SEs) may form an SE by promoting the formation of a holding SE. The companies promoting the formation must become majority-owned by the SE. At least two of the companies must be governed by the laws of a different Member State, or for two years have had a subsidiary company governed by the laws of another Member State or had a branch in another Member State.
3. *A subsidiary SE:* Two or more companies, firms or other legal bodies formed under the law of a Member State may form an SE by subscribing for its shares. At least two of the companies or firms must be governed by the laws of a different Member State or for two years have had a subsidiary company governed by the laws of another Member State or had a branch in another Member State.
4. *Subsidiary SE formed by another SE:* An existing SE may itself form another SE as a subsidiary company, in which it may be the sole shareholder.
5. *Plc transforming to become an SE:* An existing plc registered in the UK may transform itself into an SE registered in the UK if the plc has for two years had a subsidiary governed by the laws of another Member State. This process does not involve the winding up of the plc or the creation of a new legal person in the form of an SE.

European Economic Interest Groupings

EC Regulation No. 2137/85, allows UK businesses, corporate or otherwise, to enter into an agreement of cooperation with a business or businesses in other Member States. An agreement of this nature creates a European Economic Interest Group (EEIG). The purpose in creating the EEIG system was to facilitate cooperation between businesses located in different Member States. The businesses, which together form an EEIG, become its members although an EEIG may not exert control over the business activities of any individual member of its EEIG grouping. An EEIG has a separate legal personality, but unlike a registered company, the members of the EEIG are liable for the EEIG's debts; that is, it does not possess a limited liability status. An EEIG cannot invite investment from the public. An EEIG must not, in its individual capacity as a separate legal entity, seek to make a profit; it is not required to have a share capital nor does it need to file annual accounts or reports. Where an EEIG is registered in the UK, the UK companies legislation, insofar as it is applicable to the EEIG, will regulate its affairs.

CHAPTER 4

Accounts and reporting structures

4.1 INTRODUCTION

The accounting provisions of the Companies Act (CA) 2006 will come into force on 6 April 2008. A large amount of detail, which now partly appears in the Schedules to the Companies Act (CA) 1985, will be set out in regulations. These largely remain to be issued, but will be voluminous.

Five major developments are embodied in the new and extensive provisions which form CA 2006, ss.380–539:

1. The law has become increasingly prescriptive about what should appear in accounts, notes to accounts and directors' reports.
2. Accounting standards have become increasingly formalised, elaborate and extensive.
3. Accounting judgments are not taken by companies on a commercial basis but imposed by standard setters on a centralised basis.
4. As a counterweight to these trends, the same accounting rules are not applied to all companies. Accounting and audit standards have been simplified and abbreviated for small and medium-sized enterprises (SMEs).
5. A dualism is established whereby entity accounts (what the Act calls 'individual accounts') are to be based either upon UK accounting standards (UK Generally Accepted Accounting Practice (GAAP)) or International Accounting Standards (IAS).

The same distinction as in item 5 is found in the Tax Acts. In the Tax Acts 'generally accepted accounting practice' means:

(a) where accounts are drawn up using IAS, IAS GAAP;
(b) in any other case, UK GAAP.

(Finance Act (FA) 2004, s.50A; Income and Corporation Taxes Act (TA) 1988, s.836A.)

All companies in a group have to produce individual accounts. Additionally, the principal company of the group must produce consolidated (group) accounts, unless exempt from this requirement.

For accounting periods beginning on or after 1 January 2005, all consolidated accounts of EU listed companies have to be based on International Financial Reporting Standards (IFRSs). The use of IFRSs is likely to spread to entity accounts. UK GAAP is rapidly being aligned with IFRSs.

Hence the CA 2006 distinguishes between:

- Companies Act individual accounts;
- Companies Act group accounts;
- IAS individual accounts;
- IAS group accounts.

4.2 ACCOUNTING REFERENCE DATE

Every company must have an accounting reference date, to determine its accounting reference period, i.e. the period for which it makes up its accounts (CA 2006, s.391). The financial year begins at the start of the accounting reference period, and ends on the last day of the period, or up to seven days either side for companies which make up accounts for 52- or 53-week periods (CA 2006, s.390).

The accounting reference date will normally be:

(a) for companies incorporated before 1 April 1996, the date specified by notice to the registrar of companies; and

(b) in other cases the last day of the month in which the anniversary of the incorporation of the company falls (CA 2006, s.391).

A company can alter its accounting reference date by notice to the registrar, provided that (CA 2006, s.392):

(a) the time for filing accounts and reports has not expired;

(b) the effect of the notice would be to extend an accounting reference period beyond 18 months;

(c) the company has not extended its accounting reference period in the previous five years.

4.3 THE ACCOUNTS OBLIGATION

A company's 'statutory accounts' are the accounts for a financial year which the company is required to file with the registrar of companies under CA 2006, s.441 (CA 2006, s.434(3)).

'Annual accounts' are defined in CA 2006, s.471 by reference to the financial year as meaning the company's individual accounts and any group accounts made up for that year. A reference to the accounts includes a reference to the notes to the accounts (CA 2006, s.472). 'International accounting standards' are defined in CA 2006, s.471.

The CA 2006 applies to 'UK-registered companies', as defined by s.1158, i.e. companies registered under the UK companies legislation. Companies are artificial persons. Unlike natural persons, they are required to maintain and produce annual accounts. This is a condition imposed for the enjoyment of the privilege of incorporation. Accounts serve four purposes:

1. They provide information to creditors and other lenders who may deal with the company.
2. They provide information to investors who hold or may acquire shares in the company.
3. They provide a record of the directors' stewardship for the existing shareholders.
4. They provide a means of supervising and regulating the operation of companies.

The obligations imposed by the CA 2006 with regard to accounts are essentially threefold, and apply alike to all companies:

*   companies must prepare accounts which give a true and fair view;
*   the accounts must be filed with the registrar of companies;
*   the accounts must be circulated to members.

The duty to prepare annual accounts applies to *all* UK-registered companies. Such company accounts are called 'individual accounts' (previously referred to as 'entity accounts'). The basic duty is set out in CA 2006, s.394:

> The directors of every company must prepare accounts for the company for each of the financial years. These accounts are referred to as the company's 'individual accounts'.

Individual accounts can be Companies Act individual accounts or IAS individual accounts (CA 2006, s.395(1)). A charity can only prepare Companies Act individual accounts (s.395(2)). Once IAS accounts are adopted, IAS must be retained, unless there is a 'relevant change of circumstance' (s.395(3)–(5)). A relevant change of circumstance would, for example, occur if a company became a subsidiary of another company which did not prepare IAS individual accounts.

Companies Act individual accounts must comprise (CA 2006, s.396):

*   a balance sheet which gives a true and fair view of the state of affairs of the company at the end of the financial year; and
*   a profit and loss account which gives a true and fair view of the profit or loss of the company for the financial year.

Accounting standards additionally require:

(a) a Statement of Total Reported Gains and Losses (STRGL);
(b) a cash flow statement.

The function of the STRGL is to ensure that the income statement and the balance sheet reconcile by taking the surplus (or loss) for the year in the income statement, and adding to that figure (or deducting from it) changes in balance sheet figures which do not go through the income statement, e.g. asset revaluations, and changes in pension scheme deficits.

IAS individual accounts comprise (CA 2006, ss.397, 474):

• an income statement;
• a balance sheet.

Such accounts must state that they have been prepared in accordance with IAS.

The nature and extent of the accounts obligation depends upon the type of company. Where provisions do not apply to all companies, the legislation sets out the provisions in the order:

• small companies;
• public companies;
• quoted companies.

Where a small company or medium-sized company prepares Companies Act accounts, the directors may deliver a balance sheet and a profit and loss account with items specified in regulations omitted. These are called 'abbreviated accounts' (CA 2006, ss.444(3), 445(3)). If abbreviated accounts are delivered, then the obligation to deliver the auditor's report is replaced by the obligation to deliver the auditor's special report in accordance with CA 2006, s.449 (CA 2006, ss.444(4), 445(4)).

Where the directors propose to deliver abbreviated accounts to the registrar, they must include, in a prominent position above the director's signature on the balance sheet, a statement that the abbreviated accounts are prepared in accordance with the SME regime. The ability to file abbreviated accounts does not apply where the directors have taken advantage of the audit exemption (CA 2006, s.477). If a small group company prepares group accounts, it cannot use simpler form accounts for its individual accounts.

The normal currency of account will be sterling. However, companies may draw up accounts which also give the accounts figures in euros (CA 2006, s.469). In *Re Scandinavian Bank Corp plc* [1987] BCLC 220 it was held that a company may have a multi-currency share capital, provided that in the case of a public company it has allotted share capital of not less than the authorised minimum denomination in sterling.

Accounting formats

The form and content of accounts, the additional information to be provided, details of any departure from accounting standards in order to give a true and fair view ('the true and fair override') and reasons for such departure must accord with regulations to be issued by the Secretary of State (CA 2006, s.396(3)–(5)).

Hence the accounting formats in the CA 1985 are not reproduced in the CA 2006, and accordingly the CA 1985 formats will continue to apply, until replaced by new formats contained in regulations.

The prescribed accounting formats are:

Companies Act 2006	Companies Act 1985 format	Type of company	Type of accounts
s.396(3)	Schedule 4	General companies	Individual
s.404(3)	Schedule 4A	General companies	Group accounts
s.409(1)	Schedule 5	Requirement to prepare group accounts	
	Schedule 8	Small companies	Individual
	Schedule 8A	Small companies	Group accounts
	Schedule 9	Banking companies and groups	Individual and consolidated
	Schedule 9A	Insurance companies and groups	Individual and consolidated

CA 1985, Sched.4 contains a number of fundamental accounting principles which are to be observed in drawing up accounts, including (CA 1985, Sched.4, paras.9–14):

- going concern;
- consistency;
- prudence.

These will presumably be carried over into the new regulations.

Approval of accounts

Accounts must be approved by the board of directors and signed on behalf of the board by a director signing the balance sheet. The balance sheet, and other reports must state the name of the director who has signed (CA 2006, s.433). If the accounts do not comply with the requirements of the Act, every director who knew that they did not comply, or was reckless as to their compliance, and does not take reasonable steps to secure compliance, commits an offence (CA 2006, s.414).

Information to be given in notes to the accounts

In the case of a company not subject to the small companies regime, the notes to the accounts must contain information about the average number of employees in the financial year, and the number of persons employed in each category of employee. The notes must also state the aggregate amounts of wages and salaries, social security costs and pension costs (CA 2006, s.411). Information must also be given in accordance with regulations about directors' remuneration and benefits (CA 2006, ss.412–3).

Directors' report

The directors must prepare a report for each financial year, stating the names of the directors and the principal activities of the company. Unless the company comes within the small companies regime, the directors' report must include a business review. This must include 'an analysis of key performance indicators', i.e. 'factors by reference to which the development, performance of position of the company's business can be measured effectively' (CA 2006, s.417(6)). These requirements are relaxed in the case of medium-sized companies. In the case of quoted companies the directors must report on the main trends and factors likely to influence the business's future development, performance and position, as well as providing information about environmental matters, the impact of the company's business on the environment and 'social and community issues' (CA 2006, s.417(5)). Unless the company is exempt from the audit requirement and the directors have taken advantage of that exemption, the report must include a statement from the directors that there is no relevant audit information which has not been made available to the company's auditors (CA 2006, s.418). Except in the case of companies subject to the small companies regime, the directors' report must state the amount of any proposed dividends (CA 2006, s.416(3)). The directors' report must be approved by the directors and signed on their behalf by a director or the company secretary (CA 2006, s.419).

Quoted companies must prepare a directors' remuneration report, containing additional information about the pay of directors, in accordance with regulations (CA 2006, s.421). Prior to the accounts meeting, the company must give notice to those entitled to attend the meeting of the intention to move at the meeting by way of ordinary resolution a resolution approving the report (CA 2006, s.439).

Publication of accounts and reports

Every company must send a copy of the annual accounts and reports for each financial year to every member of the company, every debenture holder and every person who is entitled to receive notice of the annual general meeting, where an annual general meeting is required (CA 2006, s.423). Private companies no longer need to hold an annual general meeting, and the accounts must be sent out by the filing date, i.e. within nine months of the end of the financial year (CA 2006, s.424). A public company must send out the accounts at least 21 days before the annual general meeting. A public company must hold an annual general meeting within six months of its accounting reference date (CA 2006, s.336(1)).

Instead of sending out the full accounts and reports, companies can send out summary financial statements, provided that they comply with regulations, and are in the forms prescribed for unquoted companies and quoted companies respectively and other provisions of the Act (CA 2006, ss.426–8).

A quoted company must ensure that its accounts and reports are available on its website (CA 2006, s.430).

Where a company publishes its accounts, they must be accompanied by the auditor's report, unless the company is exempt from audit and the directors have taken advantage of that exemption (CA 2006, s.434(1)).

If a company publishes a balance sheet or profit and loss account otherwise than as part of its annual accounts, these must be identified as 'non-statutory accounts' (CA 2006, s.435).

Filing accounts

Filing obligations vary with the type of company, and are set out as follows:

Type of company	CA 2006 section
Small companies	444
Medium-sized companies	445
Unquoted companies	446
Quoted companies	447
Unlimited companies	448

The time limits for filing are set out for all companies in CA 2006, s.442. The CA 2006 brings in shorter filing periods for annual and interim accounts. Public companies will have to file their accounts within six months of the accounting year end (instead of seven months). This coincides with the requirement to hold the annual general meeting within six months of the accounting reference date. Private companies must file within nine months (instead of 10) (CA 2006, s.442). There are provisions for calculating periods of time in CA 2006, s.443.

In the case of private companies there is no need to hold an annual general meeting (discussed at 14.2) and so there is no longer a need to lay the accounts before such a meeting. Instead, the accounts, directors' report and (if applicable) auditor's report must be circulated to members within the period in which they must be filed with the registrar of companies.

Unlimited companies are exempt from the obligation to file accounts with the registrar, provided that the company has not been the subsidiary undertaking of a limited company or the parent of a limited company, and is not a banking or insurance company (CA 2006, s.448).

Where abbreviated accounts are delivered, but the company is not exempt from audit (or the directors have not taken advantage of the exemption), the accounts must be accompanied by a special auditor's report, confirming the company's entitlement to deliver abbreviated accounts (CA 2006, ss.449–50).

Penalties for failure to file are set out in CA 2006, ss.451–3. If there is default in filing accounts and reports, all directors of such a company will commit an offence, subject to a 'reasonable steps' defence. If the directors fail to make good the default within 14 days of notification, the court can on application make a direction to the directors to remedy the default (CA 2006, s.452).

Defective accounts

After accounts have been filed, directors may find that there is an accounting error, e.g. sales have been overstated or an equity instrument classified as such when accounting standards required it to be treated as debt. In that case the directors can amend the accounts (CA 2006, s.454).

The Secretary of State can also give notice to the directors of a company requiring explanation of the matters specified in the notice (CA 2006, s.455).

The Secretary of State or a person authorised by him (i.e. an accounting regulatory body) can apply to the court for a declaration that the accounts fail to conform to accounting standards (CA 2006, ss.456, 457).

4.4 THE 'TRUE AND FAIR' REQUIREMENT

The cardinal principle is that all accounts prepared by all companies subject to CA 2006 must give a 'true and fair view'. This principle is set out in s.393(1):

> (1) The directors of a company must not approve accounts . . . unless they are satisfied that they give a true and fair view of the assets, liabilities, financial position and profit or loss –
>
>   (a) in the case of the company's individual accounts, in the case of the company;
>   (b) in the case of the company's group accounts, of the undertakings included in the consolidation as a whole, so far as concerns members of the company.

This principle is restated for individual accounts in CA 2006, s.396, and for group accounts in s.404. Likewise the auditor's report must state whether the accounts give a true and fair view (CA 2006, s.495(3)). The concept is derived from Directive 76/222/EC, art.2(3).

'True and fair' is not defined in the Directive or by statute. In 1983, 1984 and 1993 the opinion of counsel (Leonard Hoffmann QC and Mary Arden QC, as they then were) was sought on the significance of the concept. The view expressed was that:

(a) 'true and fair' was a statutory requirement;
(b) in interpreting that concept the courts would be unlikely to find that accounts would give a true and fair view; unless they had been drawn up in accordance with the relevant accounting standards;
(c) accordingly, while accounting standards had no direct legal effect as such, being simply rules of professional conduct for accountants, they were given indirect legal effect through the true and fair concept;
(d) in short, 'true and fair' means 'drawn up in accordance with accounting standards'.

The Statement of Principles for Financial Reporting issued by the Accounting Standards Board (ASB) deals with the true and fair concept in paras.10–13 and says:

> The concept of a true and fair view lies at the heart of financial reporting in the UK . . . It is the ultimate test for financial statements.

Particulars and reasons must be given for any material departures from accounting standards, and these should be disclosed in the notes to the accounts in accordance with Financial Reporting Standard (FRS) 18 (CA 2006, s.396(5)).

4.5 ACCOUNTING REGULATORS

Accounting standards are issued by professional bodies prescribed under CA 2006, s.464. The current regulations are the Accounting Standards (Prescribed Body) Regulations, SI 2005/697. The prescribed bodies are the Accounting Standards Board (ASB) and International Accounting Standards Board (ASB). The ASB was established on 1 August 1990, as the successor to the Accounting Standards Committee (ASC).

The Financial Reporting Council (FRC) has oversight regulation of all accounting and audit matters in the UK. It embraces the ASB, which issues Financial Reporting Standards (FRS). FRSs in turn take the place of Statements of Standard Accounting Practice (SSAP) formerly issued by the ASC.

Under the FRC is also the Urgent Issues Task Force (UITF), which was established in March 1991, to produce Abstracts on the interpretation of particular accounting standards, e.g. UITF 40 on income recognition for professional work in progress. Designated trade bodies produce Statements of Recommended Practice (SORP) for particular sectors, where the body in question is recognised by the ASB as a SORP-making body, e.g. the British Banker's Association SORP on Advances; the Charities Commission's SORP 'Accounting by Charities'. Since 2004 the FRC regulates auditing activities through the Auditing Practice Board (APB). The Financial Reporting Review Panel (FRRP) has power to direct that defective accounts should be remedied.

Listed companies are required to observe the Listing Rules (FSA Sourcebook) and Guidance Manual issued by the Financial Services Authority (FSA). Companies whose shares are listed on the Alternative Investment Market (AIM) have to observe the AIM Rules issued by the Stock Exchange.

The structure is thus:

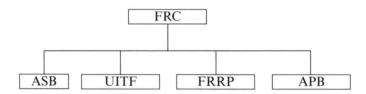

The International Accounting Standards Board (IASB) issues International Financial Reporting Standards (IFRS), which are referred to generically as International Accounting Standards (IAS). The International Financial Reporting Standard Interpreting Committee (IFRSIC) plays much the same role as UITF in relation to UK accounting standards.

For adoption within the EU, IFRSs have to be 'endorsed' as suitable for use by the European Commission. This process involves consideration by the Accounting Regulatory Committee (ARC) and the European Financial Reporting Advisory Group (EFRAG).

4.6   SMALL AND MEDIUM-SIZED COMPANIES

The definitions of companies subject to the small and medium-sized companies regime are set out in CA 2006, ss.381–4. For accounting periods beginning on or after 31 December 2006, a small company remains eligible for the small companies regime whether its individual accounts are Companies Act or IAS. A company qualifies as a small or medium-sized company if for the financial year in question and the previous financial year it meets two out of three criteria relating to maximum:

- turnover;
- assets;
- number of employees.

For accounting periods ending on or after 30 January 2004 the maximum figures are (CA 2006, s.382):

Maximum (two out of three)	Small companies		Medium-sized companies	
	Net	Gross	Net	Gross
Turnover £	5,600,000	6,720,000	22,800,000	27,360,000
Assets £	2,800,000	3,336,000	11,400,000	13,680,000
Employees	50	50	250	250

'Net' = with adjustments for intra-group transactions
'Gross' = without adjustments for intra-group transactions

Depending upon the accounting format used, the balance sheet for these purposes comprises either:

- called up share capital not paid;
- fixed assets;
- current assets;
- prepayments and accrued income;

or simply

- assets.

A parent company qualifies as a small or medium-sized parent company if its totals for turnover, assets and employees satisfy two out of three criteria (CA 2006, s.383).

Maximum (two out of three)	Small parent companies	Medium sized parent companies
Turnover £	5,600,000	22,800,000
Assets £	2,800,000	11,400,000
Employees	50	250

A parent company of a group that qualifies as an SME may take advantage of an exemption from applying group accounts if the group aggregates as a whole meet the SME requirements.

The exemptions and simplifications from which small companies can benefit include (CA 2006, ss.411, 414, 416, 417, 444, 445):

(a) use of FRSSE;
(b) omission of disclosures relating to directors' remuneration;
(c) use of 'simpler form accounts' (CA 1985, Sched.8, rather than Sched.4);
(d) simplified directors' report;
(e) simplified information relating to employee numbers and costs, financial year of subsidiary undertakings, shares and debentures held by subsidiary undertakings (CA 2006, s.411);
(f) audit exemption;
(g) ability to file 'abbreviated accounts' with the registrar of companies;
(h) small group companies need not prepare group accounts.

The following companies are excluded from the small companies regime:

• public companies;
• authorised insurance companies, banking companies, collective investment scheme management company;
• companies which belong to groups whose securities are admitted to trading on any regulated EEA market (CA 2006, s.384(2)(a)).

Medium-sized companies cannot deliver abbreviated accounts to the registrar of companies if they prepare IAS individual accounts. Likewise a medium-sized company cannot benefit from relaxations for such companies if it is a public company, is carrying on a regulated activity under the Financial Services and Markets Act 2000, is carrying on an insurance activity or belongs to a group containing a member which falls into any of these categories (CA 2006, s.467).

4.7   GROUP ACCOUNTS

There is an important distinction between companies which need only prepare individual accounts, and companies which must also produce group accounts. CA 2006, ss.380, 398, 399 distinguish between the following situations:

(a) companies subject to the small companies regime;
(b) companies outside the small companies regime and not quoted;
(c) companies outside the small companies regime and quoted;
(d) companies subject to the small companies regime which are the parent companies of a group;
(e) companies outside the small companies regime which are the parent companies of a group;

Parent companies not subject to the small companies regime are required to prepare group accounts as well as individual accounts. A company which at the end of the financial year is a parent company must prepare consolidated accounts, unless (broadly speaking) it is itself a subsidiary undertaking (CA 2006, s.399).

'Parent undertaking' and 'subsidiary undertaking' are defined in CA 2006, s.1162 and Sched.7. An undertaking is a parent undertaking in relation to a subsidiary undertaking if it:

(a) holds the majority of voting rights;
(b) has the right to appoint or remove directors;
(c) has the right to exert dominant influence by virtue of the articles or a control contract;
(d) controls a majority of voting rights;
(e) has power to exercise or actually exercises a dominant influence;
(f) is managed on a unified basis with the subsidiary.

The terms 'dominant influence' and 'managed on a unified basis' are defined in FRS 2 'Accounting for Subsidiary Undertakings'.

There are three exemptions:

1. The first case is for companies whose accounting figures are included in the IAS group accounts of an EEA parent undertaking, where the imme- diate parent company (a) owns all the shares in the subsidiary, or (b) owns more than 50 per cent of the shares and no notice requesting group accounts has been served by shareholders. The securities of the subsidiary must not be traded on an EEA exchange (CA 2006, s.400).
2. The second case is for companies whose accounting figures are included in the group accounts of a parent undertaking established outside the EEA, where the immediate parent company (a) owns all the shares in the subsidiary, or (b) owns more than 50 per cent of the shares and no notice requesting group accounts has been served by shareholders. The securities of the subsidiary must not be traded on an EEA exchange. The company must state in its individual accounts the name of the parent undertaking, and the fact that it is exempt from the requirement to draw up group accounts.
3. The third case is where a parent company prepares Companies Act group accounts and all the subsidiary undertakings of the parent are included in the consolidation (CA 2006, ss.401, 405).

Companies Act group accounts comprise (CA 2006, s.404):

• a consolidated profit and loss account;
• a consolidated balance sheet.

Parent companies that are charities must use UK GAAP (CA 2006, s.403(3)).

All subsidiary undertakings must be included in the consolidation, unless such consolidation is not material for the purpose of giving a true and fair view or the parent company is subject to long-term restrictions over the exercise of its powers (CA 2006, s.405).

IAS group accounts must state that they have been drawn up in accordance with IAS (CA 2006, s.406).

Financial reporting in a group should be made on a consistent basis, i.e. 'using the same financial reporting framework' (CA 2006, s.407(1)(a)). This does not apply if both the group and the individual accounts are prepared using IAS.

Accounting basis for group accounts

For accounting periods beginning on or after 1 January 2005, all companies governed by the law of an EU Member State were required to adopt endorsed IAS for their consolidated (group) accounts, if their securities were listed on an exchange in a Member State (Regulation 2002/1606/EC). As this was a Regulation, it did not require implementation in Member States to take effect as a legal obligation.

The Regulation left individual Member States free to decide whether to allow or require listed companies to adopt IAS for individual company accounts within the group, or to continue with national generally accepted accounting practice.

Under the UK regulations:

(a) companies subject to the small companies regime which are the parent companies of a group and ordinary limited companies may adopt either IAS or UK GAAP;

(b) parent companies of listed groups must require group companies to adopt either IAS or IK GAAP, unless there are good reasons not to do so;

(c) in general, the decision as to accounting standards, once made, cannot be reversed.

(Companies Act 1985 (International Accounting Standards and Other Accounting Amendments) Regulations, SI 2004/2947; CA 2006, ss.395, 396.)

'UK GAAP' in turn embraces both 'old UK GAAP' and 'new UK GAAP'. This is because some FRSs (replacing previous SSAPs or FRSs) apply only to particular types of company. For example, until 2009 FRS 25 and FRS 26 only apply to listed companies, but other companies can voluntarily adopt them.

4.8 THE AUDIT REQUIREMENT

A company's annual accounts must be audited in accordance with the Act, unless the company is exempt from audit (CA 2006, s.475). A company may be exempt from audit under s.477 (small companies) or s.480 (dormant companies). There is also an exemption for non-profit-making companies subject to public sector audit. A company is not entitled to the exemption unless its balance sheet contains a statement to that effect, above the director's signature.

The members of a company otherwise entitled to audit exemption can require an audit (CA 2006, s.476).

To qualify for the small companies exemption:

(a)   a company must be small;
(b)   its turnover must not exceed £5.6 million in the financial year;
(c)   its balance sheet total must not exceed £2.8 million (CA 2006, s.477).

A company is not entitled to the small companies exemption if it is a group company unless:

(a)   the group is a small group;
(b)   aggregate group turnover does not exceed £5.6 million (net) or £6.72 million (gross);
(c)   aggregate balance total does not exceed £2.8 million (net) or £3.36 million (gross) (CA 2006, s.479).

Dormant companies are also exempt from the audit requirement (CA 2006, ss.480, 481).

Non-profit-making companies subject to public sector audit are exempt from audit under ss.482–4 if they are, in England, subject to audit by the Comptroller and Auditor General under the Government Resources and Accountability Act 2000, s.25(6), or equivalent provisions in other parts of the UK.

Auditors for private companies must be appointed each year (CA 2006, s.485). Because an annual general meeting is no longer required under the Act, the auditor is no longer appointed by resolution at the annual general meeting. In the first year the auditor will be appointed by the directors. Thereafter the auditor must be appointed by the members by ordinary resolution. The 'period for appointing auditors' is the period of 28 days beginning with the time by which the accounts and report are required to be circulated to members under ss.423, 424, or beginning from the date of sending out the accounts and report, if earlier. If no auditor is appointed, the existing auditor is deemed to be reappointed (CA 2006, s.487(2)). If a casual vacancy arises, the directors have power to appoint an auditor.

Auditors of private companies hold office for the term of their appointment, and cannot take office until the previous auditors have ceased to hold office. They cease to hold office at the end of the next 'period for appointing auditors' unless reappointed (CA 2006, s.487).

In the case of public companies, the auditor is initially appointed by the directors and thereafter by the members by ordinary resolution at the 'accounts meeting' (CA 2006, s.489). The accounts meeting is 'a general meeting of the company at which the company's annual accounts and reports are . . . laid' (CA 2006, s.437(3)). The directors have power to fill a casual vacancy. In default of appointment under s.489, the Secretary of State has a default power of appointment (CA 2006, s.490).

Auditors or public companies hold office for the term of their appointment, and cannot take office until the previous auditors have ceased to hold office. They cease to hold office at the end of the next accounts meeting unless reappointed (CA 2006, s.491).

Where the auditor is appointed by the members, his remuneration is fixed by ordinary resolution (CA 2006, s.492).

The prime function of the auditor's report is to say whether or not in the auditor's opinion the accounts give a true and fair view of the company's financial affairs for the financial year to which they relate (CA 2006, s.495(3)). The auditor's report must be unqualified or qualified (CA 2006, s.495(4)(a)). The auditor's report must state whether the directors' report is consistent with the accounts (s.496). In the case of quoted companies the auditor's report must also state whether the auditable part of the directors' remuneration report has been compiled in accordance with the Act. The auditor's report must be sent out with the annual accounts and directors' report (CA 2006, s.495(1)).

The duties of the auditor are (CA 2006, s.498):

- to be satisfied as to the adequacy of the company's accounting records and procedures;
- to obtain all the information and explanations which to the best of his knowledge and belief are necessary for the purposes of the audit.

The auditor has extensive rights to information relating to the company's financial affairs and it is an offence to withhold information from the auditor or provide misleading information (CA 2006, ss.499–502).

If the auditor is an individual, the auditor's report must be signed by that individual. If the auditor is a firm, the auditor's report must be signed by the 'senior statutory auditor', i.e. the professionally qualified auditor named by the firm as responsible for the audit (CA 2006, s.504).

The auditor can be removed at any time by ordinary resolution (CA 2006, s.510).

The auditor can resign and require the directors to convene a general meeting at which the auditor can explain the circumstances connected with this resignation (CA 2006, s.516). Where an auditor ceases for any reason to hold office, in unquoted companies the auditor must in all cases make a statement, whether of the circumstances or to say that none were relevant (CA 2006, s.519(1), (2)). In quoted companies the auditor must outline the circumstances (CA 2006, s.519(3)).

Any provision for exempting the auditor from liability for breach of duty or for indemnification of the auditor by the company for breach of duty are void, except as provided by CA 2006, s.533 (indemnification by company for costs of successfully defending proceedings) and ss.534–6 (limitation of liability agreements). Such agreements may not limit liability to 'less than such an amount is fair and reasonable in all the circumstances' (s.537). There is provision for the issue of regulations to specify what matters can and cannot be included in such agreements (CA 2006, s.535(2)).

Accounting records

A company must maintain adequate accounting records, and retain them for three years in the case of private companies and six years in the case of public companies. Officers but not members are entitled to access to the accounting records. In particular the records must account for receipts and payments of money on a day-to-day basis, and provide a record of the assets and liabilities of the company (CA 2006, s.386(2)). In the case of a company dealing in goods, the accounting records must record the stocks, and (except in the case of ordinary retail sales) provide means of identifying suppliers and customers (CA 2006, ss.386–9).

CHAPTER 5

Taxation of companies

5.1 INTRODUCTION

As legal persons, companies are liable to taxation by analogy with the taxation of individuals. Individuals pay income tax and capital gains tax. Companies pay corporation tax on income and capital gains. The scope of corporation tax is extended by including in the term 'companies' bodies of persons which are not companies. 'Company' means 'any body corporate or unincorporated association'. However, a 'company' does not include 'a partnership, a local authority or a local authority association' (Income and Corporation Taxes Act (TA) 1988, s.832(1); Taxes Management Act (TMA) 1970, s.118(1)).

Companies are liable to corporation tax on their 'profits'. 'Profits' comprise two components: income and capital gains. A separate corporation tax was introduced in 1965. However, it was grafted on to income tax (which had existed continuously since 1842) and capital gains tax (which was also introduced in 1965, to tax gains which would escape income tax). In its original conception the income and gains of companies were computed in much the same way as the income and gains of individuals, but then charged to corporation tax. Hence, the income of companies is computed in accordance with income tax principles, and the capital gains of companies are computed in accordance with capital gains principles (TA 1988, s.9(1); Taxation of Chargeable Gains Act (TCGA) 1992, s.8(3)). In both cases, however, these principles only apply to the extent that they are not modified by law. Increasingly, corporation tax has become based on rules which are quite distinct from those which apply for income tax and capital gains tax. The chief reason for this has been the increasing importance of the principle that the corporation tax computation should follow the commercial computation of profits, and the increasing elaboration and formalisation of accounting standards.

As explained in **Chapter 4,** unlike individuals, companies are required to maintain accounts which 'give a true and fair view of the company's assets, liabilities, financial position and profit and loss'. Hence companies are broadly taxed on an accounts basis, and pay corporation tax on income and capital gains, while individuals are taxed on a cash basis, and pay income tax on income and capital gains tax on capital gains.

Corporation tax applies *instead* of income tax or capital gains tax. If corporation tax does not apply, the charge to income tax or capital gains tax is reinstated. For example, a non-UK resident investment company pays income tax on its UK source income, not corporation tax.

5.2 LEGISLATION

The legislation imposing corporation tax is based on a number of legislative sources:

1. Corporation tax is an annual tax, which is renewed by annual Finance Acts (FA).
2. TA 1988 imposes the charge to corporation tax, has rules relating to accounting periods, and lays down the rules for income taxation. Income is classified into a number of schedules, of which the most important for companies is Schedule D Case I, which applies to trading profits. The schedular system has been formally relinquished for income tax purposes. Hence the TA 1988 applies for corporation tax purposes, but not for income tax purposes. The income tax legislation is now contained in a number of new Acts, enacted as part of the Tax Law Rewrite, which will in due course encompass the corporation tax legislation.
3. TCGA 1992 contains the rules for the computation of capital gains, which in the case of a UK resident company are charged to corporation tax on capital gains.
4. Annual Finance Acts contain special rules for corporation tax. In particular, where a profit does not fall within the 'income' or 'gains' categories, but falls in a no man's land between the two, the rules are placed in a separate Finance Act.
5. Hence rules on corporate debt ('loan relationships') are found in FA 1996. Rules of derivative contracts are contained in FA 2002, Sched.26. The scheme for the taxation of intangible assets is set out in FA 2002, Sched.29.
6. The rules on capital allowances for incorporated and unincorporated businesses alike are contained in the Capital Allowances Act (CAA) 2001.
7. The administrative provisions for corporation tax are set out in FA 1998, Sched.18 and the Taxes Management Act (TMA) 1970. These also contain the rules for tax appeals.
8. There are numerous statutory instruments relating to corporation tax, e.g. Corporation Tax (Instalment Payments) Regulations, SI 1998/3175.
9. As noted in **Chapter 4**, Financial Reporting Standards (FRS) are issued by the Accounting Standards Board. International Financial Reporting Standards (IFRS) are issued by the International Accounting Standards

Board. While not legislation, they are given statutory recognition by the Companies Act (CA) 1985, s.256 and Sched.4, para.36A (Companies Act (CA) 2006, s.464).

5.3 PROFITS

Corporation tax is charged on the 'profits' of companies, which comprise 'income' and 'chargeable gains' (TA 1988, s.6(4)(a)). Income is calculated according to the law applicable to income tax, while chargeable gains are calculated according to the law applicable to capital gains tax. A company is only liable to corporation tax on sources of income which fall within the income tax Schedules, or capital gains. However, there are numerous special rules for corporation tax.

The general rule is that trading profits are a matter of fact to be determined by the application of the ordinary principles of commercial accountancy, subject to such adjustments as are required by law. The classic formulation of this method is by Pennycuick V-C in *Odeon Associated Theatres Ltd* v. *Jones* 48 TC 257 at 273 and is now codified in FA 1998, s.42, which states:

> For the purposes of Case I or II of Schedule D the profits of a trade, profession or vocation must be computed on an accounting basis which gives a true and fair view, subject to any adjustments required or authorised by law in computing profits for those purposes.

Where an 'all income' treatment applies, profits are ascertained in accordance with the commercial accounts, in the usual way, but the taxable profit is then regarded solely as income and not as gains. The areas where the all income treatment applies are:

1. *Loan relationships*: 'Loan relationships' are types of corporate debt defined in the FA 1996. Profits and gains on loan relationships include interest, capital accruals, expenses, fluctuations in capital values, foreign exchange differences and losses.
2. *Derivative contracts:* 'Derivative contracts' are defined in the FA 2002, and are contracts for differences, futures and options. However, gains on certain notional derivative contracts may be treated as capital gains for corporation tax purposes.
3. *Intangibles:* 'Intangibles' are defined in the FA 2002. The definition follows the accounting definition in FRS 10 but expressly includes intellectual property. Patents, copyrights, trademarks, registered design, design rights and goodwill all fall under this concept.

Capital gains for companies are computed by deducting the base cost of the asset from the proceeds of sale. The base cost is increased by index-linking (TCGA 1992, s.53).

Companies can also deduct charges on income from total profits. This is confined to qualifying donations to charity (TA 1988, ss.338, 338A).

Trading and investment companies

A trading company is a company whose business consists wholly or mainly in carrying on a trade whose profits are taxable under Schedule D Case I. Investment companies derive the bulk of their income from holding investments, being companies whose business consists wholly or mainly in making or holding investments (TA 1988, s.130). Non-trade profits will be taxable under Schedule A (profits from land); Schedule D Case III(a) (interest and profits from non-trading loan relationships); Schedule D Case V (income from possessions out of the UK); and Schedule D Case VI (other income). Dividends from foreign subsidiaries will always be Schedule D Case V items. All foreign source items which constitute profits on loan relationships which are not trading items are taxable not under Schedule D Case V but under Schedule D Case III(a).

From total profits received from those sources and capital gains a company with investment business deducts expenses of management, by reference to the accounting period in which they are charged against profits (TA 1988, ss.75, 75A). These will include reasonable directors' fees, interest, office and administrative expenses. Capital expenditure is excluded.

Losses

Losses may be revenue losses or capital losses. Revenue losses in turn may be trading losses or non-trading losses. Trading losses can be set against capital gains of the same or the previous accounting period, but capital gains cannot be set against trading losses. Losses on other forms of income can in general only be carried forward and set against income from the same source. Capital losses can likewise be carried forward and set against future capital gains. The rules are that trading losses may (TA 1988, ss.393, 393A, 402):

(a) be used for set-off against the profits (including chargeable gains) of the same accounting period; or
(b) be used to carry back the loss against the profits (including chargeable gains) for a period of 12 months prior to the period in which the loss occurred; or
(c) be carried forward against trading income from the same trade; or
(d) be made available for group relief.

If the company carries on a trade, trading losses are computed in the same way as trading income. A trading loss may be set off against other profits, including chargeable gains of the same accounting period. Claims must be made within two years of the end of the accounting period in which the loss is made, or such longer period as Her Majesty's Revenue and Customs

(HMRC) may allow. The balance of loss unrelieved by a claim for the year in which the loss occured may be carried back to be set against profits of preceding accounting periods for a period of 12 months ending immediately before the loss period, provided that the trade was carried on in that period. The balance of trading losses not relieved in an earlier period may be carried forward so set against income of the same trade (TA 1988, s.393(1)).

5.4 COMPANY RESIDENCE

The connecting factor for corporation tax purposes is residence. UK legislation is limited in territorial scope to persons or subject-matter which comes within the scope of its jurisdiction. There are two tests of company residence, a statutory test and a common law test. The statutory test is that all companies incorporated in the UK are UK resident (FA 1988, s.66(1)). The common law test is that a company is resident in the country where its central management and control is exercised: *De Beers Consolidated Gold Mines* v. *Howe* 5 TC 198.

Double tax treaties, which may override domestic law, use a 'place of effective management' test.

The case-law concept of 'central management and control' is broadly directed to the highest level of control of the business of the company concerned. It has to be distinguished from the place where the main operations of the business are to be found, although of course the two places may often coincide. Moreover, the exercise of control does not necessarily demand any minimum standard of active involvement: it may in some cases be exercised tacitly through passive oversight.

HMRC has indicated that where there are doubts about a particular company's residence status it adopts the following approach.

1. HMRC first tries to ascertain *whether* the directors of the company in fact exercise 'central management and control'.
2. If so, HMRC seeks to determine *where* the directors exercise this central management and control (which is not necessarily where they meet).
3. In cases where the directors apparently do *not* exercise central management and control of the company, HMRC will look to establish where and by whom it is exercised.

The common law test has been reviewed in *Wood* v. *Holden* [2006] STC 443.

In the High Court Park J observed [2005] STC 789 at 824–5:

> In all normal cases the central control and management is identified with the control which a company's board of directors has over its business and affairs, so that the principle almost always followed is that a company is resident in the jurisdiction where its board of directors meets . . .

There is a difference between, on the one hand, exercising management and control and, on the other, being able to influence those who exercise management and control.

The key issue is where the constitutional organs of the company perform their functions, provided that their authority is not usurped by another body.

If a non-resident company is carrying on a trade in the UK through a permanent establishment, it is liable to corporation tax by reference to the profits of the permanent establishment (TA 1988, s.11). 'Permanent establishment' is defined as (FA 2003, s.148):

(a) a fixed place of business . . . through which the business of the company is wholly or partly carried on; or
(b) an agent acting on behalf of the company [who] has and habitually exercises their authority to do business on behalf of the company.

'Fixed place of business' includes a place of management, a branch, an office, a factory or a building site. In double taxation agreements a building or construction site will normally constitute a permanent establishment 'only if it lasts more than twelve months' OECD Model Convention, art.6(3). A representative office is not a permanent establishment.

5.5   CLOSE COMPANIES

The close company has no counterpart in company law. There are numerous special tax rules which apply only to close companies. Broadly, a close company is defined as one which is controlled by five or fewer participators or is controlled by participators (of whatever number) who are directors (TA 1988, s.414).

Control is widely defined in terms of (TA 1988, ss.416, 417):

(a) ownership of majority voting control or ownership of the greater part of the share capital;
(b) being entitled on a winding up to receive the greater part of the assets available for distribution either through ownership of ordinary or redeemable share capital;
(c) ownership of sufficient share capital to ensure that the greater part of the whole income of the company if distributed would be received by the owner.

Two or more persons jointly together possessing 'control' are taken to have control.

The definition of 'participator' proceeds in the same way as the definitions of control. A person is a 'participator' if he falls under any of these headings:

(a) a person who owns share capital in that company;
(b) a person who has voting rights in that company;

(c) any loan creditor of that company except where the loan is made in the ordinary course of banking;

(d) any person who has a right to receive 'distributions' or amounts payable to loan creditors by way of premium on redemption of a loan; or

(e) any person entitled to secure that income or assets of that company, whether present or future, will be applied directly or indirectly for his benefit.

In general, entitlement rather than actual possession is sufficient.

The powers of an associate or any number of associates may be added to those of a participator in order to determine whether a company is a close company. Associates are, briefly, close relations and partners of a participator, trustees of a settlement of which the participator or any close relation of his is a settlor, co-beneficiaries of any trust or under any will who possess some interest in 'shares or obligations' of a company along with the participator. The second addition is that any person who exercises the function of a director, for example, a shareholder with a preponderant controlling shareholding who could bring pressure to bear on directors, is counted as a director. A person who does not own shares and is not a loan creditor cannot be a participator nor have associates.

If at least 35 per cent of the shares in a company (excluding preference shares or other shares with a fixed dividend) carrying voting power are owned by the public, then the company is not a close company. A subsidiary of a close company will itself be close.

Where a close company, otherwise than in the ordinary course of a business which includes lending money, makes a loan to a 'participator' or 'associate', the company is obliged to pay corporation tax at the rate of 25 per cent of the amount of the loan (TA 1988, s.419).

If such a loan is written off or released, the borrower is treated as receiving by way of income the amount written off or released, grossed up at the lower rate of income tax and carrying a non-repayable tax credit of the corresponding amount. If the loan is repaid, the corporation tax is refunded.

5.6   CHARGE TO CORPORATION TAX

Corporation tax is fixed for financial years, which begin on 1 April (as opposed to 6 April for individuals). The 'financial year 2008' means the period 1 April 2008 to 31 March 2009. UK-resident companies are chargeable to corporation tax on all profits wherever arising. Companies not resident in the UK are only chargeable to corporation tax if they carry on a trade in the UK through a permanent establishment, by reference to the trading income arising directly to the company through the permanent establishment.

Dividends and other distributions of a UK-resident company are exempt from corporation tax in the hands of the recipient company if it is UK-resident. By the same token, they cannot be deducted in computing the paying company's taxable income: (TA 1988, s.208). A dividend plus the assoicated tax credit are known as franked investment income (FII). Dividends from foreign companies received by UK-resident companies are relieved from tax by a credit system, whereby credit is given for foreign tax on the dividends up to the maximum of the UK tax of the profits.

The full rate of corporation tax has been 30 per cent since 1 April 2000. From 1 April 2008 the rate will be 28 per cent. This full rate applies to companies whose profits exceed £1,500,000. Reduced rates apply for 'small companies' whose profits are under £1,500,000. 'Profits' for these purposes includes franked investment income, i.e. dividends plus the associated tax credit, but excluding dividends from 51 per cent subsidiaries.

Profits up to the 'lower relevant maximum amount' (LRMA) are charged to corporation tax at 20 per cent (from 1 April 2007). Profits between the LRMA and the 'higher relevant maximum amount' (HRMA), attract marginal relief, i.e. the company is charged to tax at the full rate, but the tax payable is then reduced by the marginal relief fraction of an amount produced by applying a formula.

For financial years from 1 April 2007 onwards the marginal relief fraction is one-quarter. The formula for calculating small companies marginal relief is:

$$(M - P) \times \frac{I}{P} \times F$$

Where:

M = upper relevant maximum amount
P = profits
I = basic profits (i.e. profits chargeable to tax)
F = Marginal relief fraction

The lower and higher amounts are:

Lower relevant maximum amount (LRMA)	£300,000
Higher relevant maximum amount (HRMA)	£1,500,000

The upper and lower units are reduced where a company has 'associated companies', by dividing the amount in question by one plus the number of associates. A is an associate of B if either: (i) B controls A, or (ii) A and B are under common control. 'Control' means possession or entitlement, direct or indirect, of up to 51 per cent of the share capital, voting power, income distributions or assets on a winding up. Where a person is not a 'participator', the rights and powers of his associates are not to be attributed to him, so as to make one company 'associated' with another.

A 'close investment-holding company' is a close company which is an investment company other than a property investment company. A close investment-holding company pays corporation tax at the full rate and cannot claim the small companies' rate (TA 1988, s.13A).

Accounting periods

Companies pay corporation tax by reference to accounting periods, which will normally be the period for which the company makes up its annual accounts, i.e. the 12 months ending on the accounting reference date (TA 1988, s.12). An accounting period begins:

(a) when a company becomes UK resident; or
(b) when it acquires a source of income, e.g. by commencing a business; or
(c) when a previous accounting period comes to an end, without the company ceasing to be within the charge to corporation tax.

An accounting period ends in the first occurrence of any of the following:

(a) the expiration of 12 months from the beginning of the accounting period;
(b) the occurrence of the company's accounting reference date;
(c) the company's beginning or ceasing to trade;
(d) the company's beginning or ceasing to be resident in the UK;
(e) the company's ceasing to be within the charge to corporation tax.

An accounting period may not exceed 12 months. Corporation tax rates are fixed by reference to financial years. Where an accounting period straddles a change in corporation tax rates, the profits will be apportioned on a time basis between the financial years which overlap the accounting period.

Example

Trading company with no associated companies

Accounting period: 1 April 2007 – 31 March 2008

Basic profits:	£440,000
Franked investment income: 90,000 × 10/9	100,000
Profits:	540,000
Corporation tax: 30% × 440,000	132,000
Less: marginal relief	
1/4 x (1,500,000 – 540,000) × (440,000/540,000)	19,555
Tax payable	112,445

5.7   ADMINISTRATION AND PAYMENT OF CORPORATION TAX

Corporation tax self-assessment (CTSA) operates. This requires companies to file a corporation tax return and pay the corporation tax shown to be due in it. 'Large companies' (i.e. companies with profits of at least £1.5 million a year in-cluding franked investment income and which accordingly pay the main rate of corporation tax) are required to pay corporation tax by quarterly instalments (Corporation Tax (Instalment Payments) Regulations 1998, SI 1998/3175, reg.5). The instalments fall in months seven, 10, 13 and 16 after the start of the accounting period to which they relate. The quarterly instalments are based on the anticipated corporation tax liability for the accounting period, net of all reliefs and set-offs (such as income tax suffered by deduction). Payments are based on current estimated tax liabilities, with interest payable on underpayments and receivable on overpayments. Interest charged will be deductible in computing profits, and interest received will be taxable.

In establishing whether or not a company is 'large', and so required to pay quarterly instalments, the taxable profits limit of £1.5 million has to be split between associated companies, in the same way as is used to determine whether or not a company qualifies for small companies' relief.

Other companies are required to pay corporation tax nine months after the end of the accounting period (TMA 1970, s.59D).

The company's tax return is to be filed before a specified filing date, which is usually 12 months from the end of the accounting period. While an amendment is possible, no amendment can be made more than 12 months after the filing date. HMRC can amend the return to correct obvious errors or omissions up to nine months after the filing date. If a company does not make a self-assessment in response to a notice requiring the company to make such a return, HMRC may 'determine to the best of their information and belief the amount of tax payable by the company'. This determination has effect as if it were a self-assessment and no appeal is possible. The determination can only be displaced by filing a return within 12 months of the determination and five years of the filing date.

5.8   INTEREST AND DISTRIBUTIONS

Withholding tax

There is a general obligation on a company to deduct income tax from certain categories of interest payment which it makes (TA 1988, s.349). All Eurobond interest can be paid gross. The definition of 'quoted Eurobond' means any security that (i) is issued by a company, (ii) is listed on a recognised stock exchange, and (iii) carries a right to interest (TA 1988, s.349(4)). Where companies make or receive payments from which income tax has to be or has been deducted, such payments are accounted for on a quarterly return under which the company accounts to HMRC for the net income tax due.

Distributions

Where the company's business is continuing, all payments by a company to its shareholders in respect of their shares will be income distributions, paid from distributable reserves, save where capital is returned to shareholders. All payments to shareholders in respect of share capital on a winding up are capital distributions, because once the winding up resolution is passed, the undistributable reserves of the company become distributable, to the extent that they exceed the liabilities of the company. In particular circumstances, a distribution may be accorded a capital gains tax treatment (demergers; redemption of redeemable shares; purchase of own shares).

Tax law expands the company law definition of distribution, so that certain transactions which would not for company law purposes be distributions are such for tax purposes, for example:

(a) a payment of interest in excess of a 'reasonable commercial return' for the use of the principal advanced is a distribution (TA 1988, s.209(2)(d));
(b) a payment of interest by reference to the profits of the business, insofar as it exceeds a reasonable commercial return for the principal is treated as a distribution (TA 1988, s.209(2)(e)(iii));
(c) a purchase of own shares will ordinarily be a distribution, even if paid for out of capital.

The normal form of distribution will be a cash dividend, though dividends in specie also occur. Distributions are an application of profits, not a charge on profits, and so are non-deductible for accounting and tax purposes.

Distributions are classified as qualifying or non-qualifying (TA 1988, s.14(3)). Qualifying distributions carry tax credits, non-qualifying do not. Distributions resulting in an immediate distribution out of the reserves of the company in respect of shares are qualifying. Distributions causing a potential claim on reserves are non-qualifying. Hence all distributions are qualifying distributions, apart from two exceptions:

(a) issue of bonus redeemable shares and bonus securities;
(b) issue of any share capital or security which the company making the distribution has directly or indirectly received from another company in the form of bonus redeemable shares or securities.

A payment by a company to its shareholders is excluded from the qualifying distribution treatment if and to the extent that it represents a repayment of capital on the shares or if and to the extent that 'new consideration' is received by the company making the distribution. Consideration is new if it is external to the company, i.e. it is not provided directly or indirectly by the company itself. A bonus issue is not a distribution because there is no cost to the company. A rights issue where the rights are exercised is not a distribution because the consideration is new. A purchase of own shares from the shareholder direct is a distribution, but a purchase in the open market is not.

Rules on the re-characterisation of interest as a distribution do not apply where the payment is from one UK-resident company to another, except for the rule that interest in excess of a reasonable commercial return for the use of the principal will be regarded as a dividend (TA 1988, s.212(1)).

Dividends are 'treated as paid on the date when they become due and payable'. Unless the memorandum or articles provide otherwise a dividend is not payable until it has been declared. Final dividends are declared by the annual general meeting. The articles may give the directors power to pay interim dividends (see the 1985 Table A Regulations, regs.102 and 103). An interim dividend is paid on account of the final dividend. An interim dividend is due only when actually paid by the company. A final dividend is due when it is sanctioned by the annual general meeting, i.e. it then becomes a debt immediately due from the company to shareholders.

Stock dividends

An option conferred on a shareholder to take additional share capital as the alternative to a dividend is a 'stock dividend'. Although they may be declared out of distributable profits, stock dividends can also be paid out of share premium account, thus leaving distributable reserves unaffected.

Where the shareholder who is liable to income tax has an option to take shares instead of a cash dividend, the stock dividend is treated as an income distribution (TA 1988, s.249; Income Tax (Trading and Other Income) Act (ITTOIA) 2005, s.410). The shareholder who opts for a stock dividend instead of cash is treated as receiving a dividend of the 'appropriate amount in cash' plus the 'tax-credit fraction', while for capital gains tax purposes he acquires the shares for 'the appropriate amount in cash'. The amount of the distribution is the tax credit plus 'the appropriate amount in cash'. The 'appropriate amount in cash' is either:

(a) the amount of the cash dividend which the shareholder would have received, unless the market value of the shares received is significantly different on the date of first dealing from the cash dividend, i.e. varies by more than 15 per cent; or

(b) if the 'significantly different proviso applies', because the value of the shares has risen or fallen sharply since the declaration of the dividend, the 'appropriate amount in cash' is the market value of the shares. In that case, the amount of the notional tax dividend has to be correspondingly adjusted.

Purchase of own shares

For tax purposes a purchase of own shares is a hybrid transaction, comprising in part a return of capital and in part a distribution. The proceeds of sale must be divided into two parts:

(a) the part (if any) which corresponds to whatever amount of value was received by the company upon the issue of the shares in question. This part is always treated as capital for tax purposes;

(b) the balance ('the income element'), if any. The shareholder receives income of an amount which is ten-ninths of the distribution, which carries a non-repayable tax credit of 10 per cent.

On a purchase of own shares, CA 2006, s.706(b) provides that the shares redeemed or repurchased are to be cancelled on redemption. The nominal value of shares purchased or redeemed has to be carried to a capital redemption reserve. Thus if 20 £1 shares are to be repurchased at £20 per share, £200 of distributable profits will be required for this purpose. Reserves will be reduced by £200 and share capital by £20. This £20 has to be taken to capital redemption reserve, otherwise the balance sheet will not balance.

Example

A company has an issued share capital of 10,000 £1 ordinary shares. Its capital and reserves are:

Share capital	10,000
Reserves	10,000
	20,000

The company decides to purchase 2,000 ordinary shares at par. The accounting entries are:

	Dr	Cr
Share capital	2,000	
Cash		2,000
Reserves	2,000	
Capital redemption reserve		2,000

After the transaction, the capital and reserves are:

Share capital	8,000
Capital redemption reserve	2,000
Reserves	8,000
	18,000

Where unquoted trading companies (or holding companies of trading groups) purchase their own shares, the transaction may be treated as giving rise to a capital gains rather than an income receipt. Where the purchase is made to benefit the trade carried on by the acquiring company, the vendor is resident and ordinarily resident in the UK and has owned the shares or stock for five years, the income element of the purchase will not be treated as a distribution, but will instead be subject to capital gains tax treatment (TA 1988, ss.219–29).

The operation of the relief is subject to two restrictions:

(a) the holding of the shareholder must be 'substantially reduced' after the acquisition, so that not more than 75 per cent of his former interest is retained; and

(b) the vendor must not be 'connected' with the acquiring company or any other company in its group after the purchase. This term is specially defined, so that a person will be connected if he directly or indirectly possesses or is entitled to acquire more than 30 per cent of the issued ordinary shares, loan capital and issued shares, or votes of a company.

Because of business asset taper relief, which gives a capital gains tax rate of 10 per cent for all 'business assets' (which include all shares in unquoted trading companies, subject to certain restrictions) a capital gains tax treatment is generally more advantageous for individuals (TCGA 1992, Sched.A1).

As far as corporate shareholders are concerned, corporation tax is not chargeable on the dividend itself (by reason of TA 1988, s.208) but on a chargeable gain.

Imputation system

In the hands of a UK-resident shareholder a dividend paid by a company is liable to income tax at the dividend ordinary rate or dividend upper rate. A dividend carries with it a tax credit of one-ninth of the dividends. This tax credit franks the dividend from ordinary dividend rate taxation of 10 per cent on the sum of the dividend and the tax credit. Thus, part of the corporation tax paid by the company is imputed to the shareholder, and treated as tax paid by the company on behalf of shareholders (TA 1988, s.231).

If the taxpayer is liable to higher rate tax, he is subject to dividend upper rate tax at 32.5 per cent, and additional tax is payable. If the taxpayer is exempt (e.g. a pension fund) or not liable to tax, the tax credit is non-repayable (TA 1988, s.1B; ITTOIA 2005, s.383).

Example

	Ordinary Rate	Upper rate
Dividend	90	90
Tax credit	10	10
Income	100	100
Tax at 10%	10	
Tax at 32.5%		32.5
Tax credit	(10)	(10)
Additional tax		22.5

5.9   GROUPS OF COMPANIES

There are extensive special tax rules for groups of companies. The principal reliefs relate to:

(a)   surrender of losses within a group ('group relief');

(b)   transfer of assets within a group.

There are also rules which extend group relief to consortium companies.

A group consists of a parent and one or more subsidiaries. Group relationships are defined in terms of ownership 'directly or indirectly' by the parent of the given percentage (or more) of the 'ordinary share capital' of the subsidiary. 'Ordinary share capital' is defined as meaning 'all the issued share capital (by whatever name called) of the company, other than share capital the holders of which have a right to a dividend at a fixed rate but have no other right to share in the profits of the company' (TA 1988, s.832(1)).

For group relief purposes, a group consists of a parent company and its 75 per cent subsidiaries (TA 1988, s.413(3)). Two companies are members of a group for group relief purposes if one is the 75 per cent subsidiary of the other, or both are 75 per cent subsidiaries of a third company. The parent must have 75 per cent of the ordinary share capital of the subsidiary. TA 1988, s.413, supplemented by Sched.18, paras.2 and 3, sets out in great detail two additional tests which a parent must satisfy if another company is to be regarded as its 75 per cent subsidiary:

(a)   the parent must be beneficially entitled to 75 per cent of any profits available for distribution to equity holders of the subsidiary ('profit distribution' test); and

(b)   the parent must be entitled to at least 75 per cent of any assets of the subsidiary available for distribution to equity holders on a winding up ('notional winding up' test).

Trading losses of one company (the surrendering company) can be transferred to another company (the claimant company) to be allowed to the claimant company by way of relief from corporation tax (group relief) (TA 1988, s.402(1)). Group relief is only be available when the surrendering company and claimant company are members of the same group, and such a claim is a 'group claim' (s.402(2)). Where the conditions for group relief are satisfied, trading losses for the current year can be surrendered to other group companies. Within a group, losses can be surrendered upwards, downwards or sideways.

If the conditions are satisfied in respect of part of an accounting period, but not in respect of another part, the subsidiary will be treated as part of the group during that part of the period in which both conditions are satisfied. The subsidiary's loss would be apportioned between the two parts of the accounting period. The effect of group relief is simply to transfer the use of loss to another company that has an immediate use for it. The company receiving the surrender of losses may make a payment to the surrendering company not exceeding the amount surrendered, and such a payment is left out of account in computing the profits and losses for corporation tax of both parties.

Following decisions of the European Court of Justice, the scope of group relief has been extended where there is an international element. The decisions which have led to these changes are:

- *Imperial Chemical Industries plc* v. *Colmer* (Case C-264/96) [1998] STC 874;
- *Marks & Spencer plc* v. *Halsey* (Case C-446/03) [2006] STC 237.

Group membership can be traced through a non-UK-resident parent. A permanent establishment of a non-resident company will be treated as a UK resident company for these purposes. Further, a subsidiary resident in the EEA which has suffered trading losses which cannot be utilised in the country of residence can surrender these losses to a UK parent. The qualifying loss conditions restrict claims to those which cannot be given qualifying loss relief for any period, past, current or future in the territory where the loss has occurred, nor have been otherwise relieved outside the UK.

Consortium relief

A consortium consists of at least two and not more than 20 companies which together own 75 per cent or more of the ordinary share capital of a company (a consortium company) and each of them owns separately at least 5 per cent of the ordinary share capital. A consortium company is a company *owned* by a consortium, not a company which belongs to a consortium.

Within a consortium, losses can only be surrendered upwards from the consortium company to the members of the consortium company (TA 1988, s.402(3)). Each member of a consortium can claim a share of a consortium company's losses which corresponds to its percentage ownership of the consortium company.

A member's share in a consortium in relation to an accounting period of the surrendering company is whichever is the *lowest* of the following percentages:

(a) the percentage of ordinary share capital beneficially owned by the member;
(b) the percentage to which the member is beneficially entitled to any profits available to equity holders; and
(c) the percentage to which the member would be beneficially entitled to any assets available to equity holders on a winding up.

Intra-group transfers of assets

For capital gains tax purposes, groups are defined differently than for group relief. There are two limbs to the definition of a capital gains tax group (TCGA 1992, s.170):

1. A group consists of a principal company and 75 per cent subsidiaries and sub-subsidiaries.
2. All members of a group must be effective 51 per cent subsidiaries of the principal company, and satisfy the profit distribution and notional winding up tests.

For capital gains tax purposes, disposals between connected persons are transactions 'otherwise than by way of a bargain at arm's length', which are deemed to take place at market value (TCGA 1992, ss.17(1), 18. Members of a group are 'connected persons' (TCGA 1992, s.286). Where *capital* assets are transferred within a capital gains tax group, there is a disposal on a no gain/no loss disposal, instead of a disposal at market value (TCGA 1992, s.171(1)). Hence, if a capital gains tax group exists, when one member of the group disposes of an asset to another member of the group, no corporation tax on capital gains arises at that point. The deemed consideration is taken to be equal to the transferor's indexed base cost.

Example

P, a non-resident company, owns all the share capital of A and B, which are both UK resident companies. A holds land acquired for £0.2 million. When its market value is £1 million, it sells the land to B for £0.6 million. The indexation factor is 0.287.

B's acquisition cost is:		£200,000
Indexation allowance:	£200,000 × 0.287	£57,400
		£257,400

Notional transfers

Where A and B are members of the same capital gains tax group, and A disposes of an asset to a third company C which is not a member of the group, A and B may jointly elect that the disposal may be treated as having been made by B rather than A, and that A may be treated as having transferred the asset intra-group to B immediately before the disposal (TCGA 1992, s.171A). Thus if B has capital losses brought forward, a gain on the disposal of the asset can be set against B's losses, without the need for an actual transfer of the asset to B prior to sale.

Degrouping

Where the company leaving a group owns an asset acquired from another group member within the previous six years, a degrouping charge is imposed, i.e. the transferee company is treated as if it had disposed of and reacquired the asset at its market value at the time of the intra-group transfer (TCGA 1992, s.179(1)–(3)). This is the primary degrouping charge.

There is a secondary degrouping charge which applies where, on a takeover, a company in the acquired group does not become a member of the new enlarged group and, within six years of having acquired the asset intra-group, ceases to be either a 75 per cent or a 51 per cent subsidiary of companies in the new group (TCGA 1992, s.179(5)–(8)).

The rules do not apply in a number of situations:

(a) where a company leaves a group in consequence of another company 'ceasing to exist', e.g. subsidiary transfers asset to parent, subsidiary is liquidated, and the parent has no other subsidiary;

(b) where associated companies leave a group together, one having acquired an asset from another (TCGA 1992, s.179(2)). Two or more companies are associated if by themselves they would form a group. So two companies are associated if they are parent and subsidiary or if they are linked by a sub-holding company;

(c) where the transferee company reinvests the notional gain in a new asset (TCGA 1992, s.179A);

(d) where on the joint election of the transferee company and another company in the transferor company, that other company claims rollover relief, so saving the transferee company from the recapture tax charge (TCGA 1992, s.179B).

5.10 ALL INCOME TREATMENT

Loans of companies and securities representing the indebtedness of companies (e.g. loan notes) are classified as 'loan relationships' for tax purposes, and are subject to a special set of rules. The definition of 'loan relationship' covers all debts arising from transactions for the lending of money, and all securities, payments on which are not distributions for tax purposes (FA 1996, s.81). Only companies can have loan relationships.

The legislation requires a company to bring into account as revenue items all profits and gains and losses on loan relationships, whether or not of a capital nature, i.e. all interest receivable, premiums and discounts received plus fluctuations in the value of loan relationships, including all foreign exchange differences on loan relationships and trade debts.

Expenses are deducted from receipts and the balance charged to corporation tax (or made allowable as a loss).

For tax purposes, positive items (income, an increase in an asset, a decrease in a liability) are called 'credits', while negative items (expenditure, decreases in an asset, and increase in a liability) are called 'debits'. This terminology does not conform with accounting terminology.

If the company is party to a loan relationship for the purposes of a trade, profits and gains arising from the loan relationship are included in the Schedule D Case I computation as receipts or expenses of that trade. If the company is party to a loan relationship other than for the purposes of a trade, profits and gains arising from the loan relationship are included in the Schedule D Case III(a) computation as non-trading credits and non-trading debits. The amounts to be taxed or relieved are determined in accordance with the accounts, depending upon whether the company uses an amortised cost or fair value basis for the financial instrument in question, subject to various statutory overrides.

Trading losses arising from loan relationships will be available in the same way as trading losses general: see pp.77–8. Non-trading losses on loan relationships ('non-trading deficits') are pooled with non-trading losses in respect of derivative contracts.

Non-trading deficits on loan relationships (thus augmented) may be used as follows:

(a) treated as trading losses and surrendered by way of group relief;
(b) set off against any profits for the deficit period;
(c) carried back to set against Schedule D Case III profits from loan relationships for 12 months immediately preceding the deficit period;
(d) carried forward against non-trading profits (including capital gains) for subsequent accounting periods.

A carried forward deficit is not available for relief under (a) to (c). If non-trading loan relationship losses are utilised for group relief, relief is granted as if they were a trading loss.

Where companies are connected, a number of special rules apply. 'Connection' is defined in terms of control. Control is defined in terms of the ability to control through the holding of shares, voting power or powers in the articles how a company's affairs are conducted (FA 1996, ss.87, 87A). The principal rules for connected company loan relationships are (FA 1996, Sched.9, paras.5(5), 6(3)):

(a) if the creditor company releases the debt, the debtor company does not have to bring in a credit;
(b) if the debtor company cannot repay the loan or interest, the creditor company cannot bring in a debit and so gets no impairment relief.

Derivative contracts

Profits and losses on derivative contracts are taxed under special rules (FA 2002, Sched.26). Derivative contracts are 'relevant contracts' which are classified for accounting purposes as 'derivative financial instruments'. A relevant contract is a future, an option or a contract for differences. A derivative contract is a relevant contract which is treated as a 'derivative financial instrument' for accounting purposes.

The same terminology of 'credits' and 'debits' is applied as is used in the loan relationship rules. Under accounting standards, all derivative contracts are required to be taken to the balance sheet at fair value, with changes in value going through the income statement. For tax purposes credits and debits on equity derivatives, property derivatives and embedded derivatives which are share options are treated as capital gains and losses.

Intangible property

The taxation of intangibles acquired or created after 1 April 2002 is also subject to special rules (FA 2002, Sched.29). The rules apply to copyright, patents, trademarks, registered designs, know-how, secret knowledge, goodwill. An 'all income' approach is to be adopted, using the 'credits' and 'debits' terminology. 'Intangible asset' has the meaning which it has for accounting purposes. Goodwill, as defined for accounting purposes, is included in intangible property and ceases to be an asset which qualifies for rollover relief. Relief for expenditure on intangibles is to be given as a revenue deduction, based on the amortisation rate used in a company's accounts. Tax broadly follows. The same trading/non-trading distinction is used: trading – Schedule D Case I; non-trading – Schedule D Case VI.

There is an option to adopt a 4 per cent straight-line amortisation rate.

Profits on the sale of assets are also taxed as income, subject to a rollover relief if the company invests in newly acquired intangibles. The rollover relief will operate by reducing the amortisation relief that can be claimed on replacement assets. The new rollover relief will apply to items acquired after commencement date.

With certain exceptions the rules do not apply to acquisitions of intangibles from related companies. A definition of group is introduced based on the capital gains tax definition of group. Transfers of intangibles intra-group are on a no gain/no loss basis.

5.11   TRANSFER PRICING

Transfer pricing is a technique to shift profits from one enterprise to another related enterprise by charging 'transfer prices', i.e. prices which do not conform to an arm's length standard. If both enterprises are resident in the same jurisdiction, the overall result is likely to be neutral on profits and tax consolidation. If the two enterprises are resident in different jurisdictions, the result will be to move profits from one jurisdiction to the other. The transfer pricing rules only apply where one company stands in a control relationship to another company, or both companies are under common control (TA 1988, Sched.28AA, para.4). 'Control' is defined in terms of possession of the majority of voting rights.

For accounting periods beginning on or after 1 April 2004 the transfer pricing rules, including the thin capitalisation rules, apply to arrangements between related UK companies and arrangements between related UK and non-UK companies alike. In domestic situations, transfer pricing situations will arise where one company loans money on non-commercial terms to another group member, or intra-group supplies are made on favourable terms.

In a thin capitalisation situation, one company provides debt finance to a related company in circumstances where a commercial lender would not make a loan at all, or a loan of a smaller amount, or would make the loan on different terms. Where transfer pricing arrangements or thin capitalisation exist, the company which gains a UK tax advantage because a non-arm's length price has been used has to adjust its accounts to conform to an arm's length standard of pricing and calculate its taxable profits accordingly (TA 1988, Sched.28AA, para.1(1)).

To mitigate the effect of applying the transfer pricing rules in domestic situations, there are a number of broad exclusions, e.g. for small or medium sized enterprises. A company qualifies as a SME if it meets two out of three tests (pp. 66–7):

(a) turnover not more than £11.2 million;
(b) balance sheet total not more than £5.6 million;
(c) not more than 250 employees.

5.12 TAXATION OF FOREIGN PROFITS

A UK company with a foreign permanent establishment will be subject to foreign tax in respect of the trading profits of the foreign branch. At the same time it will be subject to UK tax on its worldwide income. Where a UK-resident company has a foreign subsidiary or portfolio shareholding (under 10 per cent), dividends may be subject to withholding and underlying tax in the country where the investee company is resident. The Schedule D Case V income which is taxable in the UK will be the net dividend ultimately received in the UK plus the total foreign underlying tax and withholding tax suffered on the various constituents of the dividend as it is paid up a chain of companies to the UK. In the case of portfolio holdings relief is normally given only for foreign withholding tax. However, the European Court of Justice has indicated that relief should also be given for foreign underlying tax, i.e. the tax on the profits out of which the dividends are paid.

Double taxation relief is conferred by one of two methods:

1. *Exemption method:* Profits which have borne foreign tax are exempt from domestic tax.
2. *Foreign tax credit (FTC) method:* Foreign income is subject to domestic tax, but credit is allowed against domestic tax for the foreign tax suffered.

The UK gives relief by the credit method. For credit for foreign tax against UK tax to be available:

(a) the foreign tax must be charged on income;
(b) it must correspond to corporation tax;
(c) the income must arise in the foreign country;
(d) the foreign and UK tax must be applied to the same tax base.

Questions about foreign tax credits will be decided by the terms of a double tax treaty between the UK and the country where the foreign income arises and the foreign tax is imposed.

Example

Cash dividend received		80
Add: withholding tax	15	
Add: underlying tax	5	
Taxable income		20
Corporation tax at 28%		100
Less: FTC		28
Less underlying tax		(20)
Corporation tax payable:		8

Under onshore pooling, surplus foreign tax can be relieved against other dividends received from non-resident companies by a UK-resident company, or UK permanent establishments of non-resident companies. The onshore pooling rules thus allow excess credits on one foreign source to be set against residual UK tax on income from low tax foreign dividends (TA 1988, ss.806A–M).

5.13 CAPITAL ALLOWANCES

Commercial accounts must provide for depreciation of fixed assets, i.e. the reduction in value of fixed assets arising from their use in the business. Depreciation is not an allowable deduction for tax purposes. Instead uniform capital allowances are granted by statute – principally the Capital Allowances Act 2001.

The working of the capital allowances system will be modified from 2008–9 when the rate of writing down allowances for plant and machinery will be reduced from 25 per cent to 20 per cent. The main feature of the system is that all expenditure on machinery or plant is pooled. If the total expenditure carried forward from previous periods exceeds the value of any plant or machinery sold or disposed in that period, the owner obtains a writing down allowance on the excess. In the converse instance, where the value of the machinery sold or disposed of exceeds the expenditure carried forward, then the owner suffers a balancing charge on the excess.

In the case of short-life assets, an option can be made to write down their values individually (depooling). In that case a balancing allowance (or charge) arises when they are disposed of. If after four years they have not been disposed of, they are transferred to the general pool at their tax written down value (CAA 2001, ss.83–9).

Long-life assets, i.e. assets with a useful economics life of more than 25 years, are separately pooled and qualify for writing-down allowances of 6 per cent per year on a straight-line basis (CAA, ss.91–104).

CHAPTER 6

A company's constitution

6.1   INTRODUCTION

A company's constitution comprises the company's articles of association and any resolutions and agreements provided for under the Companies Act (CA) 2006, Part 3, Chapter 3. In effect, Part 3 is defined by CA 2006, s.29. Section 29 applies to the following resolutions and agreements:

(a)   any special resolution;
(b)   any resolution or agreement agreed to by all the members of a company that, if not so agreed to, would not have been effective for its purpose unless passed as a special resolution;
(c)   any resolution or agreement agreed to by all the members of a class of shareholders that, if not so agreed to, would not have been effective for its purpose unless passed by some particular majority or otherwise in some particular manner;
(d)   any resolution or agreement that effectively binds all members of a class of shareholders though not agreed to by all those members;
(e)   any other resolution to which this chapter applies by virtue of any enactment.

A copy of every resolution or agreement that affects a company's constitution and to which CA 2006, s.29 applies must be forwarded to the registrar within 15 days after it was passed or made and a failure to do so constitutes an offence by the company and every officer of it who is in default (CA 2006, s.30).

   Prior to the implementation of CA 2006, a company's constitutional structure was governed by the terms of the memorandum of association and the articles of association. The primary constitutional function of the memorandum was concerned with the regulation and external appearance of the company in its dealings with third parties. For example, the memorandum contained compulsory clauses (Companies Act (CA) 1985, s.2) to provide and regulate the name of the company, whether the company's registered office was situated in England and Wales, or specifically, Wales or Scotland, the objects clause of the company stating the business or other activities for which the company is incorporated, that the liability of the company's membership was limited or that it was a public limited company and in the case of a company with a share capital, the amount of share capital with which it proposed to be registered and the manner by which the share capital was to be divided into shares of a fixed amount.

Under the CA 1985, the articles of association were concerned with matters related to the internal affairs of the company, for example, clauses governing the regulation of general meetings, the appointment, regulation and powers of company directors, and the class rights attached to shares, share capital and dividends. Following the implementation of the CA 2006, while companies will still be required to be registered with both a memorandum and articles, the former is to be devoid of any significance in respect of the constitutional framework of a company, being relegated to the status of a procedural registration document (discussed in **Chapter 1**). The effect of the CA 2006 deems that the company's articles become the primary source of a company's constitutional structure. For companies incorporated prior to the CA 2006, the contents of the memorandum are deemed (in respect of the constitutional functions attached to the same), to have effect as if they had been incorporated into the company's articles (see CA 2006, s.28).

6.2 THE ARTICLES OF ASSOCIATION

Companies have the freedom to include regulations in their articles to govern the company's internal affairs in any manner they see fit, subject to the qualification that if a company's articles contain a regulation that is contrary to a provision of the companies legislation, or a regulation contrary to the general law, then the offending regulation will have no effect. In accordance with CA 2006, s.18, a company must have articles of association prescribing regulations for the company. A company may register its own distinct set of articles (CA 2006, s.18(2)) but if it declines to do so the terms of the company's articles will be determined by reference to the relevant model form of articles in place at the time of the company's registration (CA 2006, s.19). Where a company does register its own distinct form of articles and the same do not exclude or modify the relevant model articles, then the model articles will automatically take effect in relation to the matter not covered by the company's own distinct set of articles (CA 2006, s.20). For companies registered prior to the enactment of the CA 2006, but after the introduction of the CA 1985, the model form of articles is found in Table A of the Companies (Tables A–F) Regulations 1985, SI 1985/805 ('Table A articles'). It should be noted that where a company was incorporated prior to 1985, the model articles will be in the format of Table A of the 1948 Companies Act. However, a company that was, for example, registered before the implementation of the CA 2006, may amend its articles by special resolution (CA 2006, s.21) to a format corresponding to the model articles prescribed by the CA 2006. For companies registered in compliance with the CA 2006, the applicable form of model articles may be dependent on the type of company in question given that CA 2006, s.19 enables the Secretary of State, by regulations, to prescribe different model articles for different descriptions of companies. (See **Appendix 2** of this book for the model articles prescribed in relation to a private company.)

The contractual nature of the articles (CA 2006, s.33)

In accordance with CA 2006, s.33, the provisions of a company's constitution, when registered, bind the company and its members to the same extent as if they were covenants on the part of the company and of each member to observe those provisions. Money payable by a member to the company under its constitution is a debt due from him or her to the company. In England and Wales and Northern Ireland it is of the nature of an ordinary contract debt and as such is subject to a limitation period of six years.

CA 2006, s.33 significantly alters the contractual effect of a company's constitution, as previously determined by CA 1985, s.14. Section 14 provided that a company's constitution was, in a contractual sense, binding between the company and its members but only 'to the same extent as if it had been signed and sealed by each member'. Section 14 made no mention of the fact that a company, as a distinct legal entity, was bound as if it had signed and sealed the constitution. Therefore, while the courts construed a company's constitution as a commercial/business document (see, e.g. *Tett* v. *Phoenix Property Ltd* [1986] BCLC 149), a company's written constitution was not afforded full contractual force and was not liable to be set aside on the grounds of misrepresentation, mistake, undue influence or duress. Moreover, absent terms could not be implied into the constitution (see, e.g. *Bratton Seymour Service Co Ltd* v. *Oxborough* [1992] BCC 471). A court would only interfere with the terms of a constitution in a situation where terms were construed to be so vague as to warrant 'interpretation', i.e. to give them sense and clarity (see, e.g. *Folkes Group plc* v. *Alexander* [2002] 2 BCLC 254).

Enforceable obligations under the constitution

Obligations regulating the relationship between the company and its membership are enforceable by the company. The said obligations have full contractual effect. For example, in *Hickman* v. *Kent and Romney Sheepbreeders Association* [1915] 1 Ch 881, it was held that a member of the Association was subject to a requirement within the company's constitution that he should first submit to arbitration before pursuing litigation against the Association. However, as a qualification to the *Hickman* case, it should be noted that a requirement on the part of a member to abide by the terms of an arbitration clause, or any other type of restrictive clause contained within the constitution, may not be enforceable where the effect of the restrictive clause is overridden by a statutory right afforded to the membership. For example, in *Exeter City AFC Ltd* v. *The Football Conference Ltd & Anor* [2004] BCC 498, Exeter City AFC (E) was a member of the Conference League (C) and the Football Association (FA). E was insolvent and under the terms of C's articles, was compelled, in respect of the repayment of its debts, to favour a particular set of creditors. The said preferred creditors did not include the Inland Revenue, to which E was in debt. If E abided by the terms of the articles, the Inland Revenue would not be paid and E would be made subject to a winding-up order. E therefore sought to escape the terms of the articles by presenting a petition under CA 1985, s.459 (this provision, unaltered in its wording, is now CA 2006, s.994 discussed in **Chapter 15**), alleging that the affairs of the C/FA were being conducted in a manner unfairly prejudicial to E's interests. The C/FA sought a declaration under the Arbitration Act 1996, s.9 for a stay of the s.459 proceedings, with the objective of compelling E to comply with the articles and referring the dispute to arbitration. In refusing to grant the stay, the High Court concluded that a right to petition to wind up a company and the right to present a petition under s.459 were statutory rights conferred on every single shareholder. Compliance with such rights amounted to a condition of incorporation under the Companies Act. E's statutory rights outweighed the requirement on the part of E to abide by the terms of C's articles.

Obligations enforceable by the membership against the company

Much of the controversy associated with the interpretation of CA 1985, s.14 related to the extent by which obligations, contained within a company's articles, could be enforced by the membership of the company, against the company. The said controversy would now appear redundant in the context of CA 2006, s.33 as all obligations within a company's constitution should be enforceable where a member seeks enforcement, qua member. Under the CA 1985, only one class of obligation was definitely enforceable, namely an obligation often described as a pure membership or insider right. Such rights are rights common to all the members of any given class of shares. Examples of insider rights include the following.

- The right of a member to insist that once a company has declared a dividend, that the dividend should be paid in accordance with the terms of the articles (see, e.g. *Wood* v. *Odessa Waterworks Co* (1889) 42 Ch D 639).
- The ability of a member to enforce a right to a share certificate (see, e.g. *Burdett* v. *Standard Exploration* (1899) 16 TLR 112).
- On the winding up of a company, after the company has paid its creditors, a member's right to a return of capital (see, e.g. *Griffith* v. *Paget* (1877) 6 Ch D 511; note that preferential shareholders may have priority to a return of capital over other shareholders: see **Chapter 9**).

- On a valid transfer of shares, the right of a member to have his or her name entered in the register of members (see, e.g. *Re British Sugar Refining Co* (1857) 3 K & J 408).
- The right of a member to insist that an organ or a constituent part of an organ of the company (the board of directors or general meeting) is allowed to exercise its functions in accordance with the terms of the company's constitution (see, e.g. *Quinn & Axtens* v. *Salmon* [1909] AC 442).
- The entitlement of a member holding voting shares in a company, to exercise his or her vote at company meetings in any way and for whatever purpose he or she so chooses (see, e.g. *Pender* v. *Lushington* (1870) 6 Ch D 70). However, a member's entitlement to enforce a right to vote could be lost where a resolution to which the vote related was concerned with a matter of internal procedure as opposed to a substantive issue affecting the constitutional rights of the membership (see, e.g. *MacDougall* v. *Gardiner* (1875) 1 Ch D 13) where the voting issue was concerned with the right to a poll vote in relation to a motion to adjourn a meeting. A more exceptional example of the courts' ability to refuse a member's entitlement to vote was be found in a situation where, if the vote was cast, its effect would be to threaten the very existence of the company (see, e.g. *Standard Chartered Bank v Walker* [1992] BCLC 603). In this case the court prevented a member of a company from exercising his votes to defeat a resolution the purpose of which was to facilitate a rescue package by the company's bankers.

Unenforceable membership rights

Although insider right obligations contained in a company's constitution were regarded as enforceable under CA 1985, s.14, other obligations relating to the rights of members were regarded as unenforceable; such rights were referred to as 'outsider rights'. An 'outsider right' was an obligation that did not correspond to the collective constitutional rights of any given class of shareholder. For example, in *Eley* v. *Positive Government Security Life Insurance* (1876) 1 Ex D 88, the articles of the company provided that the plaintiff (E) was to be appointed as the company's solicitor for the duration of his life. E was also a member of the company. The Court of Appeal held that E could not enforce the right to lifelong employment as the company's solicitor because the obligation to maintain E in that position was one which did not affect the constitutional rights of the shareholding body; the obligation was unrelated to rights commonly held by the members of the company. However, following the enactment of CA 2006, s.33 the position in *Eley* is altered providing the right is enforced as a membership right, not as a right held in some other capacity. Therefore, in *Eley*, E's right to be maintained as a solicitor of the company for life could now be enforced where E sought to enforce the right qua member, i.e. as a member of the company, as opposed to the pursuit of the right in a personal capacity as the solicitor of the company.

Obligations enforceable between members inter se

CA 2006, s.33 makes no mention of whether obligations contained within the articles are directly enforceable between members *inter se*. As such, it would appear that these obligations should only be enforceable through the company (see, e.g. *MacDougall* v. *Gardiner* (1875) 1 Ch D 13). However, in specific circumstances a member may be able to directly enforce obligations against a fellow member without the need to pursue the action through the company. The principal justification for allowing a membership action is that the company should not become involved in what would essentially be a dispute between its members; namely, the company should not be involved in unnecessary litigation. Support for this view may be found in cases where preemption rights have been enforced between members of a company, i.e. rights contained within a company's articles which provide that a member must, on deciding to sell his or her shares, offer them to existing members of the company (see, e.g. *Rayfield* v. *Hands* [1960] Ch 1). However, membership disputes that are personal in nature with no connection to the constitutional functioning of a company are likely to remain unenforceable under CA 2006, s.33 for example, an obligation within the articles relating to a trading transaction between two members of the company (see, e.g. *London Sack & Bag Co Ltd* v. *Dixon & Lugton Ltd* [1943] 2 All ER 767).

Members

In accordance with CA 2006, s.32, a company must, following the request of any of its members, send to that member any or all of the following documents:

(a) an up-to-date copy of the company's articles;
(b) a copy of any resolution or agreement relating to the company to which CA 2006, s.29 applies (resolutions and agreements affecting a company's constitution) and that is for the time being in force;
(c) a copy of any document required to be sent to the registrar under:

    (i)   s.34(2) (notice where company's constitution altered by enactment); or
    (ii) s.35(2)(a) (notice where order of court or other authority alters company's constitution);

(d) a copy of any court order under s.899 (order sanctioning compromise or arrangement) or s.900 (order facilitating reconstruction or amalgamation);

(e)   a copy of any court order under s.996 (protection of members against unfair prejudice: powers of the court) that alters the company's constitution;

(f)   a copy of the company's current certificate of incorporation, and of any past certificates of incorporation;

(g)   in the case of a company with a share capital, a current statement of capital. The statement of capital required is a statement of:

   (i)   the total number of shares of the company;
   (ii) the aggregate nominal value of those shares.

   and for each class of shares:

   (i)   prescribed particulars of the rights attached to the shares;
   (ii)   the total number of shares of that class; and
   (iii) the aggregate nominal value of shares of that class; and
   (iv)   the amount paid up and the amount (if any) unpaid on each share (whether on account of the nominal value of the share or by way of premium).

(h)   in the case of a company limited by guarantee, a copy of the statement of guarantee.

If a company makes default in complying with s.32, an offence is committed by every officer of the company who is in default.

6.3   INDEPENDENT CONTRACTUAL RIGHTS

Although under CA 1985, s.14 an 'outsider right' was not directly enforceable, it may have been indirectly enforceable where it was supported by an independent contract. Accordingly, a member of a company (or indeed a non-member) would have been capable of entering into a separate enforceable contractual agreement with the company, an agreement that would have been unenforceable had it been contained within the company's constitution. A typical example of a separate enforceable contractual agreement which, under CA 1985, s.14, would have been viewed as unenforceable was a director's service contract. In accordance with CA 2006, s.33, a service contract contained within a company's constitution will be enforceable by the director in question (provided he or she is a member of the company and sues qua member) or by any other member of the company. However, notwithstanding the effect of CA 2006, s.33, it is most probable that service contracts will continue to be held as independent contracts given the practical flexibility and need to update and change the terms of the contract (if contained within the articles, terms could only be changed by altering the articles, i.e. by passing a special resolution). It should be noted that where a director's service contract is silent as to a specific matter, for example, the length of the service contract, the relevant term may be implied into the independent service contract if it is included within the company's articles (e.g. *Re New British Iron Co, ex p. Beckwith* (1898) 1 Ch 324 and *Read* v. *Astoria Garage (Streatham) Ltd* [1952] Ch 637). It must also be observed that the appointment of a person to a directorship is not, in itself, evidence of an independent contract between the director and company (e.g. *Newtherapeutics Ltd* v. *Katz* [1991] Ch 226), although upon being appointed to a directorship, the newly appointed director will be bound by the provisions of the company's constitution even in circumstances where the director is not a member of the company (e.g. *Re Anglo Austrian Printing & Publishing Union* [1892] 2 Ch 158).

Finally, a potential twist to the effect of CA 2006, s.33 is that it should now be possible for a director, pursuing the matter qua member of a company, to enforce a term of the constitution that provides that the director should hold his or her post for life or, for example, hold his or her post other than where a specific majority of the membership (greater than 50 per cent, up to 100 per cent) determine that the director be removed from office. Prior to the CA 2006, CA 1985, s.303 provided that the terms of a company's articles could not in any way preclude the right of a company to pass an ordinary resolution to remove a director. Under CA 2006, s.168 a director may still be removed by an ordinary resolution, however, the provision is without any mention of the fact that a company's articles cannot disturb the effect of the provision. CA 2006, s.168 provides that:

> A company may by ordinary resolution at a meeting remove a director before the expiration of his period of office, notwithstanding anything in any agreement between it and him.

The wording of CA 2006, s.168, especially in the absence of a requirement that a company's articles cannot preclude the enforcement of the provision, may imply that although a director can be removed by an ordinary resolution, if, however, the articles require, for example, a special resolution to effect the director's removal, then the intent of the articles should be followed.

Remedies following a breach of an independent contract

Other than where a statutory power specifically provides that its effect cannot, in any way, be impugned by the articles or otherwise, it would appear quite legitimate for an independent contractual agreement between a company and a third party to include a provision which seeks to restrain the company's exercise of a statutory power. Therefore, in an independent contractual agreement a third party could legitimately prohibit a company from altering a term of its articles, see, e.g. *Punt* v. *Symons & Co Ltd* [1903] 2 Ch 506. However, if after entering into such a contract, the company breached the agreement by reasserting its right to alter its articles, would the breach give rise to the usual remedies associated with a breach of contract? Would it be possible for the third party to obtain an injunction to restrain the company from breaching the terms of the contract? In *Punt* v. *Symons & Co Ltd*, the remedy for the breach of the agreement was restricted to a claim for damages, whereas in *British Murac Syndicate* v. *Alperton Rubber Ltd* [1915] 2 Ch 168, the Court of Appeal granted an injunction to prevent the company from altering the terms of its articles. However, *in Southern Foundries Ltd* v. *Shirlaw* [1940] AC 701, the House of Lords came to the conclusion (albeit in *obiter* comments) that an injunction should not be granted to prevent a company from altering its articles, notwithstanding that the company would be in breach of a contract by acting on new articles; a breach which could, however, be remedied by an award of damages. This approach (an award of damages), is, it is submitted, the correct approach. A company should not be prohibited from acting in accordance with a statutory power, a power the use of which the other contracting party is deemed to be aware. Nevertheless, a company should not be allowed to breach a contractual obligation without fear of the imposition of some form of penalty, namely, it should be made liable to a claim in damages.

6.4 ALTERING A COMPANY'S ARTICLES

A company may not alter its articles where the effect of the alteration would be inconsistent with a provision of the companies legislation. Otherwise a company may alter its articles by passing a special resolution, namely by a three-quarters majority vote of those members who attend and are entitled to vote at a general meeting (CA 2006, s.21) (save for where a provision of a company's articles is entrenched, see below). However, a member of a company is not bound (unless he or she otherwise agrees in writing) by an alteration to the company's articles after the date on which he or she became a member in circumstances where the effect of the alteration is to require him or her to take or subscribe for more shares in the company or in any way to increase his or her liability to contribute to the company's share capital or otherwise to pay money to the company (CA 2006, s.25). Where a company alters its articles, an offence is committed if the company fails to send a copy of the amended articles to the registrar (not later than 15 days after the amendment takes place). The offence is committed by the company and any officer in default (CA 2006, s.26).

Where a company's constitution is altered by an order of the court or other authority, or by an enactment, other than an enactment amending the general law, the company must give notice to the registrar of the alteration not less than 15 days after the alteration takes effect or the enactment comes into force (CA 2006, ss.34–5).

Assessing a valid alteration

To alter a company's articles, the alteration must also comply with requirements formulated by the courts to safeguard minority interests. As such, an alteration of a company's articles must not be retrospective in its effect, see, e.g. *Swaeby* v. *Port Darwin Mining Co* (1899) 1 Meg 385. Further, an alteration of a company's articles must be made bona fide for the benefit of the company as a whole. This rule is necessary to prevent a three-quarters majority of the membership adopting an article, the effect of which would be to exploit the interests of minority shareholders. Nevertheless, due to the courts' general reluctance to interfere in the business decisions of a company, the fact that an alteration of articles may cause some disadvantage to minority interests will not in itself be sufficient grounds to justify the alteration as invalid (see, e.g. *Allen* v. *Gold Reef* [1900] 1 Ch 656). Therefore where the purpose of the alteration applies equally to all members, it will be valid notwithstanding that its practical effect may be to cause disadvantage to the minority.

For an alteration of articles to be declared invalid the alteration must be discriminatory. For example, in *Dafen Tin Plate* v. *Llanelly Steel Ltd* [1920] 2 Ch 124, a company altered its articles to give members who held a majority stake in the company an absolute right to purchase the shares of any minority shareholder. The reason for the alteration was to prevent a minority shareholder who had transferred business interests to one of the company's competitors from retaining his membership of the company. Although the motive behind the alteration may have been for the benefit of the commercial entity, the terms of this alteration were too wide. The alteration had the effect of permitting members holding a majority stake to expel a minority shareholder without valid excuse. Finally, although an alteration of articles may be valid on the premise that it is not discriminatory, the alteration could still be challenged under CA 2006, s.994, namely on the basis that the alteration amounted to conduct of an unfairly prejudicial nature (discussed further in **Chapter 15**).

Entrenched articles

Prior to the passing of the CA 2006, the right to entrench articles did not exist. However, as a result of CA 2006, s.22, a company's articles may now contain a general provision to the effect that specified regulations within the articles may be amended or repealed only if specific conditions are met, or procedures are complied with. The conditions or procedures are more restrictive than those applicable to the normal procedure to alter a company's articles, i.e. by a special resolution. A general provision for entrenchment may only be made in the articles on the company's formation, or by an amendment to the company's articles agreed to by all the members of the company. A company must give notice to the registrar of the inclusion of a power to entrench regulations within the articles (CA 2006, s.23). Where a company seeks to alter the terms of its articles to include a general provision for entrenchment it must send to the registrar any document making or evidencing the alteration and must also deliver a statement of compliance certifying that the alteration has been made in accordance with the terms of the company's articles (CA 2006, s.24).

It is to be noted that a company cannot attempt to entrench regulations in its articles by simply providing that the entrenched regulations cannot, in any circumstances, be removed. CA 2006, s.22 is specific of a requirement whereby the method for entrenchment must also specify a procedure for the removal of the entrenchment power. However, it will be possible to create a very restrictive power of entrenchment, for example, by providing that an entrenched regulation may only be altered by means of the unanimous written consent of the membership.

A company may amend it articles to remove its general capacity to entrench regulations contained therein, but may only do so by the agreement of all the members of the company (CA 2006, s.22(3)). Finally, it should be noted that entrenchment does not affect any power of a court or other authority to alter a company's articles.

6.5 STATEMENT OF A COMPANY'S OBJECTS

CA 2006, s.31 provides that unless a company's articles specifically restrict the objects of the company then the company's objects will be unrestricted. As such, a company is not tied to the pursuit of specified business purposes. Indeed, even before CA 2006, s.31, the significance of a company's objects clause was one steeped in redundancy (discussed further in **Chapter 12**) Where a company chooses to restrict its objects, i.e. where a company's objects are specifically listed, the effect of the restriction will not affect the ability of a third party to enforce a contract, even if the purpose of that contract falls outside the terms of the objects. However, in a case where the company purports to act outside the terms of its objects this will give rise to a potential breach of the articles (the internal contract between a company and its membership) and as such it may be possible for a member to obtain an injunction to restrain the breach of objects. However, a member will not be able to prevent a proposed transaction following the execution of a binding legal agreement between the company and third party, notwithstanding that the agreement would, when enacted, be in breach of the objects (discussed further in **Chapter 12**).

6.6 THE WEIGHTED VOTING CLAUSE

A provision(s) of a company's articles, the intent of which is to override a statutory provision, will be invalid. However, a company may insert a clause into its articles (a weighted voting clause) the practical effect of which may indeed limit or preclude the company's ability to pass a resolution in a manner consistent with the terms of a statutory provision. A weighted voting clause will enhance the voting rights of a given member of the company. For example, if a company has three members (A, B and C) and all have equal voting rights, and a weighted voting clause within the articles provides that in relation to a motion to pass an ordinary resolution concerned with matter X, member A should have three times the voting rights of any other member, then in relation to any resolution related to matter X, the company will be unable to pass the resolution, save in the unlikely event where A votes in its favour. In effect, the company's ability to pass the resolution will be dependent on the will of A (other than for the weighted voting clause A would only have held one third of the voting shares) (see, e.g. the decision of the House of Lords in *Bushell* v. *Faith* [1970] 1 All ER 53).

6.7 MEMBERSHIP AGREEMENTS

In addition to those terms of a company's articles which purport to regulate the relationship of members *inter se*, the shareholders of a company may lawfully bind themselves by way of an independent membership agreement (a contractual agreement), to act or vote in a specific way on issues governed by the terms of the agreement. A membership agreement is a common feature in small private companies and usually purports to bind the entire, or a substantial majority of the existing membership of the company. The agreement seeks to regulate matters of internal management with the effect that members who are a party to the agreement act and vote on specific issues in a predetermined way (see, e.g. *Breckland Group Holdings Ltd* v. *London & Suffolk Properties* [1989] BCLC 100, *Euro Brokers Holdings Ltd* v. *Monecor (London) Ltd* [2003] BCC 573).

The effectiveness of a membership agreement, in terms of its ability to influence the outcome of any given vote, will clearly depend on the number of members who are bound by its terms. A membership agreement will be more effective if it incorporates a majority of the company's membership, affording a degree of certainty as to the outcome of issues governed by its terms. However, the terms of a membership agreement may prove to be inflexible where, for example, a majority of the members who are party to the agreement consider that a specific term contained therein should no longer be pursued; insofar as the term is no longer viewed as beneficial to the company's interests. If a minority of those party to the agreement refuse to accept the majority view and the minority demand compliance with the disputed term by, for example, seeking an injunction to protect the terms of the agreement, then, following the House of Lords decision in *Russell* v. *Northern Bank Development Corporation Ltd* [1992] 1 WLR 588, it is probable that they will succeed. In *Russell* the House upheld the validity of a membership agreement by which all five (current) members of the company were bound. Here, the company's five shareholders agreed to refrain from voting to increase the company's share capital, save in a situation where all parties consented in writing to the increase. Subsequently, as the company's circumstances changed, four of the members proposed that the company should increase its issued share capital. However, the fifth member challenged the proposal insofar as it contradicted the terms of the membership agreement. The House of Lords, overruling the decision of the Court of Appeal [1992] BCLC 431, held that as the agreement was separate and distinct from the company's articles it was of a purely personal nature and as such was binding. If necessary, an injunction could have been sought as a remedy for the purported breach.

Therefore, the decision in *Russell* opens up the possibility of a party to a membership agreement seeking an injunction to prevent non compliance by other members party to the agreement. The membership agreement will be enforced notwithstanding that it may prevent the will of the requisite majority of the membership from exercising a statutory power. Indeed, in an extreme case, a company may become a slave to the terms of a membership agreement. Finally, it is implicit from *Exeter City AFC Ltd* v. *The Football Conference Ltd & Anor* [2004] BCC 498 (discussed above) that a membership agreement cannot exclude the right of a member to exercise his or her statutory right to present a winding-up petition or petition for relief under CA 1985, s.459 (now CA 2006, s.994). Therefore, where the terms of a membership agreement attempt to exclude a member's aforementioned statutory rights, then, although the pursuit of the statutory right may breach a term of the membership agreement, the term of the membership agreement, insofar as it seeks to restrict the statutory right of the member, will be deemed redundant. Also see *Union Music Ltd & Anor* v. *Watson & Anor* [2004] BCC 37, in which it was also held that the court's power to call a company meeting pursuant to CA 1985, s.371 (now CA 2006, s.306) could not be disturbed by the terms of a shareholder agreement.

CHAPTER 7

The legal nature and characteristics of holding shares in a limited company

7.1 INTRODUCTION

A company limited by shares is founded on an undertaking by its members to contribute capital in consideration for the allotment of shares. The minimum amount by which a share may be purchased from a company is termed the nominal value (par value) of the share (see, e.g. *Ooregum Gold Mining Co of India* v. *Roper* [1892] AC 125). Where a company offers to sell shares at a price in excess of their nominal value, the monetary difference between the price paid for the shares and the nominal value is termed the 'share premium' and must be placed in a share premium account of the company (Companies Act (CA) 2006, s.610). Once contributed, share capital becomes the property of the company. The company is not classed as a debtor in respect of the repayment or restoration of capital.

The extent of a shareholder's undertaking to contribute capital, to participate in dividend distributions and vote at general meetings are all matters related to the number and class of shares held in the company. A shareholding interest is comprised of all the legal rights of membership contained within a mutual set of covenants within the company's constitution (discussed in **Chapter 6**). However, the exact scope of a membership interest is likely to extend beyond strict legal rights; the extent of a membership interest will be dependent upon the nature and type of shares held. (The scope of a membership interest is discussed further in **Chapter 15**.)

Unless a company is unlimited or limited by guarantee, the company's 'application for registration' must indicate the manner in which the contributed capital is to be divided into shares of a fixed nominal value (CA 2006, s.10). The shares may be denominated in any currency, and different classes of shares may be denominated in different currencies (CA 2006, s.542). The total nominal allotted capital of a public company must not be less than £50,000 (CA 2006, s.763).

7.2   IDENTIFYING A MEMBER OF A COMPANY

A person may become a member of a company in one of four ways:

(a) by subscribing to the memorandum on the incorporation of the company;
(b) by making a successful application to the company for shares;
(c) by purchasing shares from an existing member of the company; or
(d) by acquiring shares as a result of a member's death or bankruptcy.

CA 2006, s.112 provides that the subscribers of a company's memorandum are deemed to have agreed to become members of the company, and on the company's registration become members and must be entered as such in its register of members. Every other person who agrees to become a member of a company, and whose name is entered in its register of members is a member of the company. For a person to assent to become a member of a company it is unnecessary to establish a binding contract between that person and the company. Accordingly, a person's membership of a company will *prima facie* be conclusive (other than where, for example, he or she became a member in contravention of a term(s) of the company's articles) where, irrespective of the absence of a binding contract, that person's name (if he or she assented) is added to the register of members (see, e.g. *POW Services Ltd* v. *Clare* [1995] 2 BCLC 205). Where the details entered in a company's register of members are incorrect in some material respect, the error may be challenged in accordance with CA 2006, ss.125–8 (there is a 10-year time limit from the date/ omission of the entry) and the register may be rectified accordingly (see, e.g. *Re Thundercrest Ltd* [1994] BCC 857). Any application to challenge the details of any entry must be made without unreasonable delay or prejudice to any innocent third party (see, e.g. *Re ISIS Factors plc* [2004] BCC 359).

While the use of the terms 'member' and 'shareholder' are often synonymous, it is nevertheless possible for a person to be a member but not a shareholder of a company. For example, a company limited by guarantee has members, but not shareholders. Conversely, it is possible to be a shareholder but not a member of a company. For example, the holders of 'bearer shares' are classed as shareholders, but although shareholders, they may not necessarily be members of the company. A holder of bearer shares is entitled to specific shares identified in a share warrant. Subject to any contrary intention within the articles, the bearer of a share warrant is entitled to have his or her name entered in the register of members only upon surrendering the share warrant (CA 2006, s.122).

The register of members

CA 2006, s.113 provides that every company must keep a register of its members. There must be entered in the register:

(a) the names and addresses of the members;

(b) the date on which each person was registered as a member; and

(c) the date at which any person ceased to be a member.

Where a company has a share capital, the register must include the names and addresses of the members and a statement of:

(a) the shares held by each member, distinguishing each share:

    (i)   by its number (so long as the share has a number); and

    (ii) where the company has more than one class of issued shares, by its class; and

(b) the amount paid or agreed to be considered as paid on the shares of each member.

CA 2006, s.113(5) specifically provides that joint holders of a share fall to be treated as a single member, although all names must be stated in the register. A company registered with only one member must include a specific statement to this effect in the register of members (CA 2006, s.123). A failure to comply with the aforementioned provisions will result in the company and every officer of the company in default being made liable on summary conviction to a fine.

In accordance with CA 2006, s.114, a company's register of members must be kept available for inspection at its registered office, or at another place in the part of the UK in which the company is registered. The registrar must be notified of the place where the register is kept available for inspection. If for a 14-day period a company fails to comply with the above requirements an offence will be committed by the company, and every officer of the company who is in default. A person guilty of an offence under s.114 is liable on summary conviction to a fine.

Index of members

In addition to keeping a register of members, CA 2006, s.115 provides that a company that has more than 50 members must also keep an index of its members, unless the register of members is in such a format to qualify its classification as an index. The index must contain, in respect of each member, a sufficient indication to enable the account of that member in the register to be readily found and the index must at all times be kept available for inspection at the same place as the register of members. The company must make any necessary alteration in the index within 14 days after the date on which any alteration is made to the register of members. A failure to comply with CA 2006, s.115 by a company or any officer in default will, on summary conviction, result in the imposition of a fine.

Inspection of the register and index

The register of members, together with any index, must be kept open to inspection by any member of the company or, on the payment of a prescribed fee, by any other person (CA 2006, s.116). CA 2006, s.117 provides that a company must accept or refuse the request for an inspection (or copy of the register) within five working days of its receipt. If the company decides to reject the request, it must defend its decision via an application to the court on the ground that the request was for an improper purpose. Where the company's objection is upheld, the person having made the request may be held liable to pay, in part or full, the company's costs. Where a company refuses an inspection or copy of the register without making an application to the court an offence is committed by the company, and every officer of the company who is in default.

The company and any person who is found guilty of the offence is liable on summary conviction to a fine. In the case of any such refusal or default the court may compel an immediate inspection or direct that the copy of the register be sent to the person who requests it (CA 2006, s.118).

In relation to public companies, following the implementation of the Uncertificated Securities Regulations 2001, SI 2001/3755 it is now possible (but not obligatory) for public companies to keep a second register in computerised form (the CREST system). Although this new system may have a potential to confuse matters, its objective is to speed up share transfers. This system of registration is only applicable to shares held in electronic form (uncertified shares); it does not apply to shares held via the traditional form of share certificates (see CA 2006, Chapter 2).

7.3   ISSUING AND ACQUIRING SHARES

A company may not allot shares to itself (see, e.g. *Trevor* v. *Whitworth* (1887) 12 App Cas 409) and as a general rule must not acquire its own shares, whether by purchase, subscription or otherwise (CA 2006, s.658). However, CA 2006, s.659(2) provides exceptions to s.658, namely:

(a)   the acquisition of shares in a reduction of capital duly made,
(b)   the purchase of shares in pursuance of an order of the court under –

    (i)   section 98 (application to court to cancel resolution for re-registration as a private company),
    (ii)   section 721(6) (powers of court on objection to redemption or purchase of shares out of capital),
    (iii) section 759 (remedial order in case of breach of prohibition of public offers by private company), or
    (iv)   Part 30 (protection of members against unfair prejudice);

(c)   the forfeiture of shares, or the acceptance of shares surrendered in lieu, in pursuance of the company's articles, for failure to pay any sum payable in respect of the shares.

It should be noted that while a private company may seek offers for its shares from persons other than existing members (but not by way of an offer to the general public), commonly the articles of a private company will restrict the class of person who may be permitted to hold shares. For example, the owner-ship of shares may be restricted to the existing members of the company or their relatives.

CA 2006, s.550 provides:

> Where a private company has only one class of shares, the directors may exercise any power of the company –
>
> (a) to allot shares of that class, or
> (b) to grant rights to subscribe for or to convert any security into such shares,
>
> except to the extent that they are prohibited from doing so by the company's articles.

In other cases an issue of shares may be allotted by a company following a resolution of the company's board of directors in accordance with powers contained within the company's articles. Alternatively shares may be issued and allotted by means of an ordinary resolution of the general meeting (CA 2006, s.551). Here, the effect of the previous law (Companies Act (CA) 1985, s.80) is retained for both private and public companies other than where a company has only one class of share. For the purposes of the Companies Acts, shares in a company are taken to be allotted when a person acquires the unconditional right to be included in the company's register of members in respect of the shares (CA 2006, s.558).

Following an allotment of shares, a share certificate may be distributed to the purchaser of the shares; this is not a document of title although it provides *prima facie* evidence of title (CA 2006, s.768). The authority to allot shares under CA 2006, s.551 is for a maximum of five years. In the case of authorisation contained in the company's articles at the time of its original incorporation, the five-year period runs from the date of incorporation, and in the case of authorisation by the general meeting the five-year period runs from the date on which the resolution was passed. Authorisation may be given for a particular exercise of the power or for its exercise generally, and may be unconditional or subject to conditions (CA 2006, s.551(2)). The authority must state the maximum amount of shares to be allotted pursuant to the authority. Authorisation may be renewed or further renewed by a resolution of the company for a further period not exceeding five years, and be revoked or varied at any time by a resolution of the company.

However, in accordance with CA 2006, s.551(7), the directors may still allot shares, or grant rights to subscribe for or to convert any security into shares, after the authorisation has expired, if:

(a) the shares are allotted, or the rights are granted, in pursuance of an offer or agreement made by the company before the authorisation expired, and

(b) the authorisation allowed the company to make an offer or agreement which would or might require shares to be allotted, or rights to be granted, after the authorisation had expired.

It is interesting to note that authorisation may be given by an ordinary resolution even if its effect would be to contradict the terms of the company's articles. (It should be noted that CA 1985, s.80A ceases to have effect. Section 80A provided that in the case of a private company, the general meeting could, by ordinary resolution, elect to authorise its directors to allot shares to a maximum specified amount over a fixed or indefinite period.)

A director who knowingly contravenes, or permits or authorises a contravention of CA 2006, s.551 commits an offence and if convicted is liable on conviction on indictment, to a fine or on summary conviction, to a fine not exceeding the statutory maximum. However, the validity of an allotment or other transaction is not affected. Therefore, a person who purchases shares that have been issued without a proper authority will obtain a good title in respect of the issued shares. Finally, it should be noted that the allotment provisions (CA 2006, ss.549–51) do not apply in the case of the allotment of shares in pursuance of an employees' share scheme, or to the grant of a right to subscribe for or to convert any security into shares so allotted (CA 2006, s.549(2)).

A company limited by share capital must, within one month of making an allotment of shares, register a return of the allotment which must be accompanied by a full and up-to-date statement of the nature of the company's share capital at the date to which the return is made (CA 2006, s.551). It is an offence to fail to comply with s.551 and every officer of the company who is in default is liable to a fine (although any person liable for the default may apply to the court for relief). The court may grant relief, extending the time period for the delivery of the document where it is satisfied that the omission to deliver the document was accidental or due to inadvertence, or that it is just and equitable to grant relief. CA 2006, Part 3, Chapter 3 (resolutions affecting a company's constitution) applies to a resolution under this section.

Nominee holdings

Shares may be registered in the name of a nominee, the nominee will hold the shares directly or indirectly for the true owner (beneficial owner). If shares are issued to a nominee of a company, the shares are treated as held by the nominee on his or her own account and the company is regarded as having no beneficial interest in them (CA 2006, s.660).

Share transfers

A share may be transferred in accordance with the terms of a company's articles (CA 2006, s.554). It is unlawful for a company to register a transfer of shares unless a proper instrument of transfer has been delivered to the company (see, e.g. *Nisbet* v. *Shepherd* [1994] BCC 91). The articles of a private company often include a restriction on a member's ability to transfer shares. A common type of restriction on the transfer of shares is one which provides a right of pre-emption, namely, a member who wishes to sell shares must first offer the shares to existing members of the company. Where a member wishing to sell shares is compelled to sell to an existing member of the company, the company's articles will normally contain a valuation procedure with the valuation ordinarily undertaken by the company's auditor. Other than where fraud or gross negligence is alleged, the auditor's valuation cannot ordinarily be challenged (see, e.g. *Jones* v. *Sherwood Computer Services plc* [1992] 1 WLR 277).

A company's articles may also provide that the directors of the company may, at their absolute discretion, refuse a transfer of shares or only approve the same on specified grounds. If a company's articles stipulate that a refusal to transfer shares may only take place in specified circumstances, then the specified circumstances must have been met, prior to the company's refusal to register a transfer (see, e.g. *Re Bede Steam Shipping Co Ltd* [1917] 1 Ch 123).

In compliance with CA 2006, s.771, where a transfer of shares is lodged with a company, the company must either:

(a) register the transfer; or
(b) give the transferee notice of refusal to register the transfer, together with its reasons for the refusal,

as soon as practicable and in any event within two months after the date on which the transfer is lodged with it.

If the company refuses to register the transfer, it must provide the transferee with such further information about the reasons for the refusal as the transferee may reasonably request although this does not include copies of minutes of meetings of directors.

If a company fails to comply with CA 2006, s.771 then an offence is committed by the company, and by every officer of the company who is in default. Liability, on summary conviction, is a fine.

Although the procedure for transferring shares is normally set out in a company's articles, the regulation of fully paid-up share transfers is also provided for by the Stock Transfer Act 1963. The Act applies to transfers of all types of transferable securities of any company limited by shares. Transfers of partly paid shares are outside the ambit of the 1963 Act. The Stock Transfer Act does not invalidate other forms of transfer but it provides for a simplified method of transfer that if adopted will override the transfer mechanism contained in the articles.

The payment for shares

CA 2006, s.580 provides that a company's shares must not be issued at a discount. Further, except in a situation where a company allots bonus shares to its existing members (discussed below), or where it resolves to extinguish any amount owing on shares which at that time were not fully paid up, the payment for the acquisition of company shares (including any premium) must be by way of a monetary consideration; the shares must be paid for with cash or something to which a monetary value can be attached, to include goodwill and know how (see CA 2006, s.582). While a private company may accept an undertaking for the future performance of services in consideration for the sale of shares, a public company is prohibited from doing so (CA 2006, s.585). Further, a public company may not allot shares for a consideration which includes any other form of undertaking which is to be, or may be performed, more than five years after the allotment of shares (CA 2006, s.587). Although the full purchase price of a share may be paid in instalments (partly paid shares), a public company may not (other than for shares allotted in pursuance of an employees' share scheme) issue a share unless at least 25 per cent of its nominal value and the whole of any premium payable on it, has been made (CA 2006, s.586).

Where the consideration to be provided for the purchase of shares is other than for a cash consideration, then clearly there is a potential possibility for an abuse of the rule that provides shares should not be issued at a discount. In relation to a private company, the court will rarely enquire into the adequacy of the consideration (see, e.g. *Re Wragg* [1871] 1 Ch 796). Nevertheless, the court may intervene where the consideration is clearly inadequate, namely, if it appears that some form of fraud or bad faith was involved in respect of the transaction (see, e.g. *Hong Kong & China Gas Co* v. *Glen* [1914] 1 Ch 527). In the case of a public company, the company must ordinarily obtain a valuation or validation of the value of the consideration to be provided (CA 2006, s.593; see generally, CA 2006, Chapter 6).

7.4 TYPES OF SHARES

A company may create different types of shares, i.e. the legal rights of a particular type of share (class rights) may vary from the other types of shares issued by the company. The legal rights of any given type of share are determined by either the terms of the company's constitution, or by the terms of the particular share issue. The legal rights attached to a share comprise:

- rights as to dividend payments;
- voting rights; and
- rights to the return of capital on an authorised reduction of capital or on the winding up of a company.

Ordinary (equity) shares

An ordinary share is issued with class rights, the nature of which may be described as of a normative nature. A share which is issued with class rights which are specific and distinctive from the norm, insofar as they confer some additional or distinctive class right in relation to dividend payments will be identified as preference shares. Where a company issues shares that have specific class rights (preference shares, discussed below), any remaining shares to which the specific rights do not attach will be construed as ordinary shares. The greatest part of a company's share capital will usually consist of ordinary shares. Where a company declares a dividend payment, the dividend payable on ordinary shares will usually be determined in accordance with the relative economic performance of the company. Dividends payable on ordinary shares will be paid after the payment of dividends to preference shareholders. An ordinary shareholder is entitled to vote at general meetings of the company's shareholding body. However, if it is authorised by its constitution, a company may issue ordinary shares as non-voting shares, shares with limited voting rights or shares with enhanced voting rights.

Preference shares

A preference share is a share having specific preferential rights. Although a preference share is without any statutory definition, its most common distinctive attribute is the preferential payment of dividends in priority to ordinary shares. The dividend payment will be set at a fixed percentage rate, although a preference share may also be of a participating nature, namely the rate of return may be fixed with an additional payment to represent a share in the company's profits. In the case of a participating preference share, the right of participation is limited to an entitlement to share in any surplus profits (i.e. to be paid after a dividend has been paid to the company's ordinary shareholders).

A preference shareholder's entitlement to a fixed payment will be dependent, in any given year, on the company's ability to declare a dividend. The entitlement to a fixed payment may be either cumulative or non-cumulative. Where the payment is of a cumulative nature and the company is unable to pay a fixed payment in any one year, it must make up the difference at some future date, namely, when it is able to declare a dividend. Unless the terms of a preference share issue states otherwise, there is a presumption that a preference share is cumulative although not of a participating nature (see, e.g. *Webb* v. *Earle* (1875) LR 20 Eq 556).

Preference shares may also carry a preference over ordinary shares in respect of the repayment of capital, and following the winding up of the company, the participation in surplus assets. The extent of the legal rights attached to a preference share will be determined by construing that part of a company's constitution (or terms of the specific share issue) that govern the particular share issue. The terms of the relevant regulations (or terms of the share issue) exclusively define the rights attached to a class of shares (see, e.g. *Scottish Insurance Corporation Ltd* v. *Wilsons & Clyde* [1949] AC 462). Ordinarily, the voting rights attached to preference shares will be defined so that preference shareholders only have an entitlement to vote in circumstances where their dividend payments are in arrears, or in a situation where a proposed variation of the rights attached to the preference share is advanced (see, e.g. *Willow International Investments Ltd* v. *Smiths of Smithfield Ltd* [2003] BCC 769). Where the voting rights of preference shareholders are not so defined, the principle in *Birch* v. *Cropper* (1889) 14 App Cas 525 applies, namely, preference shareholders will be accorded the same voting rights as the holders of ordinary shares. In the absence of specific regulations to determine the rights attached to a particular type of share, the rights of the holders of all classes of shares (ordinary and preference shareholders) will be deemed the same (see, e.g. *Birch* v. *Cropper* above). However, it is to be noted that where a preference shareholder is afforded a preference in the return of capital on the winding up of the company, the said preference will also be applicable in a situation where the company wishes to reduce its capital by returning capital to its shareholders. This implied preferential right exists irrespective of the fact that the right was not specifically attached to the preference share, (see, e.g. the decision of the House of Lords in *House of Fraser plc* v. *ACGE Investments Ltd* [1987] AC 387).

Employee shares

Many companies (usually, but not exclusively public companies) operate schemes whereby company employees are encouraged to take up shares or debentures. In accordance with CA 2006, s.1166, an employees' share scheme is for the benefit of:

(a) the bona fide employees or former employees of

    (i) the company,

    (ii) any subsidiary of the company, or

    (iii) the company's holding company or any subsidiary of the company's holding company, or

(b) the spouses, civil partners, surviving spouses, surviving civil partners, or minor children or step-children of such employees or former employees.

Where shares are offered to the employees of a company, the general pre-emption rules (discussed below) are not applicable (i.e. a company is not required to first offer the shares designated for the employees to existing members of the company (CA 2006, s.556)). However, where a general allotment of shares is proposed, the pre-emption rules operate in favour of the employees' share scheme so that a portion of the general issue of shares must first be offered to holders of existing employee shares.

Treasury shares

In accordance with the Companies (Acquisition of Own Shares) (Treasury Shares) Regulations 2003, SI 2003/1116 and No.2, SI 2003/3031, public companies have the option to purchase their own shares (providing the shares satisfy the qualifying conditions) without the need to cancel them; the company may then subsequently re-issue the shares at a later date. This allows greater flexibility in relation to the issue of shares and is a less arduous procedure than seeking a new issue of shares. Shares held in this manner are known as treasury shares. For shares to 'qualify' under the regulations, the shares must be listed or traded on the Alternative Investment Market and the purchase of the shares must be made out of distributable profits and not capital. Treasury shares must be recorded in the company's register of members although obviously the shares, whilst held by the company, do not retain their voting rights. Bonus shares may be allotted to treasury shares (in the same way as other types of qualifying share) and if so, such bonus shares will also be held as treasury shares. Where treasury shares cease to be qualifying shares, the shares must be cancelled.

7.5   CLASS RIGHTS

Usually, the class rights attached to a particular type of share are determined by examining the contents of a company's constitution, the terms of a particular share issue or, the terms of a special resolution related to a particular class of shares (see, e.g. *Re Old Silkstone Collieries Ltd* [1954] Ch 169). Further, class rights may be created by the terms of a shareholders' agreement (see, e.g. the decision of the Court of Appeal in *Harman* v. *BML Group Ltd* [1994] 2 BCLC 674, where the terms of a shareholder agreement were upheld in respect of affording the holder of a class of shares an absolute right to be present at all shareholder meetings). In addition, class rights may also be created where, by the terms of a company's constitution, rights have been conferred on a particular member of the company notwithstanding that the rights are not specifically attached to the shares held by the said member (see, e.g. *Cumbrian Newspapers Group Ltd* v. *Cumberland & Westmorland Herald Newspaper & Printing Co Ltd* [1987] Ch 1, where as a condition of the acquisition of shares in Cumberland the company's articles were altered to provide the purchaser with specific rights designed to prevent an outside party from acquiring control of the company).

The variation of class rights

The companies legislation provides little guidance as to the factors which may establish a variation of class rights. However, CA 2006, s.630(5) provides that an alteration of a provision contained in a company's articles to vary the rights of a class of shareholders or the insertion of such a provision into the articles, is to be construed as a variation of class rights. Further, the abrogation of the class rights of a class of shareholders is deemed to be a variation of those rights (CA 2006, s.630(6)). However, the cancellation of an entire class of shares may not always be construed as a variation of the rights of the shareholders of that class. For example, if a company chooses to reduce its capital it may cancel all of its preference shares in circumstances where the preference shares were afforded a preferential return of capital. Here, the reduction of the company's capital and the subsequent return of capital to the preference shareholders will be in accordance with the class rights of the preference shareholders (see, e.g. *Re Saltdean Estate Co Ltd* [1968] 1 WLR 1844). However, in determining whether preference shareholders have a preferential right to a return of capital in circumstances resulting in a cancellation of the shares, it is essential to construe the company's constitution or the terms of the share issue. For example, where a company's articles expressly provide that the rights of any class of shares will be varied by a reduction of the capital paid up on the shares, then in such a case, the company will not be permitted to cancel its preference shares without the permission of the preference holders notwithstanding that preference shares are afforded an implied priority to the return of capital on a reduction of capital (see, e.g. the decision of the Court of Appeal in *Re Northern Engineering Industries plc* [1994] 2 BCLC 704).

As a general rule, in determining whether a variation of class rights has taken place the court draws a distinction between the rights of a class of shareholder and the enjoyment of those rights. Therefore, to establish a variation of class rights, the rights of a class of shareholder must be specifically altered. Accordingly, if the rights of a particular class of shareholders are impliedly affected by the company's actions but the said rights are not expressly altered there can be no variation in class rights but merely a change in the enjoyment and quality of those rights. For example, if a company has two classes of ordinary shares, class A, £1 shares with five votes per share and class B, 50p shares with five votes per share and chooses to convert its class A, £1 ordinary shares into two 50p class C ordinary shares, each 50p share having five votes, here the class rights of holders of class B shares will not have been varied albeit the class rights of class A shares will have been varied (although to the advantage of shareholders of former class A shares). The class rights of B shares will not be varied in the sense that the actual physical rights of class B shareholders remain the same, prior to the restructuring of the class A shares. However, in a practical sense the enjoyment of voting rights (power) attached to the class B shares is diluted (see, e.g. *Greenhalgh* v. *Arderne Cinemas Ltd* [1946] 1 All ER 512).

It should be noted that in accordance with CA 2006, s.618, that unless a company's articles otherwise preclude, a company may pass an ordinary resolution to sub-divide its shares, or any of them, into shares of a smaller nominal amount than its existing shares, or consolidate and divide all or any of its share capital into shares of a larger nominal amount. Where a company exercises such an authority there will prima facie be no variation of class rights. However, a variation of class rights would occur where, for example:

- there was a proposal whereby one type of share was to be converted into another type of share, for example, where a company sought to convert ordinary shares into preference shares and vice versa;
- where a company sought to alter the voting rights or dividend rights attached to a particular class of share;
- where a company sought to alter the pre-emption rights (discussed below) of a class of shareholder (see, e.g. *Willow International Investments Ltd* v. *Smiths of Smithfield Ltd* [2003] BCC 769).

If a company decides to vary the rights attached to a particular class of its issued shares it must follow the procedure contained in CA 2006, s.630. Section 630 simplifies the previous procedure, regulated by CA 1985, s.125.

CA 2006, s.630

Where a company proposes to vary the rights of a given class of share, it must, prior to implementing the variation, comply with any internal constitutional procedures attached to the variation of the class of share in question. Further, the company must abide by the procedures stipulated by CA 2006, s.630. Following the implementation of the CA 2006, the procedure for a variation of class rights is instantly more straightforward given that the memorandum of a company is no longer deemed a relevant constitutional document, i.e. it is no longer necessary, as under the CA 1985, to distinguish, in terms of the variation procedure, between whether the class rights and variation procedure were contained in the articles or memorandum. Indeed, in all cases of a proposed variation and in accordance with CA 2006, s.630, the procedure for a variation of class rights will be determined by either:

- the consent in writing, from the holders of at least three-quarters in nominal value of the issued shares of the class (excluding treasury shares); or
- a special resolution passed at a separate general meeting of the holders of the class seeking to sanction the variation. (Here, the majority vote requirement may be greater (but not less) than the 75 per cent requirement, i.e. if the company's constitution so provides.)

Finally, it should be noted that nothing in s.630 affects the power of the court under:

- section 98 (application to cancel resolution for public company to be re-registered as private);
- Part 26 (arrangements and reconstructions); or
- Part 30 (protection of members against unfair prejudice).

The minority's right to object to a variation of class rights

Where a decision is taken to sanction a proposed variation of class rights under CA 2006, s.630 and a minority of the class object to the terms of the variation, the minority may, if they hold at least 15 per cent of the shares of the class to be varied and providing they did not consent to or vote in favour of the variation, apply to the court to have the variation cancelled (CA 2006, s.633). An application to the court under s.633 has the effect of suspending the variation of class rights until the court decides whether or not to confirm the variation. The minority must apply to court within 21 days of the decision affirming the terms of the variation. In deciding whether to affirm the variation, the court must consider whether the effect of the variation would be unfairly prejudicial to the class as a whole.

7.6   TYPES OF SHARE ISSUES

Rights issue (pre-emption rights)

In accordance with CA 2006, s.561, where a company offers an issue of equity securities (ordinary shares) for cash, it must, in the first instance, make the offer to its existing ordinary shareholders. A 'rights issue' must be made in direct proportion to the number of shares held by each ordinary shareholder. A contravention of s.561 (subject to the exceptions, see below) will render every officer of the company who knowingly authorised or permitted the contravention to take place, jointly and severally liable to compensate any member of the company to whom an offer of shares should have been made.

The exceptions

- Pre-emption rights may be excluded by a specific provision contained in the articles of a private company. The exclusion may be a general one in relation to the allotment by the company of equity securities, or may be in relation to allotments of a particular description.
- An existing shareholder's right of pre-emption does not apply in relation to the allotment of bonus shares.
- An existing shareholder's right of pre-emption does not apply to a particular allotment of equity securities if these are, or are to be, wholly or partly paid up otherwise than in cash.
- An existing shareholder's right of pre-emption does not apply to the allotment of securities that would, apart from any renunciation or assignment of the right to their allotment, be held under an employees' share scheme.

Disapplication of pre-emption rights

- A private company with only one class of shares may disapply pre-emption rights in relation to the allotment of shares or apply pre-emption rights to the allotment with such modifications as the directors may determine, providing the power to disapply is contained in the company's articles or the power is authorised by a special resolution (CA 2006, s.569).
- If the directors of a company are generally authorised for the purposes of s.551 (power of directors to allot shares etc: authorisation by company), they may be given power by the articles, or by a special resolution, to allot equity securities as if a right of pre-emption did not apply to the allotment, or the right of pre-emption applied to the allotment with such modifications as the directors may determine (CA 2006, s.570).
- Where the directors of a company are authorised for the purposes of s.551 (power of directors to allot shares etc: authorisation by company), whether generally or otherwise, the company may by special resolution (providing the special resolution was recommended by the directors) resolve that s.561 (existing shareholders' right of pre-emption) does not apply to a specified allotment of equity securities to be made pursuant to that authorisation, or applies to such an allotment with such modifications as may be specified in the resolution (CA 2006, s.571).

In setting out the recommendation to disapply the pre-emption rules in accordance with s.571, a person who knowingly or recklessly authorises or permits the inclusion of any misleading, false or deceptive material in the said recommendation may be liable to imprisonment or a fine or both.

A bonus issue

Shares may be issued as bonus shares to the existing ordinary shareholders of a company where a company uses reserve funds to pay up unissued shares. The articles of a company will usually require an ordinary resolution to be passed to sanction the bonus issue. A resolution to issue bonus shares as fully paid up to all shareholders will be rendered void for mistake where the shares held by a part of the membership are not fully paid up (see, e.g. the decision of the Court of Appeal in *EIC Services* v. *Phipps* [2004] 2 BCLC 589).

Redeemable shares

A share issued under the condition that it may be redeemed by the issuing company at some specified date in the future (the redemption date) at the option of the company or the shareholder is referred to as a redeemable share (CA 2006, s.684). Redeemable shares are often issued to facilitate a company's desire to raise short-term capital. Unlike a private company, the ability of a public company to issue redeemable shares is dependent on authorisation contained within its articles (CA 2006, s.684(3)).

A company may issue redeemable shares providing that the issue does not represent the totality of the company's share capital (CA 2006, s.684(4)). Repayment of the redeemable shares can only be made where the shares are fully paid up and repayment cannot be deferred beyond the redemption date (fixed by the articles or the directors). However, providing the shares are fully paid up, the shares may be redeemed at the option of the company or shareholder at a date prior to the specified redemption date. A company must redeem the shares out of its distributable profits or out of the proceeds of a new share issue (CA 2006, s.687). However, a private company may redeem shares out of its own capital. Any premium payable on the redemption of shares must be paid out of distributable profits of the company. However, if the redeemable shares were issued at a premium, any premium payable on their redemption may be paid out of the proceeds of a fresh issue of shares made for the purposes of the redemption, up to an amount equal to:

(a) the aggregate of the premiums received by the company on the issue of the shares redeemed; or

(b) the current amount of the company's share premium account (including any sum transferred to that account in respect of premiums on the new shares), whichever is the least.

CHAPTER 8

Share capital and capital maintenance

8.1 INTRODUCTION

Share capital equates to that part of a company's assets which are made up of the monetary consideration provided by members for the purchase of the company's shares. While a company will have other capital assets – for example, property, realised profits etc. – the law does not classify this 'other capital' as capital in respect of the rules and procedures relating to capital maintenance. Unlike other forms of capital, the sum of share capital must be maintained other than where the law permits a reduction in share capital (see below). Theoretically and in an accounting sense, share capital represents a notional liability to the company's shareholders, although in practice it is more readily viewed as a protective buffer offering creditors a financial safeguard should the company's fortunes fail, i.e. creditors will have a claim against this fund in priority to the claims of shareholders.

Share capital is also regarded as a measure against which asset values should theoretically correspond, i.e. if a company is valued at £100,000 one might expect the sum of the shares issued in the company to represent the worth (£100,000) of the company. If the sum representing a company's share capital is in excess of the company's net assets, this fact may give rise to a presumption of insolvency. However, in practice, the theoretical worth of share capital as a yardstick measure of a company's financial worth is often a myth as the value of assets are prone to fluctuation. The yardstick measure of capital is typically false in respect of private companies where the law does not prescribe any minimum capital requirement, i.e. a company valued at £100,000 may have only issued five £1 shares. However, in the case of a public company, the Companies Act (CA) 2006, s.656 deems that it is an offence punishable by fine where the company's net assets fall to an amount that is equal to or below half of its called-up share capital and the company fails, within 28 days of that fact becoming known to one of the company's directors, to convene a general meeting for not later than 56 days thereafter, to consider whether any, and if so what, steps should be taken to deal with the situation.

Called-up share capital is the total amount of consideration received from shareholders for issued shares, whereas uncalled share capital is the difference between the total nominal value of a company's issued share capital and the value of the company's called-up share capital. Therefore, shares may be issued as partly paid shares, although in the case of a public company, partly paid shares must be paid up to a minimum of 25 per cent of their nominal value.

A company's share capital is made up of sums received from the issue of shares, together with any sums held in the company's share premium account or other statutory capital reserves. The most common types of capital reserve accounts are as follows:

- the share premium account which equates to the difference in value between a share's nominal value and any premium paid on the share (CA 2006, s.610);
- the capital redemption reserve: If a company is permitted to redeem or purchase its own shares out of distributable profits it must maintain its capital balance by placing an amount equal to the reduction in share capital into its capital redemption reserve (CA 2006, s.733);
- the re-valuation reserve equates to an amount equal to an increase in the value of corporate assets. This amount should be transferred to the company's revaluation reserve to maintain the notional balance between capital and corporate assets.

Sums in a capital reserve fund cannot be used to pay dividends, although they may be used in financing an issue of bonus shares. A company's capital reserves are to be contrasted with its revenue reserves – the latter represent the sum of a company's retained profits. Retained profits, unlike reserve capital, may be used to pay dividends.

While a company is a going concern, the company's paid-up share capital cannot be returned to shareholders in the form of dividend payments, although in specific circumstances the sum of a company's share capital may be reduced (discussed below). Prior to the CA 2006, the total nominal value of the shares which could be issued by a company was fixed (but subject to alteration by Companies Act (CA) 1985, s.121) by its authorised share capital clause (contained in the memorandum). Following the implementation of CA 2006, this once obligatory clause, is now rendered redundant, save that a public company is still obliged to maintain a minimum authorised share capital to the value of £50,000. The removal of the authorised share capital clause deletes the need for the previous procedure concerning a company's ability to increase its authorised share capital (previously governed by CA 1985, s.121).

8.2 REDUCING SHARE CAPITAL

It may be expedient for a company to reduce its issued share capital (by returning capital to a part of the shareholding body). For example, following a hefty fall in the value of a company's assets, it may be necessary to reduce the company's share capital to retain a capacity to make future dividend payments. However, insofar as a reduction of share capital may be prejudicial to the interests of a part of the company's shareholders or cause anxiety amongst the company's creditors, the CA 2006 provides statutory confirmation of a long established principle of company law (see *Trevor* v. *Whitworth* (1887) 12 App Cas 409), namely that a company may not, as of right, reduce its share capital. However, a company may reduce its share capital in accordance with the procedures contained in CA 2006, s.641 or alternatively under the court procedure governed by CA 2006, s.645. A reserve arising from the reduction of a company's share capital is not distributable, although this rule may be subject to exceptions provided by secondary legislation (CA 2006, s.654).

Section 641 procedure (private companies)

CA 2006, s.641(1) provides that a private company may (notwithstanding that the right to reduce capital is not contained in its articles) reduce its share capital where:

(a) the company passes a special resolution to sanction the reduction; and
(b) the directors of the company, in complying with CA 2006, s.642, issue a solvency statement not more than 15 days before the date on which the special resolution is passed.

If the resolution is proposed as a written resolution, a copy of the solvency statement should be sent or submitted to the members before or at the time the resolution is forwarded to the registrar. Where the resolution is proposed at a general meeting, a copy of the solvency statement should be made available for inspection by members of the company throughout that meeting. However, non-compliance with the members' right to view the solvency statement will not render the resolution void. Nevertheless, a failure to provide a solvency statement to the members (a statement which must subsequently be sent to the registrar) is an offence committed by every officer of the company who is in default.

It should be noted that a company may not reduce its capital under s.641 if, as a result of the reduction, the only shares held by its members are redeemable shares (CA 2006, s.641(2)).

Solvency statement

The solvency statement required by the CA 2006 must, as of the date of the statement, state that the company was solvent, specifying that there was no ground on which the company could, at that time, be found to be unable to pay (discharge) its debts. The solvency statement must provide that if the company was to be wound up within a year from the date of the statement, it would be able to pay its debts in full within 12 months commencing from the date of the winding up, or alternatively that the company would be able to pay (or otherwise discharge) its debts as they fell due within 12 months commencing from the date of the winding up. The directors of the company (all named in the statement) must be of the opinion that the solvency statement is accurate, and any director who is a party to a solvency statement without having reasonable grounds for the opinions and statements expressed therein, is liable to imprisonment for a maximum term of two years or a fine, or both. A copy of the solvency statement together with a statement of capital must be delivered to the registrar within 15 days of the passing of the resolution (CA 2006, s.643).

In accordance with CA 2006, s.644(2), the statement of capital must, in relation to the company's share capital, as altered by the order, state:

(a) the total number of shares of the company,
(b) the aggregate nominal value of those shares,
(c) for each class of shares –

  (i) prescribed particulars of the rights attached to the shares,
  (ii) the total number of shares of that class, and
  (iii) the aggregate nominal value of shares of that class, and

(d) the amount paid up and the amount (if any) unpaid on each share (whether on account of the nominal value of the share or by way of premium).

The court procedure

Alternatively, a private company may follow what is, in effect, a more time-consuming but possibly more secure procedure to reduce its share capital. This alternative procedure is the governing procedure for the reduction of capital in a public company. Prior to the passing of the CA 2006, this procedure (see CA 1985, s.143) represented the only permissible way to achieve a reduction of share capital in relation to both a private and public company.

The procedure, now governed by CA 2006, s.645, provides that:

- the company must pass a special resolution to sanction the reduction in share capital; and
- the company must obtain the court's approval for the reduction.

Creditors' right to object

If the proposed reduction of capital involves either a diminution of liability in respect of unpaid share capital, or the payment to a shareholder of any paid-up share capital, then creditors of the company may object to the court under CA 2006, s.646, unless the court directs otherwise. It is for the court to determine a list of creditors who are entitled to object. However, if an officer of the company intentionally or recklessly conceals the name of a creditor entitled to object to the reduction of capital, or misrepresents the nature or amount of the debt or claim of a creditor, or is knowingly concerned in any such concealment or misrepresentation, he or she commits an offence and is liable on conviction on indictment, to a fine or on summary conviction, to a fine not exceeding the statutory maximum.

Where a creditor entered on the list does not consent to the reduction, the court may, if it thinks fit, dispense with the consent of that creditor providing the company secures the payment of the debt in question. In accordance with CA 2006, s.648, the court may make an order confirming the reduction of capital on such terms and conditions as it thinks fit. However, the court must not confirm the reduction unless it is satisfied, with respect to every creditor of the company who is entitled to object to the reduction of capital, that the consent of the creditor has been obtained or the creditor's debt has been discharged, determined or secured. Where the court confirms the reduction, it may order the company to publish (as the court directs) the reasons for the reduction of capital, or such other information that the court thinks expedient with a view to giving proper information to the public, and (if the court thinks fit) the causes that led to the reduction. Further, the court may make an order directing that the company must, on or at any time after the date of the order, add to its name as its last words the words 'and reduced'. If such an order is made, the words 'are reduced' will be deemed part of the company's name until the end of the period specified in the order.

CA 2006, s.649 provides that the order and statement of capital must be registered following the delivery to the registrar of a copy of the order of the court confirming the reduction of a company's share capital and the delivery of a statement of capital (approved by the court). The statement of capital is in the form prescribed by CA 2006, s.649(2). This prescribed form is identical to that provided by CA 2006, s.644(2) (see above).

If a company reduces its capital (as confirmed by the court) and a creditor who was legitimately entitled to object to the reduction, did not object because of his or her ignorance of the proceedings, or the effect of the proceedings, or because he or she was not entered on the list of creditors, then, in such circumstances, if the company is unable to repay that creditor's debt after the reduction, all the members of the company as at the date on which the resolution for reducing capital took effect are deemed liable to contribute for the payment of the debt or claim. The liability is to the extent of an amount not exceeding that which the members would have been liable to contribute had the company commenced to be wound up on the day before that date (CA 2006, s.653).

The justification for maintaining a private company's ability to obtain court approval in respect of a reduction in share capital is that the court approval system affords a degree of certainty, the reduction is 'rubber stamped' by the court and it is unlikely to be challenged. The court approval method also affords the directors of the company some security in the sense that they will not be required to personally issue a solvency statement and accordingly will not be held potentially liable should the company be wound up within the 12-month period so specified under CA 2006, s.642.

In deciding whether to sanction a company's reduction of share capital, the court's principal concern will be to consider the effect of the reduction on the company's ability to repay its debts (see *Poole* v. *National Bank of China* [1907] AC 229). The court must be satisfied that the effect of the reduction in capital will not leave the company's creditors in a perilous position. In addition to considering the effect of a reduction of capital on the company's creditors, the court may also consider the effect of the reduction upon the various classes of company shareholder (see, e.g. *Re Ratners Group plc* [1988] 4 BCC 293). The consent of a class of shareholders must be obtained where a proposed reduction of capital would result in a variation of class rights.

8.3 THE PURCHASE OF A COMPANY'S OWN SHARES

CA 2006, ss.690–1 (previously CA 1985, s.162) provide that a limited company (with a share capital) may, subject to any restriction in its constitution, purchase its own shares (providing they are fully paid up), irrespective of the fact that the shares were not issued as redeemable shares. Where a limited company purchases its own shares, the shares must be paid for on purchase. A purchase/redemption of shares will not constitute a reduction of capital in the context of capital maintenance rules providing the capital reserves of the company are maintained at the level pre the company's purchase of its shares. However, a limited company may not purchase its own shares if, as a result of the purchase, there would no longer be any issued shares of the company other than redeemable shares or shares held as treasury shares.

In accordance with a company's ability to purchase its own shares (see CA 2006, s.692), a private limited company may purchase its own shares out of capital (discussed below) or, as in the case of a public limited company, out of its profits or from the proceeds of a new issue of shares; the new issue having been specifically created for the purpose of purchasing the company's existing shares. Where shares are purchased (or redeemed) wholly or partly out of profits, then a transfer of funds, equal to the par value of the shares must be made to the capital redemption reserve. Any premium payable on the shares must normally be paid out of profits. However, if a company's shares were initially issued at a premium, any premium attached to the shares as of the date on which the company purchases the shares may be paid out of the proceeds of an issue of new shares up to an amount not exceeding the lesser of:

- the total amount of premium obtained from the shares when they were first issued; and
- the amount standing to the credit of the share premium account at the time of issue. This amount includes any premium obtained on the new issue.

The amount of the company's share premium account must be reduced by a sum corresponding (or by sums in the aggregate corresponding) to the amount of any payment.

Purchase procedures

A company may purchase its own shares by means of either an off-market purchase (CA 2006, s.694) or a market purchase (CA 2006, s.701). An off-market purchase ordinarily describes a purchase of shares otherwise than on a recognised UK investment exchange but the purchase may still be described as off-market if shares purchased on a recognised investment exchange are not subject to a marketing arrangement on the exchange (CA 2006, s.693(2)). A market purchase (other than one that is not subject to a marketing arrangement) is one made on a recognised investment exchange (CA 2006, s.693(4)). An off-market transaction can only be executed by means of private contract between a company and one of its existing shareholders and must be approved by a special resolution (CA 2006, s.694(2)). It is to be noted that a copy of the proposed purchase contract (or memorandum detailing the terms of the contract) should be made available for inspection by the company's membership at least 15 days prior to the meeting at which the proposed resolution is to be considered (or in the case of a written resolution, by being sent or submitted to every eligible member at or before the time at which the proposed resolution is sent or submitted) (CA 2006, s.696(2)). The member of the company with whom the contract for sale is made is not permitted to vote on the resolution where the effect of that vote permits the resolution to be passed (CA 2006, s.695). If passed, the resolution will be invalid if the above requirements of the CA 2006 are not met. Where the company is a public company, the authority contained in the resolution will last no longer than a period of 18 months (CA 2006, s.694(5)).

A contract of purchase may be contingent giving either the company or member, or both, an option to purchase (CA 2006, s.694(3)). A payment made by a company in consideration of acquiring any right with respect to the purchase of its own shares in pursuance of any contingent purchase contract must be made from its distributable profits (see CA 2006, s.705).

In making either an off-market purchase or market purchase of shares, the company must deliver a return to the registrar which must notify the details of the transaction to the registrar and be delivered no later than 28 days from the date of purchase (CA 2006, s.707). Where a company purchases its own shares, the shares will be treated as cancelled and the amount of the company's share capital will be diminished by the extent of the nominal value of the shares cancelled. Accordingly, the shares cannot be kept in reserve and resold at a later date (other than if the shares are held as treasury shares) (CA 2006, s.706). A copy of the purchase contract must be kept at the company's registered office (CA 2006, s.702(2)). In the case of a public company, the return to the registrar must specify the aggregate amount paid for the shares, together with details of the maximum and minimum prices paid for each class of share purchased (CA 2006, s.707(4)).

Public company

A market purchase of a company's shares is relevant to a public company's purchase of its own shares. The purchase will be made on a recognised UK investment exchange. A public company may authorise a market purchase by means of an ordinary resolution (CA 2006, s.701). In addition, the resolution granting the authority to purchase must specify a maximum number of shares to be acquired and the maximum and minimum price to be paid for the shares. The resolution must also specify a date when the authority will expire; the maximum duration for the authority is 18 months after the date on which the resolution was passed.

8.4 PAYMENT OUT OF CAPITAL (PRIVATE COMPANIES ONLY)

A private company may redeem or purchase its own shares out of capital providing it is authorised to do so by its constitution (CA 2006, s.709). However, a private company may only expend capital (the permissible capital payment) to purchase its own shares if, together, any available profits and the proceeds of any new issue of shares made for the purposes of the redemption or purchase are of an insufficient value to facilitate the redemption or purchase. The availability of distributable profits is determined in accordance with the steps provided under CA 2006, s.712. Here, the company must examine its relevant accounts for the relevant period. Relevant accounts are any accounts that are prepared as at a date within the relevant period, and are such as to enable a reasonable judgment to be made of the calculated amounts. The relevant period means the period of three months ending with the date on which the directors' statement is made. In seeking to determine the availability of distributable profits the first step is to calculate gross profits by reference to the following items as stated in the relevant accounts:

(a) profits, losses, assets and liabilities;
(b) provisions of the following kinds:

    (i) where the relevant accounts are Companies Act accounts, provisions of a kind specified by regulations under CA 2006, s.396, i.e. in relation to the balance sheet as at the last day of the financial year and the profit and loss account;

    (ii) where the relevant accounts are international accounting standards (IAS) accounts, provisions of any kind;

(c) share capital and reserves (including undistributable reserves).

The second step is to reduce the calculated amount by reference to:

(a) any distribution lawfully made by the company; and

(b) any other relevant payment lawfully made by the company out of distributable profits, after the date of the relevant accounts and before the end of the relevant period. For this purpose 'other relevant payment lawfully made' includes:

- financial assistance lawfully given out of distributable profits;
- payments lawfully made out of distributable profits in respect of the purchase by the company of any shares in the company; and
- payments of any description specified in CA 2006, s.705 (payments other than purchase price to be made out of distributable profits) lawfully made by the company.

The resulting figure is the amount of the available distributable profits.

However, a company's purchase or redemption of shares from capital will be unlawful unless the company complies with the following procedures.

Directors' statement and auditor's report

A private company that intends to expend capital for the purpose of purchasing its own shares will, in accordance with CA 2006, s.714, require a statement from the company's directors specifying the amount of the permissible capital payment for the shares in question. The statement must state that immediately following the date on which the payment out of capital is proposed to be made and for the year immediately following that date the directors hold the opinion that there will be no grounds on which the company will be unable to pay its debts. The directors' statement must be in the prescribed form. The statement must also include an annexed report from the company's auditor confirming the company's financial viability and the amount specified in the statement as the permissible capital payment for the shares in question. It is an offence for the directors to make a statement under s.714 without having reasonable grounds for the opinion expressed therein. A person found to be guilty of the offence is liable on conviction on indictment to imprisonment for a term not exceeding two years or a fine (or both) and on summary conviction to imprisonment for a term not exceeding 12 months or a fine not exceeding the statutory maximum (or both).

Further, in accordance with Insolvency Act 1986, s.76, where a company redeems or purchases its shares out of capital, but within a year immediately following the capital expenditure, falls into liquidation and cannot pay its debts, the directors who made the declaration of solvency, together with the person from whom the shares were redeemed or purchased, will be liable, at the discretion of the court, to contribute to the assets of the company. A director may escape liability if he or she had reasonable grounds to believe in the accuracy of the statement.

Payment approved by special resolution

A private company that intends to expend capital to purchase its own shares will require the general meeting to authorise the reduction by means of a special resolution (CA 2006, s.716). The resolution must be passed on, or within the week immediately following the date on which the directors make the statement required by s.714. In order to consider the resolution, a copy of the directors' statement and auditor's report must be made available to members (CA 2006, s.718(2)). Where the resolution is proposed as a written resolution, a member who holds shares to which the resolution relates is not an eligible member and where the resolution is passed at a meeting of the company, it will not be effective if any member holding shares to which the resolution relates, votes on the resolution, if, without the said votes, the resolution would not have been passed (CA 2006, s.717).

In accordance with CA 2006, s.719, a private limited company that makes payment out of capital for the redemption or purchase of its own shares must, within the week immediately following the date of the resolution under s.716:

- publish details of the reduction of capital to include a statement providing that any creditor of the company may apply to the court within five weeks of the resolution for an order preventing the payment out of capital;
- publish said notice in the *Gazette*. It must also be published in an appropriate national newspaper or alternatively, notification of the same must be given in writing to each of the company's creditors;
- deliver to the registrar a copy of the directors' statement and auditor's report.

Objection to a reduction in capital

Any member of the company who did not vote in favour of the resolution, or any creditor of the company, may, within five weeks from the date of the special resolution sanctioning the reduction in capital, apply to the court for an order to prohibit the payment (CA 2006, s.721). The applicant must give immediate notification to the registrar and the company (upon receipt of the notice of the application). On hearing the application the court may either adjourn the proceedings to enable the company to enter into an arrangement to compensate the dissentient member(s) or the claims of the dissentient creditors, and/or make an order either confirming or cancelling the resolution for the purchase or redemption of the company's own shares on such terms and conditions as it thinks fit. Where the court confirms the resolution it may also order the company to purchase the shares of any member and for the reduction accordingly of the company's capital. The court may also make any alteration in the company's articles that may be required. Within 15 days of the making of the court's order (or a longer period if the court so directs) the company must deliver a copy of the order to the registrar.

8.5   FINANCIAL ASSISTANCE FOR THE PURCHASE OF A COMPANY'S SHARES

The definition of financial assistance provided for by CA 2006, s.677 is far ranging and covers any type of financial assistance that is given by a company for the purpose of assisting the acquisition of its shares, the effect of which is to reduce the company's net assets by a material extent. Financial assistance may be by way of gift, guarantee, security or indemnity, release or waiver, loan or any other agreement (see, e.g. *Belmont Finance Corporation* v. *Williams Furniture Ltd* (*No.2*) [1980] 1 All ER 393, *Charterhouse Investment Trust Ltd* v. *Tempest Diesels Ltd* [1985] 1 BCC 99, 544, *Barclays Bank plc* v. *British & Commonwealth Holdings plc* [1996] 1 BCLC 1 and *MacPherson & Anor* v. *European Strategic Bureau Ltd* [2002] BCC 39). Financial assistance also covers a situation where the assistance seeks to reduce or discharge liabilities incurred as a result of the acquisition of the company's shares.

Private companies

Prior to the passing of the CA 2006, CA 1985, s.151 generally prohibited (but with exemptions for private companies, see CA 1985, ss.153–8) both private and public companies from giving financial assistance (whether directly or indirectly, see CA 1985, s.152) to aid a person's acquisition of shares in a company or the company's subsidiary. An act contrary to the general prohibition (subject to the exemptions) was also a criminal offence. Following the CA 2006, the general rule prohibiting a company from providing financial assistance for the acquisition of its own shares has been removed in the context of private companies but remains intact for public companies. However, it should be noted that where a person is acquiring, proposing to acquire shares or has acquired shares in a private company, it is not lawful for a public company as a subsidiary of that private company to give financial assistance, directly or indirectly, for the purpose of the acquisition before or at the same time as the acquisition takes place.

Public companies

As a general rule, a public company (or any of its subsidiaries) is precluded from giving financial assistance to a person who is acquiring, proposing to acquire or who has acquired shares in the company or its holding company (CA 2006, s.678). However, financial assistance may be given for the purchase of shares in a public company if the company's principal purpose in giving the assistance was not to specifically acquire its own shares, or the giving of assistance was but an incidental part of some larger purpose, the assistance being given in good faith and in the interests of the company. Further, financial assistance may be given (providing it is given in good faith and in the interests of the company) where the company's principal purpose in giving the assistance is not to reduce or discharge any liability incurred by a person for the purpose of acquiring shares in the company or its holding company, or the reduction or discharge of any such liability was but an incidental part of some larger purpose of the company.

Following the decision of the House of Lords in *Brady* v. *Brady* [1989] AC 755, the term 'larger purpose' will not to be construed liberally and is certainly not to be viewed as a 'blank cheque'. For example, in *Brady* although the objective of providing financial assistance was to facilitate a necessary reorganisation of the companies involved, the actual purpose of providing the financial assistance was to enable the acquisition of the company's shares. In *Brady*, although the financial assistance would have been devoid of any meaningful reason had it not been used to facilitate the reorganisation of the companies, the 'meaningful reason' was ignored in the interpretation of the concept of a 'larger purpose'. Basically, the House of Lords sought to distinguish the 'reason' behind the acquisition (i.e. the reorganisation of the companies) from the 'purpose' of the financial assistance, i.e. the acquisition of the shares. In so doing, the House of Lords emphatically restricted the ability of a company to give financial assistance for the acquisition of its shares. (Also see, *Chaston* v. *SWP Group plc* [2003] BCLC 675, where the Court of Appeal applied the reasoning adopted in *Brady*. However, contrast the more liberal interpretation of the financial assistance rules by the Court of Appeal in *M T Realisations Ltd (in liq.)* v. *Digital Equipment Co Ltd* [2003] 2 BCLC 117 and *Dyment* v. *Boyden* [2005] BCC 79.)

Additional exemptions

The prohibition against a public company providing financial assistance does not apply to transactions governed by CA 2006, s.681. These exemptions include a distribution of the company's assets by way of dividends lawfully made, an allotment of bonus shares, a reduction of capital, and a redemption of shares. Conditional exceptions are also provided by CA 2006, s.682. The exceptions provide that financial assistance is not prohibited where the company in giving the assistance has net assets that are not reduced by the giving of the assistance, or to the extent that those assets are so reduced, the assistance is provided out of distributable profits. In addition, a company may provide financial assistance where the lending of money is part of a company's ordinary business activities.

Criminal offence

If a public company contravenes the financial assistance rules, the company and every officer of the company who is in default commits an offence. A person guilty of an offence is liable on conviction on indictment, to imprisonment for a term not exceeding two years or a fine (or both) and on summary conviction to imprisonment for a term not exceeding 12 months or to a fine not exceeding the statutory maximum (or both).

CHAPTER 9

Loan capital and the registration of charges

9.1 INTRODUCTION

A company's ability to obtain loan funds or other forms of credit is often essential to the survival and future prosperity of the enterprise. Creditors may demand security to counter the potential risk of default and this will often take the form of a charge on the assets of the debtor company. The law was subject to radical reforms in the context of the enforcement and priority rights of security interests following the enactment of the Enterprise Act 2002.

9.2 THE DEBENTURE

A document which purports to acknowledge a credit arrangement between a company and its creditor(s) is commonly referred to as a debenture. The Companies Act 2006 (CA) 2006, s.738 provides that a debenture includes debenture stock, bonds and any other securities of a company, irrespective of whether it constitutes a charge on the assets of the company.

A debenture holder is entitled to obtain payment of the sums due to him, whether principal or interest; the prescribed rate of interest, which is stipulated in the debenture, must be paid to the debenture holder irrespective of whether the debtor company is in profit.

Many of the statutory rules that regulate the issue of shares are equally applicable to an issue of debentures. However, unlike an issue of shares, a company may offer debentures at a discounted price providing the debentures do not confer an immediate right of conversion into shares (see, e.g. *Campbell's case* (1876) 4 Ch D 470). A debenture may be offered on the basis that it may be converted into shares at a future date (CA 2006, s.551). Convertible debentures must first be offered to existing shareholders or debenture holders before being offered to the general public (CA 2006, s.561).

Following an allotment of a debenture(s) the company must, within two months after the date of the allotment, register the same with the registrar of companies (CA 2006, s.741). A failure to do so will result in the company, and every officer of the company in default, being made subject to a fine. Where a company elects to keep a register of debenture holders (there is no statutory requirement to demand that a register must be kept by the company) the register must be kept available for inspection at the company's registered office, or at another place in the part of the UK in which the company is registered (CA 2006, s.743). In accordance with CA 2006, s.744, a register of debenture holders must, except when duly closed, be open to the inspection (without charge) of a registered debenture holder or any shareholder of the company and any other person on payment of such fee as may be prescribed (note that an inspection request may be challenged by an application to the court on the ground that the request was not for a proper purpose). A register is 'duly closed' if it is closed in accordance with a provision contained in the articles or in the debentures. The total period for which a register is closed in any year must not exceed 30 days.

CA 2006, s.739 provides that a debenture(s), or a deed for securing a debenture(s), may be issued whereby the debenture is made irredeemable, or redeemable only on the happening of a contingency (however remote), or on the expiration of a specified period (however long). Where a company redeems debentures previously issued, then unless otherwise provided by its articles, the company may re-issue the debentures, either by re-issuing the same debentures or by issuing new debentures in their place. On a re-issue of redeemed debentures the person entitled to the debentures has (and is deemed always to have had) the same priorities as if the debentures had never been redeemed.

Debenture stock

As with a company share, a debenture is transferable; it may be sold on by its original holder. Nevertheless, a debenture may only be transferred in its original form (i.e. a debenture for £200 cannot be sold off in units of £10). However, an issue of debentures can be made in the form of debenture stock; the company may create a loan fund to the sum of £50,000 out of which a holder of the stock obtains a certificate for, say, £5,000 worth of the loan fund (debenture stock). The holder of the loan stock is then able to transfer units of whatever minimum denomination is attached to the particular debenture stock issue, for example costs of £200. Where debenture stock is issued, holders of the stock will, in terms of priority of repayment of the funds invested in the stock, take equally (i.e. *pari passu*). Where a company issues loan stock, it is usual practice for the company to enter into a trust deed with a trustee company. The purpose of this trust relationship is to confer on the trustee the power to enforce the conditions laid down in the debenture in favour of the holders of the stock, namely, the beneficiaries of the trust agreement.

9.3   SECURITY INTERESTS

The mortgage/legal charge

A mortgage is a conveyance of an interest in property with a provision for redemption. A legal mortgage may be created over personal or real property and when taken over land is ordinarily created by a charge by deed expressed to be by way of legal mortgage; this is often referred to as a legal charge. A mortgage may also be of an equitable character, for example, where a mortgage of land is created in writing other than by deed. The available remedies for enforcing a legal or equitable mortgage include possession, foreclosure and sale.

The fixed/specific charge

A fixed charge (alternatively referred to as a specific charge) is equitable in character but unlike a mortgage, it does not involve a conveyance of any interest in the assets that form the subject matter of the security. The precise rights of the chargee will be contained within the debenture creating the charge. However, subject to the requirements of registration (discussed below), a fixed charge will confer an immediate security over the charged property. Having created a fixed charge over its property, the company cannot sell or deal with the charged asset without first obtaining the permission of the fixed chargeholder. It is inconsistent with the nature of a specific charge for the chargor to be at liberty to deal with the charged property (see, e.g. *Re Yorkshire Woolcombers* [1903] 2 Ch 284).

To create a fixed charge over a corporate asset, the asset in question must be identifiable, although it need not be in existence at the time the charge was created (i.e. a fixed charge may attach to future property). Property which is subject to a fixed charge and which is sold on to a third party without the chargee's consent will remain subject to the charge unless the third party is a *bona fide* purchaser without notice of the existence of the charge. However, providing the charge is registered, the third party will be deemed to have constructive notice of its existence.

The floating charge

While it may be advisable for a person, when loaning funds to a company, to secure the funds by means of a fixed charge or mortgage, priority issues and the nature of the charged property may require a subsequent creditor to secure his or her interest by means of a floating charge. The floating charge is a device which can only be given as security for a debt incurred by a limited company, a device created by the Court of Chancery, see the *Panama* case (1870) 5 Ch App 318. The nature of a floating charge is that the charge (unlike a fixed charge) does not attach itself to a specific corporate asset until an event referred to as 'crystallisation' occurs. The floating charge is created over a class of assets which by their very nature are deemed to be of a constantly changing nature, thus preventing them being readily identified.

Property to which a floating charge is likely to attach will include stock, plant, tools and other transient assets of a company. It is common for a floating charge to be expressed to encompass the whole of the company's undertaking (i.e. the charge will, following its crystallisation, be intended to take priority over all corporate assets other than those subject to a fixed charge or mortgage). In effect, the floating charge is created over assets of a shifting nature; the sale of such assets is one of the means by which the company will earn income from which it can meet its obligations under the terms of the debenture by which the floating charge was created. In *Re Yorkshire Woolcombers Association Ltd* [1903] 2 Ch 284 (sum nom *Illingworth* v. *Houldsworth* (HL)), Romer LJ tentatively identified the floating charge as possessing the following characteristics:

- a charge on all of a class of assets of the company present and future;
- a charge on a class of assets which in the ordinary course of a company's business would be changing from time to time;
- a charge which would allow the company to carry on its business in the ordinary way (i.e. the company would have the ability to trade in the assets which were subject to the floating charge).

Crystallisation of the floating charge

A company may continue to deal with assets which form the subject matter of a floating charge up until the time the charge crystallises (see, e.g. *Re Borax* [1901] Ch 326). The floating charge will crystallise into a fixed charge. Ordinarily, a floating charge will crystallise when a creditor takes action to realise the security following the happening of a specified event (i.e. the event will be specified within the debenture document, for example, non payment of interest). Prior to the implementation of the Enterprise Act (EA) 2002 (in force from 15 September 2003), the actual time of the crystallisation of a floating charge normally occurred:

- at the time of the appointment of an administrative receiver;
- on the happening of a specified event stipulated in the debenture which automatically crystallised the charge. Here, the charge would crystallise into a fixed charge without the need for the chargee to appoint an administrative receiver (see, e.g. *Re Brightlife Ltd* [1986] BCLC 418 and *Griffiths* v. *Yorkshire Bank plc* [1994] 1 WLR 1427).
- where the crystallisation of the charge was triggered by an event implied by law – for example, where the company was subject to the appointment of a liquidator, the appointment of a receiver (by another secured

creditor) or the cessation of the company's business; (see, e.g. *Re Woodroffes (Musical Instruments) Ltd* [1985] BCLC 227 and *Re The Real Meat Co Ltd* [1996] BCC 254).

In addition to the above list, and following the enactment of the EA 2002, the crystallisation of a floating charge may additionally take place as a result of the appointment of an administrator (the administrator replacing the role previously undertaken by an administrative receiver in respect of floating charges created after 15 September 2003). Although a floating charge may still be subject to an automatic crystallisation clause, it is to be noted that in relation to priority interests, the advantage afforded to an automatic crystallisation clause may have been seriously disturbed because the Insolvency Act (IA) 1986, Sched.B1, para.15(2) (as amended by the EA 2002) now provides that a qualifying floating charge takes in priority to another floating charge if it is either *prior in time* or if it is to be treated as having priority in accordance with an inter-creditor agreement. The term 'prior in time' would, for example, appear to suggest that floating charge X (albeit with an attached automatic crystallisation clause), may no longer have priority over floating charge Y, where floating charge Y was created prior in time to floating charge X. If so, the effectiveness of an automatic crystallisation clause will be nullified in relation to priority issues between competing floating charges.

An inter-creditor agreement is one whereby a creditor with a charge over corporate property (the first chargee) transfers his or her priority interest in favour of another creditor, the other creditor having previously held an inferior ranking charge. In practice, a contractual agreement between the first and second chargees to effect such an alteration in the priority position may afford some commercial advantage to the first chargee. The first chargee's priority rights may be transferred without the need to seek the approval of the company having created the charge (see, e.g. *Cheah Theam Swee* v. *Equiticorp Finance Group Ltd* [1992] BCC 98, *Re Portbase (Clothing) Ltd* [1993] BCC 96).

Appointment of receiver/administrator

Where a floating charge was created prior to the implementation of the EA 2002 (i.e. pre-15 September 2003) the chargeholder will be able to appoint an administrative receiver (defined by IA 1986, s.29(2)) to realise the security interest. An administrative receiver acts as an agent to protect the interests of the chargeholder; the position carries extensive powers (see IA 1986, Sched.1). However, following the implementation of the EA 2002, a floating chargeholder, having taken a floating charge security after 15 September 2003, will be obliged to appoint an administrator to realise the security (save in very exceptional and well defined circumstances, relating to larger corporate lending agreements, for example, capital market investments of a minimum of £50 million).

The objective of the new administration system is, where possible, to promote corporate rescue. However, where in the circumstances of a case corporate rescue is not possible, the administrator must seek to benefit the interests of the company's creditors as a whole. A holder of one or more qualifying floating charge(s) may appoint an administrator (IA 1986, Sched.B1, para.14). A qualifying charge is defined as an instrument which expressly stipulates that para.14 is to apply or a charge which, on its own or taken with other securities, extends to the whole or substantially the whole of the company's property. Where there is more than one qualifying floating chargeholder, a qualifying chargeholder may not appoint an administrator if the chargeholder holds a charge created at a date subsequent to a charge held by another qualifying chargeholder, unless the following conditions are satisfied (para.15(1)):

- the chargeholder gives at least two business days' written notice to the holder of any prior floating charge; or
- the holder of any prior floating chargeholder consents in writing to the appointment (para.15(2) provides that a floating charge is defined as being prior to another if it is either prior in time or if it is to be treated as having priority in accordance with an inter-creditor agreement).

Providing a chargeholder has given notice to the holder(s) of any prior floating charge(s), the chargeholder may appoint an administrator by simply filing a notice of appointment at court, i.e. without any requirement of a court application or hearing, or without demonstrating that the company is or is likely to become unable to pay its debts. The appointment of the administrator takes effect from the date of the filing of the notice of appointment. However, in rare cases (especially those relating to cross border cases) an administrator may be appointed by the court. (It is to be noted that where a floating charge was created prior to 15 September 2003, it is unnecessary to seek the court's approval in relation to the appointment of a receiver. In addition, the appointment of an administrative receiver will prevent the subsequent appointment of an administrator, i.e. unless the receiver consents to the subsequent appointment of an administrator.)

An administrator may also be appointed, without the involvement of the court, by the company (by a members' resolution in general meeting or a resolution of the company's directors (IA 1986, Sched.B1, para.22)). However, this type of appointment may be overturned by a debenture holder who, within a five-day period from the company giving notice of its intention to appoint an administrator, may appoint his or her own administrative receiver or administrator.

Following the appointment of an administrator, there is a moratorium on actions against the company, whereby creditors are ordinarily precluded (unless authorised by administrator or by the court) from enforcing their legal rights relating to the enforcement of a security interest or debt against the company. The moratorium also covers hire purchase agreements, conditional sale agreements, chattel leasing agreements and retention of title agreements. The moratorium allows the administrator to consider and plan the best options in respect of corporate rescue and/or the realisation of the company's assets. Once in administration, the moratorium prevents a winding-up order being made against the company.

Avoidance of floating charges

In accordance with IA 1986, s.245 a floating charge may be invalidated if it was created in the period of 12 months prior to the onset of the company's insolvency, where, at the time of its creation, the company was unable to pay its debts or, as a result of the transaction creating the charge, the chargor company became unable to pay its debts. An exception to this rule is where the charge was created in consideration for money paid at the same time as or after its creation. However, in respect of a charge created in favour of a connected person, the charge will be deemed invalid where it was created two years prior to the company's insolvency, unless it was created in consideration for money paid at the same time as or after its creation.

A fixed or floating charge?

The distinguishing characteristic between a fixed and floating charge relates to the capacity of the chargor to dispose of or deal with the charged asset. With a floating charge the chargor may dispose or deal with the assets made subject to the charge without any form of substantive restriction, that is, until the charge crystallises (see, e.g. *Re G E Tunbridge Ltd* [1994] BCC 563). By contrast, if the assets over which a charge is taken cannot readily be disposed of or dealt with by the chargor, without the chargee's permission, the charge will be classed as a fixed charge.

Although a charge may be identified within a debenture as created as a fixed charge, if, in reality, the characteristics of the charge resemble that of a floating charge, the debenture will be construed as a floating charge; indeed if there is any doubt as to whether the charge is fixed or floating, the charge will be construed as a floating charge (see, e.g. *Royal Trust Bank* v. *National Westminster Bank plc* [1996] 2 BCLC 682). The decision of Hoffmann J in *Re Brightlife* [1987] Ch 200 provides a classic example of a charge being construed as a floating charge, notwithstanding that the terms of the charge purported to create a fixed charge. By the terms of the charge, Brightlife Ltd was prohibited from selling, factoring or discounting its book debts and from dealing with the same otherwise than in the ordinary course of getting in and realising the debts. As the chargor was prohibited from dealing with the unrealised debts, the effect of the charge over the uncollected book debts appeared to be that of a fixed charge. However, as the charge failed to restrict Brightlife Ltd from disposing of the proceeds of its book debts in the ordinary course of its business, here, the nature of the charge appeared to be a floating charge. Notwithstanding the restrictions placed upon the chargor's ability to sell, factor or discount the unrealised debts and given the ability of the chargor to freely dispose of the realised assets, the overall nature of the charge was held to be floating in nature. Hoffmann J sought to explain this finding on the premise that the nature of a floating charge allowed some form of restriction to be placed on the company's ability to deal with the charged assets; albeit that the usual form of restriction was a negative pledge clause (discussed below) (see also *Re Armagh Shoes Ltd* [1982] NI 59 and *Norgard* v. *DFCT* (1987) ACLR 527).

In contrast to the decision of Hoffmann J in *Re Brightlife*, it is to be noted that in *Siebe Gorman & Co Ltd* v. *Barclays Bank* [1979] 2 Lloyd's Rep 142, Slade J construed a debenture as having created a specific charge over the present and future book debts of a company. Here, the debenture was similar to the one in *Re Brightlife* save that during the continuance of the security interest the company was obliged to pay the proceeds received from all present and future book debts into its current account held by the chargee bank. The charge stipulated that subject to the prior consent of the bank in writing, the company would not charge or assign the proceeds in favour of any other person. Although the company's current account was associated with its day-to-day business expenditure, Slade J considered that the bank's general lien and rights over the funds in the current account (in operation until the charge had been extinguished) enabled it to control and restrict the account, even if in credit, thus removing any contention that the company had a freedom to draw on the account at its absolute will. The charge was construed to be a fixed charge notwithstanding that it must have been contemplated by the parties that whilst in credit to the bank, the company would be at liberty to draw on its current account (which it did without having to obtain the permission of the chargee) to satisfy its everyday commercial commitments. Although as an authority *Siebe Gorman* was followed for over 25 years, the precedent of this decision was finally overturned by the House of Lords in *National Westminster* v. *Spectrum Plus Ltd* [2005] 2 AC 680.

A more satisfactory method of creating a fixed charge over book debts may be found, for example, within the debenture considered by the Supreme Court of Ireland in *Re Keenan Bros Ltd* [1986] 2 BCC 98, 970 (approved by the House of Lords in the *Spectrum* case). Here the terms of the charge specified that the chargor could not, without the prior consent of the chargee, waive, assign or otherwise deal with the book debts in favour of any other person. The charge also obliged the company to pay all monies received from realised book debts into a designated account held with the chargee; an account specific to the purpose of collecting the proceeds of book debts. Therefore, once realised, the proceeds of the book debts were paid into a special account and as such were isolated and identifiable as separate funds.

It should be pointed out that it is most improbable that the terms of a charge (so found in *Re New Bullas Trading Ltd* [1994] 1 BCLC 485) purporting to deal with book debts as divisible between a fixed charge and a floating charge (the fixed charge attaching to the unrealised proceeds and the floating charge applied to realised proceeds) will now be upheld as anything other than an all embracing floating charge (see the decision of the House of Lords (*obiter* comments) in *National Westminster Bank plc* v. *Spectrum Plus*, confirming, in this respect, the decision of the Privy Council in *Agnew* v. *Commissioner of Inland Revenue* (*Re Brumark*) [2001] 2 AC 710). In *Agnew* v. *Commissioner of Inland Revenue*, the intention of the parties had been to create a fixed charge over the uncollected book debts, which would, following the realisation of the debts, be converted into a floating charge over the proceeds of the debts (the same intention as in *Re New Bullas*). However, according to the Privy Council, this intention could not be equated with its desired object because the chargor's freedom to convert assets away from the fixed charge was in essence destructive of the nature of a fixed charge, i.e. the objective of a fixed charge was to wrest absolute control of the charged assets into the hands of the chargee and not into the hands of the chargor. Further, it was held that an express power contained in the debenture, permitting the chargee to intervene, at will, to prevent the disposal of the realised debts in the ordinary course of the company's business, was an inadequate method of control in respect of confirming the charge to be of a fixed nature.

9.4 THE REGISTRATION OF CHARGES

CA 2006, s.860 provides that in creating a charge, a company must deliver to the registrar of companies for registration the prescribed particulars of the charge, together with the instrument (if any) by which the charge is created or evidenced. The time period for delivery of the same is 21 days beginning with the day after the day on which the charge is created (CA 2006, s.870). The registrar must keep, with respect to each company, a register of all the charges that require registration (CA 2006, s.869).

Charges requiring registration

Charges requiring registration are listed in CA 2006, s.860(7) (there is no change in content from the previous list, i.e. Companies Act 1985, s.396(1)). The list is as follows:

(a) a charge on land or any interest in land other than a charge for rent or any other periodical payment;

(b) a charge created or evidenced by an instrument, which, if executed by an individual, would require registration as a bill of sale;

147

(c) a charge for the purpose of securing an issue of debentures;

(d) a charge on uncalled share capital of the company;

(e) a charge on calls made but not paid;

(f) a charge on book debts of the company;

(g) a floating charge on the company's undertaking or property;

(h) a charge on a ship or aircraft, or any share in a ship;

(i) a charge on goodwill, trademarks, patent, copyright, etc.

Examples of interests not requiring registration

Hire purchase agreements

Where a company has acquired goods on hire purchase (HP) terms, owner-ship in those goods will not pass to the company until it has fulfilled all of its obligations under the HP agreement. A company cannot create a charge over goods subject to a HP agreement because while the HP agreement is in force, the company is not the legal owner of the goods.

The retention of title clause

A retention/reservation of title clause, also sometimes referred to as a *Romalpa* clause (after the decision of the Court of Appeal in *Aluminium Industrie Vaasen BV* v. *Romalpa Aluminium Ltd* [1976] 2 All ER 552) is a contractual provision inserted into a contract of sale which purports to allow the seller to retain title in the goods he or she sells. The seller reserves title in the goods until such a time as the buyer has fulfilled certain conditions contained within the contract of sale. In terms of priority interests, a supplier of goods with a valid retention of title clause, will, in the event of a company going into administration or liqui-dation, be paid monies owing to him or her in priority to a creditor secured by means of a registerable charge. Where a seller successfully reserves the right of ownership in goods, the buyer will be unable to create a charge over the goods (i.e. it is impossible for the buyer to create a charge over something that he or she does not legally own). The legal effect of a valid retention of title clause is therefore similar to a HP contract, save that under a HP contract the prospec-tive buyer of the property has no legal right to pass title in the goods. By con-trast, a term will be implied into a contract containing a valid retention of title clause to the effect that the prospective buyer of the goods has the legal right to pass title in the goods. In relation to priority issues, the principal criticism of the retention of title clause is that there is no requirement to register such a clause. Accordingly, a creditor wishing to take a charge over corporate assets will find it difficult to establish whether the assets, which are to be the subject of the charge, are already the subject of a retention of title clause.

In terms of determining the validity of a retention of title clause, a retention of title clause that does no more than to retain the legal ownership in goods until such a time as the full purchase price of the goods is paid, will be upheld as reserving title in the property (see, e.g. *Clough Mill* v. *Martin* [1984] 3 All ER 982). Further, a retention of title clause may, by giving effect to the contractual intentions of the parties, be upheld where it seeks to retain ownership in goods even where the goods have already been paid for by the buyer (see, e.g. the decision of the House of Lords in *Armour & Anor* v. *Thyssen Edelstahlweke AG* [1990] BCC 929). However, a retention of title clause that purports to retain equitable and beneficial ownership will not be upheld (see, e.g. *Re Bond Worth* [1980] Ch 228) and the same conclusion will apply to a retention of title clause that purports to retain title in goods manufactured from those supplied under the contract of sale, on the premise that goods supplied by the seller having been through the manufacturing process, inevitably lose their original identity, to the extent that the manufactured goods can no longer be identified as those over which the retention of title clause was placed (see, e.g. *Clough Mill* v. *Martin* [1984] 3 All ER 982). Finally, a retention of title clause that contains a proceeds of sale restriction to restrict the buyer's ability to deal with the proceeds of sale is unlikely to be upheld (although it was upheld in *Aluminium Industrie Vaasen BV* v. *Romalpa Ltd* [1976] 1 WLR 676). The subsequent authorities have not accepted such a clause on the basis of a failure to establish an agency (fiduciary) relationship between the contracting parties (see, e.g. *Re Bond Worth* [1979] 3 All ER 919, *Pfieffer Weinkellerei Weineinkauf GmbH & Co* v. *Arbuthnot Factors Ltd* [1988] 1 WLR 150, *Compaq Computers Ltd* v. *Abercorn Group Ltd & Ors* [1991] BCC 484 and *Modelboard Ltd* v. *Outer Box Ltd* [1992] BCC 945). Where the validity of a retention of title is not upheld, the seller's interest will be deemed to be an interest by way of charge which will be rendered void as a consequence of its non-registration.

The registration certificate

In registering a charge, specific information must be registered – for example, the date of the creation of the charge, the amount secured by the charge, short particulars of the property charged and the persons entitled to the charge. The registration certificate is deemed to be conclusive evidence that, in terms of registration, the requirements of the Companies Act have been satisfied (CA 2006, s.869). The registrar has the ultimate responsibility for checking the contents of particulars sent to him. It is for the registrar to decide what charges have been created and if the registrar makes a mistake as to the contents of the particulars he or she may be liable for any loss suffered as a consequence of the mistake. The actual instrument creating the charge must be delivered to the registrar within 21 days of the charge's creation.

A company and any officer of the company in default in failing to register a charge are punishable by way of a fine. The failure to register may be taken into account in any disqualification proceedings instigated against a director.

A charge that has not been registered within the requisite period, will be void against the liquidator, administrator and any creditor of the company, although the obligation to repay the money secured by the charge is not invalidated by a failure to register; indeed, it becomes immediately repayable upon demand (CA 2006, s.874).

Rectification

The certificate of registration is conclusive; errors in the filed particulars of a charge do not prevent enforcement of the rights contained therein (see, e.g. *Re Nye* [1971] Ch 1052). However, CA 2006, s.873 permits rectification of the register in circumstances where the court is satisfied:

- that an omission or misstatement of any particular was accidental;
- an omission or misstatement was due to inadvertence or to some other sufficient cause;
- the omission or misstatement was of a nature to prejudice the position of creditors or shareholders of the company; and
- it is just and equitable to grant relief on other grounds.

Rectification will not be permitted where, for example, the subject matter of a claim for rectification is not concerned with the particulars which the registrar is required to enter on the register of charges (see, e.g. *igroup Ltd* v. *Owen* [2004] BCLC 61).

Late delivery

The only method by which particulars may be registered after the elapse of the 21-day period is by a court order via an application under CA 2006, s.873 (see above and, e.g. *R* v. *Registrar of Companies, ex p. Central Bank of India* [1986] 2 QB 1114). In considering an application under s.873, there must be evidence justifying the court's decision to allow registration out of time; the court must consider whether it is equitable to grant relief and in doing so must consider the effect of allowing late registration in respect of the interests of other creditors (see, e.g. *Re Telomatic Ltd* [1993] BCC 404).

The company register

In accordance with CA 2006, ss.875–6 a company must keep at its registered office a copy of every instrument creating a charge, irrespective of whether the charge requires to be registered in accordance with the CA 2006. The company must keep a register of its charges. The register is open to public inspection (CA 2006, s.876). A failure to enter a charge on the register will not invalidate the charge but the company and any officer of the company in default of not registering the charge will be liable to a fine.

9.5 PRIORITY RIGHTS

Where a receiver, administrator (under the rules post 15 September 2003) or liquidator of a company is entrusted with the responsibility of selling a corporate asset(s) to discharge the debts of a company, the realisation of such an asset(s) may be insufficient to discharge the full amount of the debt owed to individual creditors. To determine whether a particular creditor is entitled to a priority in the repayment of his or her debt it is necessary to examine the priority interests of competing chargeholders.

Priority between fixed charges

A legal or equitable fixed charge, acquired *bona fide* for value will, subject to compliance with the registration procedure, take in priority to a subsequently created and registered legal or equitable fixed charge because any subsequent chargee, having taken security over the same assets, is deemed to have constructive notice of the earlier charge. However, if the prior created legal or equitable fixed charge is not duly registered, the holder of the subsequently created and registered legal or equitable fixed charge will take priority over the first created charge.

Priority between fixed and floating charges

A fixed charge created over a particular asset (an asset to which a floating charge may later become attached on the date of its crystallisation) will, if it is duly registered, take in priority to the floating charge (see, e.g. *Re Hamilton Windsor Ironworks Co Ltd* (1879) 12 Ch D 707). A fixed charge will take priority over an earlier created floating charge, even if the floating charge expressly includes a covenant (negative pledge clause) on the part of the company not to create a charge ranking in priority or *pari passu* with the floating charge (i.e. provided that the subsequent fixed charge was created without *actual* notice of the covenant (see, e.g. *English & Scottish Mercantile Investment Trust* v. *Brunton* [1892] 12 Ch D 707)). While the subsequent chargeholder will be deemed to have constructive notice of the earlier created floating charge, he or she will not be deemed to have constructive notice of the covenant (negative pledge clause) (see, e.g. *Wilson* v. *Kellard* [1910] 2 Ch 306). Nevertheless, it should be noted that a fixed charge will not take in priority to a floating charge that crystallised prior to the creation and registration of that fixed charge.

Priority in relation to competing floating charges

Where a company creates more than one floating charge over a class of assets, the floating charge that was the first in time (if duly registered) will take priority. This priority rule applies notwithstanding that the first in time

151

floating charge failed to include a negative pledge clause (see, e.g. *Re Benjamin Cope & Sons Ltd* [1914] Ch 800). However, in accordance with *Griffiths* v. *Yorkshire Bank plc* [1994] 1 WLR 1427, for floating charges created prior to the implementation of the EA 2002 (15 September 2003), where a subsequent registered floating charge crystallises prior to an earlier created registered floating charge (i.e. because the subsequent charge contains an automatic crystallisation clause), the subsequent charge will take in priority because following its automatic crystallisation, the charge is fixed in nature, outranking the floating charge created first in time. In respect of the position after 15 September 2003, priority would appear to be determined solely in accordance with the date on which a charge was created. In effect, any former priority advantage afforded to an automatic crystallisation clause may have ceased following the implementation of the EA 2002.

It should also be noted that where a company creates a first floating charge and that charge contains a negative pledge clause which is expressed to govern a specific and defined class of assets, then a subsequent floating charge with *actual notice* of the terms of the negative pledge clause, may still take priority over the first floating charge but only in respect of the class of assets that are absent from the terms of the negative pledge clause (see, e.g. *Re Automatic Bottle Markers Ltd* [1926] Ch 412).

Preferential creditors

The preferential debts of a company are listed in IA 1986, Sched.6. Preferential debts rank equally amongst themselves. Prior to the implementation of the EA 2002, preferential creditors were categorised as debts due to:

- the Inland Revenue (now Her Majesty's Revenue and Customs (HMRC));
- Customs and Excise (now HMRC);
- social security contributions, contributions to occupational pension schemes, remuneration of employees; and finally
- levies on coal and steel production.

However, following the implementation of the EA 2002, the Crown's preferential rights have been abolished to the extent that debts due to HMRC and social security contributions are no longer deemed to be preferential debts and as such are no longer contained within IA 1986, Sched.6.

- Therefore, preferential debts now comprise contributions to occupational pension schemes, the remuneration of employees and levies on coal and steel production.

In a situation where a company is not in the course of being wound up, the priority position of preferential creditors in relation to the floating charge-holders is such that preferential debts are to be paid out of the assets coming into the hands of the receiver (administrator) in priority to any claims for principal or interest in respect of the debentures; irrespective of whether the floating charge crystallised prior to the appointment of the receiver (IA 1986, s.40 applies where an administrative receiver is appointed (pre 15 September 2003 debenture) and CA 2006, s.767 applies in the case of administration (post 15 September 2003 debenture)).

IA 1986, s.175 deals with the priority position of preferential debts when a company is in the process of being wound up. Where a company is in the course of being wound up, the preferential debts are also paid in priority to debts expressed to be secured by means of a floating charge (see, e.g. *Re Oval 1742 Ltd (in liq.); Customs & Excise Commissioners* v. *Royal Bank of Scotland Plc* [2006] EWHC 2813 (Ch)). Prior to the decision of the House of Lords in *Buchler* v. *Talbot* [2004] 2 WLR 582, s.175 was interpreted in a manner whereby liquidation expenses were paid in priority out of the realised assets of the company, over the claims of both preferential creditors and the holder of a floating charge (see *Re Barleycorn Enterprises Ltd* [1970] Ch 465). However, in overruling *Barleycorn*, the *Bulcher* case held that liquidation expenses could not to be taken ahead of the claims for principal and interest owing to the holder of a floating charge. The position post *Bulcher* equated to a dramatic change in the application of the law having serious consequences in relation to a liquidator's planned expenditure following the realisation of assets. However, following the CA 2006, IA 1986, s.176 is made subject to an amendment, the effect of which is to reverse the decision in the *Bulcher* case. The 2006 Act introduces a new IA 1986, s.176ZA which provides that winding-up expenses take in priority over any claims by preferential creditors or to property comprised in or subject to any floating charge created by the company.

The effect of the Enterprise Act 2002

As a consequence of the implementation of the EA 2002, the priority position of creditors has been changed (see the Transitional Provisions (Insolvency) Order 2003, SI 2003/2332) with the objective of improving the position of unsecured creditors. To effect a more equitable distribution of assets, the EA 2002 abolishes the Crown's preferential rights by removing paras.1 and 2 (debts due to Inland Revenue, now HMRC), paras.3–5C (debts due to Customs and Excise, now HMRC) and paras.6 and 7 (social security contributions) from IA 1986, Sched.6. The preferential status of other contributions in Sched.6 is retained and here the preferential creditors will still take in priority to floating chargeholders (CA 2006, s.767).

To ensure that the funds (which other than for the passing of the 2002 Act would have first been distributed to Crown preferences) are made available for unsecured creditors, the EA 2002 provides for a prescribed portion (reserve fund) of the net property (i.e. after the payment of fixed chargeholders and liquidation/administration fees) to be set aside specifically for unsecured creditors (see below). Other than where the administration of the reserve fund would be uneconomic to administer, for example, the cost in terms of the administration of the fund was in excess of the size of the fund, unsecured creditors will take the prescribed portion of the available assets in priority to the holder of a floating charge. However, save for the prescribed portion, floating chargeholders gain in terms of climbing the priority tree and do so at the expense of the Crown's preferential rights, which are now relegated to the position of unsecured debts. It should be noted that for floating charges created prior to 15 September 2003, there is an additional bonus, insofar as the distribution here will be absent any reduction in respect of the prescribed portion. The rules relating to the prescribed portion do not apply retrospectively to floating charges created prior to 15 September 2003.

The prescribed part of the company's net property available for the repayment of the company's unsecured debts will be calculated in accordance with IA 1986, s.176A, namely:

- where the company's net property is no more than £10,000 in value, 50 per cent of that property is reserved to the prescribed part;
- where the company's net property exceeds £10,000 in value, then 50 per cent of the first £10,000 in value will be set aside for the prescribed part; and 20 per cent of any sum in excess of £10,000 will be set aside for the prescribed part;
- however, the value of the prescribed part to be made available for the satisfaction of unsecured debts of the company cannot exceed £600,000.

The revised priority position (order of ranking)

(1st)   Fixed chargeholders.
(2nd)   Liquidation/administration expenses.
(3rd)   Preferential creditors (but *not* Crown debts).
(4th)   Floating chargeholders (minus the sum representing the prescribed part, i.e. the reserve fund for unsecured creditors).
(5th)   Unsecured creditors (this group will now include previous preferential creditors, i.e. comprising Crown debts).

CHAPTER 10

Directors and the management of a company

10.1 INTRODUCTION

The management of a company's affairs will ordinarily reside in persons specifically appointed to hold office as company directors. Collectively, persons appointed to act as company directors will be members of the company's board of directors. In addition to a formally appointed director, the law may also class a person as a director of a company in circumstances where the degree of his or her responsibility and authority in the management of a company's affairs equates to the position of either a *de facto* or shadow director. The significance of a person being labelled as a director will be particularly pertinent in circumstances where the law imposes a personal liability against directors in respect of delinquent conduct, for example, a breach of duty or in relation to acts of fraudulent trading (Insolvency Act (IA) 1986, s.213), wrongful trading (IA 1986, s.214) and disqualification (Company Directors Disqualification Act 1986, s.6). Where a person is found to be a *de facto* director, that person will be subject to the responsibilities and liabilities of a formally appointed director. A person classed as a shadow director will be subject to the responsibilities and liabilities of a formally appointed director in circumstances specified by the companies legislation. Ordinarily, the responsibilities and liabilities of a shadow director will be akin to those of a formally appointed director.

10.2 IDENTIFYING COMPANY DIRECTORS

The Companies Act (CA) 2006 provides little assistance in defining the managerial characteristics of a company director. CA 2006, s.250 (affording no change from the previous position under the Companies Act (CA) 1985, s.741(1)) states that the term 'director' includes:

> Any person occupying the position of director, by whatever name called.

Accordingly, a person may be classified as a director where that person is formally appointed to hold office (a *de jure* director) or in a situation where a person, in the absence of any formal appointment, performs tasks and duties ordinarily associated with the office of a director (a *de facto* director). A person may also be classed as a shadow director. CA 2006, s.251 (again affording no change from the position under the CA 1985 (s.741(2))) defines a 'shadow director' as:

> A person in accordance with whose directions or instructions the directors of the company are accustomed to act ... A person is not to be regarded as a shadow director by reason only that the directors act on advice given by him in a professional capacity.

However, in respect of the regulation of the general duties of directors, transactions requiring members' approval, or contracts with a sole member who is also a director, a body corporate is not regarded as a shadow director of any of its subsidiary companies by reason only that the directors of the subsidiary are accustomed to act in accordance with the directions or instructions of its holding company.

10.3   THE *DE JURE* DIRECTOR

Unless a company's constitution provides otherwise, a *de jure* director will be formally appointed by the passing of an ordinary resolution. Following a person's appointment as a director, the person's authority to act in that capacity and his or her ability to bind the company will, in accordance with CA 2006, s.161, be valid for the period during which office is held, notwithstanding any defect in the appointment process or the fact that he or she had been disqualified from holding office. Further, the validity of a corporate act may not be impugned even in a situation where a director voted on a matter that he or she was not entitled to vote on.

CA 2006, s.154 stipulates that a private company must have at least one director, whereas a public company must have at least two directors. CA 2006, s.155 provides that a company must have at least one director who is a natural person, although this requirement is met if the office of director is held by a natural person as a corporation sole or otherwise by virtue of an office. This provision overturns the previous law, i.e. under the CA 1985, any legal entity could be formally appointed as the director of another company. Where a company fails to satisfy the ss.154 and 155 requirements, the Secretary of State may give the company a direction under s.156(4) to make the necessary appointment or appointments.

Although the CA 2006 stipulates that the ss.154 and 155 requirements must be met in relation to the *appointment* of a director, it is to be assumed that a *de facto* or shadow director will not be counted in relation to satisfying the numerical and status requirements (i.e. both a *de facto* and shadow director will not be appointed to hold office).

The details of a person appointed to hold office as a director must be entered into the register of directors (CA 2006, s.162). Every company must keep a register of its directors that must contain the required particulars of every person so appointed. The register must be kept available for inspection at the company's registered office. The required particulars must, *inter alia*, include:

- the director's name;
- any former name by which the individual was formerly known for business purposes;
- a service address;
- the country or state (or part of the UK) in which the director is usually resident;
- nationality;
- business occupation (if any);
- date of birth.

The register must be open to inspection by any member of the company without charge, and any other person on payment of such a fee as may be prescribed. It is to be noted that the previous requirement (under CA 1985, s.289) for a director to provide details of any other directorships held or directorships held within the preceding five years, is no longer a prescribed requirement of the CA 2006. The company must also keep a register of the residential addresses of its directors (CA 2006, s.165) and must, within the period of 14 days from the occurrence of any change in its directors, or any change in the particulars contained in its register of directors or its register of directors' residential addresses, give notice to the registrar of the change and of the date on which it occurred (CA 2006, s.167). Given the imprecise nature of the definition and identification of a person occupying the position as a shadow director (discussed below), a shadow director is nevertheless treated as an officer of the company for the purposes of a person who may incur liability for non compliance with procedures relating to CA 2006, s.162 (register of directors) and s.165 (register of directors' residential addresses).

Qualifications

Other than where a company's constitution specifically provides that a person must hold a specified number of shares before his or her appointment as a director of the company (a share qualification), a person may be appointed to a directorship without the necessity of having attained any specific qualifications for the post. Prior to the passing of the CA 2006, it was even possible for an infant to hold office as a director, notwithstanding a minor's legal incapacity to contractually bind a company (see, e.g. *Marquis of Bute's case* [1892] 2 Ch 100). As a consequence of CA 2006, s.157, a person must now be at least 16 years old before he or she can hold office as a director. This provision applies retrospectively to persons under 16 years of age who held office prior to the implementation of s.157. However, a minor may be provisionally appointed to a directorship at any age on the understanding that he or she does not legally hold office until attaining the age of 16. It is to be noted that s.157 is, however, subject to a peculiar exemption in the form of s.158, namely the latter permits the Secretary of State to make provision by regulations to permit cases in which a person who has not attained the age of 16 years to be appointed to take up office as a director of a company. An appointment made in contravention of s.157 (but subject to s.158) is deemed void. A person who acts in contravention of s.157 remains liable for any breach of the companies legislation during the period in which he or she purported to act as a director.

Types of *de jure* directors

The executive director

An executive director will normally be a full-time officer of the company, employed under a contract of employment. A company's articles will normally specify that the company may appoint one or more of their number to the office of managing director or to any other executive office. An obvious example of a person holding an executive office will be where that person has been appointed to the post of managing director/chief executive. A managing director is normally appointed to oversee the day-to-day running of a company. The terms of an executive director's service contract (discussed below) and the specific powers delegated to the office held, are determined by the collective board of directors.

The non-executive director

A person who holds the position of a non-executive director will ordinarily be devoid of any contract of employment and as such will not be a salaried employee of the company. Nevertheless, a non-executive director may be held liable for a breach of corporate duty or other statutory obligation in a manner akin to that of an executive director. A non-executive director, once appointed, will hold office for a period determined by the company's articles. However, in public companies, following the trend of recent corporate governance initiatives, the role of a non-executive director has now taken on a far more important position in management structures. The role of non-executive directors has been elevated to a position akin to that of independent protectors of the public interest. In public companies non-executive directors will be expected to contribute to the development of corporate strategy by, for example, scrutinising the performance of executive directors and by satisfying themselves that financial controls and systems of risk management are robust and defensible.

The company chairman

The company chairman is an appointed director of the company, ordinarily an executive director, with responsibilities of a supervisory nature. The chairman presides over meetings of the board of directors. The chairman of the board, or in his or her absence some other director, will ordinarily preside over general meetings of the company. Although a company chairman will normally have no special powers, where a vote at a meeting of the board or general meeting is tied, he or she may ordinarily, but subject to the terms of the company's articles, be entitled to a second or casting vote.

The alternate director

Where a director is to be absent from board meetings, he or she may appoint a nominee, an alternate person, to act in his or her place. A person appointed to act as an alternate director may be an existing director of the company or any other person. An authority to appoint an alternate director must be provided for in a company's articles and the appointment must be approved by the board of directors. Although an alternate director acts as a director's replacement, an alternate director is not an agent for the absent director, accordingly, he or she may act and vote according to his or her own conscience and as such is responsible for his or her own acts.

Retirement

Prior to the CA 2006, a director of a public company was obliged to retire at the age of 70, unless he or she continued to hold office with the approval of the company's general meeting (previously CA 1985, s.293(1)). The CA 2006 provides no compulsory retirement age for a director.

10.4 THE *DE FACTO* AND SHADOW DIRECTOR

The *de facto* director

A person may be deemed to act as a *de facto* director where that person performs managerial tasks properly associated with the office of a director. The tasks performed by that person must exceed those of a mere employee; they must extend to an authority in matters related to the administration and management of the company's affairs in a manner associated with those performed by a *de jure* director. Although the courts have attempted to define the nature and degree of control considered necessary to identify a person as a *de facto* director, formal guidelines have not always been of a uniform nature. Indeed the courts have recognised, irrespective of any given formula or test, that the question as to whether a person acted as a *de facto* director will ultimately be one of fact to be determined from the circumstances of each individual case (see, e.g. *Re Kaytech International plc. Portier* v. *Secretary of State for Trade and Industry* [1999] BCC 390, the first case to reach the Court of Appeal on the question relating to the interpretation of a '*de facto*' director). However, in determining what is ultimately a 'jury question' the court will consider specific factors, to include:

- whether there was a holding out by the company of the individual as a director;
- if the individual used the title 'director';
- whether the individual had proper information (e.g. management accounts) on which to base decisions;
- if the individual had or exercised a capacity to exercise control, make or take part in major decision-making; and
- whether the individual contributed management skills in the running of the company.

Taking, for example, the above factors into account, the court must ultimately consider whether the individual was a part of the governing structure of the company (see, e.g. *Secretary of State for Trade and Industry* v. *Hollier* [2007] BCC 11). Obviously, there will be a strong presumption that a person acts as a *de facto* director where that person contributes skills and knowledge to the internal management of a company and being concerned with its affairs, portrays to the outside world an obvious understanding and relationship with functions ordinarily exercised by a director of the company.

The shadow director

In contrast to a *de facto* director, a shadow director will rarely be held out as an officer of a company (albeit this assumption may be questioned in the context of ss.162–5 (see above). Following the Court of Appeal's decision in *Secretary of State* v. *Deverell* [2001] Ch 340, the scope of the definition previously afforded to a shadow director has been extended. Prior to *Deverell*, the case law identified a shadow director as any person who, from outside formal management structures, exerted a dominant and controlling influence over the company's affairs, i.e. a person who was responsible for engineering and directing corporate activity through what may be described as a 'puppet' board of directors. However, this definition can no longer be viewed with authority. Following *Deverell*, a controlling and dominant, but hidden, influence in the affairs of a company must be considered to be an exaggeration of the level and degree of involvement deemed necessary to identify a shadow director.

In *Deverell* the Court of Appeal considered that it was unnecessary to establish a subservient relationship between a person and the board of directors in seeking to conclude that the said person acted as a shadow director.

The court held that it was incorrect to view CA 1985, s.741(2) (now CA 2006, s.251) in the use of the term 'accustomed to act' as being conclusive of establishing that the board must always be compelled to obey the guidance of a shadow director. Accordingly, a person is capable of acting as a shadow director even if the board is given a capacity to exercise independent judgment. Further, the Court of Appeal concluded that the giving of advice could, in relation to the language of s.741(2) (now CA 2006, s.251), be equated with a direction or instruction in circumstances where the advice was given on a regular and consistent basis. Following the judgment of the Court of Appeal, advice may be considered in the same vein as a direction or instruction because a direction, instruction, or the giving of advice all share the common characteristic of an act of guidance.

In accordance with the judgment of the Court of Appeal in *Deverell*, a shadow director may be identified in the following manner, namely, as a person who is not formally appointed to the company's board of directors but a person who nevertheless customarily tenders advice, instructions or directions to the company's board, of a type which, as an act of guidance, carries real influence in relation to a part or the whole of the company's business affairs. While the company's board will normally follow the guidance tendered by a shadow director, it is not essential that it is habitually followed or that there is any expectation that it will be followed. A shadow director may be independent from or form a part of the internal management structures of the company.

The need to attach a level of responsibility to a person who directs and influences corporate activity through a formally appointed board of directors is patently obvious. A person who exerts influence over a company's affairs must be regulated and be made subject to duties and responsibilities ordinarily associated with the company appointed directors.

Although CA 2006, s.251 would appear expressly to exempt a person acting in a professional capacity from being construed as a shadow director, the exemption is limited and will not cover a situation where, for example, a professional offers advice beyond the reasonable scope of advice one would normally expect from a person occupying a similar professional status. For example, a bank manager, an accountant or solicitor who exercises a degree of control over a company's affairs in a manner to suggest influence as opposed to routine professional advice, may be classed as a shadow director (see, e.g. *Re Tasbian Ltd* (*No.3*) [1992] BCC 358 and *Re a Company* (*No.005009 of 1987*) (1988) 4 BCC 424).

10.5   THE BOARD OF DIRECTORS

A company's board of directors comprises the individually appointed *de jure* directors of the company. The scope of a board's management powers is determined by the company's constitution. A company's articles will ordinarily confer the general management powers of a company to the company's board (or expressed as the general meeting of directors), albeit specific powers may be retained by the general meeting. For example the general meeting may be afforded a power by the articles (usually by means of a special resolution) to challenge the decisions of the board of directors.

An individual director's management functions are delegated to him or her by the board. The directors can pursue and authorise any corporate act in relation to third-party dealings even in a situation where the corporate act is outside the company's own contractual capacity (discussed in **Chapter 12**).

Board meetings

The regulation of board meetings is determined by the company's constitution. In accordance with a company's articles, the ability to call and regulate board meetings will ordinarily be decided upon by the directors. Usually, any director of the company will be permitted to call a board meeting. Unless the directors decide otherwise, or unless the company comprises a sole director, a board meeting must have a quorum of two directors. Resolutions of the directors should, unless otherwise provided for by the articles, be passed at properly convened board meetings, each director being entitled to one vote per resolution. However, if all the directors agree on the outcome of a motion, the informal agreement of members of the board of directors may pass the resolution. A formal resolution will be passed by a simple majority of directors; where there is an equality of votes the resolution will be lost (see, e.g. *Re Hackney Pavilion Ltd* [1924] 1 Ch 276). To avoid the possibility of a deadlock situation, a company's constitution may specify that the company's chairman should be afforded a casting vote.

Notice requirements

Subject to a contrary indication in a company's articles and except for directors absent from the UK, notice of board meetings must be given to all the members of the board. However, a resolution passed by a single director in the absence of a co-director will be invalid where it impugns the quorum requirement, notwithstanding the fact that a co-director may have been absent from the UK and therefore not entitled to notice of the meeting (see, e.g. *Globalink Telecommunications Ltd* v. *Wilmbury Ltd & Ors* [2002] BCC 958). Nevertheless, a company may be estopped from denying the validity of a resolution in circumstances where it acted on the terms of the resolution and where it would have been unconscionable to subsequently deny its validity.

In determining a time period amounting to an appropriate period of notice, the court will be influenced by whether, given the period of notice and the individual circumstances surrounding the calling of the meeting, it was reasonable to expect a director to attend a particular meeting. For example, inadequate notice was found in a situation where a letter was sent to a director on a Sunday, convening a meeting of the board for the morning of the next day (Monday). The director in question had been away on a weekend holiday and did not discover the letter until the Monday evening, by which time the board meeting had taken place (see, e.g. *Bentley-Stevens* v. *Jones* [1974] 1 WLR 638). However, despite the fact that a period of notice may be inadequate, where a director's absence would not have altered the outcome of the board meeting, the resolution as passed will ordinarily be allowed to stand (see, e.g. *Browne* v. *La Trinidad* (1887) 37 Ch D 1).

Delegation of the board's powers to individual directors

It is commonplace for a company's constitution to empower its board to appoint committees of one or more of the directors to exercise powers normally reserved to the board. The necessity for permitting the board of directors to delegate its powers arises from the practical difficulties that occur in the day-to-day management of a corporate enterprise. Obviously, a company would cease to function if all senior managerial decisions could only be justified on the basis of a resolution of the company's board.

10.6   SERVICE CONTRACTS AND DIRECTORS' REMUNERATION

Remuneration

A director's remuneration is a payment received by a director for services provided to the company in which he holds office. The method of remuneration may be in cash or other financial incentives, for example, share options. It should be noted that a director is not entitled, as of right, to any remuneration other than in a situation where the director holds a service contract under which a level of remuneration representing an annual salary package is included as a contractual term of the contract. The articles of a company will normally provide that directors are entitled to receive such remuneration as the company by ordinary resolution determines (this will not apply to the determination of the level of salary in respect of a director's service contract). A remuneration award may be paid to a director in addition to his or her annual salary. As the power to grant remuneration is ordinarily vested in the general meeting, the board has no authority to delegate this power to individual directors or a committee of directors. However, a company's constitution may provide that remuneration awards should be determined by the board (see, e.g. *Guinness* v. *Saunders* [1990] 2 AC 663).

The majority of company directors appointed to executive posts hold service contracts. The salary package for the services of such directors may often be negotiable on an annual basis. The terms of a director's service contract will be determined in accordance with the procedure specified in the company's constitution, albeit the salary package for the services of executive directors will usually be determined by the board of directors. A director is prohibited from voting on the terms of his or her own service contract and nor can a director be counted as part of the quorum for the meeting at which his or her service contract is to be considered. Other than where CA 2006, s.189 applies (discussed below), the terms of a director's service contract will not require the approval of the general meeting, although CA 2006, s.229 provides that a director's service contract must be made available for inspection by the general meeting. Following the introduction of the Directors' Remuneration Report Regulations, SI 2002/1986 (see CA 2006, s.426), for financial years ending on or after 31 December 2002, quoted companies are required to publish a directors' remuneration report as part of their annual reporting cycle and to file a copy at Companies House. In amending the CA 1985, the regulations inserted a new Sched.7A to incorporate the disclosure requirements. The remuneration report must disclose details of the directors' pay packages, details of the board's consideration of directors' pay, the membership of the remuneration committee; the names of any remuneration consultants used, a statement of the company's policy on directors' remuneration, an explanation of how the remuneration packages relate to performance, together with details and an explanation of policy on contract and notice periods and a performance graph providing information on the company's performance in comparison with an appropriate share market index. A shareholder vote must be held on the report at the company's annual general meeting. However, where the report is not approved, the company is not obliged by law to adhere to the wishes of the general meeting.

Service contracts

In accordance with CA 2006, s.227, a director's 'service contract', is a contract under which:

- a director of the company undertakes personally to perform services (as director or otherwise) for the company, or for a subsidiary of the company; or
- services (as director or otherwise) that a director of the company undertakes personally to perform are made available by a third party to the company, or to a subsidiary of the company.

By CA 2006, s.228, a company must keep available for inspection, a copy of every director's service contract (or a variation of the contract) with the company or with a subsidiary of the company, or if the contract is not in writing, a written memorandum setting out the terms of the contract. The copy or memorandum must be open to inspection by any member of the company without charge. All the copies and memoranda must be kept available for inspection at the company's registered office. The copies and memoranda must be retained by the company for at least one year from the date of termination or expiry of the contract and must be kept available for inspection during that time.

The company must give notice to the registrar of the place at which the copies and memoranda are kept available for inspection, and of any change in that place unless they have at all times been kept at the company's registered office. If default is made in complying with the notice requirement, an offence is committed by every officer of the company in default and a person guilty of this offence is liable on summary conviction to a fine.

Although a director's service contract will not normally require the approval of the general meeting, approval will be required (other than where the company is a wholly owned subsidiary of another company) in circumstances where it is set for a guaranteed period, defined by CA 2006, s.189, as a period in excess of two years (previously the duration period was set to a maximum of five years, see CA 1985, s.319) and the contract contains a term under which the company cannot terminate the employment by notice (or, if giving notice, the notice period would, on its own, or together with the duration of the contract, be for a period in excess of two years). Instead of seeking a formal resolution approving the contract, approval may also be by way of a written resolution and it is probable that it may also be informally approved by the entire body of shareholders (see, e.g. *Atlas Wright* (*Europe*) *Ltd* v. *Wright* [1999] BCC 163). CA 2006, s.189 is also applicable where, for the guaranteed period, a term(s) of the contract restricts the company's ability to terminate a director's employment in 'specified circumstances'. Here the Act is somewhat vague, as it fails to attribute any meaning to the term 'specified circumstances'.

It will be unnecessary for a company to seek the subsequent approval of the shareholders if it intends to extend an existing service contract for a further period in excess of two years, providing the ability to extend the contract was included within the terms of the previous contract. In all other cases, if more than six months before the end of the guaranteed term of a director's employment, the company enters into a further service contract, s.189 will need to be complied with, where the unexpired period of the guaranteed term when added to the guaranteed term of the new contract, is in excess of the two-year period. A contravention of s.189 will render the offending provision of the contract void and the company may terminate the contract at any time by the giving of reasonable notice.

10.7 THE REMOVAL OF DIRECTORS

It is commonplace for a company's constitution to contain conditions which relate to circumstances whereby directors can be removed from office. For example, a director may be obliged to cease to hold office if he resigns, is prohibited by law from holding office, becomes bankrupt or is absent from board meetings without due excuse for a period of six months. It is also commonplace to find that the constitution of a public company will provide that a director may be removed by a simple resolution of the board.

In accordance with CA 2006, s.169, a company may, by ordinary resolution, remove a director before the expiration of his or her period of office, notwithstanding anything in any agreement between the company and the director (but note the possibility of a weighted voting clause (discussed in **Chapter 3**) or a clause within a membership agreement restricting a director's removal (discussed in **Chapter 3**)). Section 169 replaces CA 1985, s.303(1). At first sight, the wording of s.169 appears similar to CA 1985, s.303; however, s.169 fails to specify (unlike s.303) that its terms cannot be overridden by a contrary provision within the company's articles. As such, where a clause within the company's articles specifies, for example, that a director may only be removed by the passing of a special resolution, such a clause would appear valid (the clause could even be entrenched (discussed in **Chapter 6**)). Given the said interpretation, the only challenge to the validity of the clause, albeit a very unlikely one, would be that the director as (if) a member of the company, is (as with all other members of the company) impliedly bound by the terms of the constitution to the extent that the same may equate to an 'agreement' between the company and the member/director. If construed as an 'agreement' then in accordance with s.169, the example clause (see above) relating to removal by special resolution would be deemed invalid.

CA 2006, s.169(5) provides that the power of the general meeting to dismiss a director will not, however, deprive the director's claim to compensation or damages for a breach of his or her service contract (see, e.g. *Southern Foundries Ltd* v. *Shirlaw* [1940] AC 701). Special notice (28 days) must be given to the company of the intention to introduce a motion calling for the dismissal of a director (CA 2006, s.169(2)). A director must be given a copy of the form of motion together with the opportunity (even if not a member of the company) to present representations at the meeting at which the motion is to be heard. A copy of a written form of the representations may, if requested by the director (and providing they are of a reasonable length), be distributed to members, providing the delivery would be practicable given the date on which the representations were delivered by the director to the company and the proposed date of the meeting. If a copy of a director's representations is received too late or because of the company's default, the director may (without prejudice to his or her right to be heard orally) require that the representations be read out at the meeting (CA 2006, s.170). An exception to a director's right to present representations is provided by CA 2006, s.170(5), namely, in a situation where, on the application of either the company or of any other person who claims to be aggrieved, the court is satisfied that the rights conferred by s.170 are being abused. This extends the ambit of the exemption beyond the previous law where, under CA 1985, s.304, the director's 'abuse' had to be for the purpose of securing needless publicity for a defamatory matter.

Payments for loss of office

A payment made to a director or past director of a company by way of compensation for loss of office must be approved by an ordinary resolution of the members of the company (CA 2006, s.217). A resolution approving a payment must not be passed unless a memorandum setting out the particulars of the proposed payment (including its amount) is made available to the members of the company:

- in the case of a written resolution, by being sent or submitted to every eligible member at or before the time at which the proposed resolution is sent or submitted to him or her;
- in the case of a resolution at a meeting, by being made available for inspection by the members both at the company's registered office for not less than 15 days ending with the date of the meeting, and at the meeting itself.

However, approval is not required under s.217 for a payment made in good faith:

- in discharge of an existing legal obligation that was not entered into in connection with, or in consequence of, the event giving rise to the payment for loss of office, or by way of damages for breach of such an obligation;
- by way of settlement or compromise of any claim arising in connection with the termination of a person's office or employment;
- by way of pension in respect of past services; or
- where the value of the payment made by the company does not exceed £200.

If a payment is made in contravention of s.217, then the payment must be held on trust for the company. Any director who authorised the payment is jointly and severally liable to indemnify the company for any loss resulting from it (CA 2006, s.222).

10.8   THE COMPANY SECRETARY

Although a company secretary's responsibilities are primarily of an administrative, as opposed to a managerial nature, the role of a company secretary may be vital to the proper functioning of the corporate entity. The specific responsibilities of a company secretary will naturally depend upon the size and nature of the company in which office is held. However, tasks common to all company secretaries will include:

- maintaining the company's registers;
- sending relevant details to the registrar of companies;
- preparing share certificates;
- making arrangements for board meetings;
- drafting the minutes of such meetings;
- keeping the company's documentation in order;
- keeping up to date with the relevant companies legislation insofar as it affects the running and administration of the company.

As a company secretary's responsibilities are geared to the administration of the company's affairs, the post may carry an authority to bind the company in contracts related to the ambit of a particular secretary's actual or ostensible authority (see, e.g. *Panorama Developments Ltd* v. *Fidelis Furnishing Fabrics Ltd* [1971] 2 QB 711).

Private companies

Previously, under CA 1985, s.283(1), every company was required to appoint a company secretary. However, following the implementation of CA 2006, s.12(2), private companies are no longer obliged to appoint a company secretary. The change in the law recognises that, in respect of private companies, the obligatory requirement of appointing a company secretary was often an unnecessary burden. Indeed, in small private companies the requirement of having to appoint a company secretary was often complied with via the 'artificial' appointment of a secretary from family members or friends.

Public companies

A company secretary must be appointed by a public company. The secretary is appointed by the directors of the company on such terms as they may determine. The power to remove the secretary is vested in the directors. A company must keep details at its registered office (similar to those kept for directors) of its company secretary (CA 2006, s.277). It must also send the relevant details of its secretary to the registrar who must be notified of any change in the person appointed as company secretary. The company secretary must be a suitably qualified person, that is, he or she must, as determined by the board of directors, have the necessary experience to perform the secretary's functions and/or must have a professionally recognised qualification.

A director may be authorised by the board to act in the place of a formally appointed secretary; the director may act as a secretary providing that a task which requires the act of both the secretary and director is not performed by one person, i.e. a person acting as both the director and secretary (CA 2006, s.280). A company may also act as the secretary of another company. It may so act notwithstanding that the appointment of a company as the sole director of another company is prohibited by CA 2006, s.155.

10.9 THE AUDITOR

This is discussed further at **4.6**.

An auditor holds office (CA 2006, s.487), but the nature of an auditor's office cannot be equated with the office held by a director or company secretary. An auditor is not a part of a company's general management team; the auditor is an independent contractor. With the exception of companies with a turnover below £5.6m and a balance sheet total of £2.8m (see CA 2006, s.477), limited companies (other than a dormant company) are obliged to prepare and file accounts at Companies House and to appoint an auditor to report on and undertake statutory prescribed tasks for the financial year. An auditor is appointed by the directors or by an ordinary resolution of the general meeting (CA 2006, s.485 (private company) and s.489 (public company)). If a company fails to appoint an auditor in accordance with s.485 or s.489, the Secretary of State may appoint one or more persons to fill the vacancy. CA 2006, s.492 provides that the remuneration of an auditor appointed by the members of a company must be fixed by the members by ordinary resolution or in such manner as the members may by ordinary resolution determine. The remuneration of an auditor appointed by the directors of a company must be fixed by the directors.

The statutory audit aims to provide an independent, external professional opinion of a company's accounts and financial returns. An auditor's task is primarily to advise the shareholding body in respect of the financial affairs of the company. CA 2006, s.495(2) prescribes that the auditor's report must include:

(a) an introduction identifying the annual accounts that are the subject of the audit and the financial reporting framework that has been applied in their preparation; and

(b) a description of the scope of the audit identifying the auditing standards in accordance with which the audit was conducted.

The report must have been properly prepared in accordance with the relevant financial reporting framework and statutory rules and must state clearly whether, in the auditor's opinion, the annual accounts give a true and fair view (s.495(3)(a)):

(i) in the case of an individual balance sheet, of the state of affairs of the company as at the end of the financial year;

(ii) in the case of an individual profit and loss account, of the profit or loss of the company for the financial year;

(iii) in the case of group accounts, of the state of affairs as at the end of the financial year and of the profit or loss for the financial year of the undertakings included in the consolidation as a whole, so far as concerns members of the company.

The auditor's report must be either unqualified or qualified, and must include a reference to any matters to which the auditor wishes to draw attention by way of emphasis without qualifying the report. The auditor must also state in the report on the company's annual accounts whether in his or her opinion the information given in the directors' report for the financial year for which the accounts are prepared is consistent with those accounts. Where the company is a quoted company, the auditor, in his or her report on the company's annual accounts for the financial year, must report to the company's members on the auditable part of the directors' remuneration report (see CA 2006, s.421), and state whether in his or her opinion that part of the directors' remuneration report has been properly prepared in accordance with the CA 2006.

Removal of an auditor

Notwithstanding any form of agreement between a company and its auditor, an auditor may be removed by an ordinary resolution. Nevertheless, dismissal will not preclude the auditor from seeking compensation for a breach of any service contract. Special notice is required by CA 2006, s.551 in respect of a resolution to remove an auditor in circumstances where the removal would take place prior to the expiration of the auditor's term of office (i.e. those proposing the motion to dismiss the auditor must give at least 28 days' notice to the company before the meeting at which the motion to remove is to be heard). Before calling the meeting to consider an auditor's removal, the auditor (in a like manner to a director's removal from office) may make written representations to the company and these must be distributed to the company's members.

CHAPTER 11

Directors' duties

11.1 INTRODUCTION

In an attempt to eradicate potential abuses of the powers afforded to the board of directors and persons expressly or impliedly authorised to act on the board's behalf, the regulation of company law incorporates a series of statutory, common law and compliance rules, designed to provide a mechanism for both the internal and external governance of company directors. The rules and duties relating to the internal governance of directors are ultimately concerned with a company's ability to prevent, curb and penalise the delinquent conduct of directors. Prior to the passing of the Companies Act (CA) 2006, the said rules and duties were largely, albeit not exclusively, regulated by the common law and equitable principles. In the 2006 Act, the legislature has sought to codify the common law/equitable rules and duties. However, in accordance with the CA 2006, the codified rules and duties will, where appropriate, be interpreted and applied in the same way as common law rules and equitable principles (CA 2006, s.170(4)).

The rules of external governance which comprise a voluntary code of best practice (the Combined Code) are tied to Stock Exchange listing requirements and are essentially concerned with the regulation of public companies. An analysis of the rules of external governance extends beyond the scope of this work.

11.2 THE DUTIES

Directors and other authorised company officers owe duties to the company in which they hold office. The duties also apply to shadow directors. The most common analogy of the duties owed by a director of a company is that of a trust and/or agency relationship. While a director may be regarded as a trustee in a situation where he or she is responsible for the management of corporate funds, a more apt analogy of the general relationship between a director and company is that of agency. As agents, the directors stand in a fiduciary relationship to the principal, i.e. the company. A fiduciary may be defined as a person who undertakes to act for or on behalf of another in a particular matter in circumstances which give rise to a relationship of trust and confidence. The distinguishing obligation of a fiduciary is the obligation of loyalty. A fiduciary must act in good faith; he or she must not make a personal profit from his or her position of responsibility and must not place him or herself in a position resulting in a conflict of interest (see, e.g. *Bristol & West Building Society* v. *Mothew* [1998] Ch 1).

The statutory list of duties

The CA 2006 codifies the previous common law duties of company directors in an attempt to clarify and simplify what, by many, was often perceived as a complex and uncertain set of rules. The codification of the general duties has effect subject to any rule of law enabling the company to give authority, specifically or generally, for anything to be done (or omitted) by the directors (or any of them), that would otherwise be a breach of duty.

The codified duties are as follows.

The duty to act for a proper purpose (CA 2006, s.171)

CA 2006, s.171 provides that:

A director of a company must –

(a)   act in accordance with the company's constitution, and
(b)   only exercise powers for the purposes for which they were conferred.

Although a director may honestly believe that in entering into a transaction he or she is acting in the best interests of the company as a whole, he or she will nevertheless be held to be in breach of a fiduciary duty if, objectively, the director's conduct amounts to conduct outside or in abuse of the director's allocated powers (see, e.g. *Hogg* v. *Cramphorn* [1967] Ch 254). The duty amounts to one whereby a director must act for a proper purpose in the exercise of his or her powers. For example, if a director exercises a power to issue unissued shares with a principal objective of manipulating the voting control of the company, (notwithstanding that a subsidiary purpose for the issue may be to raise additional capital), the director's dominant purpose in issuing the shares will be viewed objectively as one for an improper purpose, i.e. the proper purpose attached to an issue of shares is to raise capital (see, e.g. the Privy Council's decision in *Howard Smith Ltd* v. *Ampol Petroleum Ltd* [1974] AC 821). The court must therefore seek out the dominant purpose in relation to the use of a power to determine whether the proper purpose duty has been infringed (also see *Lee Panavision Ltd* v. *Lee Lighting Ltd* [1992] BCLC 22).

However, it is to be noted in the context of the above example, that while the directors of a company may not ordinarily use their powers to issue shares for the purpose of manipulating voting control, an exception may be made where, with a view to resisting a takeover bid, the exercise of the power, in manipulating voting control, is objectively viewed as one essential to the company's survival as a going concern. For example, if A Ltd and B Ltd are in competition and B seeks to destroy A's share of the marketplace by obtaining a controlling interest in A and running down the company to obtain a greater share of the marketplace for itself, then the directors of A may be justified in issuing further shares in A with the objective of maintaining their control over the company. Here the dominant and legitimate purpose of the power use would be to prevent the demise of A Ltd (see, e.g. *Cayne v. Global Natural Resources plc* [1984] 1 All ER 225).

The duty to act bona fide in good faith in the interests of the company (CA 2006, s.172)

CA 2006, s.172 states that:

(1) A director of a company must act in the way he considers, in good faith, would be most likely to promote the success of the company for the benefit of its members as a whole, and in doing so have regard (amongst other matters) to –

    (a) the likely consequences of any decision in the long term,

    (b) the interests of the company's employees,

    (c) the need to foster the company's business relationships with suppliers, customers and others,

    (d) the impact of the company's operations on the community and the environment,

    (e) the desirability of the company maintaining a reputation for high standards of business conduct, and

    (f) the need to act fairly as between members of the company.

(2) Where or to the extent that the purposes of the company consist of or include purposes other than the benefit of its members, subsection (1) has effect as if the reference to promoting the success of the company for the benefit of its members were to achieving those purposes.

(3) The duty imposed by this section has effect subject to any enactment or rule of law requiring directors, in certain circumstances, to consider or act in the interests of creditors of the company.

In conducting the business of a company a director must, in accordance with CA 2006, s.172, act for the benefit of the company as a whole and not for some other collateral purpose (see, e.g. *Re Smith & Fawcett Ltd* [1942] Ch 304, *Fusion Interactive Communication Solutions Ltd v. Venture Investment Placement Ltd* [2006] BCC 187). In considering whether a director is in breach of this duty the court must determine whether the director considered that he or she (applying a subjective test) was acting for the benefit of the company as a whole (see, e.g. *Extrasure Travel Insurances Ltd v. Scattergood*

[2003] 1 BCLC 598). Therefore a director will not be in breach of this duty where he or she honestly believed his or her actions were in the best interests of the company even if, objectively, the court considered the director's actions to be unreasonable. However, where objectively, a director's conduct is considered to be unreasonable, the extent of that unreasonable behaviour may, in extreme cases, be so out of line with all reasonable perceptions of expected conduct to the extent that the director's conduct cannot, in any logical sense, be viewed as beneficial to the company as a whole. For example, if a director believed that the sale of a corporate asset for a price of £2,000 was for the benefit of the company, notwithstanding that the asset had been independently valued at £200,000, it is most probable that the director's belief would be considered so unreasonable that it negated any suggestion that his or her conduct could be perceived to have any legitimate degree of benefit to the company as a whole.

In construing the *bona fide* duty it must also be observed that even if a director is not in breach of this particular duty, his or her conduct may still be viewed as being contrary to the proper purpose rule (CA 2006, s.171, see above) (see, e.g. *Bishopsgate Investment Management Ltd* v. *Maxwell* [1993] BCC 140).

The CA 2006 specifies that, in purporting to act in good faith and for the benefit of the company, a director must act in a manner most likely to promote the success of the company for the benefit of its members as a whole. Accordingly, a director owes his or her duty to the company (in the form of the shareholders as a collective body) in which he or she holds office and does not, for example, owe duties to specific individual shareholders or other third parties (see, e.g. *Percival* v. *Wright* [1902] 2 Ch 421). CA 2006, s.171(1) provides that a director's primary responsibility in the exercise of his or her duties is one geared to benefiting the collective interests of the shareholders. For example, in *Heron International* v. *Lord Grade* [1983] BCLC 244, the Court of Appeal suggested that in considering competing takeover bids, the directors of a company were under a duty to ensure that they did not exercise their powers to prevent shareholders obtaining the best possible price available for their shares. However, it should be noted, following the decision of the Court of Appeal in *Peskin* v. *Anderson* [2001] BCC 874, that directors will not be in breach of their fiduciary duty in circumstances where they fail to disclose to the membership that they are in the process of considering (but without any actual commitment) plans to invite offers for the sale of the business.

Although a director must seek to promote the success of the company for the benefit of its members as a whole, CA 2006, s.172(1)(a)–(f) does provide that in aiming to achieve corporate success, directors must act fairly between members and take into account the interests of employees, suppliers and customers. Indeed, in the context of defining the success of a 'company', the view that a company can have a separate and distinct interest in any given project which is independent from the interests of the company's human constituents and players, is, in reality, a myth. A company's interest is, in effect, dominated by a collection of parties, all of whom may be said to share a financial stake in the success of the company. Directors must also take account of the interests of affected communities and the environment. However, here the intent of the legislation is vague and in part confusing because if a director takes account of the interests of communities and the environment to the detriment of generating profits, will this not prejudice the company's shareholders and other parties with a financial interest in the company? Further, will a shareholder in a company with a reputation for high standards of business conduct view that as a benefit when in achieving such high standards the company is unable to declare a favourable dividend? Will a company really enforce such third-party obligations?

A creditor's interest (CA 2006, s.172(3))

When a company is close to or actually enters into a state of insolvency (defined by the Insolvency Act (IA) 1986, s.123 as a situation where a company's liabilities exceed its assets), it is apparent that the interests of creditors will begin to outweigh those of the general body of shareholders (see, e.g. *Mercia Safetywear Ltd* v. *Dodd* [1988] BCLC 250 and *Whalley (Liquidator of MDA Investment Management Ltd)* v. *Doney* [2004] BPIR 75). The insolvency of a company mirrors a substantial risk that the company will be unable to discharge its debts. Accordingly, CA 2006, s.172(3) makes mention of the interests of creditors. The interests of creditors will become paramount following a company's slide into an insolvent state, to the extent that company directors will owe a primary duty to creditors in respect of the maintenance of corporate assets.

The duty to act with independent judgment (CA 2006, s.173)

CA 2006, s.173 provides that:

(1) A director of a company must exercise independent judgment.
(2) This duty is not infringed by his acting –

    (a) in accordance with an agreement duly entered into by the company that restricts the future exercise of discretion by its directors, or
    (b) in a way authorised by the company's constitution.

A director of a company must exercise independent judgment and should not be subject to considerations or influences that would deter him or her from acting otherwise than in the best interests of the company as a whole. However, this duty will not be infringed where a director acts in accordance with the terms of the company's constitution or in respect of an agreement duly entered into by the company restricting the future exercise of discretion by its directors.

Although a director will exercise corporate powers in a fiduciary capacity and as such it may be assumed that he or she may not, by a contractual agreement or otherwise, fetter the future exercise of such powers, commercial reality dictates that it may be necessary for a director to bind the company to a specific course of future conduct. The case of *Fulham Football Club Ltd* v. *Cabra Estates plc* [1992] BCC 863 validates this point of view. Here, the directors of Fulham Football Club (F) undertook to support, in preference to a plan proposed by the local authority, a planning application by the ground's owners (Cabra Estates plc (C)) for the future development of 'Craven Cottage' (the football ground). At the time of giving the undertaking, given in return for substantial financial support by C to the football club, the directors believed that their decision had been taken in the best interests of the company. However, subsequent events resulted in the directors and shareholders of F changing their minds in relation to the terms of the agreement on the pretext that it could no longer be construed as beneficial to F. The Court of Appeal held that F was bound by the terms of its agreement with C. F had obtained a substantial benefit at the time of entering into the agreement and it had been permissible for the directors of F to act to bind the company to an agreed future course of conduct.

The duty of care (CA 2006, s.174)

CA 2006, s.174 states that:

(1) A director of a company must exercise reasonable care, skill and diligence.
(2) This means the care, skill and diligence that would be exercised by a reasonably diligent person with –

 (a) the general knowledge, skill and experience that may reasonably be expected of a person carrying out the functions carried out by the director in relation to the company, and
 (b) the general knowledge, skill and experience that the director has.

Although a director is expected to exhibit a reasonable degree of care in the performance of his or her duties, it is nevertheless essential to the promotion of an enterprise culture that the expectation of due care is balanced against the potential benefit of risk. In managing the affairs of a company, a director may be placed in a position where, in entering into a business transaction, he or she is aware that the particular venture carries a risk of failure. A commercial gamble may be necessary to secure economic stability and/or growth. Therefore, mere errors of judgment or acts of imprudence will not necessarily equate to a breach of a duty of care.

To comply with the duty of care, a director must pay diligent attention to the business affairs of the company in which he or she holds office. The standard of care required of a director is not measured by a universal professional standard applicable to directors as a class, but, in part, is dependent upon the abilities and qualifications of the individual director in question. For example, directors who are qualified in a particular business-related area will be expected to exhibit a reasonable standard of skill appropriate to that area of expertise. A director's non-performance of an act which it is his or her duty to perform may result in a breach of his or her duty of care. For example, in *Re Duomatic* [1969] 2 Ch 365, a director who failed to seek specialist help or guidance (in this case from the general body of shareholders), when it was reasonable in the circumstances for him to do so, was found to be in breach of his duty of care.

In accordance with cases such as, *Lister* v. *Romford Ice & Cold Storage Ltd* [1957] AC 555, *Norman* v. *Theodore Goddard* [1991] BCLC 1028 and *Re D'Jan of London Ltd* [1993] BCC 646, a director need not exhibit in the performance of his or her duties any greater degree of skill than could be expected from a reasonable diligent person in circumstances where the diligent person is imputed with the general knowledge, skill and experience that may reasonably be expected of the holder of the position in question. However, where, for example, the knowledge, skill and experience of a director falls below the standard expected of a reasonable diligent person, the director cannot rely on his or her poor standards in an attempt to argue that he or she did not breach the duty of care. The test to determine a breach of a duty of care is therefore comparable to the one used to determine wrongful trading under IA 1986, s.214 (discussed in **Chapter 2**).

Although the standard of care expected from executive directors may ordinarily be expected to be of a higher standard than for non-executive directors, the expectation may be displaced where, for example, non-executive directors are entrusted with specific business matters or deal with matters in which they have a personal expertise (see, e.g. *Dorchester Finance Co Ltd* v. *Stebbing* [1989] BCLC 498).

The conflict of interest duty (CA 2006, s.175)

CA 2006, s.175 provides that:

(1) A director of a company must avoid a situation in which he has, or can have, a direct or indirect interest that conflicts, or possibly may conflict, with the interests of the company.

(2) This applies in particular to the exploitation of any property, information or opportunity (and it is immaterial whether the company could take advantage of the property, information or opportunity).

(3) This duty does not apply to a conflict of interest arising in relation to a transaction or arrangement with the company.

(4) This duty is not infringed –

    (a) if the situation cannot reasonably be regarded as likely to give rise to a conflict of interest; or

    (b) if the matter has been authorised by the directors.

(5)   Authorisation may be given by the directors –

(a)   where the company is a private company and nothing in the company's constitution invalidates such authorisation, by the matter being proposed to and authorised by the directors; or

(b)   where the company is a public company and its constitution includes provision enabling the directors to authorise the matter, by the matter being proposed to and authorised by them in accordance with the constitution.

(6)   The authorisation is effective only if –

(a)   any requirement as to the quorum at the meeting at which the matter is considered is met without counting the director in question or any other interested director, and

(b)   the matter was agreed to without their voting or would have been agreed to if their votes had not been counted.

(7)   Any reference in this section to a conflict of interest includes a conflict of interest and duty and a conflict of duties.

The conflict of interest duty specified in CA 2006, s.175 may, in its simplest form, be described as a duty of loyalty and fidelity which prohibits a company director from exploiting or potentially exploiting his or her position in respect of a corporate opportunity, corporate property or information. A director of a company will be in breach of the conflict of interest duty where, by virtue of his or her fiduciary position, he or she uses to his or her own advantage information which came into his or her hands whilst holding office; information in which the company had, or potentially had, an interest (see, e.g. *Bhullar* v. *Bhullar* [2003] 2 BCLC 241). A director will be in breach of the conflict of interest duty even in circumstances where the company in which he or she holds or has held office could not, of itself, have benefited from the opportunity in question.

The conflict of interest duty is strict in the sense that it fails to distinguish between, on the one hand, directors who have purposely set out to exploit a corporate opportunity for their own benefit (an intentional or reckless abuse of the rule and an obvious breach of fiduciary duty), and, on the other hand, directors who personally profit from a corporate opportunity where the company was, at the time of the opportunity, unable or unwilling to act upon it. For example, in *Regal (Hastings) Ltd* v. *Gulliver* [1942] 1 All ER 378, reported at [1967] 2 AC 134, a company (R) was the owner of a cinema. The directors of R wished to obtain two more cinemas with a view eventually to selling the company as a going concern. R formed a subsidiary company (A) for the purpose of obtaining a leasing agreement for the two other cinemas in question. In order to secure the leasing agreement the subsidiary company was required to raise £5,000. However, R was unable to meet this requirement. R's directors injected their own personal funds (£3,000) to finance the balance between R's contribution and the total amount required. The directors subsequently sold their shares in both A and R, making a substantial profit in the process. The new controllers of R sought to recover the profit which the directors had made from the sale of the shares in A on the premise that the directors had made that profit as a result of an exploitation of a corporate opportunity. The House of Lords unanimously held the directors to be liable to account for the profits made from the sale of the shares. Notwithstanding the directors' honest and well informed intentions, the liability resulted from the mere fact of a profit having been made.

The prohibition against a director benefiting from a corporate opportunity is operative for the duration of a director's term of office but may also be enforced against the director following his or her departure from the company, albeit that an ex-director will not be precluded from using his or her general fund of skill and knowledge, or his or her personal connections, to compete with his or her former company. In relation to the potential liability of an ex-director, liability will arise in circumstances where he or she exploited information which was directed towards the company in which he or she held office and which came to his or her attention during the period in which office was held (see, e.g. *Industrial Development Consultants Ltd* v. *Cooley* [1972] 1 WLR 443, *Export Finance Ltd* v. *Umunna* [1986] BCLC 460). For example, where a director of a company resigns from the company with the objective of diverting a maturing business opportunity of the company to a new business venture in which he or she is involved. In circumstances where a director exploits a corporate opportunity for the benefit of another company which then takes advantage of the said opportunity, then both the director and the new company will be liable to account having both jointly participated in a breach of trust (see, e.g. *CMS Dolphin Ltd* v. *Simonet* [2002] BCC 600 and *Quarter Master UK* v. *Pyke* [2005] 1 BCLC 245).

However, in relation to the exploitation of a business opportunity, a director of a company (or ex-director) will not be in breach of the duty where the company itself successfully exploits a business opportunity and as a result of that exploitation the director obtains an ancillary benefit. A director may accrue an ancillary benefit from a business opportunity that falls to the company, providing the benefit was obtained without prejudice to the company's interests (see, e.g. *Framlington Group plc* v. *Anderson* [1995] BCC 611). For example, if company A decides to sell a part of its business (GG) to company B, and X, a director of A and previously the head of GG, resigns his position to take up a directorship with B, to manage GG, X will not be in breach of any duty to A, providing X obtains no undue advantage at the expense of A. Here, in this situation, A exploits the corporate opportunity and not X. Further, X would not be in breach of duty where, on becoming a director of B, he or she receives an additional payment from B in consideration of his or her continued management of GG. However, in this instance the payment to X must be made as a genuine incentive to X and not as a 'back handed' payment to reward X for a misappropriation of information etc. in respect of the business transaction between A and B.

Duty not to accept any benefits from a third party (CA 2006, s.176)

CA 2006, s.176 states that:

(1) A director of a company must not accept a benefit from a third party conferred by reason of –

    (a) his being a director, or

    (b) his doing (or not doing) anything as director.

(2) A 'third party' means a person other than the company, an associated body corporate or a person acting on behalf of the company or an associated body corporate.

(3) Benefits received by a director from a person by whom his services (as a director or otherwise) are provided to the company are not regarded as conferred by a third party.

(4) This duty is not infringed if the acceptance of the benefit cannot reasonably be regarded as likely to give rise to a conflict of interest.

(5) Any reference in this section to a conflict of interest includes a conflict of interest and duty and a conflict of duties.

CA 2006, s.176 expands the definition of a conflict of interest to encompass a situation precluding a director of a company from personally benefiting from the provision of a service or information to a third party, a benefit conferred on the basis of the director's office. A service may be equated with non-activity on the part of a director, for example, where the director is, by receiving a benefit, influenced by a third party to abstain from voting on a specific matter in his or her capacity as a director. The s.176 duty covers any inducement or incentive type of payment to a director but may also cover a situation where, for example, a director is 'wined and dined' or provided with some other type of inducement by a third party.

Disclosure and the waiver of the conflict of interest duty (CA 2006, s.177)

If a director of a company is, in any way, directly or indirectly interested in a proposed transaction or arrangement between the company and a third party, the conflict of interest may be excused where it is disclosed to the directors of the company. CA 2006, s.177 provides that:

(1) If a director of a company is in any way, directly or indirectly, interested in a proposed transaction or arrangement with the company, he must declare the nature and extent of that interest to the other directors.

(2) The declaration may (but need not) be made –

    (a) at a meeting of the directors, or

    (b) by notice to the directors in accordance with –

        (i) section 184 (notice in writing), or

        (ii) section 185 (general notice).

(3) If a declaration of interest under this section proves to be, or becomes, inaccurate or incomplete, a further declaration must be made.

(4) Any declaration required by this section must be made before the company enters into the transaction or arrangement.

(5) This section does not require a declaration of an interest of which the director is not aware or where the director is not aware of the transaction or arrangement in question.

For this purpose a director is treated as being aware of matters of which he ought reasonably to be aware.

(6) A director need not declare an interest –

   (a) if it cannot reasonably be regarded as likely to give rise to a conflict of interest;

   (b) if, or to the extent that, the other directors are already aware of it (and for this purpose the other directors are treated as aware of anything of which they ought reasonably to be aware); or

   (c) if, or to the extent that, it concerns terms of his service contract that have been or are to be considered –

      (i) by a meeting of the directors, or

      (ii) by a committee of the directors appointed for the purpose under the company's constitution.

Following the decision of the Court of Appeal in *Lee Panavision Ltd* v. *Lee Lighting Ltd* [1992] BCLC 22, disclosure of an interest may be given informally without any need for the interest to be declared at a formal board meeting (also see *Runciman* v. *Walter Runciman plc* [1992] BCLC 1084). The disclosure must specify the nature and extent of the conflict of interest. However, a sole director of a company is not subject to the formal disclosure requirement and here the effect of the CA 2006 overturns the decision of Lighman J in *Neptune (Vehicle Washing Equipment) Ltd* v. *Fitzgerald* [1995] BCC 474.

The board of directors (i.e. members of the board who are independent of the conflict) may vote to waive any potential conflict of interest, other than where the company's constitution prohibits waiver. However, it is to be noted that in the case of a public company, the company's constitution must specifically allow for a waiver of the conflict of interest (in effect, this duplicates the previous position under the Companies Act 1985 (CA 1985), i.e. Table A, art.85). Further, in respect of both a public and private company, a transaction giving rise to a conflict of interest may (if it is not waived by the directors), as with any breach of duty, be waived by the general meeting (albeit the director with the conflict of interest will not be allowed to vote on the matter (i.e. as a member of the company).

It is to be noted that as the CA 2006 now classifies a conflict of interest as a duty (previously a conflict of interest was deemed a distinct rule of equity and was not strictly speaking a fiduciary duty), a potential problem may have arisen in respect of the operation and application of CA 2006, s.232 (previously CA 1985, s.310) i.e. this provision prohibits a company's ability to waive a breach of duty. Previously, a conflict of interest (because it was not classified as a duty) could be waived without disturbing CA 1985, s.310 (see, e.g. *Movitex Ltd* v. *Bulfield* [1988] BCLC 104). However, in respect of the CA 2006, this potential problem is eradicated insofar as the general duties have effect notwithstanding any other enactment or rule of law (CA 2006, s.180(5)), i.e. a company's ability to waive a breach of the conflict of interest duty is, in accordance with s.180(5), not defeated by the effect of CA 2006, s.232.

Competing directorships

Although there is no specific statutory provision or common law principle which prohibits a person from holding a directorship in two or more companies (see, e.g. *London & Mashonaland Exploration Co Ltd* v. *New Mashonaland Exploration Co Ltd* [1891] WN 165), the test to determine a breach of the conflict of interest duty may, in theory, be indicative of a finding of conflict in cases of competing directorships; especially in circumstances (as, for example, in the Mashonaland case, above) where a director holds office in two distinct companies which by virtue of their business purposes may be viewed as being in direct competition with each other. The potential conflict is apparent. How for example, can a director who holds office in company A, ignore information, projects, dealings or potential contracts in relation to that company when, in also acting as a director of company B, he or she is considering business matters, projects, dealings and potential contracts of a type which are equally relevant to company A? How in such circumstances can a director act in the best interests of both companies? (See the *obiter* comments of Sedley LJ in *Plus Group Ltd & Ors* v. *Pyke* [2003] BCC 332.)

Consequences of non-compliance with the conflict of interest duty

Although the non-disclosure of an interest will not, in itself, invalidate the proposed transaction in which a director has an interest (see, e.g. *Coleman Taymar Ltd* v. *Oakes* [2001] 2 BCLC 749), the resulting transaction will become voidable and may be avoided by the company in general meeting (see, e.g. *Hely Hutchinson* v. *Brayhead Ltd* [1968] 1 QB 549). In circumstances where a director fails to declare a conflict of interest and the subsequent breach of duty is not ratified by the general meeting, the director must reimburse the company for any benefit gained or loss sustained as a result of entering into the transaction to which the conflict of interest is linked. A dishonest agreement between a company's directors to impede the exercise of the company's right to recover any benefit gained as a result of a director entering into a transaction involving a conflict of interest will constitute a conspiracy to defraud (see, e.g. *Adams* v. *R* [1995] BCC 376 (Privy Council)).

A conflict of interest in respect of an existing transaction or arrangement (CA 2006, s.182) (criminal liability)

In a situation where a director fails to declare an interest in a proposed transaction or arrangement (and so acts in breach of duty, see CA 2006, s.177) and the proposed transaction/arrangement materialises into an existing transaction/arrangement, then providing the director is deemed to be directly or indirectly aware of the interest in the existing transaction or arrangement, the director must, in accordance with CA 2006, s.182, declare the nature and extent of the interest to the board of directors. CA 2006, s.182 will also be operative where a director is deemed to have an interest in an existing transaction without having had a prior interest in the transaction before it materialised into an existing transaction. This latter scenario will be a rare one, but may for example, arise where a person is appointed to a directorship at a time after a contract (in which the newly appointed director has an interest) was concluded.

A failure to declare the interest is deemed an offence punishable by way of a fine (disclosure under s.177 will satisfy the disclosure requirements under s.182). A director is deemed to be aware of an interest if, by the application of an objective test, he or she is considered to have been aware of matters of which he or she ought reasonably to be aware. Ordinarily, disclosure should be made at a meeting of the directors (but may also be made by notice in writing or by general notice). A breach of CA 2006, s.182 results in the imposition of criminal liability and as such the effect of s.182 is akin to the previous law represented by CA 1985, s.317. However, where an interest is disclosed in accordance with CA 2006, s.182, the interest cannot (in relation to the civil consequences of the breach) be subject to a right of waiver by the board of directors in the sense that the directors are not afforded a power to waive a breach of duty unless permitted to do so by a statutory provision (CA 2006, s.232). Unlike CA 2006, s.175, s.182 is absent of the directors' ability to waive a breach of duty. However, the breach could, but only in relation to its civil consequences, still be ratified by a resolution of the general meeting.

The consequences attached to any breach of duty

Where a director is discovered to be contemplating the pursuit of a transaction that would, if completed, amount to a breach of duty, the company may apply for an injunction to restrain the commission of the breach. In circumstances where a breach of duty has actually occurred, the director in breach may be liable to account for any profit made or loss sustained as a result of his or her transgression. However, save possibly in a situation where a breach of duty results in a fraud on the minority (discussed in **Chapter 15**), the company may legitimately excuse the breach by the passing of an ordinary resolution. However, in an equitable and logical change to the previous law (which was silent on the issue) it is to be noted that any director who is in breach of a duty (or connected person), will not (if he or she is a member of the company) be permitted to vote at the general meeting (or take part in a written resolution) where the motion to excuse the breach is to be considered (CA 2006, s.239). However, nothing in s.239 affects the validity of a decision taken by unanimous consent of the members of the company, or any power of the directors to agree not to sue, or to settle or release a claim made by them on behalf of the company.

Relief available from the court

In accordance with CA 2006, s.1157 (formerly CA 1985, s.727), the court may relieve, partly or wholly, the liability of any officer of the company (or auditor) in proceedings involving negligence, default, breach of duty or breach of trust. Liability may be relieved on such terms as the court sees fit. A director (or auditor) may apply for relief in the course of proceedings (see, e.g. *Re Kirby's Coaches Ltd* [1991] BCC 130) or may make an anticipatory application.

The courts' jurisdiction under s.1157 arises, notwithstanding that the applicant may have been in breach of a duty, where the court considers that the applicant acted in an honest and reasonable manner. The provision permits the court to take account of the economic realities of a case in seeking to do justice between a variety of interests, including the interests of creditors (see, e.g. *Re Loquitur Ltd* [2003] 2 BCLC 442). The burden of satisfying the s.1157 defence lies upon the applicant who must persuade the court that he or she did not intend to cause prejudice to the interests of the company as a whole. Even where the court is satisfied that an applicant acted honestly and reasonably, the court, under its general discretion, may still decide to decline relief (see, e.g. *Coleman Taymar Ltd* v. *Oakes* [2001] 2 BCLC 749). Following the decision of Hoffmann LJ in *Re D'Jan of London* [1993] BCC 646, s.1157 may even prove an appropriate defence in circumstances where a negligent breach of duty is alleged, notwithstanding that a negligent act necessarily equates to an unreasonable act. Here, Hoffmann LJ opined that, although in an objective sense an applicant's conduct may be considered negligent and unreasonable, nevertheless, CA 1985, s.727 (now CA 2006, s.1157) lends itself to a subjective consideration of the applicant's conduct and while negligent conduct cannot be ignored, an applicant's error of judgment may, in a particular case, be viewed with some understanding (in *Re D'Jan* the applicant was negligent in the completion of an insurance document). However, it is suggested that the decision of Hoffmann LJ should be viewed with caution, because in *Re D'Jan of London*, the s.727 defence was construed with, it is submitted, a more than generous leaning towards a subjective consideration of events. A director's honesty is, in itself, insufficient in circumstances where the breach of duty is deemed an unreasonable act (see, e.g. *Re MDA Investment Management Ltd; Whalley (liquidator of MDA Investment Management Ltd)* v. *Doney* [2005] BCC 783).

Protection for directors – indemnities

The Companies (Audit, Investigations and Community Enterprise) Act 2004 introduced provisions relevant to indemnifying (but not exempting) company directors against liability in specified circumstances. These matters are now dealt with under CA 2006, ss.232–8. As a starting point, a company is generally precluded from providing any form of indemnity for a director of the company or associated company in respect of any negligence, default, breach of duty or breach of trust on the part of the director (CA 2006, s.232). However, a company may purchase insurance for a director in respect of the consequences of a director's negligence, default, breach of duty or breach of trust (CA 2006, s.233). Further, an indemnity may be provided in specific instances, namely in cases involving qualifying third party proceedings (CA 2006, s.234) and in relation to qualifying pension scheme indemnity provisions (CA 2006, s.235). The details of all qualifying indemnity provisions must be disclosed in the directors' report and if a provision is in force for the benefit of one or more of the directors (to include former directors within the financial year) of the company (or an associated company) the directors' report must specify that fact (CA 2006, s.236). Copies of all qualifying indemnity provisions must be kept by the company (for at least one year from the expiry date of the provision) at either the company's registered office, the place where its register of members is kept, or its principal place of business; the nominated place must be notified to the registrar. A company commits an offence in respect of a failure to abide by any of the aforementioned requirements (CA 2006, s.238). Any member of a company is entitled, on request and on payment of such fee as may be prescribed, to be provided with a copy of any indemnity provision.

Third party indemnities (CA 2006, s.234)

CA 2006, s.234 defines a 'qualifying third party indemnity provision', to include any indemnity, other than where:

- the director's liability is incurred directly to the company or an associated company;
- liability is in the form of a fine imposed in criminal proceedings or a sum payable to a regulatory authority (e.g. the Financial Service Authority) by way of a penalty;
- a director incurs liability in defending criminal proceedings in which he or she is convicted, or civil proceedings brought by the company or an associated company in which judgment is made against him or her; and
- the court refuses a director relief in an application under CA 2006, s.1157 (formerly CA 1985, s.727).

11.3   OTHER STATUTORY DUTIES AND OBLIGATIONS

Substantial property transactions

In accordance with CA 2006, s.190 (previously regulated under CA 1985, s.320), a company is prohibited from entering into an arrangement whereby a director of the company or a director of its holding company, or a connected person of such a director, acquires, or is to acquire, directly or indirectly, a substantial non-cash asset(s) of the requisite value from the company. However, the arrangement may be approved by an ordinary resolution (or may be validated conditional on the approval being obtained). In addition, s.190 prohibits an arrangement whereby the company (directly or indirectly) acquires or is to acquire a substantial non-cash asset(s) of the requisite value from a director or director of its holding company or connected person of such a director. As the s.190 provision prohibits 'corporate conduct' as opposed to the conduct of a director, regrettably there would appear to be no restriction on an 'interested' director voting on the matter, i.e. where the director has an interest in the transaction he or she will still be allowed to vote on any resolution to approve the substantial property transaction. Accordingly, CA 2006, s.239 (discussed above) would appear to be inapplicable in relation to the application of s.190. However, note that the transaction may involve a distinct breach of the conflict of interest duty (discussed above).

Where an arrangement involving a substantial property transaction with a director or connected person has not been approved by the general meeting of the company, the transaction may be avoided (CA 2006, s.195). However, a company will lose its right to avoid the transaction where restitution of the subject matter is no longer possible or where the company is indemnified by any other person for the loss or damage that it has suffered, or where rights to the property have been acquired by a *bona fide* third party for value without actual notice of the contravention. Regardless of whether the transaction is (or can be) avoided, the director or connected person in breach of CA 2006, s.190 (and any other director who authorised the transaction) will be liable to account to the company for any profit or loss sustained as a result of the breach of the provision (the loss sustained may be measured in relation to any depreciation in value of the asset(s) acquired in contravention of s.190) (see, e.g. *Re Duckwari plc (No.2)* [1998] 2 BCLC 315 and *Re Duckwari plc (No.3)* [1999] 1 BCLC 168). However, where the breach of s.190 was committed by a connected person, the director with whom the person is connected will not be liable if he or she can prove that all reasonable steps had been taken to secure the company's compliance with s.190. The connected person and any authorising director may also escape liability if they can establish that at the time of the transaction they were unaware of the relevant circumstances giving rise to the contravention of s.190.

Requisite value

The requisite value of a substantial asset is currently set at £100,000 or 10 per cent of the company's net assets (transactions of less than £5,000 are not included). Asset value is measured (at the time of the arrangement) by the company's most recent statutory accounts, or if no statutory accounts have been prepared, the amount of the company's called-up share capital (CA 2006, s.191).

Connected person

A connected person is defined by CA 2006, ss.252–5 to include, *inter alia*, the director's spouse, child or step-child and a company with which the director is associated, i.e. if the director and the persons connected with him or her, hold at least one-fifth of the associated company's share capital, or are entitled to exercise or control the exercise of more than one-fifth of the voting power at any general meeting of that body.

Exceptions to CA 2006, s.190

There are the following exceptions to CA 2006, s.190:

- *Group transactions:* CA 2006, s.192 permits holding companies to acquire or transfer assets from or to their wholly owned subsidiaries. The section also permits two wholly owned subsidiaries of the same holding company to acquire or transfer assets between each other.
- *Members:* CA 2006, s.192 provides that a person may acquire an asset from the company in which he or she is a member providing the arrangement is made with that person in his character as a member and not in any other capacity.
- *Winding up or administration:* Where a company in administration or in the course of being wound up (other than by means of a members voluntary winding-up order) enters into an arrangement for the acquisition of a non-cash asset (CA 2006, s.193).
- *Transactions on a recognised investment exchange:* Membership approval is not required where the transaction is on a recognised investment exchange and is effected by a director or a person connected to the director through the agency of a person who in relation to the transaction acts as an independent broker (CA 2006, s.194).

Contracts for loans and guarantees

The statutory rules (see CA 2006, s.197 et seq) alter the previous regulatory regime (see CA 1985, s.330 et seq). Under the terms of the CA 1985, a company was generally prohibited from entering into a loan agreement for the benefit of a director. The position under CA 2006, s.197 is now that a company may enter into loan agreements with directors and connected persons providing the transaction in question is approved by an ordinary resolution (approval may take place within a reasonable period after the transaction, see CA 2006, s.203). A resolution approving the transaction must not be passed unless a memorandum setting out the nature and amount of the transaction and the extent of the company's liability under any transaction connected with the loan, etc. has first been made available to the members (CA 2006, s.197(3)). Additional rules exist in the case of relevant companies (public companies). These additional rules (not applicable to private companies other than where the private company is connected via a group relationship with a public company) are concerned with quasi loans and other credit transactions. In the case of relevant companies, the following also require shareholder approval:

- *Quasi-loans (CA 2006, s.198):* A 'quasi-loan' is defined by CA 2006, s.199 as an arrangement under which a company meets a financial obligation of a director, a connected person, or its holding company on terms that the director, etc. will reimburse the company. Shareholder approval will also be required in the case of guarantees entered into by a relevant company in respect of a quasi-loan made by a third party for the benefit of a director, connected person or holding company.

- *Credit transactions (CA 2006, s.201):* A credit transaction is a transaction under which one party (the creditor) supplies, hires or leases goods or sells land under a hire purchase contract, or for periodical payments, or otherwise disposes of land or supplies goods or services on the understanding that payment (whether in lump sum or instalments or by way of periodical payment) is to be deferred (CA 2006, s.202). A credit transaction that is entered into by a relevant company for the benefit of a director, connected person or holding company must be approved by a resolution of the members. The same is true of a guarantee given by the company in respect of a credit transaction between a director, connected person or holding company and third party.

- *Related arrangements (CA 2006, s.203):* Shareholder approval is required where a relevant company takes part in an arrangement under which another person enters into a transaction and in doing so obtains a benefit from the company or an associated company in circumstances where, if the transaction had been entered into by the company, the company would have been subject to CA 2006, s.198 or s.200.

General exceptions to CA 2006, s.197

The CA 2006 provides exceptions to the requirement that shareholder approval must be sought in respect of loan transactions. The exceptions are as follows.

Shareholder approval is not required in respect of loan funds, etc. made available (maximum amount of £50,000) to a director of the company or holding company (or connected person) to facilitate the performance of the director's duties (CA 2006, s.204). Likewise, shareholder approval is not required where a company provides a director (or a director of its holding company) with loan funds, etc. (here no maximum amount is specified) to meet expenditure incurred in defending any criminal or civil proceedings in connection with any alleged negligence, default, breach of duty or breach of trust (CA 2006, s.205). Loan funds may be given providing the director repays the said funds should judgment be given against him or her. Further, shareholder approval is not required where a company provides loan funds, etc. (no maximum amount specified) for a director or a director of its holding company to meet expenditure incurred in relation to defending an investigation by a regulatory body (CA 2006, s.206).

CA 2006, s.207 provides that shareholder approval is not required in respect of an arrangement that does not exceed £10,000 in respect of a loan or quasi-loan (£15,000 in respect of a credit transaction). Likewise CA 2006, s.208 states that a loan, quasi-loan, credit transaction or guarantee or security made in respect of an associated company is not subject to shareholder approval.

Finally, CA 2006, s.209 provides wide exceptions in the case of a company which pursues a money lending business, i.e. one whose ordinary business includes the making or guaranteeing of loans or quasi-loans. Any loan, quasi-loan or guarantee made by a money lending company is permissible without shareholder approval providing it is made within the ordinary course of business on terms which the company might reasonably have afforded to an unconnected person of the same financial standing. A loan made to a director or employee of the company or a director of the company's holding company enabling the director to purchase or improve his or her main residence is permissible without shareholder approval, providing loans are ordinarily made by the company to employees and the terms of the loan in question are no more favourable than those on which such loans are ordinarily made.

Civil penalties

CA 2006, s.213 provides that a breach of CA 2006, ss.197, 198, 200, 201 or 203 will render the transaction in question voidable (see, e.g. *Re Ciro Citterio Menswear plc* v. *Thakra*r [2002] 1 BCLC 672, decided under CA 1985, s.330). The company may (although it is not obliged to) avoid the transaction (by ordinary resolution). However, although a transaction may be avoided, the following persons will remain liable to account (whether jointly or severally) to the company for any gain or loss sustained as a consequence of the transaction. The said persons are listed in s.213(4) as:

(a) any director of the company or of its holding company with whom the company entered into the transaction or arrangement in contravention of section 197, 198, 201 or 203,

(b) any person with whom the company entered into the transaction or arrangement in contravention of any of those sections who is connected with a director of the company or of its holding company,

(c) the director of the company or of its holding company with whom any such person is connected, and

(d) any other director of the company who authorised the transaction or arrangement.

In the case of a transaction or arrangement entered into by a company in contravention of ss.200, 201 or 203 with a person connected with a director of the company or of its holding company, that director is not liable by virtue of s.213(4)(c) if he or she shows that all reasonable steps were taken to secure the company's compliance with the section concerned.

It should be noted that a transaction may not be avoided if restitution of the subject matter of the transaction is no longer possible, the company has been indemnified for the loss resulting from the transaction, or the rights acquired by a third party, having been acquired in good faith, for value and without actual notice of the contravention, would be affected by an avoidance.

Removal of criminal sanctions

Previously, under CA 1985, s.342, the directors of relevant companies were also subject to criminal sanctions by way of imprisonment or fine in circumstances indicative of an intentional or reckless contravention of the provisions relating to loans and guarantees (see CA 1985, s.330). The relevant company was also subject to a fine although it could escape liability where it could be established that at the time the transaction or arrangement was entered into, it did not know (i.e. the company's directing mind did not know) of the relevant circumstances giving rise to the contravention. As a result of the CA 2006, criminal liability is removed from the provisions dealing with loans, etc., albeit that CA 2006, s.212 provides that nothing in s.212 shall be read as excluding any other legal rule which may be brought into operation by a contravention of CA 2006, ss.198, 220 or 202 (i.e. the other legal rule in question may result in a criminal sanction; for example, the loan transaction may incorporate a fraudulent act which may be made subject to the criminal law).

CHAPTER 12

Directors' authority and the validity of corporate transactions

12.1 INTRODUCTION

The ability of a company to enter into a transaction or other obligation with a third party is dependent upon the company's contractual capacity and issues relating to the directors' authority to bind the company, or delegate others to do so. In a historical context, a company's contractual capacity was at one time determined by the *ultra vires* rule. During the twentieth century the significance of the *ultra vires* rule declined and today it has no role in the context of determining the contractual capacity of a company in relation to its dealings with third parties. In effect, the abrogation of the *ultra vires* rule affords a company an unrestricted capacity to enter into any type of legal transaction or other legal obligation. However, despite an unrestricted corporate capacity, a transaction or other obligation may still be deemed voidable in circumstances where the corporate act was of an unauthorised nature.

12.2 CORPORATE CAPACITY – THE *ULTRA VIRES* RULE

Historically, a company's capacity to enter into a contractual obligation was dominated by the *ultra vires* rule. In its strictest sense, the rule provided that if a contractual transaction exceeded a company's corporate capacity, the transaction would be deemed void. If void, not even the unanimous consent of the company's shareholders could validate the transaction (see, e.g. *Ashbury Railway Carriage and Iron Co* v. *Riche* (1875) LR 7 HL 653). A company's corporate capacity to enter into a particular transaction was determined by the company's objects clause so it was contained within the company's memorandum. The objects clause specified the company's intended business purposes. Potential creditors and shareholders of the company could inspect the objects clause to discover the company's business purposes with a view to determining whether to lend or invest funds. As the objects clause was contained within the memorandum, a document available for public inspection, a person contracting with a company was deemed to have constructive notice of its contents, irrespective of whether any actual inspection of the document had actually taken place. Therefore, a party who dealt with a company could not subsequently complain if a transaction in which he or she was involved conflicted with the company's objects clause; the company could avoid the transaction. The strict application (or potential application) of the *ultra vires* rule handicapped business efficiency to the extent that over time objects clauses were ingeniously and often elaborately constructed in an attempt to avoid the severity of the *ultra vires* rule (see, e.g. *Bell Houses Ltd* v. *City Wall Properties* [1966] 2 QB 656, where the scope of a company's objects clause authorised the company to carry on any business whatsoever which, in the opinion of the directors, could be advantageously carried out by the company in conjunction with or ancillary to any of the ventures specified in the objects clause).

Statutory reform of the *ultra vires* rule

The first statutory reform of the *ultra vires* rule followed the UK's requirement to comply with art.9 of the EC First Company Law Directive. The basic intent of the reform, incorporated as Companies Act (CA) 1985, s.35, was that where a third party dealt with a company in good faith, then any transaction authorised by the directors would be permissible. However, the language of the provision failed fully to achieve its objective (in seeking to comply with art.9) (see, e.g. *International Sales and Agencies Ltd* v. *Marcus* [1982] 3 All ER 551 and *Barclays Bank Ltd* v. *TOSG* [1984] BCLC 1). As problems associated with the wording of s.35 persisted, the ghost of the *ultra vires* rule remained intact and companies, in drawing up object clauses, continued to create elaborate and well-defined clauses in an attempt to avoid any potential conflict with the *ultra vires* rule.

Further reform was advanced by Companies Act (CA) 1989, s.110, which amended CA 1985, s.35. The effect of the amendment was one which, in relation to a company's dealings with third parties, finally abolished the *ultra vires* rule. Section 35(1) (as amended) provided that:

> The validity of an act done by a company shall not be called into question on the ground of lack of capacity by reason of anything in the company's memorandum.

The intention behind s.35 was to remove the *ultra vires* rule in respect of third-party interests. Although the provision did not afford a company the capacity of a natural person, corporate capacity was nevertheless unrestricted by the contents of the memorandum. Although the CA 1989 did not remove the need for an objects clause, it sought to avoid the practice of prolonged clauses via the introduction of a standard type of objects clause (introduced by CA 1985, s.3A). The standard clause allowed companies to pursue any activity within a commercial context. In adopting an objects clause in line with s.3A, it should be noted that if a company wished to place a limitation on a power to exercise the general commercial objects (limitations on the exercise of objects were found in cases decided pre Companies Act 1989; see, e.g. *Simmonds* v. *Heffer* [1983] BCLC 298 and *Rosemary Simmons Memorial Housing Association Ltd* v. *UDT Ltd* [1986] 1 WLR 1440), then the limitation had to be separately provided for as an 'additional extra' to the '3A type' objects clause. However, where limitations on the '3A type' objects were included, such limitations would not defeat the commercial capacity of a company in its dealings with third parties; s.35(1) prevented this from happening. Nevertheless, limitations contained in the objects clause would regulate the powers of the board of directors and a transaction falling foul of a stipulated limitation, while not *ultra vires* a third party, would render any director acting contrary to the terms of the limitation (subject to a special resolution of the general meeting ratifying the director's act) liable to contribute personally to any loss sustained as a consequence of the transaction (see CA 1985, s.35(3)).

Political donations

In a like manner, corporate powers untouched by the CA 1985, s.3A definition but which the company wished to include additionally within its objects clause needed to be expressly provided for; such powers included the ability to make charitable or political donations. However, it is to be noted that in respect of the latter and following the enactment in February 2001, of the Political Parties, Elections and Referendum Act 2000, a company, if it wished to make a political donation, could do so, providing it required the approval of the general meeting by an ordinary resolution. Political donations are now governed by CA 2006, ss.362–79. Again, under the CA 2006, an ordinary resolution is required to confer a company with authorisation to make a political donation where the donation exceeds £5,000 in the period of 12 months ending with the date on which that donation is made. Any authorisation has effect for a period of four years beginning with the date on which it was passed unless the directors determine, or the articles require, that it is to have effect for a shorter period. The power of the directors to propose a political donation is subject to any provision of the articles that operates to prevent them from doing so. If the directors breach this requirement they will be collectively liable to repay the amount of the donation, to the company. The holders of not less than 5 per cent of the company's issue share capital may, with the leave of the court, enforce this right in the company's name against the directors.

Shareholder protection

By retaining the concept of an objects clause, the CA 1989 maintained one of the initial justifications of the *ultra vires* rule, namely, shareholder protection.

Indeed, the ability of a shareholder to prevent the company from pursuing a transaction which fell outside its objects clause was expressly maintained by the 1989 Act (introduced as CA 1985, s.35(2)). Nevertheless, s.35(2) contained a severe limitation on the ability of a shareholder to intervene, insofar as intervention was not possible where the company acted in furtherance of an existing legal obligation. Therefore, a commercial transaction which went beyond a company's capacity, would, insofar as it was subject to a prior contractual agreement, be outside the ambit of shareholder control, i.e. following the agreement relating to the transaction, a legal obligation would be created to negate the effect of CA 1985, s.35(2).

The effect of the CA 2006

The CA 2006 no longer compels a company to register an objects clause and as such a company's objects may be unrestricted. However, a company may include an objects clause within its articles (note, the objects clause will no longer be contained in the memorandum as the memorandum ceases to have any constitutional effect).

CA 2006, s.31 provides that:

(1) Unless a company's articles specifically restrict the objects of the company, its objects are unrestricted.
(2) Where a company amends its articles so as to add, remove or alter a statement of the company's objects –

   (a) it must give notice to the registrar,
   (b) on receipt of the notice, the registrar shall register it, and
   (c) the amendment is not effective until entry of that notice on the register.

Although a company may (where it chooses to adopt an objects clause) restrict the scope of its objects, the restriction will have no effect in relation to third party dealings. However, the restriction may operate as an internal fetter in respect of limiting the powers of the directors. Therefore, at best, the significance of an objects clause will only affect the relationship between the membership and its directors. In relation to the *ultra vires* rule, the CA 2006 makes no substantive difference to the effect of CA 1985, s.35 save that the relevant provision, namely CA 2006, s.39 provides that:

> The validity of an act done by a company shall not be called into question on the ground of lack of capacity by reason of anything in the company's constitution.

It is to be noted that the CA 2006 contains no specific provision (unlike CA 1985, s.35(2)) in respect of a shareholder's ability to challenge a proposed transaction that, if pursued, would fall foul of the company's objects clause (i.e. if the objects are restricted by the articles).

12.3   THE AUTHORITY OF DIRECTORS AND OTHERS TO BIND THE COMPANY

The agency relationship

The rules of agency determine whether an individual is possessed of an authority to bind the company in a contractual relationship with a third party. There are two principal forms of valid authority: actual authority – which may be express, implied or usual (real); and second, ostensible (apparent) authority. The directors of a company, acting as a collective body, are invested with the powers of the company; the company is the principal in the agency relationship. Subject to a contrary intention within a company's articles, the actual authority to exercise the powers of the directors or part of those powers may be delegated to individual directors, a committee of directors or to directors occupying an executive position. The delegation of actual authority follows a resolution passed by the directors to appoint a director or committee of directors to take charge of specific corporate powers. A delegation of actual authority in any matter is termed an express actual authority. The delegation of actual authority may also be implied. For example, where a director is expressly or impliedly appointed to a particular executive position, the director concerned will have an implied authority to bind the company in a manner consistent with the powers associated with that position, that is, a usual (real) authority (see, e.g. *Hely Hutchinson* v. *Brayhead Ltd* [1968] 1 QB 549).

An executive position to which an implied actual authority is attached may be subject to express restrictions, imposed by either the collective will of the directors or the company's articles. Here the implied authority granted may be more restrictive than the usual authority ordinarily associated with the position in question. However, where an implied authority is subject to express restrictions imposed by the company's articles, the effect of those restrictions will be consumed in relation to a third party acting in good faith, and be made redundant in accordance with CA 2006, s.40.

Ostensible authority operates following a representation from the company (the principal) to a third party. The representation is to the effect that a particular person (the agent) possesses the necessary authority to bind the company. An officer of a company who possesses ostensible authority will have no actual authority to perform the act to which the ostensible authority relates. In effect, ostensible authority will be established where there is a express or implied representation (by conduct or acquiescence) from the directors or duly authorised executive that acknowledges the right of the company's agent to bind the company in a particular transaction (see, e.g. *Freeman & Lockyer* v. *Buckhurst Park Properties Ltd* [1964] 2 QB 480 and *First Energy Ltd* v. *Hungarian International Bank Ltd* [1993] BCC 533). However, in cases where a third party seeks to rely on ostensible authority in respect of a director's conduct or acquiescence, ostensible authority will not operate if the third party was aware that the purported agent of the company had never been afforded an authority to bind the company (see, e.g. *Heinl* v. *Jyske Bank (Gibraltar) Ltd* [1999] Lloyd's Rep 511).

Prior to European Communities Act 1972, s.9 the formation of an agency relationship was also dependent upon the potential scope of an officer's authority to act as determined by the company's constitutional documents, to the extent that a third party could not rely on an officer's authority to bind a company where the authority relied upon was outside the ambit of the officer's authority so determined by the company's constitution. A third party was deemed to have constructive notice of the contents of the memorandum and articles. However, as a consequence of the European Communities Act 1972 and subsequent legislation, the relevance of the company's constitution as the ultimate source of a company's capacity to delegate authority is no longer of importance in relation to third party transactions.

The indoor management rule (the Turquand rule)

The indoor management rule, derived from the case of *Royal British Bank* v. *Turquand* (1856) 6 E & B 327, provides that when dealing with a company, a third party is not bound to ensure that all the internal regulations of the company have been complied with in respect of the exercise of an authority to bind the company. The operation of the rule is subject to a number of exceptions, namely:

- a third party with actual knowledge that a transaction is outside the authority conferred by the company's constitution cannot plead the rule (see, e.g. *Howard* v. *Patent Ivory Manufacturing Co* (1833) 38 Ch D 156);
- a third party cannot rely on the rule in circumstances where he or she is an insider, namely where he or she is an officer of the company (see, e.g. *Morris* v. *Kansen* [1946] AC 459);
- where there are suspicious circumstances surrounding the authorisation of a transaction and the third party should reasonably have been aware of such circumstances, the third party will not be able to rely on the rule (see e.g. *Underwood* v. *Bank of Liverpool & Martins Ltd* [1924] 1 KB 755);
- the rule will not operate in circumstances where the contractual authorisation was a forgery (see, e.g. *Ruben* v. *Great Fingall Consolidated* [1906] AC 439);
- where the necessary authorisation for a transaction requires the passing of a special resolution, a third party will be deemed to have notice of the outcome of the resolution, as a special resolution must be registered and therefore is open to public inspection (see e.g. *Irvine* v. *Union Bank of Australia* (1877) 2 App Cas 366). However, the rule would apply in a situation where an ordinary resolution was required to validate an exercise of authority because an ordinary resolution does not require registration.

The indoor management rule is operative in relation to the company's internal procedures. However, a third party is not entitled to rely on the rule to assert an assumption that an officer of a company had been given an authority by the board to act in excess of his or her actual or usual authority. In abolishing the doctrine of constructive notice, the companies legislation (discussed further below) has, to a large extent, extinguished the need for the indoor management rule. However, the rule may still be of assistance in matters concerning a board's delegation of authority. For example, where the board delegates authority but in doing so places internal restrictions (other than restrictions contained in the constitution) on the ability of the agent to carry out his or her functions (a matter not covered by the legislation, see below), then, in accordance with the Turquand rule, the third party will not, unless he or she acted in bad faith, be deemed to have knowledge of the said restrictions; he or she may assume that the director in question acts with a usual authority.

The governing legislation

In addition to curtailing the *ultra vires* rule, the companies legislation, in an attempt to produce a commercial climate of contractual freedom, seeks to limit restrictions placed upon the authority of company directors. The legislation applicable to directors' authority is aimed at complementing that made in connection with matters relating to the scope of a company's capacity to enter into contractual relationships. Accordingly, providing a third party acts in good faith when entering into a contract with a company, the power of the directors to bind the company or authorise others to do so is, as a consequence of CA 2006, s.40 (substituting CA 1985, s.35A(1)) deemed free of any limitation under the company's constitution. Section 40(1) provides:

> In favour of a person dealing with a company in good faith, the power of the directors to bind the company, or authorise others to do so, is deemed to be free of any limitation under the company's constitution.

In common with its statutory predecessor (CA 1985, s.35A(1)), the effect of CA 2006, s.40 is that the directors of a company will act as the guardian of the principal's (the company's) ability to delegate authority. Section 40 specifically vests this guardianship in the 'directors' although unlike CA 1985, s.35A(1), the term 'board of directors' is not used. The significance behind the removal of the term 'board of directors' may be considered radical if, as is possible, the term 'directors' is interpreted in a manner that permits an individual director to bind the company as of right even in circumstances where the individual director does not, in seeking to bind the company, have the support or authority of the collective board of directors.

However, this 'radical' interpretation must be questionable given that the management powers of a company are ultimately vested in the directors as a collective body and not in the hands of individual directors. Further, although s.40 provides that a third party is not to be deprived of the benefit of an agreement with a company in circumstances where the directors exceed limitations placed on their powers by the company's constitution, limitations placed on a director's authority to bind the company, by the rules of agency will surely still prevail. 'Constitutional limitations' include those derived from a resolution of the company or of any class of shareholders, or from any agreement between the members of the company or of any class of shareholders.

In accordance with CA 2006, s.40(4) (following CA 1985, s.35A) a member of a company is afforded a limited right to challenge an act of the directors where the act in question is beyond the powers of the directors. This provision may, for example, be relevant where a company retains an objects clause but the directors propose to exceed the stated objects. Section 40(4) states:

> This section does not affect any right of a member of the company to bring proceedings to restrain the doing of an action that is beyond the powers of the directors. But no such proceedings lie in respect of an act to be done in fulfilment of a legal obligation arising from a previous act of the company.

Nevertheless, the difficulty with this provision is in its requirement that a member must establish that the 'challenged act' was not subject to an existing legal obligation. For example, a company will inevitably enter into some form of legal obligation with a third party prior to the commencement of an agreed act. While the ability to enter into a legal obligation (i.e. a contract) could theoretically be challenged by a member of the company on the premise that it constituted an infringement of the directors' powers, the subsequent performance of the contract could not be challenged on the basis of s.40(4). The obligation (for example, the contractual agreement), once created, will negate the effect of s.40(4).

For the purposes of CA 2006, s.40(1), a third party must deal with the company in good faith. However, a person is presumed to have acted in good faith unless the contrary is proved. The fact that a third party knows that a corporate act went beyond the powers of the directors as governed by the company's constitution is, in itself, insufficient to establish bad faith and as such this extends the protection afforded by the Turquand rule insofar as it removes the first exception to the Turquand rule (discussed above). As with the CA 1985, the CA 2006 provides no definition of 'bad faith'. However, it is suggested that bad faith will be limited to circumstances where the court deems that it was unconscionable for the third party to seek to enforce the contract. In the unlikely event that a third party is unable to rely on CA 2006, s.40, a transaction involving a breach of director's authority may nevertheless be ratified by an ordinary resolution of the general meeting. It is to be noted that CA 2006, s.40 does not affect any potential liability incurred by a director(s), or any other person, by reason of a director(s) exceeding his or her powers.

In the context of CA 2006, s.40, the abolition of the constructive notice rule is subject to one exception in the guise of CA 2006, s.41 (replacing CA 1985, s.322A). Namely, where a company enters into a transaction or other act (otherwise covered by s.40) and the parties to the transaction include an insider, i.e. a director of the company or of its holding company or a person connected with any such director, then in such circumstances, the transaction will be voidable at the instance of the company (by ordinary resolution) (CA 2006, s.41(2)). Whether or not the transaction is avoided, the insider and any director of the company who authorised the transaction, is liable to account to the company for any gain he or she has made directly or indirectly by the transaction, and to indemnify the company for any loss or damage resulting from the transaction (CA 2006, s.41(3)). However, an insider, other than a director of the company, is not liable if he or she shows that at the time the transaction was entered into he or she did not know that the directors were exceeding their powers (CA 2006, s.41(5)). Nothing in s.41 is to be read as excluding the operation of any other enactment or rule of law by virtue of which the transaction may be called in question or any liability to the company may arise.

It is to be noted that the transaction will cease to be voidable if, by CA 2006, s.41(4):

(a) restitution of any money or other asset which was the subject matter of the transaction is no longer possible, or
(b) the company is indemnified for any loss or damage resulting from the transaction, or
(c) rights acquired bona fide for value and without actual notice of the directors' exceeding their powers by a person who is not party to the transaction would be affected by the avoidance, or
(d) the transaction is affirmed by the company.

The content of CA 2006, s.41 does not affect the rights of any party to the transaction other than a director or insider (i.e. those covered by s.41(2)). Nevertheless, the court may, on the application of the company or any such party, make an order affirming, severing or setting aside the transaction on such terms as appear to the court to be just.

The judicial interpretation of CA 2006, ss.40 and 41

The judicial interpretation to be afforded to CA 2006, ss.40–1 is, given the similarity with CA 1985, ss.35A and 322A, likely to follow the interpretation of the latter provisions. In *Smith* v. *Henniker-Major & Co* [2003] Ch 182, the Court of Appeal held that a director was unable to take the benefit of s.35A, in respect of a purported agreement involving himself and the company in circumstances where there had been no delegation of authority to the director. In effect, the director (S) sought to ignore the crucial requirement of s.35A, namely, a director's authority to act must originate from the directors as a collective body. Without the requisite authority, S had no more authority to take a decision in the name of the company than its office boy; the agreement was therefore a nullity. Further, the Court of Appeal concluded that while in a technical sense, a director could be classed as a 'person' for the purposes of s.35A, nevertheless, a director was subject to and caught by s.322A. Following on from *Smith* v. *Henniker-Major & Co*, it is to be noted that in *EIC Services* v. *Phipps* [2004] 2 BCLC 589, the Court of Appeal construed s.35A in a manner whereby a 'person dealing with a company' would not include a member of the company. The court held that in the context of a company, s.35A naturally referred to persons other than the company and its members.

CHAPTER 13

The disqualification of company directors

13.1 INTRODUCTION

The disqualification process is governed by the Company Directors Disqualification Act (CDDA) 1986. The objective of a disqualification order is temporarily to remove a director's future capacity to participate in the management activities of a company. Although provisions of the CDDA 1986 may be implemented against a person involved in the management of a solvent company, examples of corporate mismanagement, giving rise to the imposition of a disqualification order, will be most evident following the collapse of a corporate enterprise. While corporate failure may be attributed to factors unrelated to managerial abuse or incompetence, it is often caused (or at least compounded) by managerial error or wrongdoing. During the period in which a person is subject to a disqualification order, the public interest will be protected by the removal of that person's capacity to repeat his or her past misconduct in respect of the future management of another company.

13.2 THE DISQUALIFICATION REGIME

Although the CDDA 1986 is permissive of a disqualification order being imposed against any person involved in the management of a company (save for ss.6, 8 and 9 where the person must be a director) in the vast majority of cases a person made subject to a disqualification order will have acted in the capacity of a company director. For the purposes of the CDDA 1986, the definition of a director is that of 'any person occupying the position of director, by whatever name called' (see CDDA 1986, s.22(4)). This vague definition is the same as that found in the Companies Act 2006 (CA 2006). A disqualification order may also be imposed against a shadow director. (For further discussion relating to the definition of a director, see **Chapter 10**.)

Under CDDA 1986, s.1(1), the effect of a disqualification order is such that the disqualified person shall not, without the leave of the court:

- be a director of a company; or
- act as an insolvency practitioner or administrator of a company; or
- be a receiver or manager of a company's property; or
- in any way, whether directly or indirectly, be concerned or take part in the promotion, formation or management of a company.

The disqualification period takes effect from the date of the order and for the duration of the order, a person is disqualified from acting in all the capacities indicated by s.1(1). In accordance with CDDA 1986, s.13, a breach of a disqualification order carries a maximum penalty of two years' imprisonment and a fine. A person in breach of the order will also be made jointly and severally liable (with the company and any other relevant person) for the debts of the company incurred during the period in which the disqualified person acted in breach of the order (CDDA 1986, s.15).

The register of disqualification orders

Under CDDA 1986, s.18(2), the Secretary of State is obliged to maintain a register of disqualification orders. The register is open to public inspection on the payment of a small fee. Where the duration of a disqualification order has expired, the Secretary of State must, in accordance with CDDA 1986, s.18(3), remove the entry from the register and all particulars relating to the order.

13.3   DISCRETIONARY DISQUALIFICATION ORDERS

CDDA 2006, s.2

Section 2 permits the court to impose a disqualification order in circumstances where a person is convicted of an indictable offence connected with the promotion, formation, management or liquidation of a company, or with the receivership or management of a company's property. It is unnecessary to establish that the indictable offence was committed in the course of the day-to-day management of the affairs of a company or that the offence was associated with an improper exercise or abuse of the administration of a company's affairs. However, to impose a disqualification order under CDDA 1986, s.2, the nature of the indictable offence must be connected to a person's involvement in the management of the company's affairs.

For the purposes of s.2, any court with a jurisdiction to wind up a company may impose a disqualification order. Alternatively, s.2(2) provides that the disqualification order may be imposed by the court in which the person was convicted of the indictable offence. The maximum period of disqualification is five years in the case of an order made by a court of summary jurisdiction and 15 years in any other case.

CDDA 1986, ss.3 and 5

Under CDDA 1986, ss.3 and 5, the court may impose a disqualification order in circumstances where a person is in persistent breach of provisions of the companies legislation that require any return, account or other document to be filed with, delivered, or sent, or notice of any matter to be given to the registrar of companies. Here the disqualification period is for a maximum period of five years. The difference between ss.3 and 5 is that under the former provision, a disqualification order may be made by a court with a jurisdiction to wind up a company, whereas under s.5, the disqualification order is restricted to the court of summary conviction at which the person was found guilty of an offence relating to a persistent breach of the companies legislation in relation to the return or filing, etc. of relevant documents.

CDDA 1986, s.4

Section 4 deals with the disqualification of a person who, during the winding up of a company, was shown to have acted in a fraudulent manner in the conduct of the company's affairs. Here the maximum disqualification period is 15 years. A person is judged to have acted in a fraudulent manner where the court considers that his or her conduct justified a guilty verdict (irrespective of whether that person has actually been convicted of an offence) in respect of a charge of:

(a)   fraudulent trading, under CA 2006, s.993; or
(b)   being otherwise guilty while an officer, liquidator, receiver of the company, or administrative receiver, of any fraud connected with the management of the company or any fraud related to any breach of duty to the company.

CDDA 1986, s.8

Section 8 of the CDDA 1986 provides that a person may be disqualified as a director of a company following a Department for Business, Enterprise and Regulatory Reform (BERR) (formerly the Department of Trade and Industry (DTI)) investigation. Here it must be established that the director's conduct was of a standard whereby he or she is judged unfit to be concerned in the management of a company. Under CDDA 1986, s.8, the maximum period of disqualification is 15 years.

CDDA 1986, s.10

Where a person is liable under the Insolvency Act (IA) 1986, s.213 (for fraudulent trading) or s.214 (for wrongful trading) then CDDA 1986, s.10 provides that the court may, of its own volition, impose a disqualification order against that person (see, e.g. *Re Brian D Pierson (Contractors) Ltd* [1999] BCC 26).

The maximum period of disqualification under s.10 is 15 years. Although s.10 offers no guidance on this matter, it may be assumed that the fraudulent or wrongful trading must be confirmed as conduct of an unfit nature of a type that would have established culpability under CDDA 1986, s.6 (discussed below). Given that both CDDA 1986, ss.6 and 10 penalise managerial misconduct in the context of an insolvent company and both carry the same maximum penalty in terms of the disqualification period, it would be inappropriate if a disqualification order could be imposed under s.10 in circumstances where the delinquent conduct was insufficient to justify a finding of unfitness. In all probability, conduct deserving of a s.10 order in the context of fraudulent trading will be classed as conduct of an unfit nature. However, in relation to wrongful trading, the delinquent conduct may not always be of a sufficiently serious nature to justify a comparison with conduct of an unfit nature. (IA 1986, ss.213 and 214 are discussed in **Chapter 2**.)

13.4   MANDATORY DISQUALIFICATION – CDDA 1986, S.6

CDDA 1986, ss.6 and 9 are the only provision within the CDDA 2006 that carry a mandatory disqualification period. CDDA 1986, s.6(4) provides for a mandatory disqualification period of a minimum period of two years. The maximum period of disqualification is 15 years. Under CDDA 1986, s.6(1), the court is under a duty to impose a disqualification order against any person in a case where:

(a)   that person is or has been a director of a company which has at any time become insolvent (while the person was a director or subsequently). An insolvent company is defined in broad terms by CDDA 1986, s.6(2) as either:

    (i)   a company which goes into liquidation at a time when its assets are insufficient for the payment of its debts and other liabilities and the expenses of the winding up;

    (ii)   where an administration order is made in relation to a company; or

    (iii)   where an administrative receiver is appointed to the company; and

(b)   that person's conduct as a director of the company (either taken alone or taken together with the person's conduct as a director of another company or companies) makes the person unfit to be concerned in the management of a company.

Commencement of proceedings

Where, in accordance with CDDA 1986, s.7(1), the Secretary of State considers it to be in the public interest, an application to impose a disqualification order under CDDA 1986, s.6, may be made:

(a) by the Secretary of State; or

(b) if the Secretary of State so directs in the case of a person who is or has been a director of a company, where the company is being wound up by the court in England and Wales, by the Official Receiver.

The prosecution of s.6 actions

In accordance with CDDA 1986, s.7(3), insolvency practitioners are under a statutory obligation to report to the BERR any director who is suspected of conducting the affairs of a company in an unfit manner. In submitting a report, the office holder must investigate conduct by reference to guidelines set out in CDDA 1986, Sched.1 (see below). The insolvency practitioner is required to consider matters of conduct on the basis of information acquired in the course of his or her normal duties and by reference to the books and records available to him or her. An insolvency practitioner is not obliged to undertake an investigation that he or she would not otherwise have considered necessary for the purposes of his or her administration. The Insolvency Service, a department of the BERR, is, through its Disqualification Unit, responsible for determining whether to commence proceedings.

A failing system

By the late 1990s, the growing number of prosecutions under CDDA 1986, s.6 was such as to endanger an already overburdened court system. For example, for the period 2000–1, 58 per cent of s.6 cases had not been concluded within two years from the commencement of proceedings and as such exceeded the two-year limit specified by CDDA 1986, s.7(2). Indeed, had it not been for the courts' willingness to adopt a summary form of procedure, the Carecraft procedure (taking its name from *Re Carecraft Construction Co Ltd* [1994] 1 WLR 172), the strain on the disqualification system would have been even more transparent. In 2000–1 the said summary procedure accounted for approximately 30 per cent of all s.6 cases. The *Carecraft* procedure was applied in circumstances where the facts relating to a director's misconduct were not disputed and where both the Secretary of State and the respondent were willing to allow the case to be dealt with on the understanding that an agreed disqualification order would be made for a period falling within one of the brackets specified in *Re Sevenoaks Stationers (Retail) Ltd* (discussed below).

The Insolvency Act 2000 – the undertaking procedure

Following the implementation of the Insolvency Act (IA) 2000, a statutory undertaking procedure was introduced for the disqualification of directors (s.6 and s.8 disqualifications). The purpose of this procedure was to create a more efficient disqualification system. The provisions of the IA 2000 which create the undertaking procedure are incorporated within the CDDA 1986.

CDDA 1986, s.1A permits the Secretary of State to accept an undertaking as an alternative to instigating disqualification proceedings through the courts. A director is not obliged to proceed via the undertaking procedure and obviously where a case is contested by a director it will continue to be heard by way of a court action. According to the Insolvency Service annual report and accounts 2005–6, close to 80 per cent of all disqualifications under s.6 now proceed by way of the undertaking procedure. The Secretary of State may accept an undertaking if it appears expedient in the public interest to do so (CDDA 1986, s.2A). Under the undertaking procedure a defendant will agree to refrain from acting as a director or in any other capacity so specified by CDDA 1986 ss.1A(1)(a) and (b) for a pre-determined period (i.e. a minimum duration of two years and a maximum duration of 15 years). However, a director who agrees to an undertaking may still seek leave to act under CDDA 1986, s.17 (discussed below).

The expected efficiency of the undertaking procedure should permit the Insolvency Service to prosecute disqualification cases with greater speed and in greater numbers, although the fact that only very serious instances of corporate malpractice will justify disqualification under s.6 may inhibit any substantial increase in the overall number of prosecutions. The statutory undertaking procedure advances the *Carecraft* procedure in a logical way and the undertaking procedure will extinguish any future need for disqualification proceedings to be determined by way of the *Carecraft* procedure. However, as delinquent directors will largely be dealt with in the absence of judicial and public scrutiny, the disqualification process has lost significant transparency (evidenced by, for example, a dramatic fall in the number of reported s.6 cases since the introduction of the undertaking procedure). Further, the Disqualification Unit will encounter additional costs and time burdens in respect of managing and administering the procedure.

Following a defendant's acceptance of the undertaking procedure, the courts will only be called upon to consider the merits or otherwise of a disqualification order in a situation where a defendant applies to have the duration of the order reduced or cancelled. The power of the court to vary the duration of an undertaking is provided for by CDDA 1986, s.8A.

Conduct of an unfit nature

In assessing whether conduct is of an unfit nature in respect of determining a director's culpability under s.6, the court, or the BERR under the undertaking procedure, must have particular regard to the matters set out in CDDA 1986, Sched.1, both Parts 1 and 2 (CDDA 1986, s.9). The matters mentioned in Sched.1, Part 1 require the court to consider whether a director against whom a disqualification order is sought was responsible for:

(a) any misfeasance or breach of any fiduciary or other duty in relation to the company;

(b) any misapplication or retention by the director of, or any conduct by the director giving rise to an obligation to account for, any money or property of the company;

(c) the extent of a director's responsibility for the company entering into any transaction liable to be set aside under IA 1986, Part XVI (provisions against debt avoidance);

(d) the extent of a director's responsibility for any failure by the company to comply with any of the following provisions of the CA 2006, namely:

(i) s.386 (formerly CA 1985, s.221) companies to keep accounting records;

(ii) s.388 (formerly CA 1985, s.222) where and for how long records are to be kept;

(iii) ss.162 and 275 (formerly CA 1985, s.228) register of directors and secretaries;

(iv) s.114 (formerly CA 1985, s.352) obligation to keep and enter up register of members;

(v) s.116 (formerly CA 1985, s.353) location of register of members;

(vi) s.854 (formerly CA 1985, s.363) duty of company to make annual returns; and

(vii) ss.875–877 (formerly CA 1985, ss.399, 415) company's duty to register charges which it creates;

(e) the extent of the director's responsibility for any failure by the directors of the company to comply with the following provisions of the CA 2006, namely:

(i) s.394 (formerly CA 1985, s.226) duty to prepare annual accounts; or

(ii) s.414 (formerly CA 1985, s.233) approval and signature of accounts.

The matters mentioned in Sched.1, Part 2 (where a company is insolvent) are as follows:

(f) the extent of the director's responsibility for the causes of the company becoming insolvent;

(g) the extent of the director's responsibility for any failure by the company to supply any goods or services which have been paid for (in whole or in part);

(h) the extent of the director's responsibility for the company entering into any transaction or giving any preference, being a transaction or preference:

(i) liable to be set aside under s.127 or IA 1986, ss.238–240; or

(ii) open to challenge under IA 1986, s.242 or s.243;

(i)   the extent of the director's responsibility for any failure by the directors of the company to comply with IA 1986, s.98 (duty to call creditors' meeting in creditors' voluntary winding up);

(j)   any failure by the director to comply with any obligation imposed on him or her by or under any of the following provisions of the IA 1986:

    (i)   s.22 (company's statement of affairs in administration);

    (ii)   s.47 (statement of affairs to administrative receiver);

    (iii)   s.66 (statement of affairs in Scottish receivership);

    (iv)   s.99 (directors' duty to attend meeting, statement of affairs in creditors' voluntary winding up);

    (v)   s.131 (statement of affairs in winding up by the court);

    (vi)   s.234 (duty of anyone with company property to deliver it up);

    (vii) s.235 (duty to cooperate with liquidator, etc.).

It should be stressed that in determining unfit conduct, the crucial factor will be the seriousness of the conduct and not necessarily the type of conduct in question. In the majority of cases dealing with disqualification orders under s.6, it is rare to find proceedings which are commenced on the basis of just one count of alleged misconduct. Whilst it is possible to disqualify a director on the premise of one complaint of misconduct, or to indicate that a specific complaint taken from a number of complaints of misconduct, was sufficient to justify disqualification, it is more common to find that a director's unfitness will be established in relation to a series of delinquent acts. The seriousness of a particular course of conduct will be measured in accordance with its perceived prejudicial effect in relation to public interest considerations. Public interest factors will include the interests of, for example, shareholders, creditors, customers and employees.

The question of whether a director's conduct was of an unfit nature will always be one of fact, to be determined from the individual circumstances of any given case. Other than where a director conducts the affairs of a company in a manner which is established to be of a serious and fraudulent nature, it is impossible to predict with any degree of certainty whether a director's conduct may be properly labelled as unfit conduct. In considering the matters mentioned in Sched.1, it must be determined whether, on a balance of probabilities, a director's conduct was sufficiently serious to justify his or her disqualification. The courts have expressed an unwillingness to impose disqualification orders in situations whereby the fault element attached to a director's act or omission was attributable to business practices of no more than a naive and imprudent standard. The courts have emphasised that misconduct must be established at a level which is considered harmful to the public interest, namely where it conveys a clear exploitation of the privileges attributable to the limited liability status of a company. Such exploitation will ordinarily be exhibited following a deliberate or patently reckless or negligent abuse of creditor interests or a persistent failing to abide by provisions of the companies legislation (see, e.g. *Secretary of State for Trade and Industry* v. *Gray* [1995] 1 BCLC 276).

In *Re Sevenoaks Stationers (Retail) Ltd* [1991] Ch 164, the Court of Appeal stated that a disqualification order should only be made if there is conclusive proof of conduct which established that a director's conduct amounted to commercially culpable behaviour of a type constituting a threat to the commercial community. The ability to label a particular course of business malpractice as one equating to commercially culpable behaviour will be a question of fact dependent upon the circumstances of each individual case (see, e.g. *Re Civica Investments Ltd* [1983] BCLC 456).

Conduct in relation to other companies

In accordance with CDDA 1986, s.6(1)(b), and for the purpose of determining whether a director's conduct was unfit in the management of a company, the nature of a director's conduct in relation to any other company will obviously be irrelevant where that conduct was of a satisfactory nature. Prior to the Court of Appeal's decision in *Re County Farm Inns Ltd; Secretary of State* v. *Ivens* [1997] BCC 801, the courts' interpretation of s.6(1)(b) had been one whereby a director's misconduct in the affairs of another company had to be of a type which was the same as or similar in nature to the director's misconduct in relation to his or her management of the lead company. However, following the decision in *Re County Farm Inns Ltd; Secretary of State* v. *Ivens,* it is now clear that any impropriety in relation to the conduct of another company may be advanced to support a finding of unfitness in relation to the director's misconduct in respect of the lead company. There is no requirement to be inferred from the wording of s.6(1)(b) that the conduct has to be the same or similar in the other companies to that alleged in the lead company, as very different types of misconduct can be taken into account and accumulated to reach a decision that a director is unfit to be concerned in the management of a company. If there is some misconduct in relation to the lead company, there is no reason why the acts in relation to the other company(ies) need to be of the same or a similar nature, and why the same process of aggregation should not be capable of being carried out, remembering, of course, that the other companies are different companies and the acts occurred at different times and in different circumstances, so they may have a different probative force. Further, while for the purposes of s.6 the lead company must be insolvent, it is unnecessary, in respect of s.6(2)(b), for any other company in which the director's conduct is called into question to be insolvent.

Conduct falling outside the ambit of CDDA 1986, s.6

A disqualification order will not be imposed under CDDA 1986, s.6 where a director's imprudent conduct was undertaken without any form of malice, recklessness or serious neglect. Therefore, even if a director is aware that a company is trading whilst insolvent, that fact alone will not substantiate a finding of unfit conduct. However, if the said director was aware or should have been aware that, at the time of trading in an insolvent state, there was no reasonable prospect of the company avoiding insolvency, then in such circumstances there will be a strong presumption of unfitness (see, e.g. *Re Uno Plc; Secretary of State for Trade and Industry* v. *Gill* [2006] BCC 725). Further, in *Re Bath Glass Ltd* [1988] BCLC 329, Peter Gibson J concluded that two directors, party to the company's wrongful trading (over a period of two years) should not be disqualified under s.6, because although their misconduct had been imprudent, it had not been undertaken with an intention to benefit themselves at the expense of the company's creditors. This finding as to the director's honesty in the conduct of the company's affairs had been substantiated, in part, by their willingness to make a firm financial commitment to the company by, for example, taking shares in the company in return for repaying the company's overdraft. In addition, the two directors had sought to act upon professional advice, had drawn up regular and meticulous (albeit inaccurate) business plans and genuinely and reasonably believed that the company would be able to trade itself out of its difficulties.

However, other than where a director of an insolvent company honestly and reasonably believed that the company was capable of trading itself out of its financial difficulties, a director's continued involvement in the affairs of the insolvent company will provide *prima facie* evidence of his or her unfit conduct. Nevertheless, in such a case, the presumption that conduct was of an unfit nature may be overturned. For example, in accordance with the decision of Chadwick J in *Secretary of State* v. *Gash* [1997] 1 BCLC 341, a director of an insolvent company, who continues to hold office, despite realising the folly of existing corporate policy, may escape any charge of having acted in an unfit manner if it can be established that he or she objected to and took no part in, or had no responsibility for, the deployment of the ill-fated policy.

Civil proceedings and human rights

As a contravention of s.6 invokes no form of criminal liability, the proceedings are regulated by the civil law and as such a person's culpability must be established in accordance with the balance of probabilities test (see, e.g. *Secretary of State* v. *Deverell* [2000] 2 All ER 365). Given the civil nature of the proceedings, it follows that hearsay evidence and findings of primary and secondary fact will be more readily admissible than had the proceedings been dealt with under the criminal law. Further, s.6 proceedings are of a regulatory as opposed to criminal nature, and as such art.6 of the European Convention on Human Rights (ECHR) will have a limited application. The Human Rights Act 1998 gives effect to the rights and freedoms guaranteed under the ECHR. According to the ECHR, art.6(1) provides:

In the determination of his civil rights and obligations or of any criminal charge against him, everyone is entitled to a fair and public hearing within a reasonable time by an independent and impartial tribunal established by law.

As disqualification cases are of a civil nature they will not ordinarily be within the jurisdiction of art.6(1) (see, e.g. *R* v. *Secretary of State for Trade and Industry, ex p. McCormick* [1998] BCC 379, *DC, HS and AD* v. *United Kingdom* [2000] BCC 710 and *Re Westminster Property Management Ltd* [2001] BCC 121). However, a director subject to s.6 proceedings is entitled to a fair hearing (see, e.g. *WGS and MSLS* v. *United Kingdom* [2000] BCC 719) and delays in the prosecution of proceedings under the CDDA 1986, may constitute a violation of art.6(1) (see, e.g. *EDC* v. *United Kingdom* [1998] BCC 370, *Davies* v. *United Kingdom* [2005] BCC 401. However, contrast *Re Blackspur Group plc (No.3); Secretary of State for Trade and Industry* v. *Eastaway* [2003] BCC 520).

Protecting the public interest

Although a director's capacity to act in the future management of a company is the essential yardstick to determine whether, in any given instance, a disqualification order should be imposed, it must be remembered that the imposition of a disqualification order is mandatory. Accordingly, CDDA 1986, s.6 prohibits any consideration of a director's ability or potential ability to reform his or her past misconduct in respect of his or her involvement in the management of a future enterprise. Indeed, in *Secretary of State* v. *Gray* [1995] 1 BCLC 276, the Court of Appeal made it clear that notwithstanding a director's potential to reform his or her past indiscretions, the court was obliged to impose a disqualification order where it was established that the director's past conduct was of an unfit nature. Although extenuating circumstances may influence any decision in relation to whether a director's past conduct reached an appropriate standard of unfitness, the decision to impose a disqualification order must not be influenced by considering a director's capacity to reform his or her past activities. Nevertheless, a director's potential to reform past misconduct, portrayed, for example, by reason of his or her success in the management of another existing company, may be a significant mitigating factor in determining the length of any disqualification order (see, e.g. *Re Pamstock Ltd* [1994] 1 BCLC 716).

The duration of a s.6 disqualification order

CDDA 1986, s.6(4) provides that the length of a disqualification order must be for a minimum of two years and for a maximum period of 15 years. In determining the length of a disqualification period, the court (or BERR in respect of the undertaking procedure) must consider the extent and seriousness of a director's misconduct. Where a director's misconduct is founded on dishonest conduct, it is logical to assume that the disqualification period will be of a greater duration than had the misconduct been of a reckless or negligent manner. Further, it may be assumed that where a director holds a senior executive position, or otherwise has a capacity to dictate a company's operations, the extent of his or her culpability (and the duration of any disqualification order) will be greater than in a situation where the director does not occupy such a commanding position.

In *Re Sevenoaks Stationers (Retail) Ltd* [1991] Ch 164, the Court of Appeal advanced guidelines to the lower courts in respect of the duration of disqualification orders. However, notwithstanding the potential benefit of such guidance, in reality, the guidelines amounted to little more than commonsense generalisations. They were as follows:

1. The top bracket of disqualification for a period of over 10 years should be reserved for particularly serious cases of commercial abuse. Here, this bracket could also include cases where a director had a past record of being made subject to a disqualification order(s).
2. The middle bracket of disqualification for a period between six and 10 years should apply in serious cases.
3. The minimum bracket of between two and five years should be applied where a director was found to be unfit in the management of a company. However, while unfit, the conduct would not be of a sufficiently serious nature to justify disqualification within the first or second brackets.

Mitigation

In considering the length of a disqualification period or, in respect of CDDA 1986, s.17 (discussed below), whether the court should grant leave to a person made subject to a disqualification order, the courts are permitted to take account of mitigating factors. The significance and effect of a mitigating factor will be dependent upon issues relating to the justice of an individual case. In considering the justice issue, the court must attempt to balance the respective interests of the defendant against the seriousness of the unfit conduct and its perceived threat to the public interest. The following factors are examples of circumstances that may be considered.

- A director's conduct during the actual course of the disqualification process may, in appropriate circumstances, act as a mitigating factor if, for example, such conduct enables the proceedings to be dealt with in a more efficient manner. Accordingly, cooperation with the liquidator or by admitting responsibility for the alleged acts of misconduct may result in a director escaping a heftier disqualification period than would otherwise been the case.

- In at least one reported case, namely, *Re Melcast (Wolverhampton) Ltd,* [1991] BCLC 288, the age of a director (he was 75 years old) was, of itself, considered to be a mitigating factor. Here the court imposed a more lenient disqualification period than the nature of the director's conduct would ordinarily have warranted. However, a director's age may be of more relevance as a mitigating factor where the director is also suffering from very poor health. Indeed, there would seem little point in imposing a lengthy disqualification order against a person of advancing years who is physically or mentally incapable of repeating his or her past misconduct.
- A director who is to be disqualified may, in terms of the calculation of the disqualification period to be imposed, also hope to be afforded some leniency where, prior to the collapse of the company, he or she sought to expend, or put at risk, his or her own personal funds, in an attempt to secure the company's financial well being. The director's personal losses may be justified as a mitigating factor in the sense that such funds were voluntarily provided to aid the company's financial position. Indeed, as a result of the loss of personal funds the court may consider that the director has, to some extent, already been penalised for his or her misconduct of the company's affairs (see, e.g. *Re Pamstock Ltd* [1994] 1 BCLC 716).
- A director may be afforded a more lenient disqualification period where the conduct of the company's affairs was attributable to his or her reliance on the skill and expertise of a professional advisor (see, e.g. *Re Park Properties Ltd* [1997] 2 BCLC 530).

An application for leave to act (CDDA 1986, s.17)

Although a director must be disqualified when deemed unfit for the purposes of CDDA 1986, s.6, the said director may, at any time during the term of the disqualification order, apply for leave under CDDA 1986, s.17, to act in the management of a specified company (but not the company(ies) in which his or her management conduct was judged to be of an unfit nature or any future company, i.e. one that he or she was not already involved in prior to the disqualification). The practical effect of a grant of leave is the creation of a modified type of disqualification order, whereby a director is disqualified in a general sense but is nevertheless allowed to continue in the management of another company (or companies), so specified by the terms of the order (see, e.g. *Secretary of State for Trade and Industry* v. *Rosenfield* [1999] BCC 413). The justification for the grant of leave is that the director's involvement in the management of the specified enterprise is considered beneficial to the public interest, for example, beneficial in the sense of protecting the interests of the employees and creditors of the specified company.

As the modified order permits a director with a dubious past history in the management of a company(ies) to, in part, escape the consequences of his or her past indiscretions, it must be applied with caution. Obviously, when considering a grant of leave the court must ponder the likelihood of a director re-offending. The length of the disqualification order will be a relevant consideration in determining whether leave should be granted (see, e.g. *Hease v. Secretary of State for Trade and Industry* [2006] BPIR 425, where the period of disqualification was six years and the application under s.17 was refused). The court must be satisfied of the need to make the modified order and in doing so must always bear in mind that the purpose of a disqualification order is to safeguard the public interest. Where an order is made, it will normally be granted subject to specific conditions; notwithstanding that neither CDDA 1986, s.1 or s.17 provides the court with a capacity to grant leave subject to such specific conditions. The said specific conditions may include, for example, that the director provides an undertaking that he or she will set up proper financial controls in respect of the company (in which he or she continues in a management capacity), or that the director is required to appoint a further director to the company's board or a qualified accountant or auditor so approved by the court (see, e.g. *Re Gibson Davies Ltd* [1995] BCC 11).

CDDA 1986, s.9

A court is also obliged to impose a disqualification order against a director of a company, following a breach of competition law by the company. The breach must illustrate that the director is unfit to be concerned in the future management of a company. The maximum disqualification period is 15 years.

CHAPTER 14

The company in general meeting

14.1 INTRODUCTION

The powers and procedures attached to the general meeting of company shareholders is a subject area of company law that is subject to significant reform following the implementation of the Companies Act (CA) 2006. Historically, the general meeting was perceived as the ultimate source of corporate power. However, in modern society, the general meeting's position of power has declined in the management of corporate affairs. Nevertheless, the general meeting is still, in the exercise of its inherent powers, properly regarded as an essential organ of the body corporate. Although the general meeting's powers are limited, the effect of such powers may carry real influence in the management of a company's affairs.

The articles of a majority of companies are drafted in a manner whereby they confer the vast bulk of the powers of management on the company's board of directors. Nevertheless, the articles of a company normally reserve limited powers of management to the general meeting. For example, powers related to the election of directors, the remuneration of directors and the declaration of dividends up to an amount recommended by the directors. The companies legislation also reserves certain exclusive powers of management to the general meeting. The powers so reserved are few, but are nevertheless quite substantive, being concerned with the constitutional functioning of the company – for example, the power to alter the terms of the company's articles. In addition, the general meeting has a right, by ordinary resolution, to remove a director from office. This power is of some significance because where members of a company disagree with the board's management policy and command sufficient support, they may seek to alter the direction of management policy, by either threatening the directors with dismissal or, if that tactic fails, actually enforce the power of removal. (However, note **6.3**.)

The duty of the general meeting to act for the benefit of the company as a whole

In exercising its limited powers of management, the general meeting must, in a manner akin to the company's directors, apply its powers for the benefit of the company as a whole. In any given situation, the test to determine whether the general meeting acted for the benefit of the company as a whole is dominated by an objective consideration of whether the general meeting's powers were exercised for a proper purpose. However, the interpretation of the test to determine whether the general meeting acted for the benefit of the company as a whole is clouded in some confusion (see, e.g. *Clemens* v. *Clemens Bros Ltd* [1976] 2 All ER 268). Nevertheless, it is clear that a power reserved to the general meeting must not be used where its effect would be to defraud or seriously prejudice creditors. For example, in *Re Halt Garage* [1982] 3 All ER 1016, the court sought to determine whether a company's membership, which comprised a husband and wife team (both held directorships in the company) had, in authorising remuneration payments to themselves as directors, awarded payments which were in reality gratuitous distributions out of capital dressed up as remuneration. The company (which had been put into liquidation), sought (through its liquidator) the return of remuneration payments over a period of three years. In determining the matter the court, applying an objective test, considered the true nature of the payments in terms of the genuineness and honesty of the transaction and in doing so reached the conclusion that while there was no evidence that the husband's level of takings had been excessive or unreasonable, the level of takings paid to the wife had been unreasonably high. The wife had ceased to be active in the employment of the company and therefore was not entitled to remuneration during the period over which the complaint related. Although the company's articles included a power to award remuneration for the mere assumption of the office of director, Oliver J opined that the awards made to the wife were so out of proportion to the value attributed to her holding office that the court was justified in not treating them as genuine payments of remuneration but, rather, as dressed-up dividends out of capital. The payments to the wife had been invalidly authorised by the general meeting.

The general meeting's ability to ratify an irregular act of the directors

Where a company director commits a breach of duty or exceeds his or her authority in exercising a management power, the irregular act will, in most instances, be voidable. The general meeting may ratify the irregular act by an ordinary resolution (although the culpable director will not be allowed to vote on the resolution). However, an irregular act, if ratified, may be challenged by a minority shareholder(s) in circumstances where the general meeting's ratification was deemed not to be for the benefit of the company as a whole (i.e. a fraud on minority shareholders, giving rise to a derivative action, discussed in **Chapter 15**).

Although directors are not permitted to exercise powers which, by the terms of a company's articles, are vested in the general meeting, should such a usurpation of a power occur, the general meeting may nevertheless ratify the abuse of power by ordinary resolution, regardless of the fact that the power use would otherwise have required a special resolution (see, e.g. *Grant* v. *United Kingdom Switchback Railways Co* (1888) 40 Ch D 135). While in such a case the general meeting's power to ratify the abuse of power by ordinary resolution would appear contradictory to the manner in which the general meeting could otherwise have exercised the power, in reality, the power to ratify affects the approval of an unauthorised act, as opposed to an attempt to usurp the terms of the company's articles; ratification does not confer future powers on the directors, whereas an alteration of the articles would have a permanent effect.

However, if an ordinary resolution of the general meeting purports to ratify an irregular act and the nature and type of act in question contravenes the terms of a company's articles, then in such a case the general meeting's attempted ratification would be invalid. For example, in *Boschoek Proprietary Co Ltd* v. *Fuke* [1906] 1 Ch 148, the directors of a company appointed a managing director at a level of remuneration in excess of the amount prescribed in the company's articles and also in contravention of a share qualification clause. The appointment was purportedly ratified by the general meeting. The court concluded that the general meeting could not, of itself, alter the terms of the appointment in contravention of the articles and as such the purported ratification was invalid. Until and unless altered, the articles bound the membership and the board of directors.

14.2 TYPES OF GENERAL MEETING

The annual general meeting

Prior to the introduction of the CA 2006 and except in a situation where a private company resolved to dispense with the holding of an annual general meeting (AGM), the Companies Act (CA) 1985 provided that a company was required to hold an AGM once every calendar year with no more than 15 months elapsing between each AGM. Following the introduction of the CA 2006, the position is now changed for private companies, via the introduction of a prescribed default regime. The effect of this regime is that unless there is a contrary intention within a private company's constitution, a private company will no longer be required to hold an AGM. However, the AGM requirement is retained for public companies. Every public company must hold a general meeting as its AGM in each period of six months beginning with the day following its accounting reference date (CA 2006, s.336(1)). In accordance with CA 2006, s.337, a notice calling an annual general meeting of a public company must state that the meeting is to be held as an AGM. The notice required may be shorter notice than that specified by CA 2006, s.307(2) (21 days' notice) or that contained in the company's articles if all the members entitled to attend and vote at the meeting agree to the shorter notice. The matters dealt with at a company's AGM are dependent upon the business raised by the board or individual members of the company, although where the holding of an AGM is applicable, prescribed procedural tasks will be addressed. The procedural tasks will include the appointment of an auditor and adoption of accounts, the receipt of the directors' report, the election of directors and, in appropriate circumstances, the determination of directors' remuneration.

CA 2006, s.338 provides that the members of a public company may require the company to give notice of a resolution which may properly be moved and is intended to be moved at that meeting. The request from members must be received by the company not later than:

(a)   six weeks before the AGM to which the requests relate; or
(b)   if later, the time at which notice is given of that meeting.

A company is required to give notice of a resolution once it has received requests that it do so from:

(a)   members representing at least 5 per cent of the total voting rights of all the members who have a right to vote on the resolution at the AGM to which the requests relate (excluding any voting rights attached to any shares in the company held as treasury shares); or
(b)   at least 100 members who have a right to vote on the resolution at the AGM to which the requests relate and hold shares in the company on which there has been paid up an average sum, per member, of at least £100. A resolution may properly be moved at an AGM unless:

(i)   it would, if passed, be ineffective (whether by reason of inconsistency with any enactment or the company's constitution or otherwise);
(ii)   it is defamatory of any person; or
(iii)   it is frivolous or vexatious.

The general meeting

A general meeting other than an AGM is simply referred to by the CA 2006 as a 'general meeting' (previously known as an 'extraordinary general meeting' (EGM)). A general meeting may be convened by any company at the will of the company's board of directors. Alternatively, the board may be required to convene a general meeting where, under CA 2006, s.303, they are requisitioned to do so by members holding not less than 10 per cent of the company's paid-up share capital; here the share capital must carry voting rights. In the case of a company not having a share capital, a general meeting may be requisitioned by members who, together, represent 10 per cent or more of the total voting rights of members entitled to vote. However, for a private company, the

10 per cent requirement will be reduced to 5 per cent if more than 12 months has elapsed from the end of the last general meeting called in pursuance of a requirement under CA 2006, s.303, or in relation to which any members of the company had (by virtue of an enactment, the company's articles or otherwise) rights with respect to the circulation of a resolution no less extensive than they would have had if the meeting had been so called at their request.

Where, under CA 2006, s.303, the directors of a company are requisitioned to call a meeting, they must do so within 21 days of receiving the requisition and must provide the membership with notice of the meeting (see, e.g. *Re Windward Islands (Enterprises Ltd)* (1988) 4 BCC 158). The meeting must be called no more than 28 days after the notice to convene the meeting is sent out. By CA 2006, s.305, where, after receiving the requisition, the directors fail to give notice of the meeting within the 21-day period, those seeking the requisition, or any of them representing more than one-half of the total voting rights of all of them, may convene the meeting, providing that the meeting is held before the end of three months from the date after the date on which the directors become subject to the requirement to call the meeting. Any reasonable expenses incurred by the members who requested the meeting that was caused by the failure of the directors to duly call a meeting must be reimbursed by the company. Any sum reimbursed by the company may be taken out of any sums due (or to become due) from the company to its directors in connection with the payment of fees or other remuneration in respect of the services of such of the directors that were in default.

14.3   FORMAL REQUIREMENTS FOR MEETINGS

The quorum requirement

CA 2006, s.318 states that unless a company's articles provide otherwise, two members (or proxies) must be present at a general meeting in order to satisfy the quorum requirement. In the case of single-member companies, one member present in person or by proxy will constitute a quorum. Where, at a general meeting, the quorum requirement is not satisfied, the meeting will be null and void, other than in a situation where the court employs its powers under CA 2006, s.306.

The notice requirement

CA 2006, s.308 provides that notice of an intention to call a general meeting of a company must be given in hard copy form and in either electronic form or by means of a website. Notice of a general meeting of a company must state the time and date of the meeting, and the place of the meeting together with the general nature of the business to be dealt with at the meeting (CA

2006, s.311). Notice of a general meeting must be sent to every member of the company, and every director. A previous requirement contained in CA 1985, s.387, that notice of a general meeting had to be given to the company's auditor, is no longer present within the CA 2006. The reference to members includes any person who is entitled to a share in consequence of the death or bankruptcy of a member, i.e. if the company has been notified of their entitlement. In the case of electronic or website communication, notice may be given partly by one such means and partly by another. Where notice is to be posted on a website, notice is not validly given by a company unless, as of the date of notifying a member of the presence of the notice on the website, the notification states that it concerns notice of a company meeting, specifying the place, date and time of the meeting. In the case of a public company the notification must also state whether the meeting will be an annual general meeting. The notice must be available on the website throughout the period beginning with the date of the notification and ending with the conclusion of the meeting (CA 2006, s.309).

In accordance with CA 2006, s.307, a general meeting of a private or public company (other than an adjourned meeting) must be called by notice of at least 14 days. A provision in a company's articles which seeks to increase the prescribed notice period will be valid although where a provision in the articles declares a shorter time period, the relevant provision will be deemed void, unless, in relation to the proposed meeting, it is agreed to by the holders of 90 per cent of the nominal value of the shares (the 90 per cent of members must have been entitled to attend and vote at the meeting).

Although an accidental failure on the part of a company to give notice to a member will rarely invalidate a meeting (see CA 2006, s.313), a deliberate act or omission on the part of a company that prevents a member from receiving proper and adequate notice of the meeting will render the meeting invalid (see, e.g. *Royal Mutual Benefit Building Society* v. *Sharman* [1963] 1 WLR 581).

Special notice

Where a provision of the companies legislation expressly stipulates a requirement to provide special notice of an intention to pass a resolution (e.g. the removal of a director or auditor), CA 2006, s.312 provides that the resolution, if passed, will not be effective if the proposers of that resolution failed to give at least 28 days' notice to the company before the date of the meeting at which the resolution was moved. On receiving special notice, a company must, where practicable, also provide its membership with 28 days' notice of the proposed resolution and must do so at the same time that it gives notice of the meeting at which the resolution is to be heard. Where this is not practicable, the company must give its members at least 14 days' notice before the meeting by way of an advertisement in a newspaper having an appropriate circulation, or in any other manner allowed by the company's articles. It should be noted that the validity of a meeting and any resolution passed at the meeting will not be called into question where, after notice of the intention to move such a resolution was given to the company, a meeting is called for a date 28 days or less after the notice was given (although at least 14 days' notice must be given).

Members' statements

CA 2006, s.314 provides that a company may be obliged to circulate to its membership a statement of not more than 1,000 words with respect to a matter referred to in a proposed resolution that will be dealt with at a general meeting. Providing the request to issue the statement is received by the company at least one week before the meeting to which it relates, the company is required to circulate a statement if it has received requests to do so from:

(a) members representing at least 5 per cent of the total voting rights of all the members who have a relevant right to vote (excluding any voting rights attached to any shares in the company held as treasury shares); or
(b) at least 100 members who have a relevant right to vote and hold shares in the company on which there has been paid up an average sum, per member, of at least £100.

A company that is required to circulate a statement (under s.314) must, in accordance with CA 2006, s.315, send a copy of the statement to each member of the company entitled to receive notice of the meeting in the same manner as the notice of the meeting and at the same time as, or as soon as reasonably practicable after, it gives notice of the meeting. In the event of non-compliance with s.315, an offence is committed by every officer of the company who is in default. Here, a person guilty of an offence is liable on conviction on indictment, to a fine and on summary conviction, to a fine not exceeding the statutory maximum.

However, an exception to s.315 is provided by CA 2006, s.317. The latter states that a company is not required to circulate a members' statement if, on an application by the company or another person who claims to be aggrieved, the court is satisfied that the rights conferred by s.314 and s.315 are being abused. In such a case the court may order the members who requested the circulation of the statement to pay the whole or part of the company's costs.

Expenses of circulating members' statement

The expense involved in complying with s.315 need not be incurred by the members who requested the circulation of the statement if:

(a) the meeting to which the request relates is an annual general meeting of a public company; and

(b) requests sufficient to require the company to circulate the statement are received before the end of the financial year preceding the meeting.

Otherwise:

(a) the expense of complying with s.315 must be paid by the members who requested the circulation of the statement unless the company resolves otherwise; and

(b) unless the company has previously so resolved, it is not bound to comply with s.315 unless a sum reasonably sufficient to meet its expenses is deposited with or tendered to it, not later than one week before the meeting.

Circulars

When giving notice of a general meeting, a company may issue circulars. The usual purpose of a circular is to inform the membership of the views of the company's board. Although it is possible for dissentient members to issue circulars (e.g. to explain an opposing view to the one taken by the board), the expense of issuing circulars may prove prohibitive. As a company's board is authorised to represent the company's interests, the expense of the board issuing circulars may be met from company funds. However, the board of directors must not issue information for the purpose of personal gain or advantage, nor must the purpose of the circular be to paint a false and misleading picture of a company's affairs. Where, in issuing a circular, a company misrepresents a state of affairs, then, in relation to a meeting for which a misleading circular was issued and at which a resolution favoured by those responsible for the circular was passed, the resolution may be set aside. The misrepresentation may take the form of an omission to provide accurate information.

The courts' discretion to call meetings

In accordance with CA 2006, s.306 (previously CA 1985, s.371), if it is impracticable to call or conduct a meeting of a company by a manner prescribed by either the Companies Act or the company's articles or a shareholders' agreement, the court may, on an application from a director or a member of the company, otherwise entitled to attend and vote at the meeting, order a meeting to be called and held in a manner prescribed by the court. The provision will ordinarily be invoked where a minority shareholder purports to employ quorum tactics to prevent a majority shareholder from exercising the voting rights attached to his or her shares.

Section 306 is a procedural provision and is not designed to affect substantive voting rights or class rights or shift the balance of power between shareholders in circumstances where there is an agreement to share power equally or where a potential deadlock was a matter that must be taken to have been expressly or impliedly foreseen as relevant to the protection of each of the parties (see, e.g. *Alvona Developments Ltd* v. *The Manhattan Loft Corporation (AC) Ltd* [2006] BCC 119). Further, in deciding whether to grant relief the court will consider other options available to the applicant, for example, a right to petition under CA 2006, s.994. An example of the application of the provision is in the case of *Re Opera Photographic* [1989] 5 BCC 601. Here the court directed a meeting to be held to overcome a quorum requirement in order to enable a resolution to be passed to dismiss a director of the company. The director against which the dismissal was sought had refused to attend a convened meeting of the members (there were only two members). Here, the quorum requirement was prevented from being used as a device to curb the implementation of a statutory power, namely, the ability of the general meeting to pass an ordinary resolution to remove a director from office.

A more recent application of the provision is in *Union Music Ltd & Anor* v. *Watson & Anor* [2004] BCC 37. Here, the Court of Appeal accepted that CA 1985, s.371 (now CA 2006, s.306) was not intended to allow the court to break a deadlock between two equal shareholders. However, in this case the shareholdings were not equal. The issued share capital of the company was held by two shareholders, one holding 49 per cent and the other 51 per cent and both the shareholders were directors of the company. Although a shareholders' agreement included a clause which provided that 'the company could not without the prior consent of both shareholders hold any meeting or transact any business at such a meeting unless there were present duly authorised representatives or proxies for each shareholder', nevertheless, the shareholders' agreement was not designed to ensure that power was shared equally. The shareholders' agreement could not prevent the court from making an order under s.371 where the order was necessary to allow the company to manage its affairs in an effective and proper manner; in this instance, to allow the right of a majority shareholder to remove or appoint a director in accordance with a majority voting power (see also *Vectone Entertainment Holding Ltd* v. *South Entertainment Ltd* [2004] BCLC 224).

14.4   TYPES OF RESOLUTION

Other than in the case of an informal resolution (discussed below), CA 2006, s.281 specifies that for a private company a resolution must be passed as a written resolution or at a meeting of the members, whereas in a public company a resolution must be passed at a meeting of the members.

The ordinary resolution

An ordinary resolution is one passed by a simple majority of the members who are present (or present by proxy) and entitled to attend and vote at a company meeting. Unless the companies legislation or articles deem otherwise, resolutions passed by a company in general meeting will be by ordinary resolution (CA 2006, s.282).

The special resolution

In some instances, the companies legislation or a company's articles will specify that a resolution may only be passed by not less than a 75 per cent majority of those members present (or present by proxy) and entitled to attend and vote at a company meeting. This type of resolution is a special resolution. Where a resolution is passed at a meeting the resolution is not a special resolution unless the notice of the meeting included the text of the resolution and specified the intention to propose the resolution as a special resolution (CA 2006, s.283).

It is to be noted that prior to the CA 2006, a form of resolution, referred to as an extraordinary resolution, was also in use. An extraordinary resolution was required in specific instances to, for example, commence a voluntary winding up of a company (Insolvency Act 1986, s.84(1)) or to pass a resolution of a class of members where the company proposed to vary the rights of the class. As with a special resolution, an extraordinary resolution would be passed by a 75 per cent majority of those members entitled to attend and vote at a company meeting (CA 1985, s.378(1)). In reality the effect of an extraordinary resolution was the same as a special resolution and, as such, its removal from the CA 2006, as a defined type of resolution, is of no consequence.

The written resolution

In the case of private companies, CA 2006, s.288 provides that the passing of a resolution in general meeting or at a separate meeting of a specific class of shareholders may be achieved by means of a written resolution. The directors or members of the company may instigate the written resolution procedure. Any resolution may properly be moved as a written resolution unless it would, if passed, be ineffective, be defamatory of any person, or it is frivolous or vexatious. Where the members require the company to circulate a motion to pass a written resolution they may also compel the company to circulate a statement of not more than 1,000 words on the subject matter of the resolution. A company is required to circulate the motion and any accompanying statement if it receives requests to do so from members representing not less than 5 per cent or such lower percentage of the total voting rights as is specified by the company's articles. Where the directors wish to instigate the written resolution procedure, the company must send or submit a copy of the motion to every member who would have been entitled to vote on the resolution on the circulation date of the motion. In relation to the circulation of any proposed written resolution, the resolution will lapse if it is not passed before the end of the period specified for this purpose in the company's articles, or if no period is specified, the period of 28 days beginning with the circulation date.

The written resolution takes effect as if agreed by the company in a general meeting or by a meeting of the relevant class of members of the company. A written resolution may be passed by the same majority required had the resolution been passed at a formal meeting, although companies may, in their articles, adopt a stricter requirement in terms of the requisite majority. This is a significant change to the position represented under the CA 1985: in accordance with CA 1985, s.381A, a written resolution could only be passed where all the members of the company who, as of the date of the resolution, would have been entitled to attend and vote at a general meeting of the company, agreed (in writing) to the terms of the resolution.

It should be noted that a written resolution may be invoked to pass any type of resolution other than the exceptions stipulated by CA 2006, s.288(2). The exceptions stipulated by CA 2006, s.288, are as follows:

(a) a resolution under CA 2006, s.168 removing a director before the expiration of his or her period of office;
(b) a resolution under CA 2006, s.510 removing an auditor before the expiration of his or her term of office.

Further, by CA 2006, s.300 a provision in the articles of a private company will be void where its effect would be to deny a company the ability to propose and pass a written resolution in accordance with a provision of the CA 2006.

The informal resolution at common law

At common law, a motion to pass a resolution may be approved, without a formal resolution of the general meeting, if the resolution carries the unanimous support of those members who would have been entitled to attend and vote had the motion been put before a formal general meeting (see, e.g. *Parker & Cooper Ltd* v. *Reading* [1926] Ch 975). The common law makes no requirement to the effect that an informal resolution must be in writing. For example, in *Re Duomatic* [1969] 2 Ch 365, an informal agreement to authorise directors' remuneration (a matter which would normally require approval via an ordinary resolution of the general meeting) was upheld, despite the fact that the agreement was not in writing.

It would appear unclear whether any specified notice requirement of an intention to pass an informal agreement must, as with a formal resolution (or impliedly with a written resolution), be sent to all members of the company. An informal agreement is as valid as if the resolution had been passed in a general meeting, irrespective of whether the informal agreement approves a matter that would ordinarily have required a vote from either a simple or a

75 per cent majority vote. For example, in *Cane* v. *Jones* [1980] 1 WLR 1451, the court approved an alteration to a company's articles by the unanimous but informal agreement of the company's voting members. The flexibility of the common law approach (referred to as the Duomatic principle after the case of that name (see above)) allows members of a company to reach an agreement without any strict and arbitrary adherence to formal procedures.

In *Re Home Treat Ltd* [1991] BCC 165, Harman J suggested that the informal consent of the membership could be found in a situation where the members of a company did not seek to oppose it. However, if consent by acquiescence is acceptable (and this may be doubted) it would surely only suffice where there was, on the part of the shareholders, actual knowledge of the nature, extent and content of the proposed resolution and no evidence of dissent. It will not be sufficient to show that a shareholder's assent would have been given if he or she had been presented with the facts and then asked to give an assent (see, e.g. *EIC Services Ltd & Anor* v. *Phipps & Ors* [2003] BCC 931).

It may also be possible for a shareholder agreement to be viewed as an implied mechanism to sanction an informal resolution in circumstances where the subject matter of the resolution is specifically dealt with by the terms of the shareholders' agreement and where the agreement comprises the will of the entire membership of the company. However, a shareholder agreement will not be capable of impliedly sanctioning an informal resolution where the agreement is absent of some material matter, so specified and required by the terms of the resolution (see, e.g. *Demite Ltd* v. *Proctec Health Ltd* [1998] BCC 638).

Statutory provisions – conflict with the Duomatic principle

Where a statutory provision is linked to the passing of a resolution but in addition to the required resolution, the provision requires some other additional requirement, an informal resolution may, in such a case, be ineffective, and if relied upon may be liable to be set aside. For example, an informal resolution would not be effective to pass a resolution to remove a director or auditor. In effect, whether the Duomatic principle can be relied upon will depend on the underlying purpose and effect of the additional requirement(s) of the provision and whether in such circumstances formal as opposed to informal compliance with the provision is deemed absolutely necessary. Generally, the courts adopt a strict approach to the formal requirements laid down by statutory provisions (see, e.g. *Re R. W. Peak (King's Lynn) Ltd* [1998] BCC 596). However, much will depend upon the terms and purpose of the actual provision under consideration. For example, in *Re Barry Artist Ltd* [1985] BCLC 283, a case concerned with a reduction of the company's capital, the court was reluctant to accept an informal resolution because the relevant provision stated that the court had to exercise its discretion in relation to determining whether to approve a special resolution passed in general meeting for the purpose of reducing share capital. In *Re Barry Artist* there was no formal resolution which the court could approve or disapprove. However, the informal resolution was accepted because the court was still able to exercise its discretion (which had not been affected by the informal resolution) in respect of whether or not to permit the reduction of capital.

Copies of resolutions or agreements to be forwarded to registrar

Where a company passes any special resolution or any resolution or agreement agreed to by all the members of a company that, if not so agreed to, would not have been effective for its purpose unless passed as a special resolution, then a copy of the resolution or agreement (or a written memorandum setting out its terms) must be forwarded to the registrar within 15 days after it is passed or made (CA 2006, s.30). Where a company fails to comply, it commits an offence, as does every officer (to include a liquidator of the company) who is in default. A person guilty of an offence is liable on summary conviction to a fine.

Section 30 also applies to:

- any resolution or agreement agreed to by all the members of a class of shareholders that, if not so agreed to, would not have been effective for its purpose unless passed by some particular majority or otherwise in some particular manner;
- any resolution or agreement that effectively binds all members of a class of shareholders though not agreed to by all those members;
- any other resolution or agreement by virtue of any enactment.

14.5 VOTING PROCEDURE

At general meetings the standard procedure for casting votes in favour of or against proposed resolutions is by the members present at the meeting to vote, by a show of hands (each member will have one vote irrespective of the number of shares held). In effect, this means that if, for example, a motion is required to be carried by a special resolution and only 50 members, out of a total membership of 500, attend the meeting at which the motion is proposed, the resolution may be carried by just 38 members voting in its favour. Indeed, it is not an uncommon feature at company meetings for resolutions to be passed by but a small percentage of the total membership.

However, as an alternative to a vote by a show of hands, a member may demand that a poll vote be taken. A poll vote entitles members to cast votes in proportion to the number of voting shares held; that is, if a member holds 20 shares, each carrying one vote, he or she will be entitled to cast 20 votes.

Yet, on a poll taken at a general meeting of a company, a member entitled to more than one vote need not, if he or she votes, use all his or her votes or cast all the votes he or she uses in the same way (CA 2006, s.322). CA 2006, s.321 provides that any provision contained within a company's articles which seeks to exclude the right to demand a poll on any matter other than the election of a chairman or the adjournment of a meeting, will be void. CA 2006, s.321(2) further provides that any provision contained within a company's articles will be void where it prohibits a poll from being demanded by:

- not less than five members; or
- by a member or members representing not less than 10 per cent of the total voting rights of all the members having the right to vote on the resolution (excluding shares held as treasury shares); or
- by a member or members holding voting shares on which an aggregate sum has been paid up equal to not less than 10 per cent of the total sum paid up on all the voting shares (excluding shares held as treasury shares).

Proxies

A proxy is a person appointed by a member of a company to represent that member's voting interests at a general meeting. CA 2006, s.324 provides that any member of a company who is entitled to attend and vote at a general meeting may appoint a proxy to attend in his or her place. Previously, under the CA 1985, a proxy was only allowed to vote on a poll vote, but in accordance with s.324, the ability of a proxy to vote is no longer so restricted. A proxy need not himself be a member of the company and any member of a company entitled to vote at a general meeting is permitted to appoint one or more proxies to attend, speak at, vote, and be counted as a part of the quorum requirement of the meeting. In the case of a company with a share capital, a member may appoint more than one proxy in relation to a meeting, provided that each proxy is appointed to exercise the rights attached to a different share or shares held by him, or (as the case may be) to a different £10, or multiple of £10, of stock held by him.

As a member's agent, a proxy should vote in accordance with the wishes of his or her principal. Nevertheless, where a proxy acts contrary to his or her principal's instructions, the votes cast will not normally be discounted other than where they are considered to be crucial to the final outcome of the vote (see, e.g. *Oliver* v. *Dalgleish* [1963] 3 All ER 330).

Adjournments

In certain circumstances, it may be necessary for the chairman of a general meeting to adjourn a meeting and, if so, unfinished matters of business will be postponed to a new date. By exercising the power to adjourn a meeting the chairman must act *bona fide* in the best interests of the company. The decision to adjourn a meeting must be a reasonable one to take in the light of all the relevant circumstances. A meeting must not be adjourned as a means to prevent, delay or handicap the will of the company in general meeting. An example of a chairman's decision to adjourn a meeting that attracted judicial disapproval is to be found in *Byng* v. *London Life Association Ltd* [1990] Ch 170. Here, the Court of Appeal considered it impracticable for a chairman to adjourn a meeting for a period of two hours. The meeting was adjourned to a venue located in a different part of London from the one in which the original meeting had taken place because the meeting hall was too small. The haste at which the adjourned meeting was rearranged meant that many of the members who attended the original meeting were unable to attend the rescheduled meeting. Following the adjournment, a special resolution was passed. The resolution had the support of the board of directors but attracted opposition from a part of the membership; had the original meeting not been adjourned, the outcome of the vote may have been different. The fact that the meeting was rescheduled at such short notice and at a different venue, gave rise to a finding that, in the circumstances of the case, the chairman's decision had been unreasonable. The vote to secure the special resolution in question was declared invalid.

CHAPTER 15

The protection of minority shareholders

15.1 INTRODUCTION

This chapter is concerned with the remedies available to a minority share-holder in respect of both (a) an ability to redress a wrong committed against the company as a result of delinquent management practices or the wrongful act of a third party, and (b) the personal rights available to a minority share-holder in relation to remedying corporate conduct which adversely affects a membership interest.

In relation to (a), where a wrong is committed against a company, the pro-tection of minority interests is regulated by the rule taken from the judgment of Wigram V-C in the case of *Foss* v. *Harbottle* (1843) 2 Hare 461. The rule is generally prohibitive of the availability of minority actions in a situation where the majority of the membership have declined to pursue an action, because as Wigram V-C made clear in his judgment, every individual share-holder must realise that on becoming a member of a company, majority rule will prevail, as in all other walks of society. However, by way of an excep-tion, in circumstances prescribed by the Companies Act (CA) 2006, s.260, a minority shareholder may have the capacity to pursue a derivative action.

In relation to (b), a minority shareholder may petition the court under CA 2006, s.994 in circumstances where the company's conduct is such that the shareholder's membership interest is subject to unfairly prejudicial con-duct. Under s.994 the petitioning member will seek a personal remedy. Alternatively, where a remedy for an aggrieved shareholder is unavailable under s.994 or perhaps the extent of an available remedy is considered unsat-isfactory, a minority shareholder may, in accordance with the Insolvency Act (IA) 1986, s.122(1)(g), petition to have the company wound up on the just and equitable ground. This latter remedy is one of last resort.

15.2 THE DERIVATIVE ACTION

Where a wrong is committed against a company, the company as a distinct legal entity is the proper claimant to instigate proceedings to remedy the wrong. Therefore, as a general rule, a minority shareholder will be precluded from commencing an action in the company's name unless he or she has the support of a majority of the membership. Without the support of the general meeting, the proceedings will be struck out by the court and the applicant and his or her solicitor will be personally liable to pay the costs of the litigation. Even with the support of the general meeting, the board of directors must agree to instigate proceedings in the company's name (see, e.g. *Breckland Group* v. *London & Suffolk Properties* [1989] BCLC 100). The only exception to the proper claimant rule is where a minority shareholder is able to pursue his or her complaint in the derivative form. The ability to pursue a derivative action is particularly relevant in relation to companies in which corporate malpractice may be hidden and unwittingly tolerated by a majority of the company's shareholders.

The courts will be reluctant to overturn the wishes of a majority of the membership and will only permit a derivative action in circumstances where the conduct of those in control of the company was inspired by actions other than to promote the best interests of the company as a whole. To permit a derivative action, the wrong in question must be of a serious nature and the principal motive for pursuing a derivative action must be one which seeks to benefit the company as a distinct commercial entity, as opposed to a motive which seeks to benefit the personal interests of a minority shareholder(s). Prior to the CA 2006, the derivative action was regulated by the common law and a shareholder was obliged to establish that the wrong that was the subject of the complaint constituted 'a fraud on the company'. Although there was no exact definition of 'wrongs' that would equate with a fraud on the minority, case law established that fraud was not necessarily to be identified in a manner that required a dishonest intent or deception. The nature and degree of the wrong had to be determined on a case-by-case basis. Nevertheless, case law examples indicated that it was possible to establish a 'fraud' in circumstances where the controllers of the company intentionally committed a breach of duty resulting in a misappropriation of corporate assets (see, e.g. *Cook* v. *Deeks* [1916] 1 AC 554), a negligent and self serving abuse of corporate power (see, e.g. *Daniels* v. *Daniels* [1978] Ch 406), or discriminatory act resulting in an unfair advantage to the minority (see, e.g. *Estmanco* v. *Greater London Council* [1982] 1 All ER 437). However, it should be noted that the justice of a particular case could not, in itself, be regarded as a standard exception (see, e.g. *Prudential Assurance Co Ltd* v. *Newman Industries* (*No.2*) [1982] Ch 204).

Where 'fraud' was established, ratification of the alleged wrong would be ineffective other than where, for example, an independent board of directors or a majority of the independent part of the minority shareholders (those not involved in the wrongdoing) resolved to rescind from proceeding with an action (see, e.g. *Atwool* v. *Merryweather* (1868) LR 5 Eq; *Rights and Issues Investment Trust* v. *Stylo Shoes* [1956] Ch 250; and *Smith* v. *Croft (No.2)* and *(No 3)* [1987] BCLC 206 and [1987] BCLC 355).

The statutory derivative action

In creating the statutory derivative action, the CA 2006 attempts to provide a minority shareholder with a more accessible method of challenging corporate wrongdoing; the action is regulated by CA 2006, ss.260–4. Although CA 2006, s.260(2) permits a derivative action to be brought in pursuance of an order of the court in proceedings under CA 2006, s.994 (discussed below), a distinct procedure for commencing a statutory derivative action is provided by CA 2006, s.260(3). Here, a derivative claim may be commenced in respect of a cause of action arising from an actual or proposed act or omission involving negligence, default, breach of duty or breach of trust. The cause of action may be against a director or another person (or both) and it is immaterial that it arose before or after the person seeking to bring or continue the derivative claim became a member of the company (CA 2006, s.260(4)).

Subject to the procedural conditions laid down in CA 2006, s.261, a derivative action may be commenced in circumstances where the company initially sought, but failed, to pursue an action against a director or other person in circumstances where that failure was due to a lack of diligence in the prosecution, or the prosecution otherwise amounted to an abuse of the process of the court (see CA 2006, s.262). Where the court deems it appropriate, the claimant's derivative action (to include an action covered under CA 2006, s.262) may also be taken over and pursued by another member (the applicant) in circumstances where the claimant's action failed due to a lack of diligence in respect of its prosecution, or the prosecution otherwise amounted to an abuse of the process of the court. Here, the court procedure for a derivative action pursued by an 'applicant' is provided by CA 2006, s.264(3)–(5). The said procedure is identical to that contained in CA 2006, s.261 (detailed below).

Procedure

CA 2006, s.261 provides that in commencing a derivative action, a member must apply to the court for permission to continue that action. Where the court considers the proposed application does not disclose a *prima facie* case, the court may dismiss the application and may make any consequential order it considers appropriate. Alternatively, if the application is not dismissed, the court may give directions in respect of the evidence to be provided by the company and may adjourn the proceedings to enable the evidence to be obtained. On hearing the application, the court may give permission to continue the claim on such terms as it thinks fit, refuse permission and dismiss the claim or adjourn the proceedings on the application and give such directions as it thinks fit. The court has a discretion to order that the costs of the claimant/applicant be paid by the company, even where the claimant's/applicant's action proves to be unsuccessful (see, e.g. *Wallersteiner* v. *Moir (No.2)* [1975] QB 373).

In deciding whether a derivative action should proceed, the court must refuse the application if, in accordance with CA 2006, s.263(2), it is satisfied that:

(a) a person acting in accordance with CA 2006, s.172 (duty to promote the success of the company) would not seek to continue the claim; or

(b) if the cause of action arises from an act or omission that is yet to occur, that the act or omission has been authorised by the company; or

(c) where the cause of action arises from an act or omission that has already occurred, that the act or omission was authorised by the company before it occurred, or has been ratified by the company since it occurred.

However, even if the conditions stated in CA 2006, s.263(2) do not prevent the proceedings from continuing, the court may still refuse its permission to allow the continuance of the action. In particular, in determining the matter, the court must take account of the matters specified by CA 2006, s.263(3), namely:

(a) whether the member is acting in good faith in seeking to continue the claim;

(b) the importance that a person acting in accordance with the s.172 duty to promote the success of the company would attach to continuing it;

(c) where the cause of action results from an act or omission that is yet to occur, whether the act or omission could be, and in the circumstances would be likely to be:

(i) authorised by the company before it occurs; or
(ii) ratified by the company after it occurs;

(d) where the cause of action arises from an act or omission that has already occurred, whether the act or omission could be, and in the circumstances would be likely to be, ratified by the company;

(e) whether the company has decided not to pursue the claim;

(f) whether the act or omission in respect of which the claim is brought gives rise to a cause of action that the member could pursue in his own right rather than on behalf of the company.

Here, the court, in considering whether to give its permission, must have particular regard to any evidence before it in relation to the views of the independent members of the company, i.e. those members who have no personal interest in the matter, be that interest of a direct or indirect nature (CA 2006, s.263(4)). It is important to note that the wrongful act that results in a derivative action may not be effectively ratified in circumstances where ratification is or will be effected by the votes of those classified as the wrongdoers in relation to the delinquent act. Although this requirement is not specifically spelt out in CA 2006, ss.260–4, it is applicable in respect of the general meeting's ability to sanction (or otherwise) a director's breach of duty, etc. (see CA 2006, s.239).

In accordance with CA 2006, s.264(5), the Secretary of State may by regulations:

(a) amend subsection (2) so as to alter or add to the circumstances in which permission (or leave) is to be refused;
(b) amend subsection (3) so as to alter or add to the matters that the court is required to take into account in considering whether to give permission.

A personal or corporate action?

Confusion surrounding whether an action should be of a personal or corporate nature is evident in cases where a shareholder suffers an indirect personal loss as a result of a wrong committed against the company, for example, in a situation where the value of a member's shares depreciate following the wrongful act of a third party, or a breach of directors' duty. Here, a shareholder's loss may be particularly striking, especially when, in reality, the company is little more than the *alter ego* of the shareholder. In this type of situation, a depreciation in the worth of the company may cause great financial harm to an individual shareholder.

Nevertheless, although a wrongful act that affects a company may result in a personal loss to a shareholder, such loss, being merely a reflection of the overall corporate loss, will not be recoverable, as a contrary conclusion would be unjust, giving rise to double recovery against the wrongdoer (see, e.g. *Prudential Assurance Co* v. *Newman Industries* [1982] Ch 204). More recently, in *Johnson* v. *Gore Wood & Co* [2002]2 AC 1, the House of Lords sought to explain and expand upon the *Prudential* decision. Lord Bingham advanced three propositions, namely:

1. Where a company suffers loss caused by a breach of duty owed to it, only the company may sue in respect of that loss. No action lies at the suit of a shareholder suing in that capacity and no other to make good a diminution in the value of the shareholder's shareholding where that merely reflects the loss suffered by the company. A claim will not lie by a shareholder to make good a loss which would be made good if the company's assets were replenished through action against the party responsible for the loss, even if the company, acting through its constitutional organs, has declined or failed to make good that loss. . . .
2. Where a company suffers loss but has no cause of action to sue to recover that loss, the shareholder in the company may sue in respect of it (if the shareholder has a cause of action to do so), even though the loss is a diminution in the value of the shareholding.
3. Where a company suffers loss caused by a breach of duty to it, and a shareholder suffers a loss separate and distinct from that suffered by the company caused by breach of a duty independently owed to the shareholder, each may sue to recover the loss caused to it by breach of the duty owed to it but neither may recover loss caused to the other by breach of the duty owed to that other . . . (At pp.35–6.)

In accordance with these propositions, a shareholder will generally be precluded from proceeding with a personal action to recover a loss where the wrong adversely affects (in an economic sense) the company (however, note the possibility of an action under CA 2006, s.994, discussed below). In reality, a shareholder loss, accountable as a reflection of an economic loss to the company, will not be recoverable, other than where the company is, by law, precluded from maintaining the action or alternatively, where the shareholder can establish that the defendant's conduct resulted in a breach of a distinct legal duty, a duty owed to the shareholder in a personal capacity. The defendant's conduct must cause a personal loss which is separate and distinct from any loss suffered by the company. In cases subsequent to *Johnson*, the Court of Appeal has sought to follow Lord Bingham's propositions to the letter; see, e.g. *Day* v. *Cook* [2002] 1 BCLC 1, *Ellis* v. *Property Leeds (UK) Ltd* [2002] 2 BCLC 175, *Shaker* v. *Al-Bedrawi* [2003] BCC 465, *Floyd & Ors* v. *Fairhurst & Co* [2004] EWCA Civ 604 and *Gardner* v. *Parker* [2005] BCC 46.

However, a possible diversion to Lord Bingham's propositions may be found in the Court of Appeal's decision in *Giles* v. *Rhind* [2001] 2 BCLC 582 (decided after *Johnson*). Here, the issued share capital of the company (S) was divided between G and R. G and R were the appointed directors of S. The company refinanced and G and R were left with a combined holding of approximately 20 per cent of the issued share capital. The refinance agreement was subject to a shareholders' agreement to which G and R were parties. The relationship between R and G broke down. R set up a new business, of a type similar to the business pursued by S. R took with him employees of S and a vital contract which had properly belonged to S. R used confidential information to divert the contract away from S and in doing so acted contrary to the shareholders' agreement, i.e. in breach of a contractual duty of confidence. S commenced proceedings against R but before the hearing S was placed into receivership and then subsequently, liquidation. G issued proceedings against R claiming that R's actions had resulted in personal losses equating to a loss of remuneration and the loss in the value of his shareholding. In reversing the judgment at first instance, the Court of Appeal sought to distinguish *Johnson* on two distinct grounds. First, in *Giles*, the company was unable to sustain an action against R due to a lack of funds; as such there could be no double recovery against R. (However, note that this first ground would appear to contradict the second proposition advanced in *Johnson*, namely, although the company was unable to pursue the action due to a lack of funds, the company did, nevertheless, have a cause of action). The second, and it is submitted valid, ground related to G's claim for the loss of future remuneration. While the court accepted that G's claim for the loss of accrued earnings would ordinarily be defeated on the basis of the reflective loss principle (i.e. the loss suffered by G as an employee was reflective of the company's own loss); the issue concerning future earnings was a different matter. In this context, the loss suffered by G was not reflective of any loss suffered by the company because the loss flowed from the termination of G's employment. Even if the company had been able to enforce its rights against R, following the collapse of its business, any damages recoverable by the company would not have compensated G for a loss of future earnings.

15.3 THE UNFAIR PREJUDICE REMEDY

CA 2006, s.994 (previously CA 1985, s.459) provides:

> A member of a company may apply to the court by petition for an order . . . on the ground that the company's affairs are being or have been conducted in a manner which is unfairly prejudicial to the interests of its members generally or some part of its members (including himself) or that any actual or proposed act or omission on the part of the company (including an act or omission on its behalf) is or would be prejudicial.

The s.994 provision subjects the legal rights of the membership to equitable constraints and to this end a membership interest is founded on a petitioner's relationship, qua shareholder, with the other members of the company, a relationship based on mutual trust and understanding. This type of personal relationship may be apt to describe the internal workings of a private company but is misplaced in the context of a public company. Accordingly, the s.994 provision will almost exclusively be confined to the protection of shareholder interests in the context of a private company. Although the primary function of s.994 is to afford statutory protection to minority shareholders, the provision does not preclude the possibility (albeit this is rare) of a petition from a majority shareholder (see, e.g. *Re Baltic Real Estate Ltd* [1992] BCC 629, *Re Legal Costs Negotiators Ltd* [1999] BCC 547 and *Re Ravenhart Service(Holdings) Ltd* [2004] 2 BCLC 376).

Unfairly prejudicial conduct

The court employs an objective test to determine whether a particular type of conduct is of an unfairly prejudicial nature. Prejudicial conduct relates to damaging conduct of a commercial nature (see, e.g. *Re Unisoft Group Ltd* (*No.3*) [1994] 2 BCLC 609) to the extent that for conduct to be construed as 'prejudicial' it must depreciate or fetter the financial worth of a member's shareholding interest (see, e.g. *Rock Nominees Ltd* v. *RCO (Holdings Ltd) plc* [2004] 1 BCLC 439). To justify the operation of s.994, the prejudicial conduct must be unfair. Here the underlying motive behind the pursuit of a particular course of conduct will be a key factor in construing whether the conduct was unfair. Although conduct may still be judged unfair, even in circumstances where there was no intentional act of discrimination, in the majority of cases, a petitioner will rely on establishing an intentional act of discrimination or an

236

intentional and improper exercise of the company's powers. It is doubtful whether an act of corporate misjudgment, for example, a poor investment decision, etc., will ever amount to unfair conduct insofar as s.994 does not seek to penalise commercial gambles. Indeed, it is a natural expectation for the management of a company to engage in commercial gambles. However, a ridiculous and totally unreasonable commercial gamble may be deemed unfair especially in circumstances where the conduct equates to a breach of a duty of care and where the conduct results in self-serving negligence (see, e.g. *Re Elgindata Ltd* [1991] BCLC 959). Nevertheless, note that a petition under s.994 may be sustained where, in a private company, negligent mismanagement is concerned with the internal administration and organisation of a company's affairs (see, e.g. *Re Macro (Ipswich) Ltd* [1994] 2 BCLC 354).

The effect of the conduct

To substantiate a finding of unfairly prejudicial conduct, the petitioner must show that the conduct of the company's affairs resulted in more than a trivial assault on the substance of his or her membership interest (see, e.g. *Re Saul D Harrison & Sons plc* [1994] BCC 475). Here, the crucial factor is the effect of the conduct in relation to the membership interest. For example, a small and technical breach of a director's duty may cause little harm in relation to the financial standing of a company, but the very fact that the breach occurred may result in a loss of trust and confidence in the management of the company. Although the conduct may have been trivial, the effect of that conduct may be very damaging in respect of the relationship between members. In such a case, a petition under s.994 may be sustainable (see, e.g. *Re Baumler (UK)* [2005] 1 BCLC 92).

A membership interest

Unfairly prejudicial conduct must affect a membership interest or there must be evidence to establish the likelihood of a threatened act (see, e.g. *Re Kenyon Swansea Ltd* [1987] BCLC 514). The phrase 'membership interest' incorporates the strict legal rights of the membership, for example, membership rights contained within the company's constitution and companies legislation. However, it is unclear to what extent a membership interest extends beyond a strict legal right. In *Re a Company (No.008699 of 1985)* [1986] BCLC 382, Hoffmann J opined that a membership interest encompassed a wider concept than a membership right and coupled with the word 'unfair', permitted the court to consider the legitimate expectations of the membership of a company. For example, Hoffmann J believed that in a small domestic-type company, a legitimate expectation could exist in a situation where a person became a shareholder on the premise that he or she would be allowed to participate in the management of the company, a view echoed by subsequent decisions (see, e.g. *R & H Electrical Ltd* v. *Haden Bill Electrical Ltd* [1995] BCC 958, *Quinlan* v. *Essex Hinge Co Ltd* [1996] 2 BCLC 417 and *Re Eurofinance Group Ltd* [2001] BCC 551. However, it must be noted that exclusion from management is, in itself, insufficient to justify a successful petition under s.994; the exclusion must be of an unfairly prejudicial nature. For example, a member's exclusion from management may be justified on the basis that he or she failed to participate in management issues or that he or she was unhelpful or unreasonably hostile to other board members, or that he or she acted in breach of duty (see, e.g. *Re John Reid & Sons (Strucsteel) Ltd* [2003] 2 BCLC 319, *Grace* v. *Biagioli* [2006] BCC 85).

In *Re J E Cade & Son Ltd* [1991] BCC 360, Warner J held that a shareholder's interest in a company could not be subject to expectations founded on a general concept of fairness (i.e. expectations that were unrelated to the legal rights of membership). In construing the scope of a membership interest, the learned judge maintained that the interpretation of an 'interest' should be strictly confined to legal rights or obligations related to strict legal rights, for example, the terms of a company's constitution, a director's service contract or an express shareholder agreement. While Warner J accepted that equitable considerations should be examined, he believed that considerations unconnected to the strict legal rights of membership could not, for the purposes of s.994 (and IA 1986, s.122(1)(g)), found appropriate grounds upon which relief could be sought.

The interpretation afforded to a 'membership interest' by Warner J in *Re J E Cade* would now appear settled as the acceptable norm in construing s.994. This view was confirmed in *O'Neill* v. *Phillips* [1999] 1 WLR 1092; the first case in which the House of Lords was called upon to determine s.459 (now CA 2006, s.994). Here, Lord Hoffmann, delivering the leading judgment of the House, explained that a private company was subject to equitable principles, the role of which could restrain the exercise of strict legal rights in certain relationships, namely where a reliance on strict legal rights would be contrary to good faith. His Lordship emphasised that a member of a company would have grounds to complain of unfairly prejudicial conduct where:

- there had been a breach of the legal rules which governed the manner in which the affairs of the company should be conducted; or
- alternatively, but more exceptionally, a member of a company could make a complaint in circumstances where equitable considerations made it necessary to abandon the application of strict legal rights to prevent unfairness. Unfairness equated to a breach of the rules or the use of the rules in a manner which equity would regard as contrary to good faith.

However, as a matter of protecting legal certainty, Lord Hoffmann emphasised that it was necessary to limit the scope of any applicable equitable principles and that such principles could not stand as an indefinite notion of fairness. Lord Hoffmann considered that equitable principles had to be expressly or impliedly related to a legal right of membership. In *O'Neill* v. *Phillips*, in return for his services to the company, the petitioner had been informally notified that he would participate in an equal share of the profits and be given an equal shareholding in the company. However, the petitioner's expectations could not be enforced as a membership interest because such expectations were not subject to any binding agreement or legal right (i.e. a formal agreement covering the distribution of profits or shares simply did not exist). Further, there could be no implied right and expectation relating to a share in profits and shares because the nature and structure of this particular company was not a typical quasi-partnership type company, i.e. the company had not been formed on the basis of a mutual trust and understanding in respect of the petitioner's expectations.

Therefore, post *O'Neill* v. *Phillips*, a s.994 petition will not be sustained where the alleged membership interest is not expressly or impliedly linked to an enforceable legal right. Where a legally binding agreement fails to incorporate a member's expectation, it may be possible to imply the expectation (term) as under the general law of contract, or subject the legally binding agreement to equitable considerations. However, it is most improbable that equitable considerations will ever extend to expectations which are devoid of and unconnected to a legal right.

The available remedies to a petition under CA 2006, s.994

Where a petitioner succeeds in a petition under CA 2006, s.994, the court may make an order under CA 2006, s.996. Here the court is afforded a wide discretion in the nature of the relief to be granted with an ability to make 'an order as it thinks fit'. In determining the nature of the relief there is no requirement that a petitioner should come to the court with 'clean hands'. However, any adverse conduct on the part of the petitioner may be taken into account and as such affect the extent of any remedy (see, e.g. *Richardson* v. *Blackmore* [2006] BCC 276). A list of the examples of the type of orders which are available is provided by s.996(2). This section states that without prejudice to the generality of s.996, the court's order may:

(a) regulate the conduct of the company's affairs in the future;

(b) require the company to refrain from doing or continuing an act complained of by the petitioner or to do an act which the petitioner has complained it has omitted to do;

(c) authorise civil proceedings to be brought in the name and on behalf of the company by such person or persons and on such terms as the court may direct;

(d) require the company not to make any, or any specified, alterations in its articles without the leave of the court;

239

(e)   provide for the purchase of the shares of any members of the company by other members or by the company itself and, in the case of a purchase by the company itself, authorise the reduction of the company's capital.

The most common type of order sought is the one provided by example (e), namely, the purchase of the petitioner's shares. This remedy provides the petitioner with an exit route from the company. In such cases the valuation of shares will be of paramount importance. The underlying theme in determining the value of shares is one of fairness. As such, the actual moment in time at which the valuation is to be calculated is apt to vary on a case-by-case basis, being dependent upon the individual circumstances of the case. Accordingly, the valuation of shares may be based upon the share value:

- at a time prior to the petition;
- at the date of the petition; or
- the actual date of the hearing.

In *Re London School of Electronics Ltd* [1986] Ch 211, it was advanced that the valuation procedure should normally take place at the actual date of the hearing (see also *Re D R Chemicals Ltd* [1989] 5 BCC 39). However, this presumption is rebuttable; for example, the company's financial position may have improved or worsened between the date of the petition and the hearing, rendering the valuation procedure unfair if it was to be calculated at the date of the hearing (see, e.g. *Profinance Trust SA* v. *Gladstone* [2002] 1 WLR 1024). It should also be noted that while, in the majority of cases involving a share purchase order, the order will be to the effect that the majority purchase the petitioner's shares, it is possible for the court to decide that a minority shareholder should be permitted to purchase the majority's holding (see, e.g. *Re Brenfield Squash Racquets Club* [1996] 2 BCLC 184 and *Re Nuneaton Borough AFC Ltd* (*No.2*) [1991] BCC 44). However, in *Re Ringtower Holdings plc* [1989] 5 BCC 82, Peter Gibson J opined that an order for the purchase of the shares of the majority would be inappropriate where the majority opposed the sale and the minority held less than 5 per cent of the company's share capital.

In relation to the other types of orders, an order under s.996(2)(a) will be rare because of the court's general reluctance to involve itself in issues of dispute concerning the internal management of a company. However, this type of order was used in the case of *Re Harmer Ltd* [1959] 1 WLR 62, to remove the voting control of H, the company's founder and governing director. H, aged 88, had imposed his will in the management of the company contrary to the advice and wishes of other members of the company. For example, H had entered into contracts without the board's approval. As a result of H's attitude and interference, the company's business suffered. The Court of Appeal ordered that H should be stripped of his control over the company's affairs.

An example of a s.996(2)(b) type order would be where a minority shareholder of a company sought to prevent the company from engaging in an act which, if instigated, would constitute conduct unfairly prejudicial to the interests of the shareholders (see, e.g. *Re Kenyon Swansea Ltd* [1987] 3 BCC 259). Section 996(2)(c) is, in effect, a means to a future remedy, as it affords the petitioner the right to pursue a statutory derivative action (see CA 2006, s.260(1)). Under s.996(2)(c), the court has a power to order civil proceedings to be commenced in the name and on behalf of the company. The order may be sought where, for example, a petitioner establishes that the company's affairs were conducted in a manner unfairly prejudicial to the interests of the company as a whole (members generally). In *Re a Company* (*No.005136 of 1986*) [1987] BCLC 82, Hoffmann J suggested that where a derivative action was brought by way of a s.459 petition (now CA 2006, s.994), the petitioner would be entitled to an indemnity from the company for his or her costs in line with the *Wallersteiner* v. *Moir* (*No.2*) [1975] QB 373 authority (a view impliedly confirmed by the Court of Appeal in *Clark* v. *Cutland* [2003] 2 BCLC 393). Finally, it should be stressed that the court may make any order as it sees fit under s.996 and as such is not bound to prescribe an order of the type represented by s.996(2)(a)–(e) (see, e.g. *Wilton Davies* v. *Kirk* [1997] BCC 770, where the court ordered the appointment of a receiver to oversee the company's affairs).

The relationship between CA 2006, s.994, the statutory derivative action and the no reflective loss principle

Prior to the introduction of the statutory derivative action, the rule in *Foss* v. *Harbottle* was rarely overturned. Whether the introduction of the statutory derivative action will alter this position is debatable. Although the new statutory derivative action extends the ambit of the type of conduct justifying the derivative action, the procedural requirements attached to the commencement of an action may remain an obstacle to any increase in the deployment of derivative actions.

The popularity of a derivative action is also likely to be undermined given that matters which could substantiate a corporate or derivative action may be pursued via CA 2006, s.994 (CA 1985, s.459). Indeed, here, it may be possible for a remedy to give effect to both a petitioner's interests and the interests of the company as a whole. For example in *Clark* v. *Cutland* [2003] 2 BCLC 393, the Court of Appeal accepted that the relief sought under CA 1985, s.461 (now CA 2006, s.996) could also be sought for the benefit of the company.

Where a member of a company purports to commence an action under s.994 on the ground that the company's affairs have been conducted in a manner which is unfairly prejudicial to his or her membership interest and the said conduct is of a type that would also give rise to a corporate action (i.e. it incorporates a wrong perpetrated against the company), should not the company be the proper plaintiff to the action, or if the company declines to pursue the action should it not be pursued as a derivative action? Following the case of *Johnson* v. *Gore Wood & Co* [2002]2 AC 1, it would appear that a shareholder has no personal right of action where the wrong in question adversely affects the company to the extent that the wrong should, in effect, be the substance for a corporate action. However, s.994 is a statutory claim for relief. Therefore, it is unlikely whether *Johnson* v. *Gore Wood & Co* could ever be relied upon to defeat the claims of a minority shareholder under s.994 (see, e.g. *Re Brightview Ltd* [2004] BCC 542). Indeed, there are numerous cases under s.459 (now CA 2006, s.994) that have proceeded on the basis of allowing a petition by a minority shareholder in circumstances where the wrong in question also constituted a wrong against the company (see, e.g. *Re a Company (No.005287 of 1985)* (1985) 1 BCC 99, 586, *Re a Company, ex p. Burr* [1992] BCLC 724, *Re Little Olympian Each Ways Ltd* [1994] 2 BCLC 420, *Re Macro (Ipswich) Ltd* [1994] 2 BCLC 354, *Anderson* v. *Hogg* [2002] BCC 923 and *Re Baumler Ltd* [2005] BCC 181, to name but a few).

15.4   THE JUST AND EQUITABLE WINDING-UP PROVISION

Under IA 1986, s.122(1)(g), a company may be wound up on the premise that its liquidation would provide a just and equitable remedy. IA 1986, s.124 allows any contributory to petition for an equitable winding-up order if the petitioner's shares were either originally allotted to or held by him or her and registered in his or her name for at least six months during the 18 months prior to the presentation of a petition. In all cases, the courts will require the petitioner to establish the following:

- *Tangible interest:* The petitioner must establish that the company is solvent and would be solvent after the payment of its debts (see, e.g. *Re Expanded Plugs Ltd* [1966] 1 WLR 514).
- *The qua member requirement:* A petitioner must petition in his or her capacity as a member and the interest that he or she seeks to protect must be a membership interest. For example, in *Re J E Cade & Son Ltd* [1991] BCC 360, the petitioner claimed relief under CA 1985, s.459 (now CA 2006, s.994) and in the alternative sought a winding-up order on the just and equitable ground. Warner J refused to grant relief under both heads of the petition. According to the learned judge, the petitioner, albeit a member of the company, pursued the petition to protect the ownership of his land that had been occupied by the company; the petitioner's interest was not related to a membership interest.
- *Just and equitable considerations:* As with CA 2006, s.994, a petition under IA 1986, s.122(1)(g), must be based upon an interest which is linked to a legal right of membership.

In cases where the just and equitable provision has been applied, the category of company made subject to a winding-up order has been the quasi-partnership or domestic type of company. For a petition for the just and equitable winding up of a company to succeed, it will be necessary to establish an 'underlying obligation or agreement between the shareholding parties' (see the judgment of Lord Wilberforce in *Ebrahimi* v. *Westbourne Galleries* [1973] AC 360). In the decided cases this obligation has arisen as a result of either:

- an implied agreement on the part of the shareholders to conduct the company's business in a certain manner (see, e.g. *Re Crown Bank Ltd* (1890) 44 Ch D 634 and *Loch* v. *John Blackwood Ltd* [1924] AC 783);
- an implied understanding as to a shareholder's right to participate in the management of the company (see, e.g. *Re A & BC Chewing Gum Ltd* (1975) 1 WLR 579, *Re R A Noble Clothing Ltd* [1983] BCLC 273 and *Re Zinotty Properties Ltd* [1984] 1 WLR 1249);
- an implied duty on the part of the directors to consider the distribution and proper payment of dividends to the company's shareholders (see, e.g. *Re a Company (No.00370 of 1987)* [1988] 1 WLR 1068).

A comparison between CA 2006, s.994 and IA 1986, s.122(1)(g)

CA 2006, s.994 and IA 1986, s.122(1)(g) are concerned with quasi-partnership companies and both require the petitioner to establish a membership interest, an interest that may extend beyond the strict legal rights of membership. The membership interest must be subject to inequitable conduct of a type that destroys a previous relationship of mutual trust and confidence. Indeed, unfairly prejudicial conduct and conduct justifying a winding-up order under s.121(1)(g) will often be indistinguishable; the choice of provision being dependent upon the anticipated remedy. Accordingly, it would appear point-less to plead both s.994 and s.122(1)(g) as alternatives. Indeed, Practice Direction No.1 of 1990 ([1990] 1 WLR 1089) stipulates that s.122(1)(g) should not ordinarily be pleaded as an alternative to a petition under s.994 (see, e.g. *Re Guidezone Ltd* [2001] BCC 692).

However, in some cases there may be a subtle difference in the application of the two provisions. For example, in *Re Noble (R A) & Sons (Clothing) Ltd* [1983] BCLC 273 and *Jesner* v. *Jarrad Properties Ltd* [1992] BCC 807, it was held that conduct, although not justifying a petition for unfairly prejudi-cial conduct, could, in a quasi-partnership type of company, still result in a breakdown of mutual confidence, thereby justifying a petition under s.122(1)(g). For example, a deadlock situation between the two controlling parties of a company with neither party exhibiting any greater degree of fault. In such a case it would be difficult for a petitioner to contend unfairness so justifying a petition under s.994 (see, e.g. *Re Jayflex Construction Ltd* [2004] 2 BCLC 145).

Although in exceptional circumstances a petitioner may be granted a winding-up order on the just and equitable ground in circumstances where there is an alternative remedy under s.994, it should be pointed out that IA 1986, s.125(2) provides that a winding-up order may be struck out if the court considers that it was unreasonable for the petitioner to have not pursued an alternative course of action. However, an exceptional circumstance will arise where s.122(1)(g) affords the most equitable remedy, for example, in a situation where a petitioner contends that a company's conduct and formation was directed at defrauding minority shareholders and the investing public (see, e.g. *Re Millennium Advanced Technology* [2004] 2 BCLC 77). An equitable winding-up order would also be the more appropriate remedy in circumstances similar to those evidenced in *Re Abbey Leisure* [1990] BCC 60. Here, there was an implied understanding between the shareholders that the company was to be formed with the sole purpose of acquiring, refurbishing and managing a nightclub. The nightclub in question was acquired but subsequently sold. The petitioner argued that as the principal purpose in forming the company had failed, the company should be wound up. The respondents contended that a petition under CA 1985, s.459 (now CA 2006, s.994) was a more appropriate course of action and that the petitioner's remedy should have sought the purchase of his shares in accordance with an independent valuation procedure contained in the company's articles. The Court of Appeal, in reversing the first instance judgment of Hoffmann J, held that the winding-up order was, in the circumstances of the case, the most appropriate remedy. Relying to a large extent on Lord Wilberforce's comments in *Ebrahimi* v. *Westbourne Galleries* [1973] AC 360, the court opined that the strict legal rights of the petitioner, represented by the valuation procedure in the company's articles, should be made subject to equitable considerations. Insofar as the petitioner would gain a greater financial benefit in having the company wound up, as opposed to selling his shares in accordance with the valuation procedure, the court concluded that the just and equitable provision could be employed to override the strict legal rights contained within the company's articles. Here, the circumstances of the case vindicated the application of the just and equitable winding-up order.

CHAPTER 16

The criminal liability of a company

16.1 INTRODUCTION

A company may be liable for certain torts in its own right, for example, torts where liability is imposed upon it as the occupier of property. As an employer, a company may be held vicariously liable for the tortious acts of its employees even in a situation where an employee acts in a manner inconsistent with the company's instructions, or carries out his or her duties in a dishonest manner. A company may also be held liable for the actions of its servants in a situation where, in the course of employment, the servant commits a tort for which malice is an essential ingredient. However, other than where a company adopts an unauthorised act, vicarious liability will cease if the employee acts beyond the scope of his or her authority (see, e.g. *Credit Lyonnais Bank Nederland N.V. v. Export Credits Guarantee Department* [1999] 2 WLR 540). Other than in tort, the extent of a company's culpability for an employee's unlawful act (criminal act) will be determined (with the exception of corporate manslaughter) by ascertaining whether the culpable employee is capable of being identified with the company's directing mind (the identification principle).

The identification principle

The directing mind of a company represents the physical being and will of the corporate body and is ordinarily found in the company's board of directors. However, as the board of directors may delegate some part of their functions of management, giving their delegate full discretion to act independently of instructions from them, the directing mind of a company may, in a particular instance, be found in the authorised delegate. To identify the directing mind with the actions of an employee, the employee must have been authorised to act in a specific manner by the directing mind or by a person to whom powers, ordinarily vested in the directing mind, have been delegated. Where a person commands a position within the company's directing mind, the physical act (*actus reus*) and mental state (*mens rea*) of that person may be imputed to the company for the purpose of establishing corporate liability (see, e.g. *Lennard's Carrying Co Ltd v. Asiatic Petroleum Co Ltd* [1915] AC 705).

To establish whether an employee is a part of a company's directing mind, it is often necessary, if not essential, to pierce the corporate veil to examine the company's management structure and chain of command. Such an examination will aid the determination of whether an employee's wrongful act is attributable to the company, i.e. whether the employee had or was delegated an authority to act by the directing mind or held a position in the corporate structure which could be construed to be a part of its directing mind (see, e.g. *Tesco Supermarkets Ltd* v. *Nattrass* [1972] AC 153). Therefore, the question of whether an employee's actions can be linked to the company's directing mind may only be resolved by a case-by-case analysis and examination of the nature of the employee's act and the position which that servant occupied in the corporate structure.

A company acting through its directing mind may be convicted of a criminal offence irrespective of whether the offence is of a regulatory nature (often an offence of strict liability) or one which involves proof of a guilty mind (*mens rea*). However, an ability to marry the mental state of an employee with the directing mind of the company is often marred by uncertainty and confusion. Indeed, up until 1944, there had never been a successful conviction against a company in respect of an offence involving a *mens rea* requirement. Yet, in that year there were three convictions. The convictions were sustained in: *DPP* v. *Kent & Sussex Contractors Ltd* [1944] KB 146 on a charge of deception, *R.* v. *ICR Haulage Ltd* [1944] KB 551, on a charge of conspiracy involving a company's transport officer, and *Moore* v. *I Bresler Ltd* [1944] 2 All ER 515, on a charge of fraudulent evasion of tax related to a company's sales manager.

General exceptions to criminal liability

The Interpretation Act 1978, s.5 and Sched.1 provide that a corporate entity may, unless otherwise stated, be construed as a 'person' in terms of being considered culpable for an offence which requires the wrongful act of a person. However, a company cannot be convicted of a crime which is defined in a way whereby the criminal act is incapable, in a physical sense, of being performed by an artificial entity. For example, an artificial person cannot be convicted of bigamy, rape or any other sexual offence. Following such logic, a company is incapable of being convicted of, for example, an offence specifying a requirement that involves the physical ability to drive a vehicle, so held by the Divisional Court in *Richmond-on-Thames BC* v. *Pinn* [1989] RTR 354. However, while it is impossible for a company to drive a vehicle, the logic of this decision may be questioned. Although, in relation to the *actus reus* of the offence, both a sexual offence and a driving offence require the performance of a human act by a human entity, the crucial difference is that the human act of driving a vehicle may be performed on behalf of and for the benefit of the company as part of the employee's employment. If so performed, the company should, through its employee and the chain of managerial command, be capable of being found responsible, via the identification principle, of committing the *actus reus* of the criminal offence. For example, if a company does not discourage and turns a blind eye to its drivers exceeding the speed limit to complete deliveries on time, and a driver of the company so exceeds the speed limit and as a consequence of driving at an excessive speed causes an accident, then in such circumstances, surely the company and the driver should both be capable of prosecution in relation to the driving offence.

A company may not be convicted of the offence of conspiracy in circumstances where the company and an officer of the company, representing its directing mind, are charged, as the offence of conspiracy involves at least two independent minds conspiring together, i.e. a company and its directing mind are one and the same (see, e.g. *R* v. *McDonnell* [1966] 1 All ER 193). However, where a company and a person representing its directing mind are involved in a conspiracy with other persons, the company may be charged with conspiracy (see, e.g. *R* v. *IRC Holdings* [1944] 1 All ER 691). Finally, a company may not be convicted of an offence where the sentence for that offence is incapable of being imposed on an artificial corporate entity; for example, a company cannot be convicted of murder because the punishment following the conviction for the offence is life imprisonment.

Extending corporate liability

In some exceptional cases a company may, itself, be deemed liable for the wrongful act of an employee notwithstanding that the culpable act was performed without the authority of the directing mind. Here corporate liability will be determined by reference to the language and interpretation of the specific obligation or rule. Corporate liability will be imposed where the court considers that a failure to impose liability would defeat the very purpose and intent of the legislation. For example, in *Re Supply of Ready Mixed Concrete (No.2)* [1995] 1 AC 456, a company gave an undertaking to the Restrictive Practices Court (in compliance with the Restrictive Trade Practices Act 1976) to refrain from entering into any restrictive arrangement that would amount to a breach of the undertaking. Notwithstanding the undertaking, senior employees of the company, acting within the scope of their employment, entered into a restrictive agreement. The employees acted without the consent of the company's board, which had actively encouraged its employees to abide by the terms of the restrictive agreement. In finding that the actions of the employees could be attributed to the company (rendering the company in contempt of court) the House of Lords concluded that an undertaking of this nature would have been worthless had the company been able to avoid liability for the acts of its employees by alleging (even if true) that its board of directors had been unaware of the actions of its employees.

Similarly, in *R* v. *British Steel plc* [1995] 1 WLR 1356, the defendant company was prosecuted under the Health and Safety at Work Act 1974, following the death of a worker; the death in part was caused by the ineffective supervision of the worker. The Court of Appeal found a clear breach of the statutory duty so imposed by the Health and Safety at Work Act 1974, namely to ensure that persons were not exposed to risk. The company's defence, namely that its directing mind had sought to take reasonable care by implementing safety measures, was deemed irrelevant given the terms and nature of the statute. As the statute, in seeking to protect public health and safety, imposed (subject to the defence of reasonable practicability) absolute criminal liability, it was held that the health and safety legislation would be ineffective if corporate employers could avoid criminal liability in circumstances where the wrongful act had been committed other than by the directing mind of the company.

16.2   CORPORATE MANSLAUGHTER

The operation of the identification principle

Prosecutions for corporate manslaughter are a recent phenomena and extremely rare. To date, convictions have been limited to a diminutive pool of small private companies. Indeed, prior to the Corporate Manslaughter and Corporate Homicide Act 2007, the operation of the identification principle was such that a causal link between the act of an employee and the command structure of the company (the directing mind) could, in all reality, only be established in the case of a small private company. In a small private company the relationship between the directing mind and the company's employees is often closely aligned or indistinguishable. The first recorded conviction for manslaughter was in the Lyme Bay Canoe case (noted in (1994) *The Times*, 9 December). A group of eight students and their teacher were accompanied by instructors from an outdoor centre in a canoe trip; the group were swept out to sea, and four of the students drowned. Here, the company, OLL Ltd, was also convicted of manslaughter, following the like conviction of the company's managing director. The company's managing director was the company's directing mind (the company was a small concern, the managing director was the *alter ego* of the company). Both the managing director and the company were convicted of manslaughter on the basis of ignoring and not complying with relevant safety standards and procedures.

By contrast, in a large corporation, establishing a causal link between an employee and the directing mind is much more problematic. In a large corporation, corporate policy and the implementation of corporate powers from the directing mind may become misinterpreted, confused or abused by middle management and the general workforce, to the extent that although the wrongful act of an employee may be linked to the instructions of a senior employee, it may nevertheless be devoid of any direct and binding authority emanating from the directing mind.

In *Attorney-General's Reference (No.2 of 1999)* [2000] 3 WLR 195, the Court of Appeal considered the circumstances in which a company could be convicted of involuntary manslaughter, with specific reference to the offence of manslaughter by gross negligence (i.e. the category of manslaughter associated with the prosecution of a company prior to the Corporate Manslaughter and Corporate Homicide Act 2007). The Court of Appeal's opinion was delivered at the request of the Attorney-General and followed the Southall rail disaster of 1997, in which seven train passengers were killed. The court was asked to consider two questions.

- Can a defendant be convicted of manslaughter by gross negligence without the need to establish the defendant's state of mind?
- Can a non-human defendant be convicted of manslaughter by gross negligence in the absence of evidence establishing the guilt of an identified human being for the same crime?

In relation to the first question the court gave an affirmative answer because following the decision of the House of Lords in *R* v. *Adomako* [1995] 1 AC 171, the definition of manslaughter by gross negligence is such that a defendant's guilt may, in an appropriate case, be established on the basis of the defendant having had an obvious and reckless disregard for human life, recklessness being construed in an objective sense with no prerequisite of having to prove *mens rea*. However, in respect of the second question the Court of Appeal answered in the negative. The court held that in seeking to establish a company's guilt it was still necessary to show that in causing death, the act of the employee (with the employee being liable for manslaughter) was an act attributable to the company, via its directing mind. In effect, the identification principle was as relevant to the *actus reus* as it was to the *mens rea* of a crime.

The Corporate Manslaughter and Corporate Homicide Act 2007

Over the last decade proposals to reform the law of corporate manslaughter were given prominence as a consequence of the failure to successfully prosecute larger companies following high-profile disasters such as the sinking of the 'Herald of Free Enterprise', and the Southall, Paddington and Hatfield rail disasters. The government, via the introduction of the Corporate Manslaughter and Corporate Homicide Act (CMCHA) 2007, has sought to replace the identification principle as the principal means of determining a company's liability for manslaughter. Prior to the 2007 Act, a company's potential liability for the common law offence of corporate (involuntary) manslaughter centered on the prosecution's ability to establish that an act or omission of a company employee, in causing the death of a person by gross negligence, was attributable to a constituent element of the company's direct-ing mind (see, e.g. *Attorney General's Reference (No.2 of 1999)* [2000] 3 WLR 195). It also followed that a company could not be convicted of manslaughter unless a distinct conviction could also be sustained against a person who was a part of the company's directing mind.

Under the CMCHA 2007, a company will now be guilty of the offence of corporate manslaughter if the way in which its activities are managed or organised causes a person's death and the said management or organisation of those activities amounts to a gross breach of a relevant duty of care owed by the company to the deceased. However, a company will be guilty of the offence of corporate manslaughter only if the way in which its activities are managed or organised by its senior management is a substantial element in the breach of the relevant duty. In effect, a company's guilt must be estab-lished through its senior management which is defined in two distinct ways. First, senior management may comprise persons who play a significant role in the making of decisions about how the whole or a substantial part of the company's activities are to be managed or organised. Second, senior man-agement may comprise persons who play a significant role in the actual man-aging or organising of the whole or a substantial part of those activities.

However, notwithstanding the potential difficulty of a continued depend-ency on agency rules in the identification of a senior manager, the CMCHA 2007 marks a significant change to the common law position and identifica-tion principle. In accordance with the 'senior management' test, liability for corporate manslaughter will no longer be founded on establishing an agency line of authority between a culpable company employee and the senior management (previously, the directing mind) in respect of the specific act or omission that culminates in the death of a person. In future, it will be neces-sary, in seeking to establish liability for corporate manslaughter, to assess whether a company's senior management was responsible for management practices which ultimately led to the breach of the relevant duty of care. For example, at common law, if an employee of a company negligently caused the death of a person by acting inconsistently with the health and safety legisla-tion and the general policies of the company's directing mind, the company would have escaped liability for corporate manslaughter notwithstanding any failures in the management or organisation of the company. The company would have escaped liability as the employee acted otherwise than in accor-dance with the will of the directing mind. However, under the CMCHA 2007, a company may be made potentially liable for corporate manslaughter irrespective of an employee's non-compliance with the will of the directing mind. Liability may ensue because of a failure in the organisation or manage-ment of the company's affairs – for example, a failure on the part of senior management to ensure that health and safety polices were complied with.

It should also be observed that the use of the term 'senior management' may afford a radical departure to the existing law, given the term's implied support for the aggregation of liability between members of the company's senior management. While, in any given case, it may be impossible to attribute responsibility for a breach of a relevant duty to an individual senior manager, it may be possible to establish corporate liability through the cumulative conduct of the senior managers of the company. The combined effect of the aggregated conduct of senior managers may be a substantial factor in the breach of a relevant duty of care.

Identifying whether a company owes a duty of care to an individual is a matter of law and as such must be decided by the judge at the criminal proceedings. However, in basic terms, a duty of care may be identified as a duty on the part of the company to exercise such care and skill as is reasonable in the circumstances of the case. The CMCHA 2007 requires that the duty of care must be related to specific corporate functions or activities, namely, the company as an employer, the company as an occupier of premises (which is defined to include land), the company as a supplier of goods or services, constructing or maintaining buildings, infrastructure or vehicles, and other activities carried out on a commercial basis. Where the court identifies the existence of a duty of care, the jury's task will be to determine whether there was a breach of the duty and if so whether the breach amounted to gross negligence. Here, the criminal law standard for establishing negligence is akin to the civil law standard.

In establishing the breach of a company's duty of care as an act of gross negligence the CMCHA 2007 provides that the jury must consider whether, in relation to the alleged breach of duty, the company failed to comply with any health and safety legislation. The jury must consider the extent of any such failure and how much of a risk of death it posed. The CMCHA 2007 identifies the concept of gross negligence by stipulating that negligent conduct must fall 'far below' a reasonable standard. In interpreting whether a company's breach of duty of care deviated 'far below' a reasonable standard, the jury is permitted to consider the extent to which the evidence establishes attitudes, policies, systems or accepted practices within the company that were likely to have encouraged or alternatively produced tolerance of the management or organisational failure of the company in respect of the breach. The jury may also have regard to any health and safety guidance that relates to the alleged breach and any other factor that it considers relevant to the case. Accordingly, in relation to corporate conduct resulting in a breach of duty, a company's past and current record of compliance with health and safety matters, in connection with the type of breach of duty in question, may become a paramount and decisive factor in the determination of corporate liability.

Where a company is convicted of the crime of corporate manslaughter, it will be liable to an unlimited fine. The size of the fine will be variable and will be dependent upon the nature and consequences of the managerial or organisational failure. The extent of the fine may also be influenced by the size and resources of the company in question, although the fact that the payment of a fine may propel a company into an insolvent state should be quite irrelevant to the court's determination of the level of the fine to be imposed. With some practical sense, the court may also order the convicted company to remedy any failings which led to the gross breach of duty, setting a defined period in which time the remedial steps must be undertaken. A failure to comply will result in the imposition of a fine. Under the terms of the CMCHA 2007, a company's senior management have no secondary liability in relation to the actual offence of corporate manslaughter.

The provisions of the Companies Act 2006

EFFECTIVE DATES

According to the Department for Business, Enterprise and Regulatory Reform (BERR), all the provisions of the Companies Act (CA) 2006 should be brought into force by 1 October 2008, with a majority of the provisions being in force by 6 April 2008. The implementation of the provisions of the CA 2006 was commenced in January 2007. Provisions on company communications to shareholders and others, which include provisions facilitating electronic communication were commenced from 20 January 2007. Provisions commencing Part 28 of the Act implementing the Takeovers Directive and provisions extending the community interest company regime to Northern Ireland took effect from 6 April 2007.

The remaining Parts of the Act are expected to follow the government's proposed timetable, as indicated below.

Provisions coming into force with effect from 1 October 2007

- Part 9 (Exercise of members' rights)
- Part 10 (A company's directors), other than provisions relating to directors' conflict of interest duties, directors' residential addresses and underage and natural directors
- Part 11 (Derivative claims and proceedings by members)
- Part 13 (Resolutions and meetings), and, related to this, Part 16, ss.485–8 (Audit)
- Part 14 (Control of political donations and expenditure)
- Part 15, s.417 (Contents of directors' report: business review)
- Part 29 (Fraudulent trading)
- Part 30 (Protection of members against unfair prejudice)
- Part 32 (Company investigations: amendments)

The commencement provisions in respect of Part 9 will be drafted so as to enable nominee investment operators to send indirect investors' requests to companies from 1 October 2007 to entitle indirect investors to enjoy information rights from 31 December 2007.

Provisions coming into force with effect from 6 April 2008

- Part 12 (Company secretaries)
- Part 15 (Accounts and reports), other than s.417
- Part 16 (Audit), other than ss.485–8
- Part 19 (Debentures)
- Part 20 (Private and public companies)

- Part 21 (Certification and transfer of securities)
- Part 23 (Distributions)
- Part 26 (Arrangements and reconstructions)
- Part 27 (Mergers and divisions of public companies)
- Part 42 (Statutory auditors)

Provisions coming into force with effect from 1 October 2008

- Part 1 (General introductory provisions)
- Part 2 (Company formation)
- Part 3 (A company's constitution)
- Part 4 (A company's capacity and related matters)
- Part 5 (A company's name)
- Part 6 (A company's registered office)
- Part 7 (Re-registration as a means of altering a company's status)
- Part 8 (A company's members)
- Part 10 (A company's directors) – provisions relating to directors' conflict of interest duties, directors' residential addresses and underage and natural directors
- Part 17 (A company's share capital)
- Part 18 (Acquisition by limited company of its own shares)
- Part 24 (A company's annual return)
- Part 25 (Company charges)
- Part 31 (Dissolution and restoration to the register)
- Part 33 (UK companies not formed under the Companies Acts)
- Part 34 (Overseas companies)
- Part 35 (The registrar of companies)
- Part 41 (Business names)

CA 1985, s.358 which provides a power for companies to close the register of members, will be repealed with effect from 1 October 2008.

Part 36 (Offences under the Companies Acts), Part 37 (Companies: supplementary provisions), Part 38 (Companies: interpretation), Part 45 (Northern Ireland) and Schedule 16 (Repeals) should be introduced with the relevant provisions.

It is expected that secondary legislation, including commencement orders, will be in place by the end of 2007.

HEADINGS OF THE COMPANIES ACT 2006

PART 1 – GENERAL INTRODUCTORY PROVISIONS

Companies and Companies Acts

1 Companies
2 The Companies Acts

Types of company

3 Limited and unlimited companies
4 Private and public companies
5 Companies limited by guarantee and having share capital
6 Community interest companies

PART 2 – COMPANY FORMATION

General

7 Method of forming company
8 Memorandum of association

Requirements for registration

9 Registration documents
10 Statement of capital and initial shareholdings
11 Statement of guarantee
12 Statement of proposed officers
13 Statement of compliance

Registration and its effect

14 Registration
15 Issue of certificate of incorporation
16 Effect of registration

PART 3 – A COMPANY'S CONSTITUTION

Chapter 1 – Introductory

17 A company's constitution

Chapter 2 – Articles of association

General

18 Articles of association
19 Power of Secretary of State to prescribe model articles
20 Default application of model articles

Alteration of articles

21 Amendment of articles
22 Entrenched provisions of the articles
23 Notice to registrar of existence of restriction on amendment of articles
24 Statement of compliance where amendment of articles restricted
25 Effect of alteration of articles on company's members
26 Registrar to be sent copy of amended articles
27 Registrar's notice to comply in case of failure with respect to amended articles

Supplementary

28 Existing companies: provisions of memorandum treated as provisions of articles

Chapter 3 – Resolutions and agreements affecting a company's constitution

29 Resolutions and agreements affecting a company's constitution
30 Copies of resolutions or agreements to be forwarded to registrar

Chapter 4 – Miscellaneous and supplementary provisions

Statement of company's objects

31 Statement of company's objects

Other provisions with respect to a company's constitution

32 Constitutional documents to be provided to members
33 Effect of company's constitution
34 Notice to registrar where company's constitution altered by enactment
35 Notice to registrar where company's constitution altered by order
36 Documents to be incorporated in or accompany copies of articles issued by company

Supplementary provisions

37 Right to participate in profits otherwise than as member void
38 Application to single member companies of enactments and rules of law

PART 4 – A COMPANY'S CAPACITY AND RELATED MATTERS

Capacity of company and power of directors to bind it

39 A company's capacity
40 Power of directors to bind the company
41 Constitutional limitations: transactions involving directors or their associates
42 Constitutional limitations: companies that are charities

Formalities of doing business under the law of England and Wales or Northern Ireland

43 Company contracts
44 Execution of documents
45 Common seal
46 Execution of deeds
47 Execution of deeds or other documents by attorney

Formalities of doing business under the law of Scotland

48 Execution of documents by companies

Other matters

49 Official seal for use abroad
50 Official seal for share certificates etc
51 Pre-incorporation contracts, deeds and obligations
52 Bills of exchange and promissory notes

PART 5 – A COMPANY'S NAME

Chapter 1 – General requirements

Prohibited names

53 Prohibited names

Sensitive words and expressions

54 Names suggesting connection with government or public authority
55 Other sensitive words or expressions
56 Duty to seek comments of government department or other specified body

Permitted characters etc

57 Permitted characters etc

Chapter 2 – Indications of company type or legal form

Required indications for limited companies

58 Public limited companies
59 Private limited companies
60 Exemption from requirement as to use of 'limited'
61 Continuation of existing exemption: companies limited by shares
62 Continuation of existing exemption: companies limited by guarantee
63 Exempt company: restriction on amendment of articles
64 Power to direct change of name in case of company ceasing to be entitled to exemption

Inappropriate use of indications of company type or legal form

65 Inappropriate use of indications of company type or legal form

Chapter 3 – Similarity to other names

Similarity to other name on registrar's index

66 Name not to be the same as another in the index
67 Power to direct change of name in case of similarity to existing name
68 Direction to change name: supplementary provisions

Similarity to other name in which person has goodwill

69 Objection to company's registered name
70 Company names adjudicators
71 Procedural rules
72 Decision of adjudicator to be made available to public
73 Order requiring name to be changed
74 Appeal from adjudicator's decision

Chapter 4 – Other powers of the secretary of state

75 Provision of misleading information etc
76 Misleading indication of activities

Chapter 5 – Change of name

77 Change of name
78 Change of name by special resolution

79 Change of name by means provided for in company's articles
80 Change of name: registration and issue of new certificate of incorporation
81 Change of name: effect

Chapter 6 – Trading disclosures

82 Requirement to disclose company name etc
83 Civil consequences of failure to make required disclosure
84 Criminal consequences of failure to make required disclosures
85 Minor variations in form of name to be left out of account

PART 6 – A COMPANY'S REGISTERED OFFICE

General

86 A company's registered office
87 Change of address of registered office

Welsh companies

88 Welsh companies

PART 7 – RE-REGISTRATION AS A MEANS OF ALTERING A COMPANY'S STATUS

Introductory

89 Alteration of status by re-registration

Private company becoming public

90 Re-registration of private company as public
91 Requirements as to share capital
92 Requirements as to net assets
93 Recent allotment of shares for non-cash consideration
94 Application and accompanying documents
95 Statement of proposed secretary
96 Issue of certificate of incorporation on re-registration

Public company becoming private

97 Re-registration of public company as private limited company
98 Application to court to cancel resolution
99 Notice to registrar of court application or order
100 Application and accompanying documents
101 Issue of certificate of incorporation on re-registration

Private limited company becoming unlimited

102 Re-registration of private limited company as unlimited
103 Application and accompanying documents
104 Issue of certificate of incorporation on re-registration

Unlimited private company becoming limited

105 Re-registration of unlimited company as limited
106 Application and accompanying documents
107 Issue of certificate of incorporation on re-registration
108 Statement of capital required where company already has share capital

Public company becoming private and unlimited

109 Re-registration of public company as private and unlimited
110 Application and accompanying documents
111 Issue of certificate of incorporation on re-registration

PART 8 – A COMPANY'S MEMBERS

Chapter 1 – The members of a company

112 The members of a company

Chapter 2 – Register of members

General

113 Register of members
114 Register to be kept available for inspection
115 Index of members
116 Rights to inspect and require copies
117 Register of members: response to request for inspection or copy
118 Register of members: refusal of inspection or default in providing copy
119 Register of members: offences in connection with request for or disclosure of information
120 Information as to state of register and index
121 Removal of entries relating to former members

Special cases

122 Share warrants
123 Single member companies
124 Company holding its own shares as treasury shares

Supplementary

125 Power of court to rectify register
126 Trusts not to be entered on register
127 Register to be evidence
128 Time limit for claims arising from entry in register

Chapter 3 – Overseas branch registers

129 Overseas branch registers
130 Notice of opening of overseas branch register
131 Keeping of overseas branch register

132 Register or duplicate to be kept available for inspection in UK
133 Transactions in shares registered in overseas branch register
134 Jurisdiction of local courts
135 Discontinuance of overseas branch register

Chapter 4 – Prohibition on subsidiary being member of its holding company

General prohibition

136 Prohibition on subsidiary being a member of its holding company
137 Shares acquired before prohibition became applicable

Subsidiary acting as personal representative or trustee

138 Subsidiary acting as personal representative or trustee
139 Interests to be disregarded: residual interest under pension scheme or employees' share scheme
140 Interests to be disregarded: employer's rights of recovery under pension scheme or employees' share scheme

Subsidiary acting as dealer in securities

141 Subsidiary acting as authorised dealer in securities
142 Protection of third parties in other cases where subsidiary acting as dealer in securities

Supplementary

143 Application of provisions to companies not limited by shares
144 Application of provisions to nominees

PART 9 – EXERCISE OF MEMBERS' RIGHTS

Effect of provisions in company's articles

145 Effect of provisions of articles as to enjoyment or exercise of members' rights

Information rights

146 Traded companies: nomination of persons to enjoy information rights
147 Information rights: form in which copies to be provided
148 Termination or suspension of nomination
149 Information as to possible rights in relation to voting
150 Information rights: status of rights
151 Information rights: power to amend

Exercise of rights where shares held on behalf of others

152 Exercise of rights where shares held on behalf of others: exercise in different ways
153 Exercise of rights where shares held on behalf of others: members' requests

PART 10 – A COMPANY'S DIRECTORS

Chapter 1 – Appointment and removal of directors

Requirement to have directors

154 Companies required to have directors
155 Companies required to have at least one director who is a natural person
156 Direction requiring company to make appointment

Appointment

157 Minimum age for appointment as director
158 Power to provide for exceptions from minimum age requirement
159 Existing under-age directors
160 Appointment of directors of public company to be voted on individually
161 Validity of acts of directors

Register of directors, etc

162 Register of directors
163 Particulars of directors to be registered: individuals
164 Particulars of directors to be registered: corporate directors and firms
165 Register of directors' residential addresses
166 Particulars of directors to be registered: power to make regulations
167 Duty to notify registrar of changes

Removal

168 Resolution to remove director
169 Director's right to protest against removal

Chapter 2 – General duties of directors

Introductory

170 Scope and nature of general duties

The general duties

171 Duty to act within powers
172 Duty to promote the success of the company
173 Duty to exercise independent judgment
174 Duty to exercise reasonable care, skill and diligence
175 Duty to avoid conflicts of interest
176 Duty not to accept benefits from third parties
177 Duty to declare interest in proposed transaction or arrangement

Supplementary provisions

178 Civil consequences of breach of general duties
179 Cases within more than one of the general duties

180 Consent, approval or authorisation by members
181 Modification of provisions in relation to charitable companies

Chapter 3 – Declaration of interest in existing transaction or arrangement

182 Declaration of interest in existing transaction or arrangement
183 Offence of failure to declare interest
184 Declaration made by notice in writing
185 General notice treated as sufficient declaration
186 Declaration of interest in case of company with sole director
187 Declaration of interest in existing transaction by shadow director

Chapter 4 – Transactions with directors requiring approval of members

Service contracts

188 Directors' long-term service contracts: requirement of members' approval
189 Directors' long-term service contracts: civil consequences of contravention

Substantial property transactions

190 Substantial property transactions: requirement of members' approval
191 Meaning of 'substantial'
192 Exception for transactions with members or other group companies
193 Exception in case of company in winding up or administration
194 Exception for transactions on recognised investment exchange
195 Property transactions: civil consequences of contravention
196 Property transactions: effect of subsequent affirmation

Loans, quasi-loans and credit transactions

197 Loans to directors: requirement of members' approval
198 Quasi-loans to directors: requirement of members' approval
199 Meaning of 'quasi-loan' and related expressions
200 Loans or quasi-loans to persons connected with directors: requirement of mem-
    bers' approval
201 Credit transactions: requirement of members' approval
202 Meaning of 'credit transaction'
203 Related arrangements: requirement of members' approval
204 Exception for expenditure on company business
205 Exception for expenditure on defending proceedings etc
206 Exception for expenditure in connection with regulatory action or investigation
207 Exceptions for minor and business transactions
208 Exceptions for intra-group transactions
209 Exceptions for money-lending companies
210 Other relevant transactions or arrangements
211 The value of transactions and arrangements
212 The person for whom a transaction or arrangement is entered into
213 Loans etc: civil consequences of contravention
214 Loans etc: effect of subsequent affirmation

Payments for loss of office

215 Payments for loss of office
216 Amounts taken to be payments for loss of office
217 Payment by company: requirement of members' approval
218 Payment in connection with transfer of undertaking etc: requirement of members' approval
219 Payment in connection with share transfer: requirement of members' approval
220 Exception for payments in discharge of legal obligations etc
221 Exception for small payments
222 Payments made without approval: civil consequences

Supplementary

223 Transactions requiring members' approval: application of provisions to shadow directors
224 Approval by written resolution: accidental failure to send memorandum
225 Cases where approval is required under more than one provision
226 Requirement of consent of Charity Commission: companies that are charities

Chapter 5 – Directors' service contracts

227 Directors' service contracts
228 Copy of contract or memorandum of terms to be available for inspection
229 Right of member to inspect and request copy
230 Directors' service contracts: application of provisions to shadow directors

Chapter 6 – Contracts with sole members who are directors

231 Contract with sole member who is also a director

Chapter 7 – Directors' liabilities

Provision protecting directors from liability

232 Provisions protecting directors from liability
233 Provision of insurance
234 Qualifying third party indemnity provision
235 Qualifying pension scheme indemnity provision
236 Qualifying indemnity provision to be disclosed in directors' report
237 Copy of qualifying indemnity provision to be available for inspection
238 Right of member to inspect and request copy

Ratification of acts giving rise to liability

239 Ratification of acts of directors

Chapter 8 – Directors' residential addresses: protection from disclosure

240 Protected information
241 Protected information: restriction on use or disclosure by company
242 Protected information: restriction on use or disclosure by registrar

243 Permitted use or disclosure by the registrar
244 Disclosure under court order
245 Circumstances in which registrar may put address on the public record
246 Putting the address on the public record

Chapter 9 – Supplementary provisions

Provision for employees on cessation or transfer of business

247 Power to make provision for employees on cessation or transfer of business

Records of meetings of directors

248 Minutes of directors' meetings
249 Minutes as evidence

Meaning of 'director' and 'shadow director'

250 'Director'
251 'Shadow director'

Other definitions

252 Persons connected with a director
253 Members of a director's family
254 Director 'connected with' a body corporate
255 Director 'controlling' a body corporate
256 Associated bodies corporate
257 References to company's constitution

General

258 Power to increase financial limits
259 Transactions under foreign law

PART 11 – DERIVATIVE CLAIMS AND PROCEEDINGS BY MEMBERS

Chapter 1 – Derivative claims in England and Wales or Northern Ireland

260 Derivative claims
261 Application for permission to continue derivative claim
262 Application for permission to continue claim as a derivative claim
263 Whether permission to be given
264 Application for permission to continue derivative claim brought by another member

Chapter 2 – Derivative proceedings in Scotland

265 Derivative proceedings
266 Requirement for leave and notice
267 Application to continue proceedings as derivative proceedings

268 Granting of leave
269 Application by member to be substituted for member pursuing derivative proceedings

PART 12 – COMPANY SECRETARIES

Private companies

270 Private company not required to have secretary

Public companies

271 Public company required to have secretary
272 Direction requiring public company to appoint secretary
273 Qualifications of secretaries of public companies

Provisions applying to private companies with a secretary and to public companies

274 Discharge of functions where office vacant or secretary unable to act
275 Duty to keep register of secretaries
276 Duty to notify registrar of changes
277 Particulars of secretaries to be registered: individuals
278 Particulars of secretaries to be registered: corporate secretaries and firms
279 Particulars of secretaries to be registered: power to make regulations
280 Acts done by person in dual capacity

PART 13 – RESOLUTIONS AND MEETINGS

Chapter 1 – General provisions about resolutions

281 Resolutions
282 Ordinary resolutions
283 Special resolutions
284 Votes: general rules
285 Votes: specific requirements
286 Votes of joint holders of shares
287 Saving for provisions of articles as to determination of entitlement to vote

Chapter 2 – Written resolutions

General provisions about written resolutions

288 Written resolutions of private companies
289 Eligible members

Circulation of written resolutions

290 Circulation date
291 Circulation of written resolutions proposed by directors
292 Members' power to require circulation of written resolution
293 Circulation of written resolution proposed by members

294 Expenses of circulation
295 Application not to circulate members' statement

Agreeing to written resolutions

296 Procedure for signifying agreement to written resolution
297 Period for agreeing to written resolution

Supplementary

298 Sending documents relating to written resolutions by electronic means
299 Publication of written resolution on website
300 Relationship between this Chapter and provisions of company's articles

Chapter 3 – Resolutions at meetings

General provisions about resolutions at meetings

301 Resolutions at general meetings

Calling meetings

302 Directors' power to call general meetings
303 Members' power to require directors to call general meeting
304 Directors' duty to call meetings required by members
305 Power of members to call meeting at company's expense
306 Power of court to order meeting

Notice of meetings

307 Notice required of general meeting
308 Manner in which notice to be given
309 Publication of notice of meeting on website
310 Persons entitled to receive notice of meetings
311 Contents of notices of meetings
312 Resolution requiring special notice
313 Accidental failure to give notice of resolution or meeting

Members' statements

314 Members' power to require circulation of statements
315 Company's duty to circulate members' statement
316 Expenses of circulating members' statement
317 Application not to circulate members' statement

Procedure at meetings

318 Quorum at meetings
319 Chairman of meeting
320 Declaration by chairman on a show of hands
321 Right to demand a poll

322 Voting on a poll
323 Representation of corporations at meetings

Proxies

324 Rights to appoint proxies
325 Notice of meeting to contain statement of rights
326 Company-sponsored invitations to appoint proxies
327 Notice required of appointment of proxy etc
328 Chairing meetings
329 Right of proxy to demand a poll
330 Notice required of termination of proxy's authority
331 Saving for more extensive rights conferred by articles

Adjourned meetings

332 Resolution passed at adjourned meeting

Electronic communications

333 Sending documents relating to meetings etc in electronic form

Application to class meetings

334 Application to class meetings
335 Application to class meetings: companies without a share capital

Chapter 4 – Public companies: additional requirements for AGMs

336 Public companies: annual general meeting
337 Public companies: notice of AGM
338 Public companies: members' power to require circulation of resolutions for AGMs
339 Public companies: company's duty to circulate members' resolutions for AGMs
340 Public companies: expenses of circulating members' resolutions for AGM

Chapter 5 – Additional requirements for quoted companies

Website publication of poll results

341 Results of poll to be made available on website

Independent report on poll

342 Members' power to require independent report on poll
343 Appointment of independent assessor
344 Independence requirement
345 Meaning of 'associate'
346 Effect of appointment of a partnership
347 The independent assessor's report
348 Rights of independent assessor: right to attend meeting etc
349 Rights of independent assessor: right to information

350 Offences relating to provision of information
351 Information to be made available on website

Supplementary

352 Application of provisions to class meetings
353 Requirements as to website availability
354 Power to limit or extend the types of company to which provisions of this Chapter apply

Chapter 6 – Records of resolutions and meetings

355 Records of resolutions and meetings etc
356 Records as evidence of resolutions etc
357 Records of decisions by sole member
358 Inspection of records of resolutions and meetings
359 Records of resolutions and meetings of class of members

Chapter 7 – Supplementary provisions

360 Computation of periods of notice etc: clear day rule
361 Meaning of 'quoted company'

PART 14 – CONTROL OF POLITICAL DONATIONS AND EXPENDITURE

Introductory

362 Introductory

Donations and expenditure to which this Part applies

363 Political parties, organisations etc to which this Part applies
364 Meaning of 'political donation'
365 Meaning of 'political expenditure'

Authorisation required for donations or expenditure

366 Authorisation required for donations or expenditure
367 Form of authorising resolution
368 Period for which resolution has effect

Remedies in case of unauthorised donations or expenditure

369 Liability of directors in case of unauthorised donation or expenditure
370 Enforcement of directors' liabilities by shareholder action
371 Enforcement of directors' liabilities by shareholder action: supplementary
372 Costs of shareholder action
373 Information for purposes of shareholder action

Exemptions

374 Trade unions
375 Subscription for membership of trade association

376 All-party parliamentary groups
377 Political expenditure exempted by order
378 Donations not amounting to more than £5,000 in any twelve month period

Supplementary provisions

379 Minor definitions

PART 15 – ACCOUNTS AND REPORTS

Chapter 1 – Introduction

General

380 Scheme of this Part

Companies subject to the small companies regime

381 Companies subject to the small companies regime
382 Companies qualifying as small: general
383 Companies qualifying as small: parent companies
384 Companies excluded from the small companies regime

Quoted and unquoted companies

385 Quoted and unquoted companies

Chapter 2 – Accounting records

386 Duty to keep accounting records
387 Duty to keep accounting records: offence
388 Where and for how long records to be kept
389 Where and for how long records to be kept: offences

Chapter 3 – A company's financial year

390 A company's financial year
391 Accounting reference periods and accounting reference date
392 Alteration of accounting reference date

Chapter 4 – Annual accounts

General

393 Accounts to give true and fair view

Individual accounts

394 Duty to prepare individual accounts
395 Individual accounts: applicable accounting framework

396 Companies Act individual accounts
397 IAS individual accounts

Group accounts: small companies

398 Option to prepare group accounts

Group accounts: other companies

399 Duty to prepare group accounts
400 Exemption for company included in EEA group accounts of larger group
401 Exemption for company included in non-EEA group accounts of larger group
402 Exemption if no subsidiary undertakings need be included in the consolidation

Group accounts: general

403 Group accounts: applicable accounting framework
404 Companies Act group accounts
405 Companies Act group accounts: subsidiary undertakings included in the consolidation
406 IAS group accounts
407 Consistency of financial reporting within group
408 Individual profit and loss account where group accounts prepared

Information to be given in notes to the accounts

409 Information about related undertakings
410 Information about related undertakings: alternative compliance
411 Information about employee numbers and costs
412 Information about directors' benefits: remuneration
413 Information about directors' benefits: advances, credit and guarantees

Approval and signing of accounts

414 Approval and signing of accounts

Chapter 5 – Directors' report

Directors' report

415 Duty to prepare directors' report
416 Contents of directors' report: general
417 Contents of directors' report: business review
418 Contents of directors' report: statement as to disclosure to auditors
419 Approval and signing of directors' report

Chapter 6 – Quoted companies: directors' remuneration report

420 Duty to prepare directors' remuneration report
421 Contents of directors' remuneration report
422 Approval and signing of directors' remuneration report

Chapter 7 – Publication of accounts and reports

Duty to circulate copies of accounts and reports

423 Duty to circulate copies of annual accounts and reports
424 Time allowed for sending out copies of accounts and reports
425 Default in sending out copies of accounts and reports: offences

Option to provide summary financial statement

426 Option to provide summary financial statement
427 Form and contents of summary financial statement: unquoted companies
428 Form and contents of summary financial statement: quoted companies
429 Summary financial statements: offences

Quoted companies: requirements as to website publication

430 Quoted companies: annual accounts and reports to be made available on website

Right of member or debenture holder to demand copies of accounts and reports

431 Right of member or debenture holder to copies of accounts and reports: unquoted companies
432 Right of member or debenture holder to copies of accounts and reports: quoted companies

Requirements in connection with publication of accounts and reports

433 Name of signatory to be stated in published copies of accounts and reports
434 Requirements in connection with publication of statutory accounts
435 Requirements in connection with publication of non-statutory accounts
436 Meaning of 'publication' in relation to accounts and reports

Chapter 8 – Public companies: laying of accounts and reports before general meeting

437 Public companies: laying of accounts and reports before general meeting
438 Public companies: offence of failure to lay accounts and reports

Chapter 9 – Quoted companies: members' approval of directors' remuneration report

439 Quoted companies: members' approval of directors' remuneration report
440 Quoted companies: offences in connection with procedure for approval

Chapter 10 – Filing of accounts and reports

Duty to file accounts and reports

441 Duty to file accounts and reports with the registrar
442 Period allowed for filing accounts
443 Calculation of period allowed

Filing obligations of different descriptions of company

444 Filing obligations of companies subject to small companies regime
445 Filing obligations of medium-sized companies
446 Filing obligations of unquoted companies
447 Filing obligations of quoted companies
448 Unlimited companies exempt from obligation to file accounts

Requirements where abbreviated accounts delivered

449 Special auditor's report where abbreviated accounts delivered
450 Approval and signing of abbreviated accounts

Failure to file accounts and reports

451 Default in filing accounts and reports: offences
452 Default in filing accounts and reports: court order
453 Civil penalty for failure to file accounts and reports

Chapter 11 – Revision of defective accounts and reports

Voluntary revision

454 Voluntary revision of accounts etc

Secretary of State's notice

455 Secretary of State's notice in respect of accounts or reports

Application to court

456 Application to court in respect of defective accounts or reports
457 Other persons authorised to apply to the court
458 Disclosure of information by tax authorities

Power of authorised person to require documents etc

459 Power of authorised person to require documents, information and explanations
460 Restrictions on disclosure of information obtained under compulsory powers
461 Permitted disclosure of information obtained under compulsory powers
462 Power to amend categories of permitted disclosure

Chapter 12 – Supplementary provisions

Liability for false or misleading statements in reports

463 Liability for false or misleading statements in reports

Accounting and reporting standards

464 Accounting standards

Companies qualifying as medium-sized

465 Companies qualifying as medium-sized: general
466 Companies qualifying as medium-sized: parent companies
467 Companies excluded from being treated as medium-sized

General power to make further provision about accounts and reports

468 General power to make further provision about accounts and reports

Other supplementary provisions

469 Preparation and filing of accounts in euros
470 Power to apply provisions to banking partnerships
471 Meaning of 'annual accounts' and related expressions
472 Notes to the accounts
473 Parliamentary procedure for certain regulations under this Part
474 Minor definitions

PART 16 – AUDIT

Chapter 1 – Requirement for audited accounts

Requirement for audited accounts

475 Requirement for audited accounts
476 Right of members to require audit

Exemption from audit: small companies

477 Small companies: conditions for exemption from audit
478 Companies excluded from small companies exemption
479 Availability of small companies exemption in case of group company

Exemption from audit: dormant companies

480 Dormant companies: conditions for exemption from audit
481 Companies excluded from dormant companies exemption

Companies subject to public sector audit

482 Non-profit-making companies subject to public sector audit
483 Scottish public sector companies: audit by Auditor General for Scotland

General power of amendment by regulations

484 General power of amendment by regulations

Chapter 2 – Appointment of auditors

Private companies

485 Appointment of auditors of private company: general
486 Appointment of auditors of private company: default power of Secretary of State

487 Term of office of auditors of private company
488 Prevention by members of deemed re-appointment of auditor

Public companies

489 Appointment of auditors of public company: general
490 Appointment of auditors of public company: default power of Secretary of State
491 Term of office of auditors of public company

General provisions

492 Fixing of auditor's remuneration
493 Disclosure of terms of audit appointment
494 Disclosure of services provided by auditor or associates and related remuneration

Chapter 3 – Functions of auditor

Auditor's report

495 Auditor's report on company's annual accounts
496 Auditor's report on directors' report
497 Auditor's report on auditable part of directors' remuneration report

Duties and rights of auditors

498 Duties of auditor
499 Auditor's general right to information
500 Auditor's right to information from overseas subsidiaries
501 Auditor's rights to information: offences
502 Auditor's rights in relation to resolutions and meetings

Signature of auditor's report

503 Signature of auditor's report
504 Senior statutory auditor
505 Names to be stated in published copies of auditor's report
506 Circumstances in which names may be omitted

Offences in connection with auditor's report

507 Offences in connection with auditor's report
508 Guidance for regulatory and prosecuting authorities: England, Wales and Northern Ireland
509 Guidance for regulatory authorities: Scotland

Chapter 4 – Removal, resignation, etc of auditors

Removal of auditor

510 Resolution removing auditor from office
511 Special notice required for resolution removing auditor from office

512 Notice to registrar of resolution removing auditor from office
513 Rights of auditor who has been removed from office

Failure to re-appoint auditor

514 Failure to re-appoint auditor: special procedure required for written resolution
515 Failure to re-appoint auditor: special notice required for resolution at general meeting

Resignation of auditor

516 Resignation of auditor
517 Notice to registrar of resignation of auditor
518 Rights of resigning auditor

Statement by auditor on ceasing to hold office

519 Statement by auditor to be deposited with company
520 Company's duties in relation to statement
521 Copy of statement to be sent to registrar
522 Duty of auditor to notify appropriate audit authority
523 Duty of company to notify appropriate audit authority
524 Information to be given to accounting authorities
525 Meaning of 'appropriate audit authority' and 'major audit'

Supplementary

526 Effect of casual vacancies

Chapter 5 – Quoted companies: right of members to raise audit concerns at accounts meeting

527 Members' power to require website publication of audit concerns
528 Requirements as to website availability
529 Website publication: company's supplementary duties
530 Website publication: offences
531 Meaning of 'quoted company'

Chapter 6 – Auditors' liability

Voidness of provisions protecting auditors from liability

532 Voidness of provisions protecting auditors from liability

Indemnity for costs of defending proceedings

533 Indemnity for costs of successfully defending proceedings

Liability limitation agreements

534 Liability limitation agreements
535 Terms of liability limitation agreement

536 Authorisation of agreement by members of the company
537 Effect of liability limitation agreement
538 Disclosure of agreement by company

Chapter 7 – Supplementary provisions

539 Minor definitions

PART 17 – A COMPANY'S SHARE CAPITAL

Chapter 1 – Shares and share capital of a company

Shares

540 Shares
541 Nature of shares
542 Nominal value of shares
543 Numbering of shares
544 Transferability of shares
545 Companies having a share capital
546 Issued and allotted share capital

Share capital

547 Called-up share capital
548 Equity share capital

Chapter 2 – Allotment of shares: general provisions

Power of directors to allot shares

549 Exercise by directors of power to allot shares etc
550 Power of directors to allot shares etc: private company with only one class of shares
551 Power of directors to allot shares etc: authorisation by company

Prohibition of commissions, discounts and allowances

552 General prohibition of commissions, discounts and allowances
553 Permitted commission

Registration of allotment

554 Registration of allotment

Return of allotment

555 Return of allotment by limited company
556 Return of allotment by unlimited company allotting new class of shares
557 Offence of failure to make return

Supplementary provisions

558 When shares are allotted
559 Provisions about allotment not applicable to shares taken on formation

Chapter 3 – Allotment of equity securities: existing shareholders' right of pre-emption

Introductory

560 Meaning of 'equity securities' and related expressions

Existing shareholders' right of pre-emption

561 Existing shareholders' right of pre-emption
562 Communication of pre-emption offers to shareholders
563 Liability of company and officers in case of contravention

Exceptions to right of pre-emption

564 Exception to pre-emption right: bonus shares
565 Exception to pre-emption right: issue for non-cash consideration
566 Exception to pre-emption right: securities held under employees' share scheme

Exclusion of right of pre-emption

567 Exclusion of requirements by private companies
568 Exclusion of pre-emption right: articles conferring corresponding right

Disapplication of pre-emption rights

569 Disapplication of pre-emption rights: private company with only one class of shares
570 Disapplication of pre-emption rights: directors acting under general authorisation
571 Disapplication of pre-emption rights by special resolution
572 Liability for false statement in directors' statement
573 Disapplication of pre-emption rights: sale of treasury shares

Supplementary

574 References to holder of shares in relation to offer
575 Saving for other restrictions on offer or allotment
576 Saving for certain older pre-emption requirements
577 Provisions about pre-emption not applicable to shares taken on formation

Chapter 4 – Public companies: allotment where issue not fully subscribed

578 Public companies: allotment where issue not fully subscribed
579 Public companies: effect of irregular allotment where issue not fully subscribed

Chapter 5 – Payment for shares

General rules

580 Shares not to be allotted at a discount

581 Provision for different amounts to be paid on shares
582 General rule as to means of payment
583 Meaning of payment in cash

Additional rules for public companies

584 Public companies: shares taken by subscribers of memorandum
585 Public companies: must not accept undertaking to do work or perform services
586 Public companies: shares must be at least one-quarter paid up
587 Public companies: payment by long-term undertaking

Supplementary provisions

588 Liability of subsequent holders of shares
589 Power of court to grant relief
590 Penalty for contravention of this Chapter
591 Enforceability of undertakings to do work etc
592 The appropriate rate of interest

Chapter 6 – Public companies: independent valuation of non-cash consideration

Non-cash consideration for shares

593 Public company: valuation of non-cash consideration for shares
594 Exception to valuation requirement: arrangement with another company
595 Exception to valuation requirement: merger
596 Non-cash consideration for shares: requirements as to valuation and report
597 Copy of report to be delivered to registrar

Transfer of non-cash asset in initial period

598 Public company: agreement for transfer of non-cash asset in initial period
599 Agreement for transfer of non-cash asset: requirement of independent valuation
600 Agreement for transfer of non-cash asset: requirements as to valuation and report
601 Agreement for transfer of non-cash asset: requirement of approval by members
602 Copy of resolution to be delivered to registrar
603 Adaptation of provisions in relation to company re-registering as public
604 Agreement for transfer of non-cash asset: effect of contravention

Supplementary provisions

605 Liability of subsequent holders of shares
606 Power of court to grant relief
607 Penalty for contravention of this Chapter
608 Enforceability of undertakings to do work etc
609 The appropriate rate of interest

Chapter 7 – Share premiums

The share premium account

610 Application of share premiums

Relief from requirements as to share premiums

611 Group reconstruction relief
612 Merger relief
613 Merger relief: meaning of 90% equity holding
614 Power to make further provision by regulations
615 Relief may be reflected in company's balance sheet

Supplementary provisions

616 Interpretation of this Chapter

Chapter 8 – Alteration of share capital

How share capital may be altered

617 Alteration of share capital of limited company

Subdivision or consolidation of shares

618 Sub-division or consolidation of shares
619 Notice to registrar of sub-division or consolidation

Reconversion of stock into shares

620 Reconversion of stock into shares
621 Notice to registrar of reconversion of stock into shares

Redenomination of share capital

622 Redenomination of share capital
623 Calculation of new nominal values
624 Effect of redenomination
625 Notice to registrar of redenomination
626 Reduction of capital in connection with redenomination
627 Notice to registrar of reduction of capital in connection with redenomination
628 Redenomination reserve

Chapter 9 – Classes of share and class rights

Introductory

629 Classes of shares

Variation of class rights

630 Variation of class rights: companies having a share capital
631 Variation of class rights: companies without a share capital
632 Variation of class rights: saving for court's powers under other provisions
633 Right to object to variation: companies having a share capital
634 Right to object to variation: companies without a share capital
635 Copy of court order to be forwarded to the registrar

Matters to be notified to the registrar

636 Notice of name or other designation of class of shares
637 Notice of particulars of variation of rights attached to shares
638 Notice of new class of members
639 Notice of name or other designation of class of members
640 Notice of particulars of variation of class rights

Chapter 10 – Reduction of share capital

Introductory

641 Circumstances in which a company may reduce its share capital

Private companies: reduction of capital supported by solvency statement

642 Reduction of capital supported by solvency statement
643 Solvency statement
644 Registration of resolution and supporting documents

Reduction of capital confirmed by the court

645 Application to court for order of confirmation
646 Creditors entitled to object to reduction
647 Offences in connection with list of creditors
648 Court order confirming reduction
649 Registration of order and statement of capital

Public company reducing capital below authorised minimum

650 Public company reducing capital below authorised minimum
651 Expedited procedure for re-registration as a private company

Effect of reduction of capital

652 Liability of members following reduction of capital
653 Liability to creditor in case of omission from list of creditors

Chapter 11 – Miscellaneous and supplementary provisions

654 Treatment of reserve arising from reduction of capital
655 Shares no bar to damages against company
656 Public companies: duty of directors to call meeting on serious loss of capital
657 General power to make further provision by regulations

PART 18 – ACQUISITION BY LIMITED COMPANY OF ITS OWN SHARES

Chapter 1 – General provisions

Introductory

658 General rule against limited company acquiring its own shares
659 Exceptions to general rule

Shares held by company's nominee

660 Treatment of shares held by nominee
661 Liability of others where nominee fails to make payment in respect of shares

Shares held by or for public company

662 Duty to cancel shares in public company held by or for the company
663 Notice of cancellation of shares
664 Re-registration as private company in consequence of cancellation
665 Issue of certificate of incorporation on re-registration
666 Effect of failure to re-register
667 Offence in case of failure to cancel shares or re-register
668 Application of provisions to company re-registering as public company
669 Transfer to reserve on acquisition of shares by public company or nominee

Charges of public company on own shares

670 Public companies: general rule against lien or charge on own shares

Supplementary provisions

671 Interests to be disregarded in determining whether company has beneficial interest
672 Residual interest under pension scheme or employees' share scheme
673 Employer's charges and other rights of recovery
674 Rights as personal representative or trustee
675 Meaning of 'pension scheme'
676 Application of provisions to directors

Chapter 2 – Financial assistance for purchase of own shares

Introductory

677 Meaning of 'financial assistance'

Circumstances in which financial assistance prohibited

678 Assistance for acquisition of shares in public company
679 Assistance by public company for acquisition of shares in its private holding company
680 Prohibited financial assistance an offence

Exceptions from prohibition

681 Unconditional exceptions
682 Conditional exceptions

Supplementary

683 Definitions for this Chapter

Chapter 3 – Redeemable shares

684 Power of limited company to issue redeemable shares
685 Terms and manner of redemption
686 Payment for redeemable shares
687 Financing of redemption
688 Redeemed shares treated as cancelled
689 Notice to registrar of redemption

Chapter 4 – Purchase of own shares

General provisions

690 Power of limited company to purchase own shares
691 Payment for purchase of own shares
692 Financing of purchase of own shares

Authority for purchase of own shares

693 Authority for purchase of own shares

Authority for off-market purchase

694 Authority for off-market purchase
695 Resolution authorising off-market purchase: exercise of voting rights
696 Resolution authorising off-market purchase: disclosure of details of contract
697 Variation of contract for off-market purchase
698 Resolution authorising variation: exercise of voting rights
699 Resolution authorising variation: disclosure of details of variation
700 Release of company's rights under contract for off-market purchase

Authority for market purchase

701 Authority for market purchase

Supplementary provisions

702 Copy of contract or memorandum to be available for inspection
703 Enforcement of right to inspect copy or memorandum
704 No assignment of company's right to purchase own shares
705 Payments apart from purchase price to be made out of distributable profits
706 Treatment of shares purchased
707 Return to registrar of purchase of own shares
708 Notice to registrar of cancellation of shares

Chapter 5 – Redemption or purchase by private company out of capital

Introductory

709 Power of private limited company to redeem or purchase own shares out of capital

The permissible capital payment

710 The permissible capital payment
711 Available profits
712 Determination of available profits

Requirements for payment out of capital

713 Requirements for payment out of capital
714 Directors' statement and auditor's report
715 Directors' statement: offence if no reasonable grounds for opinion
716 Payment to be approved by special resolution
717 Resolution authorising payment: exercise of voting rights
718 Resolution authorising payment: disclosure of directors' statement and auditor's report
719 Public notice of proposed payment
720 Directors' statement and auditor's report to be available for inspection

Objection to payment by members or creditors

721 Application to court to cancel resolution
722 Notice to registrar of court application or order

Supplementary provisions

723 When payment out of capital to be made

Chapter 6 – Treasury shares

724 Treasury shares
725 Treasury shares: maximum holdings
726 Treasury shares: exercise of rights
727 Treasury shares: disposal
728 Treasury shares: notice of disposal
729 Treasury shares: cancellation
730 Treasury shares: notice of cancellation
731 Treasury shares: treatment of proceeds of sale
732 Treasury shares: offences

Chapter 7 – Supplementary provisions

733 The capital redemption reserve
734 Accounting consequences of payment out of capital
735 Effect of company's failure to redeem or purchase
736 Meaning of 'distributable profits'
737 General power to make further provision by regulations

Part 19 – Debentures

General provisions

738 Meaning of 'debenture'
739 Perpetual debentures

740 Enforcement of contract to subscribe for debentures
741 Registration of allotment of debentures
742 Debentures to bearer (Scotland)

Register of debenture holders

743 Register of debenture holders
744 Register of debenture holders: right to inspect and require copy
745 Register of debenture holders: response to request for inspection or copy
746 Register of debenture holders: refusal of inspection or default in providing copy
747 Register of debenture holders: offences in connection with request for or disclosure of information
748 Time limit for claims arising from entry in register

Supplementary provisions

749 Right of debenture holder to copy of deed
750 Liability of trustees of debentures
751 Liability of trustees of debentures: saving for certain older provisions
752 Power to re-issue redeemed debentures
753 Deposit of debentures to secure advances
754 Priorities where debentures secured by floating charge

PART 20 – PRIVATE AND PUBLIC COMPANIES

Chapter 1 – Prohibition of public offers by private companies

755 Prohibition of public offers by private company
756 Meaning of 'offer to the public'
757 Enforcement of prohibition: order restraining proposed contravention
758 Enforcement of prohibition: orders available to the court after contravention
759 Enforcement of prohibition: remedial order
760 Validity of allotment etc not affected

Chapter 2 – Minimum share capital requirement for public companies

761 Public company: requirement as to minimum share capital
762 Procedure for obtaining certificate
763 The authorised minimum
764 Power to alter authorised minimum
765 Authorised minimum: application of initial requirement
766 Authorised minimum: application where shares denominated in different currencies etc
767 Consequences of doing business etc without a trading certificate

PART 21 – CERTIFICATION AND TRANSFER OF SECURITIES

Chapter 1 – Certification and transfer of securities: general

Share certificates

768 Share certificate to be evidence of title

Issue of certificates etc on allotment

769 Duty of company as to issue of certificates etc on allotment

Transfer of securities

770 Registration of transfer
771 Procedure on transfer being lodged
772 Transfer of shares on application of transferor
773 Execution of share transfer by personal representative
774 Evidence of grant of probate etc
775 Certification of instrument of transfer

Issue of certificates etc on transfer

776 Duty of company as to issue of certificates etc on transfer
777 Issue of certificates etc: cases within the Stock Transfer Act 1982

Issue of certificates etc on allotment or transfer to financial institution

778 Issue of certificates etc: allotment or transfer to financial institution

Share warrants

779 Issue and effect of share warrant to bearer
780 Duty of company as to issue of certificates on surrender of share warrant
781 Offences in connection with share warrants (Scotland)

Supplementary provisions

782 Issue of certificates etc: court order to make good default

Chapter 2 – Evidencing and transfer of title to securities without written instrument

Introductory

783 Scope of this Chapter
784 Power to make regulations

Powers exercisable

785 Provision enabling procedures for evidencing and transferring title
786 Provision enabling or requiring arrangements to be adopted
787 Provision enabling or requiring arrangements to be adopted: order-making powers

Supplementary

788 Provision that may be included in regulations
789 Duty to consult
790 Resolutions to be forwarded to registrar

PART 22 – INFORMATION ABOUT INTERESTS IN A COMPANY'S SHARES

Introductory

791 Companies to which this Part applies
792 Shares to which this Part applies

Notice requiring information about interests in shares

793 Notice by company requiring information about interests in its shares
794 Notice requiring information: order imposing restrictions on shares
795 Notice requiring information: offences
796 Notice requiring information: persons exempted from obligation to comply

Orders imposing restrictions on shares

797 Consequences of order imposing restrictions
798 Penalty for attempted evasion of restrictions
799 Relaxation of restrictions
800 Removal of restrictions
801 Order for sale of shares
802 Application of proceeds of sale under court order

Power of members to require company to act

803 Power of members to require company to act
804 Duty of company to comply with requirement
805 Report to members on outcome of investigation
806 Report to members: offences
807 Right to inspect and request copy of reports

Register of interests disclosed

808 Register of interests disclosed
809 Register to be kept available for inspection
810 Associated index
811 Rights to inspect and require copy of entries
812 Court supervision of purpose for which rights may be exercised
813 Register of interests disclosed: refusal of inspection or default in providing copy
814 Register of interests disclosed: offences in connection with request for or disclosure of information
815 Entries not to be removed from register
816 Removal of entries from register: old entries
817 Removal of entries from register: incorrect entry relating to third party
818 Adjustment of entry relating to share acquisition agreement
819 Duty of company ceasing to be public company

Meaning of interest in shares

820 Interest in shares: general
821 Interest in shares: right to subscribe for shares
822 Interest in shares: family interests
823 Interest in shares: corporate interests

824 Interest in shares: agreement to acquire interests in a particular company
825 Extent of obligation in case of share acquisition agreement

Other supplementary provisions

826 Information protected from wider disclosure
827 Reckoning of periods for fulfilling obligations
828 Power to make further provision by regulations

PART 23 – DISTRIBUTIONS

Chapter 1 – Restrictions on when distributions may be made

Introductory

829 Meaning of 'distribution'

General rules

830 Distributions to be made only out of profits available for the purpose
831 Net asset restriction on distributions by public companies

Distributions by investment companies

832 Distributions by investment companies out of accumulated revenue profits
833 Meaning of 'investment company'
834 Investment company: condition as to holdings in other companies
835 Power to extend provisions relating to investment companies

Chapter 2 – Justification of distribution by reference to accounts

Justification of distribution by reference to accounts

836 Justification of distribution by reference to relevant accounts

Requirements applicable in relation to relevant accounts

837 Requirements where last annual accounts used
838 Requirements where interim accounts used
839 Requirements where initial accounts used

Application of provisions to successive distributions etc

840 Successive distributions etc by reference to the same accounts

Chapter 3 – Supplementary provisions

Accounting matters

841 Realised losses and profits and revaluation of fixed assets
842 Determination of profit or loss in respect of asset where records incomplete
843 Realised profits and losses of long-term insurance business

844 Treatment of development costs

Distributions in kind

845 Distributions in kind: determination of amount
846 Distributions in kind: treatment of unrealised profits

Consequences of unlawful distribution

847 Consequences of unlawful distribution

Other matters

848 Saving for certain older provisions in articles
849 Restriction on application of unrealised profits
850 Treatment of certain older profits or losses
851 Application of rules of law restricting distributions
852 Saving for other restrictions on distributions
853 Minor definitions

PART 24 – A COMPANY'S ANNUAL RETURN

854 Duty to deliver annual returns
855 Contents of annual return: general
856 Contents of annual return: information about share capital and shareholders
857 Contents of annual return: power to make further provision by regulations
858 Failure to deliver annual return
859 Application of provisions to shadow directors

PART 25 – COMPANY CHARGES

Chapter 1 – Companies registered in England and Wales or in Northern Ireland

Requirement to register company charges

860 Charges created by a company
861 Charges which have to be registered: supplementary
862 Charges existing on property acquired

Special rules about debentures

863 Charge in series of debentures
864 Additional registration requirement for commission etc in relation to debentures
865 Endorsement of certificate on debentures

Charges in other jurisdictions

866 Charges created in, or over property in, jurisdictions outside the United Kingdom
867 Charges created in, or over property in, another United Kingdom jurisdiction

Orders charging land: Northern Ireland

868 Northern Ireland: registration of certain charges etc. affecting land

The register of charges

869 Register of charges to be kept by registrar
870 The period allowed for registration
871 Registration of enforcement of security
872 Entries of satisfaction and release
873 Rectification of register of charges

Avoidance of certain charges

874 Consequence of failure to register charges created by a company

Companies' records and registers

875 Companies to keep copies of instruments creating charges
876 Company's register of charges
877 Instruments creating charges and register of charges to be available for inspection

Chapter 2 – Companies registered in Scotland

Charges requiring registration

878 Charges created by a company
879 Charges which have to be registered: supplementary
880 Duty to register charges existing on property acquired
881 Charge by way of ex facie absolute disposition, etc

Special rules about debentures

882 Charge in series of debentures
883 Additional registration requirement for commission etc in relation to debentures

Charges on property outside the United Kingdom

884 Charges on property outside United Kingdom

The register of charges

885 Register of charges to be kept by registrar
886 The period allowed for registration
887 Entries of satisfaction and relief
888 Rectification of register of charges

Avoidance of certain charges

889 Charges void unless registered

Companies' records and registers

890 Copies of instruments creating charges to be kept by company
891 Company's register of charges
892 Instruments creating charges and register of charges to be available for inspection

Chapter 3 – Powers of the Secretary of State

893 Power to make provision for effect of registration in special register
894 General power to make amendments to this Part

PART 26 – ARRANGEMENTS AND RECONSTRUCTIONS

Application of this Part

895 Application of this Part

Meeting of creditors or members

896 Court order for holding of meeting
897 Statement to be circulated or made available
898 Duty of directors and trustees to provide information

Court sanction for compromise or arrangement

899 Court sanction for compromise or arrangement

Reconstructions and amalgamations

900 Powers of court to facilitate reconstruction or amalgamation

Obligations of company with respect to articles etc

901 Obligations of company with respect to articles etc

PART 27 – MERGERS AND DIVISIONS OF PUBLIC COMPANIES

Chapter 1 – Introductory

902 Application of this Part
903 Relationship of this Part to Part 26

Chapter 2 – Merger

Introductory

904 Mergers and merging companies

Requirements applicable to merger

905 Draft terms of scheme (merger)
906 Publication of draft terms (merger)
907 Approval of members of merging companies
908 Directors' explanatory report (merger)
909 Expert's report (merger)
910 Supplementary accounting statement (merger)
911 Inspection of documents (merger)
912 Approval of articles of new transferee company (merger)

913 Protection of holders of securities to which special rights attached (merger)
914 No allotment of shares to transferor company or its nominee (merger)

Exceptions where shares of transferor company held by transferee company

915 Circumstances in which certain particulars and reports not required (merger)
916 Circumstances in which meeting of members of transferee company not required (merger)
917 Circumstances in which no meetings required (merger)

Other exceptions

918 Other circumstances in which meeting of members of transferee company not required (merger)

Chapter 3 – Division

Introductory

919 Divisions and companies involved in a division

Requirements to be complied with in case of division

920 Draft terms of scheme (division)
921 Publication of draft terms (division)
922 Approval of members of companies involved in the division
923 Directors' explanatory report (division)
924 Expert's report (division)
925 Supplementary accounting statement (division)
926 Inspection of documents (division)
927 Report on material changes of assets of transferor company (division)
928 Approval of articles of new transferee company (division)
929 Protection of holders of securities to which special rights attached (division)
930 No allotment of shares to transferor company or its nominee (division)

Exceptions where shares of transferor company held by transferee company

931 Circumstances in which meeting of members of transferor company not required (division)

Other exceptions

932 Circumstances in which meeting of members of transferee company not required (division)
933 Agreement to dispense with reports etc (division)
934 Power of court to exclude certain requirements (division)

Chapter 4 –Supplementary provisions

Expert's report and related matters

935 Expert's report: valuation by another person
936 Experts and valuers: independence requirement
937 Experts and valuers: meaning of 'associate'

Powers of the court

938 Power of court to summon meeting of members or creditors of existing transferee company
939 Court to fix date for transfer of undertaking etc of transferor company

Liability of transferee companies

940 Liability of transferee companies for each other's defaults

Interpretation

941 Meaning of 'liabilities' and 'property'

PART 28 – TAKEOVERS ETC

Chapter 1 – The Takeover Panel

The Panel and its rules

942 The Panel
943 Rules
944 Further provisions about rules
945 Rulings
946 Directions

Information

947 Power to require documents and information
948 Restrictions on disclosure
949 Offence of disclosure in contravention of section 948

Co-operation

950 Panel's duty of co-operation

Hearings and appeals

951 Hearings and appeals

Contravention of rules etc

952 Sanctions
953 Failure to comply with rules about bid documentation
954 Compensation
955 Enforcement by the court
956 No action for breach of statutory duty etc

Funding

957 Fees and charges
958 Levy
959 Recovery of fees, charges or levy

Miscellaneous and supplementary

960 Panel as party to proceedings
961 Exemption from liability in damages
962 Privilege against self-incrimination
963 Annual reports
964 Amendments to Financial Services and Markets Act 2000
965 Power to extend to Isle of Man and Channel Islands

Chapter 2 – Impediments to takeovers

Opting in and opting out

966 Opting in and opting out
967 Further provision about opting-in and opting-out resolutions

Consequences of opting in

968 Effect on contractual restrictions
969 Power of offeror to require general meeting to be called

Supplementary

970 Communication of decisions
971 Interpretation of Chapter
972 Transitory provision
973 Power to extend to Isle of Man and Channel Islands

Chapter 3 – 'Squeeze-out' and 'sell-out'

Takeover offers

974 Meaning of 'takeover offer'
975 Shares already held by the offeror etc
976 Cases where offer treated as being on same terms
977 Shares to which an offer relates
978 Effect of impossibility etc of communicating or accepting offer

'Squeeze-out'

979 Right of offeror to buy out minority shareholder
980 Further provision about notices given under section 979
981 Effect of notice under section 979
982 Further provision about consideration held on trust under section 981(9)

'Sell-out'

983 Right of minority shareholder to be bought out by offeror
984 Further provision about rights conferred by section 983
985 Effect of requirement under section 983

Supplementary

986 Applications to the court
987 Joint offers

Interpretation

988 Associates
989 Convertible securities
990 Debentures carrying voting rights
991 Interpretation

Chapter 4 – Amendments to Part 7 of the Companies Act 1985

992 Matters to be dealt with in directors' report

PART 29 – FRAUDULENT TRADING

993 Offence of fraudulent trading

PART 30 – PROTECTION OF MEMBERS AGAINST UNFAIR PREJUDICE

Main provisions

994 Petition by company member
995 Petition by Secretary of State
996 Powers of the court under this Part

Supplementary provisions

997 Application of general rule-making powers
998 Copy of order affecting company's constitution to be delivered to registrar
999 Supplementary provisions where company's constitution altered

PART 31 – DISSOLUTION AND RESTORATION TO THE REGISTER

Chapter 1 – Striking off

Registrar's power to strike off defunct company

1000 Power to strike off company not carrying on business or in operation
1001 Duty to act in case of company being wound up
1002 Supplementary provisions as to service of letter or notice

Voluntary striking off

1003 Striking off on application by company
1004 Circumstances in which application not to be made: activities of company
1005 Circumstances in which application not to be made: other proceedings not concluded
1006 Copy of application to be given to members, employees, etc
1007 Copy of application to be given to new members, employees, etc

1008 Copy of application: provisions as to service of documents
1009 Circumstances in which application to be withdrawn
1010 Withdrawal of application
1011 Meaning of 'creditor'

Chapter 2 – Property of dissolved company

Property vesting as bona vacantia

1012 Property of dissolved company to be bona vacantia
1013 Crown disclaimer of property vesting as bona vacantia
1014 Effect of Crown disclaimer

Effect of Crown disclaimer: England and Wales and Northern Ireland

1015 General effect of disclaimer
1016 Disclaimer of leaseholds
1017 Power of court to make vesting order
1018 Protection of persons holding under a lease
1019 Land subject to rentcharge

Effect of Crown disclaimer: Scotland

1020 General effect of disclaimer
1021 Power of court to make vesting order
1022 Protection of persons holding under a lease

Supplementary provisions

1023 Liability for rentcharge on company's land after dissolution

Chapter 3 – Restoration to the register

Administrative restoration to the register

1024 Application for administrative restoration to the register
1025 Requirements for administrative restoration
1026 Application to be accompanied by statement of compliance
1027 Registrar's decision on application for administrative restoration
1028 Effect of administrative restoration

Restoration to the register by the court

1029 Application to court for restoration to the register
1030 When application to the court may be made
1031 Decision on application for restoration by the court
1032 Effect of court order for restoration to the register

Supplementary provisions

1033 Company's name on restoration
1034 Effect of restoration to the register where property has vested as bona vacantia

PART 32 – COMPANY INVESTIGATIONS: AMENDMENTS

1035 Powers of Secretary of State to give directions to inspectors
1036 Resignation, removal and replacement of inspectors
1037 Power to obtain information from former inspectors etc
1038 Power to require production of documents
1039 Disqualification orders: consequential amendments

PART 33 – UK COMPANIES NOT FORMED UNDER COMPANIES LEGISLATION

Chapter 1 – Companies not formed under companies legislation but authorised to register

1040 Companies authorised to register under this Act
1041 Definition of 'joint stock company'
1042 Power to make provision by regulations

Chapter 2 – Unregistered companies

1043 Unregistered companies

PART 34 – OVERSEAS COMPANIES

Introductory

1044 Overseas companies
1045 Company contracts and execution of documents by companies

Registration of particulars

1046 Duty to register particulars
1047 Registered name of overseas company
1048 Registration under alternative name

Other requirements

1049 Accounts and reports: general
1050 Accounts and reports: credit or financial institutions
1051 Trading disclosures
1052 Company charges
1053 Other returns etc

Supplementary

1054 Offences
1055 Disclosure of individual's residential address: protection from disclosure
1056 Requirement to identify persons authorised to accept service of documents
1057 Registrar to whom returns, notices etc to be delivered
1058 Duty to give notice of ceasing to have registrable presence
1059 Application of provisions in case of relocation of branch

PART 35 – THE REGISTRAR OF COMPANIES

The registrar

1060 The registrar
1061 The registrar's functions
1062 The registrar's official seal
1063 Fees payable to registrar

Certificates of incorporation

1064 Public notice of issue of certificate of incorporation
1065 Right to certificate of incorporation

Registered numbers

1066 Company's registered numbers
1067 Registered numbers of branches of overseas company

Delivery of documents to the registrar

1068 Registrar's requirements as to form, authentication and manner of delivery
1069 Power to require delivery by electronic means
1070 Agreement for delivery by electronic means
1071 Document not delivered until received

Requirements for proper delivery

1072 Requirements for proper delivery
1073 Power to accept documents not meeting requirements for proper delivery
1074 Documents containing unnecessary material
1075 Informal correction of document
1076 Replacement of document not meeting requirements for proper delivery

Public notice of receipt of certain documents

1077 Public notice of receipt of certain documents
1078 Documents subject to Directive disclosure requirements
1079 Effect of failure to give public notice

The register

1080 The register
1081 Annotation of the register
1082 Allocation of unique identifiers
1083 Preservation of original documents
1084 Records relating to companies that have been dissolved etc

Inspection etc of the register

1085 Inspection of the register
1086 Right to copy of material on the register

1087 Material not available for public inspection
1088 Application to registrar to make address unavailable for public inspection
1089 Form of application for inspection or copy
1090 Form and manner in which copies to be provided
1091 Certification of copies as accurate
1092 Issue of process for production of records kept by the registrar

Correction or removal of material on the register

1093 Registrar's notice to resolve inconsistency on the register
1094 Administrative removal of material from the register
1095 Rectification of register on application to registrar
1096 Rectification of the register under court order
1097 Powers of court on ordering removal of material from the register
1098 Public notice of removal of certain material from the register

The registrar's index of company names

1099 The registrar's index of company names
1100 Right to inspect index
1101 Power to amend enactments relating to bodies other than companies

Language requirements: translation

1102 Application of language requirements
1103 Documents to be drawn up and delivered in English
1104 Documents relating to Welsh companies
1105 Documents that may be drawn up and delivered in other languages
1106 Voluntary filing of translations
1107 Certified translations

Language requirements: transliteration

1108 Transliteration of names and addresses: permitted characters
1109 Transliteration of names and addresses: voluntary transliteration into Roman characters
1110 Transliteration of names and addresses: certification

Supplementary provisions

1111 Registrar's requirements as to certification or verification
1112 General false statement offence
1113 Enforcement of company's filing obligations
1114 Application of provisions about documents and delivery
1115 Supplementary provisions relating to electronic communications
1116 Alternative to publication in the Gazette
1117 Registrar's rules
1118 Payments into the Consolidated Fund
1119 Contracting out of registrar's functions
1120 Application of Part to overseas companies

PART 36 – OFFENCES UNDER THE COMPANIES ACTS

Liability of officer in default

1121 Liability of officer in default
1122 Liability of company as officer in default
1123 Application to bodies other than companies

Offences under the Companies Act 1985

1124 Amendments of the Companies Act 1985

General provisions

1125 Meaning of 'daily default fine'
1126 Consents required for certain prosecutions
1127 Summary proceedings: venue
1128 Summary proceedings: time limit for proceedings
1129 Legal professional privilege
1130 Proceedings against unincorporated bodies
1131 Imprisonment on summary conviction in England and Wales: transitory provision

Production and inspection of documents

1132 Production and inspection of documents where offence suspected

Supplementary

1133 Transitional provision

PART 37 – COMPANIES: SUPPLEMENTARY PROVISIONS

Company records

1134 Meaning of 'company records'
1135 Form of company records
1136 Regulations about where certain company records to be kept available for inspection
1137 Regulations about inspection of records and provision of copies
1138 Duty to take precautions against falsification

Service addresses

1139 Service of documents on company
1140 Service of documents on directors, secretaries and others
1141 Service addresses
1142 Requirement to give service address

Sending or supplying documents or information

1143 The company communications provisions
1144 Sending or supplying documents or information

1145 Right to hard copy version
1146 Requirement of authentication
1147 Deemed delivery of documents and information
1148 Interpretation of company communications provisions

Requirements as to independent valuation

1149 Application of valuation requirements
1150 Valuation by qualified independent person
1151 The independence requirement
1152 Meaning of 'associate'
1153 Valuer entitled to full disclosure

Notice of appointment of certain officers

1154 Duty to notify registrar of certain appointments etc
1155 Offence of failure to give notice

Courts and legal proceedings

1156 Meaning of 'the court'
1157 Power of court to grant relief in certain cases

PART 38 – COMPANIES: INTERPRETATION

Meaning of 'UK-registered company'

1158 Meaning of 'UK-registered company'

Meaning of 'subsidiary' and related expressions

1159 Meaning of 'subsidiary' etc
1160 Meaning of 'subsidiary' etc: power to amend

Meaning of 'undertaking' and related expressions

1161 Meaning of 'undertaking' and related expressions
1162 Parent and subsidiary undertakings

Other definitions

1163 'Non-cash asset'
1164 Meaning of 'banking company' and 'banking group'
1165 Meaning of 'insurance company' and related expressions
1166 'Employees' share scheme'
1167 Meaning of 'prescribed'
1168 Hard copy and electronic form and related expressions
1169 Dormant companies
1170 Meaning of 'EEA State' and related expressions
1171 The former Companies Acts

General

1172 References to requirements of this Act
1173 Minor definitions: general
1174 Index of defined expressions

PART 39 – COMPANIES: MINOR AMENDMENTS

1175 Removal of special provisions about accounts and audit of charitable companies
1176 Power of Secretary of State to bring civil proceedings on company's behalf
1177 Repeal of certain provisions about company directors
1178 Repeal of requirement that certain companies publish periodical statement
1179 Repeal of requirement that Secretary of State prepare annual report
1180 Repeal of certain provisions about company charges
1181 Access to constitutional documents of RTE and RTM companies

PART 40 – COMPANY DIRECTORS: FOREIGN DISQUALIFICATION ETC

Introductory

1182 Persons subject to foreign restrictions
1183 Meaning of 'the court' and 'UK company'

Power to disqualify

1184 Disqualification of persons subject to foreign restrictions
1185 Disqualification regulations: supplementary
1186 Offence of breach of disqualification

Power to make persons liable for company's debts

1187 Personal liability for debts of company

Power to require statements to be sent to the registrar of companies

1188 Statements from persons subject to foreign restrictions
1189 Statements from persons disqualified
1190 Statements: whether to be made public
1191 Offences

PART 41 – BUSINESS NAMES

Chapter 1 – Restricted or prohibited names

Introductory

1192 Application of this Chapter

Sensitive words or expressions

1193 Name suggesting connection with government or public authority
1194 Other sensitive words or expressions

1195 Requirement to seek comments of government department or other relevant body
1196 Withdrawal of Secretary of State's approval

Misleading names

1197 Name containing inappropriate indication of company type or legal form
1198 Name giving misleading indication of activities

Supplementary

1199 Savings for existing lawful business names

Chapter 2 – Disclosure required in case of individual or partnership

Introductory

1200 Application of this Chapter
1201 Information required to be disclosed

Disclosure requirements

1202 Disclosure required: business documents etc
1203 Exemption for large partnerships if certain conditions met
1204 Disclosure required: business premises

Consequences of failure to make required disclosure

1205 Criminal consequences of failure to make required disclosure
1206 Civil consequences of failure to make required disclosure

Chapter 3 – Supplementary

1207 Application of general provisions about offences
1208 Interpretation

PART 42 – STATUTORY AUDITORS

Chapter 1 – Introductory

1209 Main purposes of Part
1210 Meaning of 'statutory auditor' etc
1211 Eligibility for appointment as a statutory auditor: overview

Chapter 2 – Individuals and firms

Eligibility for appointment

1212 Individuals and firms: eligibility for appointment as a statutory auditor
1213 Effect of ineligibility

Independence requirement

1214 Independence requirement
1215 Effect of lack of independence

Effect of appointment of a partnership

1216 Effect of appointment of a partnership

Supervisory bodies

1217 Supervisory bodies
1218 Exemption from liability for damages

Professional qualifications

1219 Appropriate qualifications
1220 Qualifying bodies and recognised professional qualifications
1221 Approval of overseas qualifications
1222 Eligibility of individuals retaining only 1967 Act authorisation

Information

1223 Matters to be notified to the Secretary of State
1224 The Secretary of State's power to call for information

Enforcement

1225 Compliance orders

Chapter 3 – Auditors General

Eligibility for appointment

1226 Auditors General: eligibility for appointment as a statutory auditor

Conduct of audits

1227 Individuals responsible for audit work on behalf of Auditors General

The Independent Supervisor

1228 Appointment of the Independent Supervisor

Supervision of Auditors General

1229 Supervision of Auditors General by the Independent Supervisor
1230 Duties of Auditors General in relation to supervision arrangements

Reporting requirement

1231 Reports by the Independent Supervisor

Information

1232 Matters to be notified to the Independent Supervisor
1233 The Independent Supervisor's power to call for information

Enforcement

1234 Suspension notices
1235 Effect of suspension notices
1236 Compliance orders

Proceedings

1237 Proceedings involving the Independent Supervisor

Grants

1238 Grants to the Independent Supervisor

Chapter 4 –The register of auditors etc

1239 The register of auditors
1240 Information to be made available to public

Chapter 5 – Registered third country auditors

Introductory

1241 Meaning of 'third country auditor', 'registered third country auditor' etc

Duties

1242 Duties of registered third country auditors

Information

1243 Matters to be notified to the Secretary of State
1244 The Secretary of State's power to call for information

Enforcement

1245 Compliance orders
1246 Removal of third country auditors from the register of auditors
1247 Grants to bodies concerned with arrangements under Schedule 12

Chapter 6 – Supplementary and general

Power to require second company audit

1248 Secretary of State's power to require second audit of a company
1249 Supplementary provision about second audits

False and misleading statements

1250 Misleading, false and deceptive statements

Fees

1251 Fees

Delegation of Secretary of State's functions

1252 Delegation of the Secretary of State's functions
1253 Delegation of functions to an existing body

International obligations

1254 Directions to comply with international obligations

General provision relating to offences

1255 Offences by bodies corporate, partnerships and unincorporated associations
1256 Time limits for prosecution of offences
1257 Jurisdiction and procedure in respect of offences

Notices etc

1258 Service of notices
1259 Documents in electronic form

Interpretation

1260 Meaning of 'associate'
1261 Minor definitions
1262 Index of defined expressions

Miscellaneous and general

1263 Power to make provision in consequence of changes affecting accountancy bodies
1264 Consequential amendments

PART 43 – TRANSPARENCY OBLIGATIONS AND RELATED MATTERS

Introductory

1265 The transparency obligations directive

Transparency obligations

1266 Transparency rules
1267 Competent authority's power to call for information
1268 Powers exercisable in case of infringement of transparency obligation

Other matters

1269 Corporate governance rules
1270 Liability for false or misleading statements in certain publications
1271 Exercise of powers where UK is host member State
1272 Transparency obligations and related matters: minor and consequential amendments
1273 Corporate governance regulations

PART 44 – MISCELLANEOUS PROVISIONS

Regulation of actuaries etc

1274 Grants to bodies concerned with actuarial standards etc
1275 Levy to pay expenses of bodies concerned with actuarial standards etc
1276 Application of provisions to Scotland and Northern Ireland

Information as to exercise of voting rights by institutional investors

1277 Power to require information about exercise of voting rights
1278 Institutions to which information provisions apply
1279 Shares to which information provisions apply
1280 Obligations with respect to provision of information

Disclosure of information under the Enterprise Act 2002

1281 Disclosure of information under the Enterprise Act 2002

Expenses of winding up

1282 Payment of expenses of winding up

Commonhold associations

1283 Amendment of memorandum or articles of commonhold association

PART 45 – NORTHERN IRELAND

1284 Extension of Companies Acts to Northern Ireland
1285 Extension of GB enactments relating to SEs
1286 Extension of GB enactments relating to certain other forms of business organisation
1287 Extension of enactments relating to business names

PART 46 – GENERAL SUPPLEMENTARY PROVISIONS

Regulations and orders

1288 Regulations and orders: statutory instrument
1289 Regulations and orders: negative resolution procedure
1290 Regulations and orders: affirmative resolution procedure

1291 Regulations and orders: approval after being made
1292 Regulations and orders: supplementary

Meaning of 'enactment'

1293 Meaning of 'enactment'

Consequential and transitional provisions

1294 Power to make consequential amendments etc
1295 Repeals
1296 Power to make transitional provision and savings
1297 Continuity of the law

PART 47 – FINAL PROVISIONS

1298 Short title
1299 Extent
1300 Commencement

**SCHEDULE 1 – CONNECTED PERSONS: REFERENCES TO
AN INTEREST IN SHARES OR DEBENTURES**

**SCHEDULE 2 – SPECIFIED PERSONS, DESCRIPTIONS OF DISCLOSURES
ETC FOR THE PURPOSES OF SECTION 948**

Part 1 – Specified persons
Part 2 – Specified descriptions of disclosures
Part 3 – Overseas regulatory bodies

**SCHEDULE 3 – AMENDMENTS OF REMAINING PROVISIONS OF
THE COMPANIES ACT 1985 RELATING TO OFFENCES**

**SCHEDULE 4 – DOCUMENTS AND INFORMATION SENT OR
SUPPLIED TO A COMPANY**

Part 1 – Introduction
Part 2 – Communications in hard copy form
Part 3 – Communications in electronic form
Part 4 – Other agreed forms of communication

SCHEDULE 5 – COMMUNICATIONS BY A COMPANY

Part 1 – Introduction
Part 2 – Communications in hard copy form
Part 3 – Communications in electronic form
Part 4 – Communications by means of a website
Part 5 – Other agreed forms of communication
Part 6 – Supplementary provisions

SCHEDULE 6 – MEANING OF 'SUBSIDIARY' ETC:
SUPPLEMENTARY PROVISIONS

SCHEDULE 7 – PARENT AND SUBSIDIARY UNDERTAKINGS:
SUPPLEMENTARY PROVISIONS

SCHEDULE 8 – INDEX OF DEFINED EXPRESSIONS

SCHEDULE 9 – REMOVAL OF SPECIAL PROVISIONS ABOUT ACCOUNTS
AND AUDIT OF CHARITABLE COMPANIES

Part 1 – The Companies Act 1985 (c. 6)
Part 2 – The Companies (Northern Ireland) Order 1986 (S.I. 1986/1032) (N.I. 6)

SCHEDULE 10 – RECOGNISED SUPERVISORY BODIES

Part 1 – Grant and revocation of recognition of a supervisory body
Part 2 – Requirements for recognition of a supervisory body
Part 3 – Arrangements in which recognised supervisory bodies are required to participate

SCHEDULE 11 – RECOGNISED PROFESSIONAL QUALIFICATIONS

Part 1 – Grant and revocation of recognition of a professional qualification
Part 2 – Requirements for recognition of a professional qualification

SCHEDULE 12 – ARRANGEMENTS IN WHICH REGISTERED THIRD
COUNTRY AUDITORS ARE REQUIRED TO PARTICIPATE

SCHEDULE 13 – SUPPLEMENTARY PROVISIONS WITH RESPECT
TO DELEGATION ORDER

SCHEDULE 14 – STATUTORY AUDITORS:
CONSEQUENTIAL AMENDMENTS

SCHEDULE 15 – TRANSPARENCY OBLIGATIONS AND RELATED
MATTERS: MINOR AND CONSEQUENTIAL AMENDMENTS

Part 1 – Amendments of the Financial Services and Markets Act 2000
Part 2 – Amendments of the Companies (Audit, Investigations and Community Enterprise) Act 2004

SCHEDULE 16 – REPEALS

Draft model articles for private companies limited by shares

On 28 February 2007, the Department for Trade and Industry (DTI) (now the Department for Business, Enterprise and Regulatory Reform (BERR)) issued a consultative document entitled 'Implementation of the Companies Act 2006'. The consultation document contained draft model articles for both private and public companies. The draft model articles for a private company limited by shares were expressed as follows.

INDEX TO THE ARTICLES

PART 1 – DEFINITIONS AND INTERPRETATION

1. Defined terms

PART 2 – DIRECTORS

Directors' powers and responsibilities

2. Directors' general authority
3. Shareholders' reserve power
4. Directors may delegate
5. Committees

Decision-making by directors

6. Directors to take decisions collectively
7. Unanimous decisions
8. Majority decisions without directors' meeting
9. Calling a directors' meeting
10. Quorum for majority decisions
11. Chairing of majority decision making processes
12. Casting vote
13. Conflicts of interest
14. Records of decisions to be kept
15. Directors' discretion to make further rules

Appointment of directors

16. Methods of appointing directors
17. Termination of director's appointment

18.   Directors' remuneration
19.   Directors' expenses

PART 3 – SHARES AND DISTRIBUTIONS

Shares

20.   All shares to be fully paid up
21.   Powers to issue different classes of share
22.   Company not bound by less than absolute interests
23.   Share certificates
24.   Share transfers
25.   Transmission of shares
26.   Exercise of transmittees' rights
27.   Transmittees bound by prior notices

Dividends and other distributions

28.   Procedure for declaring dividends
29.   Payment of dividends and other distributions
30.   No interest on distributions
31.   Unclaimed distributions
32.   Non-cash distributions
33.   Waiver of distributions

Capitalisation of profits

34.   Authority to capitalise and appropriation of capitalised sums

PART 4 – DECISION-MAKING BY SHAREHOLDERS

Organisation of general meetings

35.   Attendance and speaking at general meetings
36.   Quorum for general meetings
37.   Chairing of general meetings
38.   Attendance and speaking by directors and non-shareholders
39.   Adjournment

Voting at general meetings

40.   Voting: general
41.   Errors and disputes
42.   Poll votes
43.   Content of proxy notices
44.   Delivery of proxy notices
45.   Amendments to resolutions

PART 5 – ADMINISTRATIVE ARRANGEMENTS

46.   Means of communication to be used
47.   Addresses and other contact details

48. Company seals
49. No right to inspect accounts and other records
50. Provision for employees on cessation of business

PART 1 – DEFINITIONS AND INTERPRETATION

1 Defined terms

In the articles, unless the context requires otherwise –

'articles' means the company's articles of association;

'bankruptcy' includes individual insolvency proceedings in a jurisdiction other than England and Wales and Northern Ireland which have an effect similar to that of bankruptcy;

'chairman' has the meaning given in article 11;

'chairman of the meeting' has the meaning given in article 37;

'Companies Acts' means the Companies Acts (as defined in section 2 of the Companies Act 2006), in so far as they apply to the company;

'director' means a director of the company, and includes any person occupying the position of director, by whatever name called;

'distribution recipient' has the meaning given in article 29;

'document' includes, unless otherwise specified, any document sent or supplied in electronic form;

'electronic form' has the meaning given in section 1168 of the Companies Act 2006;

'fully paid' in relation to a share, means that the nominal value and any premium to be paid to the company in respect of that share have been paid to the company;

'hard copy form' has the meaning given in section 1168 of the Companies Act 2006;

'holder' in relation to shares means the person whose name is entered in the register of members as the holder of the shares;

'instrument' means a document in hard copy form;

'majority decision' has the meaning given in article 8;

'ordinary resolution' has the meaning given in section 282 of the Companies Act 2006;

'paid' means paid or credited as paid;

'proxy notice' has the meaning given in article 43;

'securities seal' has the meaning given in article 23;

'shareholder' means a person who is the holder of a share;

'shares' means shares in the company;

'special resolution' has the meaning given in section 283 of the Companies Act 2006;

'subsidiary' has the meaning given in section 1159 of the Companies Act 2006;

'transmittee' means a person entitled to a share by reason of the death or bankruptcy of the share's holder or otherwise by operation of law;

'unanimous decision' has the meaning given in article 7; and

'writing' means the representation or reproduction of words, symbols or other information in a visible form by any method or combination of methods, whether sent or supplied in electronic form or otherwise.

Unless the context otherwise requires, other words or expressions contained in these articles bear the same meaning as in the Companies Act 2006 as in force on the date when these articles become binding on the company.

PART 2 – DIRECTORS

Directors' powers and responsibilities

2 Directors' general authority

Subject to the articles, the directors are responsible for the management of the company's business, for which purpose they may exercise all the powers of the company.

3 Shareholders' reserve power

(1) The shareholders may, by special resolution, direct the directors to take, or refrain from taking, specified action.

(2) No such special resolution invalidates anything which the directors have already done.

4 Directors may delegate

(1) Subject to the articles, the directors may delegate any of the powers which are conferred on them under the articles –

    (a)   to such persons;
    (b)   by such means (including by power of attorney);
    (c)   to such an extent;
    (d)   in relation to such matters or territories; and
    (e)   on such conditions or subject to such restrictions,

as they think fit.

(2) If the directors so specify, any such delegation may authorise further delegation of the directors' powers by any person to whom they are delegated.

(3) The directors may revoke any delegation in whole or part, or alter its terms.

5 Committees

(1) Committees to which the directors delegate any of their powers must follow procedures which are based as closely as possible on those provisions of the articles which govern the taking of decisions by directors.

(2) The directors may make rules of procedure for committees, which prevail over rules derived from the articles if they are not consistent with them.

Decision-making by directors

6 Directors to take decisions collectively

(1) The general rule about decision-making by directors is that any decision of the directors must be either a unanimous decision or a majority decision.

(2) If –

    (a)   the company only has one director, and
    (b)   no provision of the articles or rule made by the directors requires it to have more than one director (either generally or for the purposes of taking decisions other than majority decisions),

the general rule does not apply, and the director may take decisions without regard to any of the provisions of the articles relating to directors' decision-making.

(3) Subject to the articles, the directors –

    (a)   may take either a unanimous decision or a majority decision on any matter, and

    (b)   may, but need not, take any decision at a directors' meeting.

7 Unanimous decisions

(1) The directors take a unanimous decision when they all indicate to each other that they share a common view on a matter.

(2) A unanimous decision –

    (a)   may be taken without any discussion between directors, and

    (b)   may, but need not, take the form of a resolution in writing, copies of which have been signed by each director.

8 Majority decisions without directors' meeting

(1) This article applies where a majority decision is not taken in a directors' meeting.

(2) The directors take a majority decision if –

    (a)   a director has become aware of a matter on which the directors need to take a decision;

    (b)   that director has made the other directors aware of the matter and the decision;

    (c)   the directors have had a reasonable opportunity to communicate their views on the matter and the decision to each other; and

    (d)   a majority of those directors vote in favour of a particular decision on that matter.

(3) But if a director is aware that consultation with another director will make it impossible to take a particular decision as soon as the company's business requires, that director –

    (a)   may decide not to communicate with that other director in relation to that decision before it is taken, but

    (b)   must communicate any such decision not to communicate to all the other directors as soon as is practicable, explaining the reasons for it.

(4) And if a director states that he does not wish to discuss or vote on a particular matter, the directors may choose not to communicate with that director in relation to decisions to be taken on that matter.

(5) Directors participating in the taking of a majority decision otherwise than at a directors' meeting –

    (a)   may be in different places, and may participate at different times, and

    (b)   may communicate with each other by any means.

9 Calling a directors' meeting

(1) Any director may call a directors' meeting by giving notice of the meeting to the directors.

(2) Notice of any directors' meeting must indicate –

(a) its proposed date, time and subject matter;
(b) where it is to take place; and
(c) if it is anticipated that directors participating in the meeting will not be in the same place, how it is proposed that they should communicate with each other during the meeting.

(3) Notice of a directors' meeting –

(a) need not be given in writing, but
(b) must be communicated to each director.

(4) In fixing the date and time of any directors' meeting, the director calling it must try to ensure, subject to the urgency of any matter to be decided by the directors, that as many directors as practicable are likely to be available to participate in it.

(5) Notice of a directors' meeting need not be given to directors who waive their entitlement to notice, prospectively or retrospectively.

(6) Directors are to be treated as having waived their entitlement to notice of a meeting if they have not supplied the company with the information necessary to ensure that they receive the notice before the meeting takes place.

10 Quorum for majority decisions

(1) No majority decision (other than a decision to call a directors' meeting or a general meeting) shall be taken by the directors unless a quorum participates in the decision-making process.

(2) The quorum for directors' decision-making may be fixed from time to time by a decision of the directors, but it must never be less than two, and unless otherwise fixed it is two.

(3) If the total number of directors for the time being is less than the quorum required for directors' majority decision-making, the directors must not take any majority decision other than a decision –

(a) to appoint further directors, or
(b) to call a general meeting so as to enable the shareholders to appoint further directors.

11 Chairing of majority decision making processes

(1) The directors may appoint a director to chair –

(a) all of the processes by which a majority decision may be taken, or
(b) a particular process, or processes of a particular type (such as directors' meetings), by which a majority decision may be taken.

(2) The person so appointed for the time being is known as the chairman.
(3) The directors may terminate the chairman's appointment at any time.
(4) If the chairman is not participating in a directors' meeting within ten minutes of the time at which it was to start, the participating directors must appoint one of themselves to chair it.

12 Casting vote

(1) The directors may make a rule (a 'casting vote rule') that if –

(a) a majority decision is to be taken on a matter, and
(b) equal numbers of directors hold differing views on the matter,

the views of the chairman or some other specified director shall determine the majority decision which is taken on that matter.

(2) But a casting vote rule does not apply if the views of the specified director are to be disregarded as a result of an actual or potential conflict of interest.

13 Conflicts of interest

(1) If a proposed decision of the directors is concerned with an actual or proposed transaction or arrangement with the company in which a director is interested, that director is not to be counted as participating in the decision-making process for voting or quorum purposes.

(2) But if paragraph (3) below applies, a director who is interested in an actual or proposed transaction or arrangement with the company –

(a)   is to be counted as participating in the decision-making process, and

(b)   is entitled to vote on a proposal relating to it.

(3) This paragraph applies when –

(a)   the company by ordinary resolution disapplies the provision of the articles which would otherwise prevent a director from being counted as participating in, or voting at, a directors' meeting;

(b)   the director's interest cannot reasonably be regarded as likely to give rise to a conflict of interest; or

(c)   the director's conflict of interest arises from a permitted cause.

(4) For the purposes of this article, the following are permitted causes –

(a)   a guarantee given, or to be given, by or to a director in respect of an obligation incurred by or on behalf of the company or any of its subsidiaries;

(b)   subscription, or an agreement to subscribe, for shares or other securities of the company or any of its subsidiaries, or to underwrite, sub-underwrite, or guarantee subscription for any such shares or securities; and

(c)   a contract about benefits for employees and directors or former employees and directors of the company or any of its subsidiaries which does not provide special benefits for directors or former directors.

(5) For the purposes of this article, references to proposed decisions and decision-making processes include any directors' meeting or part of a directors' meeting.

(6) If a question arises at a meeting of directors or of a committee as to the right of a director to vote, the question may, before the conclusion of the meeting, be referred to the chairman of the meeting whose ruling in relation to any director other than the chairman is to be final and conclusive.

14 Records of decisions to be kept

The directors must ensure that the company keeps a record, in writing, of every unanimous or majority decision taken by the directors for at least ten years from the date of the decision recorded in it.

15 Directors' discretion to make further rules

Subject to the articles, the directors may make any rule which they think fit about how they take decisions, and about how such rules are to be recorded or communicated to directors.

Appointment of directors

16 Methods of appointing directors

Any person who is willing to act as a director, and is permitted by law to do so, may be appointed to be a director –

(a) by ordinary resolution, or
(b) by a decision of the directors.

17 Termination of director's appointment

A person ceases to be a director as soon as –

(a) that person ceases to be or is prohibited from being a director by law;
(b) a bankruptcy order is made against that person;
(c) a composition is made with that person's creditors generally in satisfaction of that person's debts (whether by means of an individual voluntary arrangement or otherwise);
(d) a registered medical practitioner who is treating that person gives a written opinion to the company stating that that person has become physically or mentally incapable of acting as a director and may remain so for more than three months;
(e) by reason of that person's mental health, a court makes an order which wholly or partly prevents that person from personally exercising any powers or rights which that person would otherwise have;
(f) a notification to the company that that person is resigning or retiring from office as director takes effect in accordance with its terms;
(g) that person receives notice signed by all the other directors stating that that person should cease to be a director.

18 Directors' remuneration

(1) Directors may undertake any services for the company that the directors decide.
(2) Directors are entitled to such remuneration as the directors determine –

(a) for their services to the company as directors, and
(b) for any other service which they undertake for the company.

(3) Subject to the articles, a director's remuneration may –

(a) take any form, and
(b) include any arrangements in connection with the payment of a pension, allowance or gratuity, or any death, sickness or disability benefits, to or in respect of that director.

(4) Unless the directors decide otherwise, directors' remuneration accrues from day to day.
(5) Unless the directors decide otherwise, directors are not accountable to the company for any remuneration which they receive as directors of the company's subsidiaries.

19 Directors' expenses

The company must pay any reasonable expenses which the directors properly incur in connection with the exercise of their powers and the discharge of their responsibilities in relation to the company.

PART 3 – SHARES AND DISTRIBUTIONS

Shares

20 All shares to be fully paid up

No share shall be issued for less than the aggregate of its nominal value and any premium to be paid to the company in consideration for its issue.

21 Powers to issue different classes of share

(1) Subject to the articles, but without prejudice to the rights attached to any existing share, the company may issue shares with such rights or restrictions as may be determined by ordinary resolution.
(2) The company may issue shares which are to be redeemed, or are liable to be redeemed at the option of the company or the holder, and the directors may determine the terms, conditions and manner of redemption of any such shares.

22 Company not bound by less than absolute interests

Except as otherwise required by law or the articles, the company shall not in any way be bound by or recognise any interest in a share other than the holder's absolute ownership of it and all the rights attaching to it.

23 Share certificates

(1) The company must issue each shareholder, free of charge, with one or more certificates in respect of the shares which that shareholder holds.
(2) Every certificate must specify –

    (a)   in respect of how many shares, of what class, it is issued;
    (b)   the nominal value of those shares;
    (c)   the amount paid up on them; and
    (d)   any distinguishing numbers assigned to them.

(3) No certificate may be issued in respect of shares of more than one class.
(4) If more than one person holds a share, only one certificate may be issued in respect of it.
(5) Certificates must –

    (a)   have affixed to them the company's common seal or an official seal which is a facsimile of the company's common seal with the addition on its face of the word 'Securities' (a 'securities seal'), or
    (b)   be otherwise executed in accordance with the Companies Acts.

24 Share transfers

(1) Shares may be transferred by means of an instrument of transfer in any usual form or any other form approved by the directors, which is executed by or on behalf of the transferor.

(2) No fee may be charged for registering any instrument of transfer or other document relating to or affecting the title to any share.

(3) The company may retain any instrument of transfer which is registered.

(4) The transferor remains the holder of a share until the transferee's name is entered in the register as holder of it.

(5) The directors may refuse to register the transfer of a share, and if they do so, the instrument of transfer must be returned to the transferee with the notice of refusal unless they suspect that the proposed transfer may be fraudulent.

25 Transmission of shares

(1) If title to a share passes to a transmittee, the company may only recognise the transmittee as having any title to that share.

(2) A transmittee who produces such evidence of entitlement to shares as the directors may properly require –

    (a)   may, subject to the articles, choose either to become the holder of those shares or to have them transferred to another person, and

    (b)   subject to the articles, and pending any transfer of the shares to another person, has the same rights as the holder had.

(3) But transmittees do not have the right to attend or vote at a general meeting in respect of shares to which they are entitled by reason of the holder's death or bankruptcy or otherwise unless the shares are transferred to them.

26 Exercise of transmittees' rights

(1) Transmittees who wish to become the holders of shares to which they have become entitled must notify the company in writing of that wish.

(2) If the transmittee wishes to have a share transferred to another person, the transmittee must execute an instrument of transfer in respect of it.

(3) Any transfer made or executed under this article is to be treated as if it were made or executed by the person from whom the transferee has derived rights in respect of the share, and as if the event which gave rise to the transmission had not occurred.

27 Transmittees bound by prior notices

If a notice is given to a shareholder in respect of shares and a transmittee is entitled to those shares, the transmittee is bound by the notice if it was given to the shareholder before the transmittee's name has been entered in the register of members.

Dividends and other distributions

28 Procedure for declaring dividends

(1) The directors may decide to declare and pay such dividends to shareholders as –

    (a)   appear to the directors to be justified by the company's profits, and

    (b)   are in accordance with shareholders' respective rights.

(2) The shareholders may by ordinary resolution decide to pay such dividends in accordance with a recommendation of the directors.

29 Payment of dividends and other distributions

(1) Where a dividend or other sum is payable in respect of a share, it must be paid by one or more of the following means –

   (a)   transfer to a bank account specified by the distribution recipient in writing or by such other means as the directors decide;

   (b)   sending a cheque made payable to the distribution recipient by post to the distribution recipient at the distribution recipient's registered address (if the distribution recipient is a holder of the share), or (in any other case) to an address specified by the distribution recipient in writing or by such other means as the directors decide;

   (c)   sending a cheque made payable to such person by post to such person at such address as the distribution recipient has specified in writing or by such other means as the directors decide; or

   (d)   any other means of payment (including by the allotment or transfer of further shares in accordance with the articles) as the directors agree with the distribution recipient in writing or by such other means as the directors decide.

(2) In the articles, 'the distribution recipient' means, in respect of a share in respect of which a dividend or other sum is payable –

   (a)   the holder of the share; or

   (b)   if the share has two or more joint holders, whichever of them is named first in the register of members (the 'senior holder'); or

   (c)   if the holder is no longer entitled to the share by reason of death or bankruptcy, or otherwise by operation of law, the transmittee.

30 No interest on distributions

The company may not pay interest on any dividend or other sum payable in respect of a share unless otherwise provided by –

   (a)   the terms on which the share was issued, or

   (b)   the provisions of another agreement between the holder of that share and the company.

31 Unclaimed distributions

(1) All dividends or other sums which are –

   (a)   payable in respect of shares, and

   (b)   unclaimed after having been declared or become payable,

may be invested or otherwise made use of by the directors for the benefit of the company until claimed.

(2) The payment of any such dividend or other sum into a separate account does not make the company a trustee in respect of it.

(3) If –

   (a)   twelve years have passed from the date on which a dividend or other sum became due for payment, and

   (b)   the distribution recipient has not claimed it,

the distribution recipient is no longer entitled to that dividend or other sum and it ceases to remain owing by the company.

32 Non-cash distributions

(1) Subject to the terms of issue of the share in question, the company may, by ordinary resolution on the recommendation of the directors, decide to pay all or part of a dividend or other sum payable in respect of a share by transferring non-cash assets of equivalent value (including, without limitation, shares or other securities in any company).

(2) For the purposes of paying a non-cash distribution, the directors may make whatever arrangements they think fit, including –

    (a)   fixing the value of any assets;

    (b)   paying cash to any distribution recipient on the basis of that value in order to adjust the rights of recipients; and

    (c)   vesting any assets in trustees.

33 Waiver of distributions

Distribution recipients may waive their entitlement to a dividend or other sum payable in respect of a share by giving the company notice in writing to that effect, but if –

    (a)   the share has more than one holder, or

    (b)   more than one person is entitled to the share, whether by reason of the death or bankruptcy of one or more joint holders, or otherwise,

the notice is not effective unless it is expressed to be given, and signed, by all the holders or persons otherwise entitled to the share.

Capitalisation of profits

34 Authority to capitalise and appropriation of capitalised sums

(1) Subject to the articles, the directors may, if they are so authorised by an ordinary resolution –

    (a)   decide to capitalise any profits of the company (whether or not they are available for distribution) which are not required for paying a preferential dividend, or any sum standing to the credit of the company's share premium account or capital redemption reserve; and

    (b)   appropriate any sum which they so decide to capitalise (a 'capitalised sum') to the persons who would have been entitled to it if it were distributed by way of dividend (the 'persons entitled') and in the same proportions.

(2) Capitalised sums must be applied –

    (a)   on behalf of the persons entitled, and

    (b)   in the same proportions as a dividend would have been distributed to them.

(3) Any capitalised sum may be applied in paying up new shares of a nominal amount equal to the capitalised sum which are then allotted credited as fully paid to the persons entitled or as they may direct.

(4) A capitalised sum which was appropriated from profits available for distribution may be applied in paying up new debentures of the company which are then allotted credited as fully paid to the persons entitled or as they may direct.

(5) Subject to the articles the directors may –

    (a) apply capitalised sums in accordance with paragraphs (3) and (4) partly in one way and partly in another;

    (b) make such arrangements as they think fit to deal with shares or debentures becoming distributable in fractions under this article (including the issuing of fractional certificates or the making of cash payments); and

    (c) authorise any person to enter into an agreement with the company on behalf of all the persons entitled which is binding on them in respect of the allotment of shares and debentures to them under this article.

PART 4 – DECISION-MAKING BY SHAREHOLDERS

Organisation of general meetings

35 Attendance and speaking at general meetings

(1) In determining attendance at a general meeting, it is immaterial whether any two or more shareholders attending it are in the same place as each other.

(2) Two or more persons who are not in the same place as each other attend a general meeting if their circumstances are such that if they have (or were to have) rights to speak and vote at that meeting, they are (or would be) able to exercise them.

(3) A person is able to exercise the right to speak at a general meeting when that person is in a position to communicate to all those attending the meeting, during the meeting, any information or opinions which that person has on the business of the meeting.

(4) A person is able to exercise the right to vote at a general meeting when –

    (a) that person is able to vote, during the meeting, on resolutions put to the vote at the meeting, and

    (b) that person's vote can be taken into account in determining whether or not such resolutions are passed at the same time as the votes of all the other persons
    attending the meeting.

(5) The directors may make whatever arrangements they consider appropriate to enable those attending a general meeting to exercise their rights to speak or vote at it.

(6) In making such arrangements, directors shall have regard to the legitimate interests of the company, individual shareholders and others attending the meeting in the efficient despatch of the business of the meeting.

36 Quorum for general meetings

(1) No business other than the appointment of the chairman of the meeting is to be transacted at a general meeting if the persons attending it do not constitute a quorum.

(2) The quorum for general meetings is as provided under the Companies Acts.

37 Chairing of general meetings

(1) If the directors have appointed a chairman, the chairman must chair general meetings at which he is present.

(2) If the directors have not appointed a chairman, or if the chairman is not present within ten minutes of the time at which a meeting was due to start –

(a) the directors present, or

(b) (if no directors are present), the meeting, must appoint a director or share-holder to chair the meeting, and the appointment of the chairman of the meeting must be the first business of the meeting.

(3) The person chairing a meeting in accordance with this article is referred to as 'the chairman of the meeting'.

38 Attendance and speaking by directors and non-shareholders

(1) Directors may attend and speak at general meetings, whether or not they are share-holders.

(2) The chairman of the meeting may permit other persons who are not –

(a) shareholders of the company, or

(b) otherwise entitled to exercise the rights of shareholders in relation to general meetings,

to attend and speak at a general meeting.

39 Adjournment

(1) If the persons attending a general meeting within half an hour of the time at which the meeting was due to start do not constitute a quorum, the chairman of the meeting must adjourn it.

(2) The chairman of the meeting may adjourn a general meeting at which a quorum is present if –

(a) the meeting consents to an adjournment, or

(b) it appears to the chairman of the meeting that an adjournment is necessary to protect the safety of any person attending the meeting or ensure that the business of the meeting is conducted in an orderly manner.

(3) The chairman of the meeting must adjourn a general meeting if directed to do so by the meeting.

(4) When adjourning a general meeting, the chairman of the meeting must –

(a) either specify the time and place to which it is adjourned or state that it is to continue at a time and place to be fixed by the directors, and

(b) have regard to any directions as to the time and place of any adjournment which have been given by the meeting.

(5) If the continuation of an adjourned meeting is to take place more than 14 days after it was adjourned, the company must give at least 7 clear days' notice of it –

(a) to the same persons to whom notice of the company's general meetings is required to be given, and

(b) containing the same information which such notice is required to contain.

(6) No business may be transacted at an adjourned general meeting which could not properly have been transacted at the meeting if the adjournment had not taken place.

Voting at general meetings

40 Voting: general

(1) A resolution put to the vote of a general meeting must be decided on a show of hands unless a poll is taken on it in accordance with the articles.

(2) If equal numbers of votes are cast for and against a resolution, whether on a show of hands or on a poll, the chairman of the meeting has a casting vote in addition to any other votes he is otherwise entitled to cast on that resolution.

41 Errors and disputes

(1) No objection may be raised to the qualification of any person voting at a general meeting except at the meeting or adjourned meeting at which the vote objected to is tendered, and every vote not disallowed at the meeting is valid.

(2) Any such objection must be referred to the chairman of the meeting whose decision is final and binding.

42 Poll votes

(1) A poll on a resolution may be demanded –

    (a)   in advance of the general meeting where it is to be put to the vote, or

    (b)   at a general meeting, either before a show of hands on that resolution or immediately after the result of a show of hands on that resolution is declared.

(2) A poll may be demanded by –

    (a)   the chairman of the meeting;

    (b)   the directors;

    (c)   two or more persons having the right to vote on the resolution; or

    (d)   a person or persons representing not less than one tenth of the total voting rights of all the shareholders having the right to vote on the resolution.

(3) A demand for a poll may be withdrawn if –

    (a)   the poll has not yet been taken, and

    (b)   the chairman of the meeting consents to the withdrawal.

(4) Polls must be taken immediately and in such manner as the chairman of the meeting directs.

43 Content of proxy notices

(1) Proxies may only validly be appointed by a notice in writing (a 'proxy notice') which –

    (a)   states the name and address of the shareholder appointing the proxy;

    (b)   identifies the person appointed to be that shareholder's proxy and the general meeting in relation to which that person is appointed;

    (c)   is executed by or on behalf of the shareholder appointing the proxy; and

    (d)   is delivered to the company in accordance with the articles and any instructions contained in the notice of the general meeting to which they relate.

(2) The company may require proxy notices to be delivered in a particular form, and may specify different forms for different purposes.

(3) Proxy notices may specify how the proxy appointed under them is to vote (or that the proxy is to abstain from voting) on one or more resolutions.

(4) Unless a proxy notice indicates otherwise, it must be treated as –

(a) allowing the person appointed under it as a proxy discretion as to how to vote on any ancillary or procedural resolutions put to the meeting, and

(b) appointing that person as a proxy in relation to any adjournment of the general meeting to which it relates as well as the meeting itself.

44 Delivery of proxy notices

(1) A person who is entitled to attend, speak or vote (either on a show of hands or on a poll) at a general meeting remains so entitled in respect of that meeting or any adjournment of it, even though a valid proxy notice has been delivered to the company by or on behalf of that person.

(2) An appointment under a proxy notice may be revoked by delivering to the company a notice given by or on behalf of the person by whom or on whose behalf the proxy notice was given.

(3) A notice revoking a proxy appointment only takes effect if it is delivered before the start of the meeting or adjourned meeting to which it relates.

(4) If a proxy notice is not executed by the person appointing the proxy, it must be accompanied by written evidence of the authority of the person who executed it to execute it on the appointor's behalf.

45 Amendments to resolutions

(1) An ordinary resolution may be amended if –

(a) notice of the proposed amendment is given to the company in writing by a person entitled to vote at the general meeting at which it is to be proposed 48 hours before the meeting is to take place (or at such time as the chairman of the meeting may direct), and

(b) the proposed amendment does not, in the reasonable opinion of the chairman of the meeting, materially alter the scope of the resolution.

(2) A special resolution may be amended by ordinary resolution, if –

(a) the chairman of the meeting proposes the amendment at the general meeting at which the resolution is to be proposed, and

(b) the amendment does not go beyond what is necessary to correct an obvious error in the resolution.

(3) If the chairman of the meeting, acting in good faith, wrongly decides that an amendment to a resolution is out of order, the chairman's error does not invalidate the vote on that resolution.

PART 5 – ADMINISTRATIVE ARRANGEMENTS

46 Means of communication to be used

(1) Subject to the articles –

(a) anything sent or supplied by or to the company under the articles may be sent or supplied in any way in which the Companies Act 2006 provides for documents or information to be sent or supplied by or to the company for the purposes of the Companies Acts, and

(b) any notice or document to be sent or supplied to a director in connection with the taking of decisions by directors may also be sent or supplied by the means by which that director has asked to be sent or supplied with such notices or documents for the time being.

(2) A director may agree with the company that notices or documents sent to that director in a particular way are to be deemed to have been received within a specified time of their being sent, and for the specified time to be less than 48 hours.

47 Addresses and other contact details

(1) Anything sent to a shareholder under the articles may be sent to that shareholder's address as registered in the register of members, unless –

(a) the shareholder and the company have agreed that another means of communication is to be used, and

(b) the shareholder has supplied the company with the information it needs in order to be able to use that other means of communication.

(2) Any notice or document sent to a director may be sent to that director's address as registered in the register of directors, unless –

(a) the director and the company have agreed that another means of communication is to be used, and

(b) the director has supplied the company with the information it needs in order to be able to use that other means of communication.

48 Company seals

(1) If the company has a common seal and it is affixed to a document, the document must also be signed by one authorised person in the presence of a witness who attests the signature.

(2) For the purposes of this article, an authorised person is –

(a) any director of the company;

(b) the company secretary (if any); or

(c) any other person authorised by the directors for the purpose of signing documents to which a company seal is applied.

(3) If the company has an official seal for use abroad, it may only be affixed to a document if its use on that document, or documents of a class to which it belongs, has been authorised by a decision of the directors.

(4) If the company has a securities seal, it may only be affixed to securities by an authorised person.

(5) For the purposes of the articles, references to the securities seal being affixed to any document include the reproduction of the image of that seal on or in a document by any mechanical or electronic means which has been approved by the directors in relation to that document or documents of a class to which it belongs.

49 No right to inspect accounts and other records

Except as provided by law or authorised by the directors or an ordinary resolution of the company, no person is entitled to inspect any of the company's accounting or other records or documents merely by virtue of being a shareholder.

50 Provision for employees on cessation of business

The directors may decide to make provision for the benefit of persons employed or formerly employed by the company or any of its subsidiaries (other than a director or former director or shadow director) in connection with the cessation or transfer to any person of the whole or part of the undertaking of the company or that subsidiary.

INDEX

abbreviated accounts 60
  filing 64
  medium-sized companies 68
accounting principles
  consistency 61
  going concern 61
  prudence 61
accounting reference date 58
  alteration 58
accounting regulators 65–6
Accounting Regulatory Committee 66
Accounting Standards Board 65
Accounting Standards Committee 65
accounts
  abbreviated 60, 68
    filing 64
    medium-sized companies 68
  accounting principles 61
  annual accounts 58–9
    duty to prepare 59
  approval of 61
  audit *see* **audit**
  balance sheet 59, 60
  CA 2006 developments 57–8
  cash flow statement 60
  circulation to members 59
  consistency principle 61
  currency 60
  defective 64
  directors' report 62
  failure to file 64
  filing 59, 63–4
  formats 61
  going concern principle 61
  group accounts *see* **group accounts**
  IAS 57, 59
  IFRSs 58
  individual accounts
    Companies Act 59–60

  IAS 60
  information in notes 62
  maintenance of records 73
  medium-sized companies 66–8
  non-statutory 63
  notes to 62
  obligations 58–64
  profit and loss account 59
  prudence principle 61
  public companies 60
  publication 62–3
  purpose of 59
  quoted companies 60
  regulators 65–6
  retention of records 73
  small companies 66–8
  small company 60
  statement of total reported gains
    and losses 60
  statutory accounts 58
  summary financial statements 63
  'true and fair' requirement 5, 59,
    64–5
  UK GAAP 57, 58, 70
  on websites 63
adjournment
  general meeting 228–9
administration
  moratorium 144–5
  substantial property transactions
    187
administrator
  appointment, by floating charge
    holder 143–5
agency
  directors and 171, 195–6
  group relationships 21–2
allotment of shares 114–15
alteration of articles

discriminatory 106
inconsistent with legislation 105
minority interests and 106
order of court 105
special resolution 105
three-quarters majority required
    1–6
validity 1–6
weighted voting clause 107–8
alternate director 159
Alternative Investment Market
    AIM Rules 66
annual general meeting 217–18
    accounts 63
    dispensing with 217
    notice of meeting 217
    notice of resolutions 218
    reports 63
annual return 5
appointment of administrator
    by floating charge holder 143–5
    moratorium following 144–5
appointment of receiver
    by floating charge holder 143
approval of accounts 61
articles of association 97, 98–103
    alteration
        discriminatory 106
        entrenched articles 106–7
        inconsistent with legislation
            105
        minority interests and 106
        order of court 105
        special resolution 105
        three-quarters majority required
            106
        validity 106
    contractual nature 99–102
    documentation requested by
        member 102–3
    enforceable obligations under
        99–100
        between member *inter se* 102
        by membership against company
            100–1
    entrenched 106–7
    independent contractual rights
        103–5
        remedies for breach 104–5
    members 102–3
    model articles 98–9
        draft 309–26

objects of company 107
'outsider right' 103–5
registration 98
requests for documents 102–3
Table A 98
unenforceable membership rights
    101–2
associated companies
    corporation tax 81
**Association of Chartered Certified
    Accountants** 12
audit
    dormant company exemption 71
    non-profit-making companies
        exemption 70, 71
    requirement 70–3
    small company exemption 70, 71
auditor
    appointment 71–2
    duties 72
    exemption from breach of duty 72
    indemnification 72
    independent contractor 169
    private companies 71
    public companies 71–2
    removal 72, 170
    remuneration 72
    report 169–70
    resignation 72
    rights to information 72
    signature on report 72
    statutory aims 169

balance sheet 59, 60
    consolidated 69
board of directors
    composition 161
    delegation of powers 163
    management powers 161–2, 163
    meetings 162
    notice of meetings 162–3
    see also **directors**
bonus issue 124

called-up share capital 126–7
capital allowances 95–6
capital of company 110
    see also **share capital**
capital redemption reserve 127
cash flow statement 60
centrebinding 37
certificate of incorporation 10–14

re-registration and 46, 47
chairman of company 159
charges
  fixed *see* **fixed charge**
  floating *see* **floating charge**
  legal 141
  mortgage 141
  preferential creditors 152–3
  priority rights 151–4
    Enterprise Act 2002 changes
      153–4
    fixed charges 151
    fixed and floating charges 151
    floating charges 151–2
    preferential creditors 152–3
  register of charges 150
  registration *see* **registration of**
    charges
  specific 141
charitable companies 51
Chartered Institute of Management
  Accountants 12
Chartered Institute of Public Finance and
  Accountancy 12
circulars 222
class rights
  general meetings 222
  variation 120–3
    CA 2006 122
    constitution and 120, 122
    objection of minority 123
close companies
  associates 80
  control 79
  participator 79–80
  taxation 79–80
close investment-holding company
  corporation tax 81
Combined Code 171
community interest company 51–2
companies
  changing status
    from private to public 42–5
    from public to private 45–6
    limited to unlimited 46–7
    unlimited company to private
      limited 47–8
  off-the-shelf 13
  Societas Europaea 55
  see also individual types e.g. **holding**
    company; limited liability; private
    companies

Companies Act 2006
  provisions of 253–308
companies limited by guarantee 2
  changing status, from limited to
    unlimited 46–7
  private 40–1
companies limited by shares 2
  changing status
    application 45
    conditions 43
    from limited to unlimited 46–7
    from private to public 42–5
    from public to private 45–6
    name after re-registration 45
    resolution 42–3
    statement of compliance 45
  private 40
  public 39–40
company secretary
  director acting in place of 168
  first 9
  private companies 168
  public companies 168–9
  role 167–8
  statement of proposed 9
conflict of interests
  breach of duty 183–4
  competing directorships 182
  directors' duty 172, 177–83
  disclosure of interest 180–2
  existing transactions or
    arrangements 183
  non-compliance with duty 182
  waiver of duty 180–2
connected persons
  capital gains tax 90
  substantial property transactions
    187
consistency principle 61
consortium relief 89
constitution of company
  articles *see* **articles of association**
  class rights 120, 122
  contractual nature 99–102
  directors and 104
  documentation requested by
    member 102–3
  enforceable obligations under
    99–100
    between member *inter se* 102
    by membership against company
      100–1

independent contractual rights 103–5
  remedies for breach 104–5
membership agreements 108–9
memorandum of association 97–8, 107, 191–2
objects clause 107, 191–2
'outsider right' 103–5
purchase of own shares 133
requests for documents 102–3
resolutions 97
unenforceable membership rights 101–2
voting *see* **voting**
contracts of company
  agency relationship 171, 195–6
  authority of directors 195–200
  constructive notice abolition 199
  corporate capacity *see* **corporate capacity**
  indoor management rule 196–7, 198
  legislation 197–200
  pre-incorporation 6–7
  Turquand rule 196–7, 198
  ultra vires rule *see* ***ultra vires* rule**
contribution order
  beneficiaries 34–5
corporate capacity
  agency relationship 171, 195–6
  authority of directors 195–200
  constructive notice abolition 199
  indoor management 196–7, 198
  legislation 197–200
  objects clause 191–2
  Turquand rule 196–7, 198
  ultra vires rule 191–4
    CA 2006 194
    political donations 193
    shareholder protection 193–4
    statutory reform 192–4
    third party interests 192–3
corporate entity 2–5
  criminal liability *see* **criminal liability of company**
  limited liability 2–5, 52–3
corporate governance 171
corporate manslaughter
  directing mind 248–9
  duty of care
    existence 250–1
    gross breach 250
  gross negligence 249, 250, 251

identification principle 248–50
legislation 249–52
penalty 251–2
'senior management' test 250–1
unlimited fine 251–2
corporate veil
  agency in group relationship 21–2
  controlling interest 20–1
  displacing 19–23
  fraud 20
  liability in tort 23
  national emergencies 19–20
corporation tax 74, 75
  accounting periods 82
  administration 82–3
  associated companies 81
  close investment-holding company 81
  exempt distributions 80
  filing of tax return 83
  financial years 80
  higher relevant maximum amount profit 81
  instalment payments 82–3
  lower relevant maximum amount profit 81
  marginal relief fraction 81
  payment 82–3
  rates 81
  self-assessment 82–3
  small companies 81
creditors
  Enterprise Act 2002 changes 153–4
  objection to reduction of share capital 129–31, 135–6
  preferential 152–3
  see also **charges; loan funding**
criminal liability of company
  conspiracy 247
  corporate manslaughter
    directing mind 248–9
    duty of care 250–1
    gross breach of duty of care 250
    gross negligence 249, 250, 251
    identification principle 248–50
    legislation 249–52
    penalty 251–2
    'senior management' test 250–1
    unlimited fine 251–2
  directing mind 245–6, 247, 248–9
  exceptions 246–7
  human act by human entity 246–7

identification principle 245–6,
  248–50
wrongful act of employee 247–8

debenture holders
  register 140
  rights 139
debenture stock 140
debentures
  discounted 139
  irredeemable 140
  issue 139
  meaning 139
  re-issue 140
  registration of allotment 139–40
defective accounts 64
derivative action 241
  benefit of company motive 231
  corporate action 234–6
  permission of court 232–4
  personal action 234–6
  procedure 232–4
  proper claimant rule 230–1
  refusal of application 233
  serious wrong requirement 231
  statutory 232–4
derivative contracts
  taxation and 76, 92–3
directing mind 245–6, 247, 248–9
directors
  agency relationship 171, 195–6
  allotment of shares 114–15
  alternate 159
  authority to bind company 195–200
    actual authority 195
    agency relationship 171, 195–6
    constructive notice abolition
      199
    indoor management 196–7, 198
    legislation 197–200
    ostensible authority 195–6
    ratification 216–17
    Turquand rule 196–7, 198
  board *see* **board of directors**
  company chairman 159
  compensation for loss of office 166,
    167
  conflict of interests *see* **conflict of
    interests**
  connected persons 187
  constitution and 104
  de facto 159–60

de jure 156–9
  definition 155–6
  disqualification *see* **disqualification
    of directors**
  duties *see* **directors' duties**
  executive 158
  exploitation of corporate
    opportunity 178–9
  first director 9
  guarantees 190
  identification of 155–6
  indemnities 185
  liability in tort 23
  loans to 187–90
    avoidance of transaction 190
    civil penalties 189–90
    credit transactions 188
    criminal sanction removal 190
    exceptions 188–9
    money lending company 189
    quasi-loans 188
    related arrangements 188
    shareholder approval 188–9
  non-executive 158
  personal liability 23–4
  protection for 185
  qualifications 157–8
  ratification of irregular acts of
    216–17
  refusal of transfer 116
  register 4, 9, 157
  removal 165–7
  remuneration 163–4
  remuneration report 62, 164
  retirement 159
  service contracts 164–5
  shadow 160–1, 171
  substantial property transactions
    186–7
directors' duties 171–85
  agency relationship 171, 195–6
  benefits from third parties 180
  bona fide in interests of company
    173–5
  breach of duty
    consequences 183–4
    relief available from court 184
  care 176–7
  competing directorships 182
  conflict of interests 172, 177–9
    breach of duty 183–4
    competing directorships 182

existing transactions or
arrangements 183
non-compliance with duty 182
waiver of duty 180–2
contracts for loans 187–90
creditor's interests 175
disclosure of interest 180–2
exploitation of corporate
opportunity 178–9
fiduciary 171–2
good faith 173–5
guarantees 190
indemnities 185
independent judgment 175–6
loyalty 172
proper purpose 172–3
secret profits 180
statutory duties 172–84
substantial property transactions
186–7
director's liability
fraudulent trading 28–30
liability in tort 23
misfeasance proceedings 25–6
personal liability 23–4
wrongful trading 30–5
directors' register 4, 9, 157
directors' remuneration report 62, 164
directors' report 5, 62
medium-sized companies 62
publication 62–3
small companies 62
disclosure requirements
director's interests 180–2
limited liability companies 4–5
disqualification of directors
application for leave to act 213–14
breach of competition law 214
conviction of indictable offence 202
disqualification order
discretionary 202–4
effect of 201–2
mandatory 204–14
objective of 201
register 202
disqualification period 202, 203, 204
fraudulent actions during winding
up 203
fraudulent trading 203–4
Insolvency Service 205–6
leave to act 213–14
legislation 201

mitigation 212–13
persistent breach of provisions 203
public interest protection 201,
211–13
regime 201–2
undertakings 205–6
unfit conduct 203, 204
application for leave to act
213–14
civil not criminal proceedings
210–11
commencement of proceedings
204–5
duration of order 211–13
factual determination 208–9
honest belief 209–10
human rights and 210–11
mitigation 212–13
nature of conduct 206–11
other companies 209
prosecution of actions 205
public interest protection 211–13
seriousness 208
undertakings 205–6
wrongful trading 203–4
distributions
purchase of own shares 85–7
recharacterisation of interest as 84
taxation 83–5
dividends
cash 84
imputation system 87
stock 85
taxation 80–1, 84–5
treated as paid 84–5
dormant company
audit exemption 71
double taxation 78, 94–5

Edinburgh Gazette
formation of company 13
electronic communication 13–14
employee shares 119
equity shares 117–18
European Economic Interest Groupings
56
name when registered in UK 14
**European Financial Reporting Advisory
Group** 66
'every step' defence
wrongful trading 34
executive director 158

extraordinary general meeting 218

filing accounts 59, 63–4
  abbreviated accounts 64
  penalties for failure to file 64
  private companies 63–4
  time limits 63
  unlimited companies 64
financial assistance for purchase of own shares
  private companies 136
  public companies 136–8
    criminal offence 138
    exemptions 137
Financial Reporting Council 65, 66
Financial Reporting Standards 65
Financial Services Authority 66
fixed charge 141
  creation 146
  floating charge distinguished 145–7
  priority rights
    competing fixed charges 151
    fixed and floating charges 151
floating charge 141–2
  administrator appointment 143–5
  avoidance 145
  crystallisation 142–5
  fixed charge distinguished 145–7
  priority rights
    competing floating charges 151–2
    fixed and floating charges 151
  property to which attached 142
  receiver appointment 143
foreign profits
  taxation 94–5
formation of company 5–7
  certificate of incorporation 10–14
  commencement of business 12–13
  Edinburgh Gazette 13
  electronic communications 13–14
  London Gazette 13
  name *see* **name of company**
  pre-incorporation contracts 6–7
  promoters *see* **promoters**
  refusal to register 14
  registration *see* **registration procedure**
Foss v. *Harbottle* **rule** 230, 241
fraud
  displacing corporate veil 20
fraudulent trading 26–30
  'blind-eye' knowledge test 30
  carrying on company's business 27–8
  establishing fraud 28
  establishing liability 28–30
  legislative provisions 27
  nature and extent of liability 30

general meetings
  acting for company as whole 215–16
  adjournment 228–9
  annual general meeting 217–18
  circulars 222
  class rights 222
  court's discretion to call 222–3
  extraordinary general meeting 218
  general meeting 218–19
    expenses 219
    requisition 219
  management powers 215
  members' statements 221–2
  notice requirement 219–21
    AGM 217–18
    failure to give 220
    special notice 220–1
  powers and procedures attached 215
  quorum 219, 222
  ratification of irregular acts 216–17
  resolutions *see* **resolutions**
  special notice 220–1
  voting
    adjournments 228–9
    poll 227–8
    procedure 227–9
    proxies 228
    rights 222
    show of hands 227
going concern principle 61
gross negligence
  corporate manslaughter 249, 250, 251
group accounts 57, 68–70
  accounting basis 70
  balance sheet 69
  contents 69–70
  definitions 50–1
  exemptions 69
  profit and loss account 69
  UK GAAP 70
groups of companies
  accounting definitions 50–1

'dominant influence' 69
holding company 48–9
    membership 49–50
individual accounts of companies 57
'managed on a unified basis' 69
parent company 50–1, 69
subsidiary company 48–9, 69
    wholly owned 49
taxation 88–91
    connected persons 90
    consortium relief 88, 89
    degrouping 90–1
    group relief 88, 89
    notional transfers 90
    'notional winding up' test 88
    'profit distribution' test 88
    transfer of assets 88, 89–90
see also **group accounts**
guarantee
    companies limited by guarantee 40–1
    personal 4
    statement of 9

hire purchase agreements 148
holding company 48–9
    agency relationship 21–2

identification principle 245–6
    corporate manslaughter 248–50
income tax
    dividends 87
incorporation
    certificate of incorporation 10–14
    commencement of business 12–13
    company creation 3
    corporate veil *see* **corporate veil**
    liability in tort 23
    management 3–4
    membership 3
    ownership of property 3
    public disclosure requirements 4–5
incorporation consequences 19–38
    centrebinding 37
    fraudulent trading *see* **fraudulent trading**
    liability in tort 23
    misfeasance proceedings 24–6
    personal liability of director 23–4
    phoenix syndrome 35–8

wrongful trading *see* **wrongful trading**
indemnities
    auditor 72
    directors 185
    third party 185
index of company names 14–15
index of members 112
    inspection 113
indoor management rule 196–7, 198
Industrial and Provident Societies 51
Institute of Chartered Accountants in England and Wales 12
Institute of Chartered Accountants in Ireland 12
Institute of Chartered Accountants of Scotland 12
Institute of Chartered Secretaries and Administrators 12
intangibles
    taxation 76, 93
interest
    recharacterisation as distribution 84
International Accounting Standards 66
International Accounting Standards Board 65, 66
International Financial Reporting Standards 66
International Financial Reporting Standards Interpreting Committee 66
investment companies
    taxation 77
issue of shares 113–15
    bonus issue 124
    pre-emption rights 123–4
    redeemable shares 124–5
    rights issue 123–4

just and equitable winding up 242–4

legislative framework 1
limited liability 2–5
    advantages 4
    disadvantages 4–5
    liability for debts 2–3
    personal guarantees 4
limited liability partnership 52–3
Listing Rules 66
loan funding
    debentures *see* **debentures**
    priority rights 151–4

security interests *see* **charges;**
   floating charge
loans to directors 187–90
London Gazette
   formation of company 13
losses
   capital 77
   revenue 77
   taxation and 92, 7708
Ltd 16

management of company 3–4
   auditor *see* **auditor**
   company secretary *see* **company**
      secretary
   directors *see* **directors**
   see also **general meetings**
medium-sized companies
   accounts 66–8
   directors' report 62
meetings
   board of directors 162
      notice 162–3
   general *see* **general meetings**
membership 3
   enforceable obligations
      between members *inter se* 102
      by members against company
         100–1
   identification of members 111–13
   index of members 112, 113
   inspection of register and index 113
   members' statements for general
      meetings 221–2
   'outsider right' 103–5
   register 111–12, 113
   request for documents 102–3
   unenforceable rights 101–2
   see also **shareholders**
membership agreements 108–9
   injunction to prevent non-
      compliance 109
   voting and 108
memorandum of association 7–8, 97–8
   application for registration 8–9
   objects clause 107, 191–2
   prescribed form 8
minority shareholders
   alteration of articles 106
   derivative action 230–6, 241
      benefit of company motive 231
      corporate action 234–6

permission of court 232–4
personal action 234–6
procedure 232–4
proper claimant rule 230–1
ratification of fraud 231
refusal of application 233
serious wrong requirement 231
statutory 232–4
Foss v. *Harbottle* rule 230, 241
just and equitable winding up 242–4
   requirements for 242
   underlying obligation or
      agreement 243
petition to court 230
protection of 230–44
unfair prejudice remedy 241–2
   conduct of company 236–9
   conduct of petitioner 239
   effect of conduct 237
   legislation 236
   membership interest 237–9
   objective test of conduct 236
   purchase of petitioner's shares
      240
   remedies to petition 239–41
   removal of voting right 240
   variation of class rights, objections
      123
misfeasance proceedings
   director's liability 25–6
   incorporation consequences 24–6
money lending company
   loans to directors 189
moratorium
   administrator appointment 144–5

name of company
   choice 14–18
   Companies Act 1985 and 17–18
   direction to change name 15
   general restrictions on use 16–17
   good will in 35–6
   index 14–15
   indication of activities 15–16
   Ltd 16
   misleading information 15–16
   passing-off action 16
   phoenix syndrome 35–8
   plc 16
   re-registration and 45, 47
nominee holdings 115
non-executive director 158

non-profit-making companies
    audit exemption 70, 71

objects of company 107, 191–2
off-the-shelf companies 13
officers of company
    auditor *see* **auditor**
    directors *see* **directors**
    secretary *see* **company secretary**
    statement of proposed officers 9
ordinary shares 117–18
'outsider right' 103–5

parent company 50–1
    group and individual accounts 68–9
participator 79–80
partnerships
    agreement 54
    business partnership 53–5
    financing 54–5
    limited liability partnership 52–3
    property 53
    sleeping partners 54
    succession 54
    vicarious liability 54
passing-off action 16
personal guarantees 4
personal liability
    of directors 23–4
phoenix syndrome
    exceptions 36
    goodwill in name 35–6
    new company after insolvency 35–8
    personal liability for debts 38
    prohibition on directors 36
    prohibition as to name 37
    re-use of name 35–6
plc 16
political donations 193
poll 227–8
pre-emption rights
    disapplication 124
    exceptions 123
pre-incorporation contracts 6–7
    promoter's liability 6–7
preference shares 118–19
    employee shares 119
preferential creditors
    priority rights 152–3
priority rights
    Enterprise Act 2002 changes 153–4
    fixed charges 151

    fixed and floating charges 151
    floating charges 151–2
    preferential creditors 152–3
private companies
    company secretary 168
    dispensing with AGM 217
    limited by guarantee 40–1
    limited by shares 40
    purchase of own shares
        approval by special resolution
            135
        auditor's report 134
        directors' statement 134
        financial assistance 136
        objections 135–6
        payment out of capital 133–6
    re-registration
        as public 42–5
        of public company as private
            45–6
    written resolutions 224–5
profit and loss account 59
    consolidated 69
profits
    'all income' treatment 76, 91–3
    chargeable gains 74, 76
    derivative contracts 76, 92–3
    foreign 94–5
    higher relevant maximum amount
        81
    intangibles 76, 93
    investment companies 77
    loan relationships 76, 91–2
    losses 77–8, 92
    lower relevant maximum amount 81
    taxation 74, 76–8
    trading companies 77
    transfer pricing 93–4
promoters 5–6
    declaration of personal interest 5–6
    fiduciary duties 5
    liability of 6–7
    undisclosed profits 6
proper claimant rule 230–1
property ownership 3
proxies 228
prudence principle 61
public companies
    company secretary 168–9
    limited by shares 39–40
    purchase of own shares 132, 133
        financial assistance 136–8

re-registration
  as private 45–6
  of private company as 42–5
purchase of own shares 131–3
  auditor's report 134
  authority of constitution 133
  contract of purchase 132
  directors' statement 134
  financial assistance
    criminal offence 138
    exemptions 137
    private companies 136
    public companies 136–8
  off-market purchase 132
  payment out of capital 133–6
  premium attached 131
  private companies 133–6
    financial assistance 136
  procedure 132–3
  public companies 132, 133
    financial assistance 136–8
  return to registrar 132
  special resolution approval 135
  taxation 85–7

quasi-partnership companies
  just and equitable winding up 243–4
quorum 219, 222

ratification
  by general meeting 216–17
  of fraud 231
  of irregular acts 216–17
re-registration
  from private to public company
    42–5
  from public to private company
    45–6
reasonably diligent person test
  wrongful trading 32–4
receiver
  appointment by floating charge
    holder 143
recognised investment exchange
  substantial property transactions
    187
redeemable shares 124–5
reduction of share capital
  court approval 130–1
  court procedure 129–31
  objections to 129–31, 135–6
  private companies 128

reasons for 127–8
s.641 procedure 128
solvency statement 128–9
register of charges 150
register of debenture holders 140
  closure 140
  inspection 140
register of directors 9
  content 157
  inspection 157
register of disqualification orders 202
register of members 111–12
  inspection 113
register of secretaries 9
registrar of companies 4
  refusal to register 14
  see also **registration procedure**
registration of charges
  certificate 149–50
    rectification 150
  failure to register 149–50
  hire purchase agreements 148
  information required 149
  interests not requiring registration
    148–9
  interests requiring registration
    147–8
  late delivery 150
  out of time 150
  retention of title clause 148–9
registration procedure 7–10
  application 8–9
  articles of association 7, 8
  memorandum of association 7,
    8–9
  refusal to register 14
  statement of compliance 8
  statement of guarantee 9
  statement of initial shareholdings 8
  statement of proposed officers 9
  statement of share capital 8–9
removal of auditor 72, 170
removal of directors 165–7
  compensation for loss of office 166,
    167
  expiration of period of office 166
  general meeting 166
  ordinary resolution 166
  representations 166
remuneration of auditor 72
remuneration of directors 163–4
  remuneration report 62, 164

reports
auditor's report 169–70
directors' remuneration report 62,
164
directors' report 62
publication 62–3
residence
taxation and 78–9
resolutions
allotment of shares 114–15
alteration of articles 105
constitution and 97
Duomatic rule conflicts 226–7
extraordinary 224
filing with registrar 5, 97, 227
informal, at common law 225–7
ordinary 223–4
special 105, 224
to change company status 42–3, 45,
48
application to cancel resolution
46
written 224–5
see also **general meetings**
retention of title clause 148–9
retirement of director 159
revaluation reserve 127
rights issue 123–4
Romalpa **clause** 148–9

secretary of company *see* **company**
secretary
security interests
mortgage 141
see also **charges**
service contracts of directors 164–5
shadow director 160–1
duties 171
share capital 110
called-up 126–7
capital redemption reserve 127
meaning 126–7
paid-up 127
purchase of own shares *see* **purchase**
of own shares
reduction *see* **reduction of share**
capital
revaluation reserve 127
share premium account 127
statement of 8–9
uncalled 126–7
unpaid 129

share premium account 127
shareholders
members of company 3
membership agreements 108–9
minority *see* **minority shareholders**
nominee 115
ultra vires rule and protection 193–4
undertaking to contribute capital
110
see also **membership**
shareholdings
initial, statement of 8
shares
acquisition 113–15
acquisition of own shares 113–14
allotment by resolution 114
cancellation 132
class rights
CA 2006 122
constitution and 120, 122
general meetings 222
minority's objection to variation
123
variation 120–3
classes 110
currency 110
employee 119
equity 117–18
issue 113–15
bonus issue 124
pre-emption rights 123–4
redeemable shares 124–5
rights issue 123–4
nominee holdings 115
ordinary 117–18
partly paid 127
payment for 116–17
preference 118–19
purchase of own shares *see* **purchase**
of own shares
redeemable 124–5
transfers 115–16
treasury shares 119–20
show of hands 227
small companies
abbreviated accounts 60
accounts 66–8
audit exemption 70, 71
corporation tax 81
directors' report 62
Societas Europaea 55
solvency statement

reduction of share capital 128–9
special resolutions 224
    copies to registrar 227
    purchase of own shares 135
statement of total reported gains and losses 60
Statements of Recommended Practice (SORP) 66
Statements of Standard Accounting Practice (SSAP) 65
subsidiary company 48–9
    individual accounts 57
    membership of holding company 49–50
    voting rights 49
    wholly owned 49
substantial property transactions 186–7
    connected persons 187
    exceptions 187
    group transactions 187
    members 187
    recognised investment exchange 187
    requisite value 187
    winding up or administration 187
summary financial statements 63

taxation
    accounts basis 74
    'all income' treatment 76, 91–3
    capital allowances 95–6
    capital gains 74
    chargeable gains 74, 76
    close companies 79–80
    company meaning 74
    corporation tax *see* **corporation tax**
    derivative contracts 76, 92–3
    distributions 83–5
    dividends 80–1, 84–5, 87
        cash 84
        imputation system 87
        stock 85
        treated as paid 84–5
    double taxation 78, 94–5
    filing of tax return 83
    foreign profits 94–5
    groups of companies 88–91
        consortium relief 89
        degrouping 90–1
        group relief 88, 89
        notional transfers 90
        transfer of assets 88, 89–90
    imputation system 87

income tax 74
intangibles 76, 93
investment companies 77
legislation 75–6
loan relationships 76, 91–2
losses 77–8, 92
non-resident company 78–9
profits *see* **profits**
purchase of own shares 85–7
residence of company 78–9
self-assessment 82–3
trading companies 77
transfer pricing 93–4
withholding tax 83
third party indemnities 185
tort
    director's liability in 23
trading companies
    taxation 77
transfer pricing 93–4
transfer of shares 115–16
    refusal by director 116
treasury shares 119–20
'true and fair' requirement
    accounts 5, 59, 64–5
***Turquand* rule** 196–7, 198

***ultra vires* rule**
    CA 2006 194
    objects clause 191–2
    political donations 193
    shareholder protection 193–4
    statutory reform 192–4
    third party interests 192–3
undisclosed profits
    directors 180
    promoters 6
unfair prejudice remedy 241–2
    conduct of company 236–9
        effect 237
        objective test 236
    conduct of petitioner 239
    legislation 236
    membership interest 237–9
    purchase of petitioner's shares 240
    remedies to petition 239–41
    removal of voting right 240
unlimited company 41–2
    change to private limited company 47–8
    change to public limited company 42–5

Urgent Issues Task Force 66

variation of class rights
    CA 2006 122
    constitution and 120, 122
    objection of minority 123
voting
    adjournments 228–9
    general meetings 222, 227–9
    membership agreements 108
    poll 227–8
    procedure 227–9
    proxies 228
    rights 222
    show of hands 227
    weighted voting clause 107–8

websites
    accounts on 63
weighted voting
    clause in articles 107–8

winding up
    fraudulent actions during 203
    just and equitable 242–4
    preferential creditors 152–3
    substantial property transactions 187
wrongful trading
    conduct giving rise to action 31–2
    contribution order 34–5
    determination of financial health 32–3
    establishing liability 32–4
    'every step' defence 34
    financing application 35
    incorporation consequences 30–5
    legislation 30–1
    no reasonable prospect of staying solvent 31, 32–3
    reasonably diligent person test 32–4
    trading in insolvent state 33–4